A Plague of Informers

THE LEWIS WALPOLE SERIES IN
EIGHTEENTH-CENTURY CULTURE AND HISTORY

The Lewis Walpole Series, published by Yale University Press with the aid of the Annie Burr Lewis Fund, is dedicated to the culture and history of the long eighteenth century (from the Glorious Revolution to the accession of Queen Victoria). It welcomes work in a variety of fields, including literature and history, the visual arts, political philosophy, music, legal history, and the history of science. In addition to original scholarly work, the series publishes new editions and translations of writing from the period, as well as reprints of major books that are currently unavailable. Though the majority of books in the series will probably concentrate on Great Britain and the Continent, the range of our geographical interests is as wide as Horace Walpole's.

A PLAGUE OF INFORMERS

*Conspiracy and Political Trust in
William III's England*

Rachel Weil

Yale
UNIVERSITY PRESS

NEW HAVEN AND LONDON

Published with assistance from the Annie Burr Lewis Fund.

Copyright © 2013 by Yale University.
All rights reserved.
This book may not be reproduced, in whole or in part, including illustrations, in any form (beyond that copying permitted by Sections 107 and 108 of the U.S. Copyright Law and except by reviewers for the public press), without written permission from the publishers.

Yale University Press books may be purchased in quantity for educational, business, or promotional use. For information, please e-mail sales.press@yale.edu (U.S. office) or sales@yaleup.co.uk (U.K. office).

Set in Fournier type by IDS Infotech, Ltd., Chandigarh, India.
Printed in the United States of America.

Library of Congress Cataloging-in-Publication Data

Weil, Rachel Judith.
A plague of informers : conspiracy and political trust in William III's England / Rachel Weil.
    pages cm. — (The Lewis Walpole series in eighteenth-century culture and history)
Includes bibliographical references and index.
ISBN 978-0-300-17104-4 (hardback)

1. Great Britain—History—William and Mary, 1689–1702. 2. Great Britain—Politics and government—1689–1702. 3. Conspiracies—Great Britain—History—17th century. 4. William III, King of England, 1650–1702—Adversaries. 5. Great Britain—Kings and rulers—Succession—History—17th century. I. Title.
DA460.W45 2013
941.06'8—dc23

2013024690

A catalogue record for this book is available from the British Library.

This paper meets the requirements of ANSI/NISO Z39.48–1992 (Permanence of Paper).

10 9 8 7 6 5 4 3 2 1

For my mother, Rose Reicherson Weil

Contents

Acknowledgments ix
Notes on Conventions and on Currency xi
Persons and Plots xii

Introduction 1

CHAPTER 1: Debates on National Security 27

CHAPTER 2: A Trusted Government? 68

CHAPTER 3: "A Tool with so Devilish an Edge": Government Officials and Political Informers in the 1690s 104

CHAPTER 4: Identity, Honor, and Gender in the Narratives of Informers 140

CHAPTER 5: Credit and Credibility in the Worlds of Richard Kingston 188

CHAPTER 6: Loyalty and Credibility in the Lancashire "Sham Plot"   217

CHAPTER 7: Representation, Politics, and Law in the Assassination Plot   248

Notes   281
Manuscript Collections Consulted   331
Index   335

Acknowledgments

Some paragraphs in chapters 1, 6, and 7 were taken from my essay "National Security and Secularization in the English Revolution of 1688," which appeared in *After Secular Law*, edited by Winnifred Sullivan, Robert Yelle, and Mateo Taussig-Rubbo (Stanford University Press, 2011). Some paragraphs in chapter 3 were taken from my essay "Matthew Smith vs. the 'Great Men': Plot Talk, the Public Sphere and the Problem of Credibility in the 1690s," which appeared in *The Politics of the Public Sphere in Early Modern England*, edited by Steve Pincus and Peter Lake (Manchester University Press, 2007).

For financial support I am grateful to the Huntington Library, the National Humanities Center, and Cornell University.

Some of my greatest debts are to people I've never met. This book would be impossible without the archivists, scholars, and editors who produced invaluable reference works like the *Calendar of State Papers*, the Historical Manuscripts Commission's *Reports*, the *Dictionary of National Biography*, and *The History of Parliament*. The computer-literate wizards who created new databases (like *Old Bailey Online*) and made so many sources and catalogues available online made my work much, much easier. It is a great pleasure to thank Virginia Cole of the Cornell University Library, whom I actually have met, for making sure I had access to what I really needed, despite budget cuts. The large and small archives in the United Kingdom that I visited while researching this book were sometimes a pain to get to but always a pleasure to work in; the people who maintain and keep them accessible have my eternal respect and gratitude.

My editors at Yale University Press—Laura Davulis, Christina Tucker, and Ash Lago—have also come through countless times with what I needed, with great patience and good cheer. Thanks also to Eliza Childs for intelligent and meticulous copyediting; to Esther Chadwick and Mark Knights for help with illustrations; to Boris Michev for the map; to Alyshia Ledlie for finding material on Robert Paterson; to Steve Pincus for a hot archival tip that sent me to Wigston Magna; to Will Deringer for teaching me how to find Secret Service payments; and to Cynthia Koepp for help deciphering John Taaffe's letters in French. For reading and commenting on various chapters, I thank Josh Chafetz, Peter Dear, Itsie Hull, Mark Knights, Paul Monod, Mary Roldán, Winni Sullivan, Daniel Szechi, Robert Travers, Carl Wennerlind, and members of the following: the historians group at the National Humanities Center (2006–7), the Johns Hopkins University History Department Seminar, the Yale University British Historical Studies Colloquium, the British History University Seminar at Columbia University, and Cornell's Comparative History Colloquium. Mary Beth Norton gave me helpful feedback on the manuscript as a whole, as did my two excellent readers for Yale University Press, Alan Houston and John Marshall.

It is a challenge for an author to resist the fear that her book is insane, trivial, or just not doable. I was lucky to have help meeting that challenge. Winni Sullivan, Sheryl Kroen, and Mary Roldán sometimes saw more potential in the project than I did myself and kept me going at critical moments. Margaret Hunt taught me, finally, how to write a grant proposal and convinced me I deserved funding. Frances Harris lured me back to the 1690s by insisting that it was, really, "heart-stopping stuff." Steve Pincus has a funny habit of asking me to write papers on things about which I think I have nothing to say. Several chapters of this book started life that way.

My life-outside-the-book stole time from writing, but without it I would not have had the strength to finish the book. I thank Lucy Goosequill and the late Laska for making sure I got my daily walks. Warm thanks, too, to Allison Bennett, whose companionship and hospitality made research trips to England so much fun. For the love, laughs, moral support, and sense of perspective that sustained me throughout this project, I thank my many friends and my extended family of Weils, Blys, Lukes, Denkers, Friedbergs, Carreras, Yearsleys (and hyphenated combinations thereof).

My greatest debt is to Becky Bly, who is joyful, fearless, and kind and (unlike the people I write about in the following pages) always tells me the truth. She lived with me through most of the stress-inducing stages of finishing this book, and nonetheless agreed to marry me (legally, in Canada), which was the best thing that ever happened.

Notes on Conventions and on Currency

Note on Conventions

Spelling and capitalization have sometimes been modernized in quotations.

Dates are given in the Old Style (in which England was eleven days behind the Continent), but the year is taken to begin on 1 January (not 25 March).

The spelling of early modern names was erratic. For example, "John Lithured" was also "John Letherhead," and "Matthew Smith" was also "Matthew Smyth." To avoid confusion, I choose one spelling and use it consistently.

I use the term *Williamite* to refer to the regime and to its supporters, not because I fail to appreciate the importance of William's wife and co-monarch, Mary II, but because (1) it was the term used by contemporaries, (2) William lived for the entire span of time covered in this book, and (3) "William-and-Maryite" is cumbersome.

In citations, place of publication is London unless otherwise specified.

Note on Currency

Values were expressed in terms of pounds, shillings, and pence: £5–8–6 is 5 pounds, 8 shillings, and 6 pence.

1 pound (£1) = 20 shillings (20 s.)
1 shilling (1 s.) = 12 pence (12 d.)
Other commonly used denominations:
guinea = 21 s.
mark = 13 s. 4 d.
crown = 5 s.
farthing = ¼ d.

Persons and Plots

Assassination Plot Alleged Jacobite plot to assassinate William III, encourage French invasion, and foment domestic rebellion. Convicted plotters include Robert Charnock, John Friend, William Parkyns, and John Fenwick. Also known as *Turnham Green Plot*.

Chaloner, William Forger of coins and bank notes, occasional informer, hanged in 1699.

Crone, Matthew Jacobite convicted of treason in 1690, on testimony of William Fuller, later became informer corroborating Preston's information.

Ellis, John Undersecretary of state for William Trumbull and later James Vernon.

Ferguson, Robert Whig pamphleteer during the Restoration, later turned Jacobite, probable author of two 1694 pamphlets defending accused Lancashire Plot conspirators.

Fuller, William Political informer, notorious con artist, autobiographer, witness against Matthew Crone, and self-described "discoverer" of the true mother of the Prince of Wales.

Lancashire Plot Alleged Jacobite plot involving wealthy gentlemen in Cheshire and Lancashire. Accused plotters were tried in Manchester in 1694 but acquitted.

Lunt, John Catholic political informer, discoverer of the alleged Lancashire Plot.

Montgomery Plot Jacobite plot discovered in 1690 involving Scottish former Whig Sir James Montgomery of Skelmorlie, in conjunction with the Earl of Annandale, Lord Ross, and Neville Payne.

Nottingham (Daniel Finch, Earl of) Tory politician, secretary of state from 1689 until November 1693.

Oates, Titus The chief "discoverer" (or fabricator) of the Popish Plot in 1678.

Preston's Plot Richard Graham, Lord Preston, a Jacobite convicted of treason in 1691, he eventually provided information against fellow conspirators, including the Earl of Clarendon. See also *Matthew Crone*.

Portland (Hans Willem Bentinck, Earl of) Close adviser to William III and manager of continental spy network.

Popish Plot Alleged plot by Catholics to assassinate Charles II, "discovered" by Titus Oates in 1678, resulting in the execution of about twenty Catholics.

Rye House Plot Alleged plot by radical Whigs to assassinate Charles II.

Shrewsbury (Charles Talbot, Duke of) Whig politician, secretary of state 1689–90 and 1695–98.

Smith, Aaron Whig activist and Treasury solicitor, responsible for management of prosecutions for treason, also active in the Superstitious Lands Commission.

Taaffe, John Ex-priest, political informer, and witness in defense of accused Lancashire plotters.

Trenchard, John Whig politician and secretary of state from March 1693 until his death in April 1695.

Trumbull, William Secretary of state, 1695–97.

Turnham Green Plot See *Assassination Plot*.

Vernon, James Undersecretary of state for both Shrewsbury and Trenchard, became secretary of state in 1697.

A Plague of Informers

Introduction

> But this I'll affirm, and if need I can swear
> We've had a sham-plot at least once a year
> And till one does take, they'll go on still I fear
> Which nobody can deny
> —ANONYMOUS, *The Lancashire Sham-Plot* [1694]

Now he that disbelieves the Lancashire conspiracy . . . his incredulity carries such dangerous symptoms with it, that I despair of seeing it ever confuted by a miracle.
　—RICHARD KINGSTON, *A True History of the Several Designs and Conspiracies against His Majesties Sacred Person and Government* (1698)

Plot Talk

In 1688, the English people deposed the Catholic king James II and installed the Protestant William and Mary as joint monarchs. Within five years, stories about plots and sham plots had become the terrain on which the credibility, lawfulness, and longevity of the new Williamite regime were tested and contested. As Paul Hopkins has noted, the "sheer number and the serious attention given to [allegations about plots] under William is unusual." Some of these alleged plots, like the Assassination Plot of 1696, are thought by even the most skeptical historians to have been real. Others, like the Lancashire Plot, may or may not have been real but in any case were not sufficiently proven in court; depending on your perspective, innocent men went free or conspirators escaped. Fierce public controversy about which plots were real and how well the authorities had handled them were occasions to ask and answer questions about the government's credit, both in the broad and narrow senses of the term: Did it tell the truth? Would it survive long enough to pay its debts? For critics, sham plots discredited the Revolution of 1688, particularly the new regime's claim that it had been created to protect the laws of England and the liberty of the subject. Supporters had different reasons to fear for the new regime's credit: plotters might be operating with impunity, perhaps even with the collusion of high-ranking officials who secretly betrayed the king.[1]

This book looks at how the "discoveries" of plots, debates about their authenticity, and controversies about how the government and the courts dealt with alleged internal enemies affected the "credit of the government" in the years immediately following the Revolution of 1688. While it is concerned with what was called at the time the "securing of their Majesties' Persons and Government" (what we today call "national security"), it is more broadly concerned with the nature of the polity created by the Revolution of 1688. Government dilemmas and public discussion about security, I suggest, are a window into the struggle of the new regime to establish its credit, to earn trust.

Why should we care about the Williamite regime and its struggles for trust? One answer is that since 1989 many societies have undergone or are striving for regime change along liberal lines. Our experience should have taught us that any kind of change in government inevitably raises tough questions: How do you tell the difference between your loyal supporters and your enemies, and how do you treat people who occupy the mushy middle ground? Do you punish those who held office under the previous regime, or do you forgive them or even invite them back into power? How does a new government establish "credit," in the sense of persuading people to trust its stories about itself, and also in the literal sense of credit (getting people to believe it will pay back debts, which in turn depends on people believing that it is here to stay)? If the change of government is made in the name of the rule of law or liberty, there are more questions still: How do you treat judicial decisions that were made in the previous regime? How do you reconcile the conflict between liberty and security? Recent experiences of "regime change" in our own world show us that even when such change is meant to bring about a more liberal order, it is never easy. It was not easy in the late seventeenth century either. Although this book is about history, my hope is that a full understanding of the challenges of liberal regime change in the past might help us think about the present.[2]

Unfortunately, acknowledgment of the difficulties inherent in any change in government is absent from much of our historical memory of the Revolution of 1688. The Puritan Revolution of 1641–60 is remembered as a chaotic and bloody affair; after the execution of Charles I there was a succession of new constitutions and governments, none of which led to stability—eventually people got so sick of disorder that they invited Charles I's son, Charles II, back to be king. The Revolution of 1688, by contrast, lasted and has been credited with laying the foundations for Britain's subsequent stability, prosperity, and imperial power. Americans think of it as the cornerstone of our own political tradition because John Locke's *Treatises of Government*, published in 1689 to justify the revolt against James II, in turn inspired the founders of the United States. It is called the Glorious Revolution or "sensible revolution." The rather staid image of the revolution as easy, consensual, and (despite Locke) conservative was enshrined by Edmund Burke, who compared it favorably to the French Revolution in his *Reflections on the Revolution in France* (1790).[3]

Such an image of the Revolution of 1688 is possible, however, only with hindsight. In the immediate aftermath of 1688, contemporaries could not be confident that the new regime would last a year, let alone three centuries. William's government in the 1690s faced serious internal and external threats. It was at war with France, with James II in Ireland, and with Jacobites and rebellious clans in Scotland. In addition to its war with declared enemies, the new government also confronted the threat of uncounted, unidentified enemies within. Newsletters, diaries, government correspondence, and transcripts of parliamentary debates from the first years of the revolution are full of reports that "papists and disaffected persons" were meeting, collecting arms and horses, and receiving commissions from King James to form an army that would rise up on his arrival. Despite government efforts to shut down the Jacobite press, copies of declarations issued by King James circulated widely, keeping alive hopes that the exiled king would soon return. Jacobite propaganda and a Jacobite liturgy helped to solidify a subculture of psychological if not physical resistance to Williamite rule and Williamite legitimacy. An otherwise upbeat pamphlet, *Vindication of the Proceedings of the Late Parliament*, estimated that one-third of the population of the three kingdoms was Jacobite.[4]

The sense of internal threat in the 1690s is dramatic. It is not the sense of threat itself, however, that is new and unique. English men and women in the reigns of Charles II (1660–85) and James II (1685–88) were also convinced that their government was threatened by Catholics in the so-called Popish Plot (1678) or by republicans and dissenters in the alleged Rye House Plot (1682). The "plot talk" of the 1690s, however, took place under very different circumstances. The regime's newness, the uncertainty of its survival, its legitimating narratives hinging on law and consent, and the intense scrutiny to which it was subjected by a Parliament frequently in session meant that plot talk would have an especially powerful impact on the new regime's capacity to earn trust and therefore on its continued survival.[5]

Trust in Historical Perspective

The political theorist John Dunn has argued that establishing and maintaining trust in itself is a necessity for any government that is worth having and possible in the real world. An authoritarian government capable of repressing its subjects may not require their trust, but we would not want to live under such a government. A pure, direct democracy eliminates the need for trust because citizens control every decision, but no such democracy is feasible for us. In a complex society, a division of political labor is inevitable: most of us are followers, some will be chosen to lead. A legitimate government will be accorded "a range of freedom to act on behalf of what the governors take to be the rights and interests of members of a society." Dunn continues:

> To possess this freedom of action the governors must in some way be released from the control of those over whom they govern. But in a legitimate political society they are accorded the discretion and the coercive power which they need, solely in order to serve their subjects. . . . In legitimate political societies, accordingly, governmental power is in fact conceived both by rulers and rules as a trust and . . . the psychic relation between rulers and ruled can also consequently aspire to be one of trust: confidence, the giving and receiving of clear, veridical, and carefully observed mutual understandings, a relation of trust deservedly received and trust rationally and freely accorded.[6]

Dunn's argument is meant to clarify the task facing polities recently liberated from authoritarian rule. Although he is addressing today's problems, it is most significant for our purposes that Dunn's argument is inspired by (and made largely through an explication of) the writings of John Locke, whom Dunn credits with having put the need for trust at the center of his account of government. The importance of trust for Locke is especially evident when he describes the circumstances under which people can rebel against their government: that is, when trust in that government has become impossible. Isolated mistakes or even illegal acts by a governor do not, Locke explains, in themselves warrant revolution. It is only when, by a ruler's "long train of actings," a subject is led to an unshakeable, involuntary belief that his liberty is in danger, making him no more able to "hinder himself from being persuaded in his own mind which way things are going, or from casting about how to save himself, than he could from believing the captain of the ship he was in was carrying him and the rest of the company to [slavery in] Algiers, when he found him always steering that course."[7]

As a theorist, Dunn is interested in whether Locke is usable in the present. As a historian, I am interested in why trust was articulated as a problem in politics and indeed in just about every other arena in the late seventeenth century. Trust or credit, I argue here, can be considered an "actor's category," that is, a problem about which seventeenth-century people consciously thought rather than a concept imposed on the past by later historians or theorists. And yet how to establish trust or credit was not simple and was not really solved at the time.

Trust and truth were, for example, conspicuous problems in religious life since at least the sixteenth century (if not before). The Protestant Reformation and Catholic Counter-Reformation raised questions about whom or what to trust in religious matters that engaged a wide public in the debate: Was truth to be found in church councils or in the Bible alone? If in the Bible, in whose interpretation of the Bible? In mid-seventeenth-century England, the collapse of ecclesiastical authority during the civil war and the ensuing multiplication of competing sects made the uncertainty of religious truth especially obvious. It is telling in this respect that when Locke wrote his *Letter Concerning Toleration*, he took it as given that there was no certainty about religious truth and that no individual, even if he wanted to, could trust the magistrate to define truth for him. The "care and salvation of men's soul's cannot belong to a magistrate" because no man can "abandon the care of his own salvation so blindly as to leave it to the choice of any other, whether prince or subject, to prescribe for him what faith or worship he shall embrace. For no man can, if he would, conform his faith to the dictates of another." What or whom to trust, how to know the truth, what method of argument could produce consensus, how much or whether consensus was necessary in a polity thus became the driving questions of the intellectual work that comprises the so-called early Enlightenment.[8]

It should not therefore surprise us that the two titans of seventeenth-century political thought, Locke and Hobbes, had diametrically opposing views of the relation between trust, truth, and government, nor that their opposing accounts were in turn entwined with their views of religion and toleration. As we saw above (following Dunn's argument), trust is a central concern for Locke, so much so that the sovereign can be the object of judgments about trust: it is possible to ask and answer the question, "Do you trust the government?" That the question is possible for Locke implies that trust is not something that the government creates; the capacity for trust (and distrust) already exists in humans independently of the state.

Trust is equally central to Hobbes's political theory. It is precisely the absence of the possibility of trust that makes life outside of a commonwealth solitary, poor, nasty, brutish, and short. Promises and contracts are meaningless in a state of nature as there is no way to ensure they will be honored. Only when we agree to be part of a commonwealth and submit to a sovereign can we expect that others will honor their engagements to us. It is the sovereign, then, that enables trust.[9]

The conflict between Locke and Hobbes over trust had ramifications for their ideas about belief and truth. Locke's argument for toleration is based on the idea that the magistrate has no monopoly on or even privileged access to truth and that none of us can trust him to pick the truth for us. Moreover, for Locke, it is precisely because we can (and must) judge truth for ourselves that we can (and must) make judgments about the trustworthiness of the government. Hobbes, by contrast, strictly curtails the ability of subjects to judge truth for themselves (or at least to judge a truth in a way that leads to outward action, to behave outwardly in accordance with their judgment of truth). Sovereigns, according to Hobbes, must have complete control over the church and the press. Even more radically, Hobbes closes the gap between what sovereigns promote as "truth" and actual truth:

> It is annexed to sovereignty, to be judge of what opinions and doctrines are averse, and what conducing to peace; and consequently, on what occasions, how far, and what, men are to be trusted withal, in speaking to multitudes of people; and who shall examine the doctrines of all books before they be

published. For the actions of men proceed from their opinions; and in the well governing of opinions, consisteth the well-governing of men's actions, in order to their peace and concord. And though in matter of doctrine, nothing ought to be regarded but the Truth; yet this is not repugnant to regulating the same by peace. For doctrine repugnant to peace, can no more be true, than peace and concord can be against the law of nature.[10]

The epistemological implication of this passage is striking: those things which the sovereign declares to be not true must by definition be false. Hobbes's argument here is not based on the assumption that a sovereign has a direct line to God. Rather, it is that the promotion or suppression of ideas is one aspect of what the sovereign does to secure the state. Because this security is (as Hobbes had previously demonstrated in *Leviathan*) necessary according to the law of God and nature, and because therefore nothing can be true which hurts sovereignty, the truth-claims that the sovereign would squelch were not true in the first place. And besides, if we behave as if what the sovereign has designated to be false is true, we destroy sovereignty, at which point truth becomes irrelevant: without sovereignty, there is no justice, no abiding by agreements, no reason to be honest. Thus, whereas Locke says that decisions about both truth and trust rest with individual members of society, Hobbes tells us that government is the enabler of trust and arbiter of truth.

If trust and truth were problems only for high philosophers, they would be of little interest. But many people in the mid to late seventeenth century, not just philosophers, daily confronted problems of trust and truth in a practical way. Such judgments were indeed hard to make yet essential to survival. Historians are now chronicling how people struggled to find methods to establish trust and credibility in a number of contexts; significantly, the late seventeenth century does appear to be the period when the need for such methods became most pressing.

How to acquire credible knowledge of natural phenomena was, for example, a live issue in this period. The Royal Society, founded in 1664, was intended to facilitate the sharing of experimental information, but whether and on what basis a member could trust data or experimental results reported by another member (or worse, a non-member) was an open question. Whom to "credit," literally, was also a question for anyone involved in commerce. Merchants large and small had grappled with how to judge the trustworthiness of customers, agents, and trading partners long before the 1690s. Still, the expansion of trade networks over longer distances, along with an increasing reliance upon paper instruments of credit, exacerbated anxiety about forgery and identity fraud. The clippers and coiners who undermined the credibility of English currency had by the late seventeenth century threatened international trade.[11]

The increasing importance of documents of all kinds was accompanied by concerns about their reliability. The discovery that forgers had replicated the seal belonging to Secretary of State Lord Nottingham, which was used as a stamp to validate passes for individuals to travel abroad and other important documents relative to national security, caused serious alarm. Meanwhile, the treason trial of Thomas Sprat, bishop of Rochester, called attention to the difficulties of identifying handwriting. Sprat was able to persuade the court that a Jacobite "Association" on which his signature was found was a forgery; however, his acquittal left many skeptical, and his own narratives of his misfortunes emphasized the nigh impossibility of separating real signatures from false ones.[12]

Printed books in the late seventeenth century were hardly more reliable than handwritten documents. As Adrian Johns has shown, readers in this period could not be sure that any given book was what the author named on the title page had written, or if it was an error-ridden, incomplete, pirated misrepresentation thereof; the eroded trust of readers in turn became a problem for authors and booksellers, whose credibility was damaged when they could not control the content of books that appeared under their names.[13]

As Mark Knights has shown, credibility was also an issue in politics. The emergence of two competing political parties making propaganda appeals to the public in the late seventeenth century undermined the grounds of certainty about anything: any narrative about truth could and would be absorbed into a counter-narrative intended to expose the first narrative as a false blind. Fake news reports and ventriloquized speeches created by one party to embarrass opponents were common, well-recognized tools in political struggle. The petitions and addresses that proliferated in the late seventeenth century purporting to express a unified voice of the people were open to the (sometimes justified) suspicion that they were really vehicles by which a partisan minority posed as a majority. In what sense a "representative" in Parliament could be said to actually "represent" a constituency became subject to doubt.[14]

There seems to have been little consensus among contemporaries about what made a person, a document, or a fact seem trustworthy. Steven Shapin

By the King and Queen,
A PROCLAMATION.

WILLIAM R.

Whereas in Order to the Holding a Correspondence with Their Majesties Enemies, and the Carrying on other Wicked and Treasonable Designs, divers Passes, and also divers Warrants for Seising of Persons have been Forged, and thereto the Hand and Seal of Daniel Earl of Nottingham, Their Majesties Principal Secretary of State have been Counterfeited; by Means whereof not only the Peace of the Kingdom may be Disturb'd, but great Danger may Ensue to Their Majesties Royal Persons, unless some Speedy and Publick Notice be given of the said Forgeries: Their Majesties therefore, with the Advice of Their Privy Council, have thought fit by this Their Royal Proclamation to Notifie the Premisses to all Their Loving Subjects. And to the End they may not hereafter be Deceived or Imposed upon by such forged Warrants or Passes, the Impression of the said Counterfeited Seal is Described, and Imprinted in the Margin of this Their Majesties Proclamation.

And for the future and more certain Avoiding the Mischiefs which may be Occasioned by the said Forgeries, and lest well meaning Persons may be Deceived by any Resemblance between the said Counterfeit Seal and the True and Real Seal formerly made use of (Their Majesties said Principal Secretary of State having, by Their Express Command, Caused a New Seal of a different Impression to be Prepared, which is to be Used for the Future) Their Majesties do by this Their Proclamation, with the Advice of Their Privy Council, Revoke and Discharge all Passes, and all Warrants whatsoever for Apprehending or Seising any Person or Persons heretofore Sealed with any Seal which shall Resemble the Impression made in the Margin of this Proclamation, hereby Willing and Requiring all Justices of Peace, Mayors, Sheriffs and Officers belonging to the Ports, and all other Officers and Persons whatsoever, to take Notice hereof, and Commanding them, and every of them upon their Duty and Allegiance, That they do not at any time hereafter Yield Obedience to any Warrants or Passes whatsoever, which shall be Sealed with the said Counterfeit Seal, or any Seal which shall Resemble the said Impression in the Margin hereof. And also that they and every of them do use their utmost Endeavours to Apprehend and Seise such Persons as shall use or produce any of the said Counterfeit Warrants or Passes, and cause them to be Committed to the next Goal, there to remain until they shall be delivered by due Course of Law: And that as soon as such Persons shall be Apprehended, they do give Notice thereof immediately to Their Majesties, or Their Privy Council, or to Their Principal Secretary of State. And Their Majesties are Graciously Pleased hereby to Promise and Declare, That whosoever shall Discover any Person who has been Guilty of making or Forging the said Counterfeit Warrants or Passes, or of Dispersing or Using the same, so as such Person may be Convicted by due Course of Law, shall have and receive as a Reward for such good Service, immediately upon the Conviction of any such Offender, the Sum of Five hundred Pounds.

Given at Our Court at *Whitehall*, the Ninth Day of *March* 1693. In the Fifth year of Our Reign.

God save King William and Queen Mary.

L O N D O N,
Printed by *Charles Bill*, and the Executrix of *Thomas Newcomb* deceas'd, Printers to the King and Queens most Excellent Majesties. 1693.

By the King and Queen, a Proclamation. Whereas in Order to the Holding a Correspondence with Their Majesties Enemies (Charles Bill, [9 March] 1693). The trustworthiness of government documents was uncertain. In 1692 the official seal of the secretary of state was counterfeited. This proclamation warns local officials not to honor passes and warrants bearing the counterfeit seal, which is illustrated in the left margin. Copy in Kent History and Library Centre, Maidstone, used by kind permission of New Romney Town Council, Romney Marsh, Kent.

has famously contended that trust was constructed in the Royal Society not by the infallibility of the experimental method but by the presumed disinterestedness of its members. The presumption of disinterestedness was established in turn by social identity (membership was confined to gentlemen, who alone were presumed to have the necessary economic independence to be disinterested) as well as by a range of rhetorical practices that conveyed cool and humble objectivity rather than arrogant, polemical enthusiasm. The Shapinesque account has been questioned by Barbara Shapiro, who suggests that even within the Royal Society social status was not so powerful a determinant of credibility. However, even if a gentlemanly model of credibility prevailed inside the Royal Society, it probably did not satisfy outsiders. Thomas Hobbes, a trenchant critic of the Royal Society's methods, denied that experiments witnessed by a closed group of gentlemen could reliably establish facts.[15]

Moreover, even if Shapin's model holds for the community of natural philosophers, it is still unclear whether gentlemanliness was a sufficient or primary guarantor of credibility in other arenas. For one thing, it was well known that gentility could be faked. For another, as we will see, political informers were rarely gentlemen. The important point for our purposes is that there were in the late seventeenth century several different lines of effort and experiment aimed at providing surer foundations for trust in a variety of arenas, but they were not all the same and they did not produce quick solutions.

Recognizing that late seventeenth-century people could not agree amongst themselves as to what made something credible should lead us to problematize a purely Lockeian narrative of the Revolution of 1688. Granted, it is possible and tempting to describe the revolution in terms of Locke's account of trust and as a vindication of his account over that of Hobbes: the English people had decided they could not trust the government of James II, so they withdrew their allegiance from it; pace Hobbes, society did not immediately dissolve into a war of all against all. In the weeks between James's flight and the crowning of William and Mary, there was enough social cohesion, enough trust, to allow people to collectively improvise a new government. However, although Locke's account of trust and revolution may be the one that most of us prefer, it has some glitches. First, who are "the people" who make the decision about whether to trust the government? Given the multiplicity of judgments about religious truth that Locke recognizes in his writings on toleration, why would we expect people to reach a consensus about the trustworthiness of the government? Moreover, for "the people" to be cohesive enough to make this decision about the trustworthiness of the government, they would have to trust one another. But on what basis would they do that? Doesn't the state itself have a role to play in creating the conditions of trust? Many of these questions are Hobbes-inspired. If Hobbes tried to create a theory that eliminated the need for spontaneous judgments about trust, perhaps it was because such judgments are so hard to make. The Revolution of 1688 was in significant ways a Lockeian revolution, but as such it was beset with problems that Hobbes would have (gleefully) predicted.

The study of political informers helps to address the questions that Locke left unanswered: How does a government earn trust, how do people know when to trust one another, and how do those two things connect? It illuminates the complex interplay of the credit of the state with the credit of individuals. It is hard to say which one gave credit to the other. In the Hobbesian model, it would be in the power of the state to define truth and to pronounce judgment on whether an informer was to be trusted. To an extent, this happened. Parliament sometimes passed resolutions on the trustworthiness of particular informers: it voted that William Fuller was a fraud who "scandalized their Majesties and the government and abused this House and falsely accused several persons of honor and quality," and that John Fenwick's informations were "false and scandalous, and a contrivance to undermine the government." Judges validated informers from the bench: in the 1696 trial of William Charnock for treason, Lord Chief Justice Holt instructed the jury that the chief witness, George Porter, might be a good witness despite the fact that he had participated in Charnock's conspiracy himself and had turned witness to avoid prosecution. We can imagine that as a result of successful informing, persons not normally trustworthy were seen to become so. It is hard to gauge public reactions to individual informers after they informed. But certainly the fact that informers writing to government officials mentioned the indebtedness they incurred through service to the state as a reason to trust them suggests that while an insolvent debtor is normally not a person to be trusted, a debtor who became insolvent in the service of the state might remain honorable.[16]

Nonetheless, the Hobbesian model of an all-powerful state conferring credit upon informers can take us only so far. Even when, in the example given above, Lord Chief Justice Holt told the jury that Porter might be a good witness, the jury had the ultimate power to decide whether to believe him. As the ballad about the so-called Lancashire Sham Plot quoted at the head of this introduction shows, people made their own judgments about whether informers told the truth. The relationship between the credit of informers and the credit of the government was thus sometimes mutually supportive and sometimes mutually destructive. Following informers lets us see how often, in the 1690s, the credit of the government could be dragged down by the very people upon whom it depended for survival.

A consideration of plot discoveries and informers brings home the multidirectional dynamics of trust. The public needs to trust the government (to detect real plots, not to persecute the innocent). But for the government to be trustworthy it has to trust the members of the public to tell it the truth about plots. It relied on informers for both security *and* legitimacy, and in doing so it always took a risk. To make matters more complicated, what affected the legitimacy of the regime was not just whether informers told the truth but whether the public believed they did, which was a separate matter. Clearly, the regime was not entirely in control of the fate of its own trustworthiness. This book seeks to capture the complex interplay between the credit of informers and the credit of the government and to show how that complexity made politics in the 1690s dynamic and unpredictable.

Trust as an Issue for the Williamite Regime

To see how trust had become so central to the Williamite regime, some definition of trust is helpful. According to the sociologist Diego Gambetta:

> Trust (or, symmetrically, distrust) is a particular level of the subjective probability with which an agent assesses that another agent or group of agents will perform a particular action, both before he can monitor such action (or independently of his capacity to ever be able to monitor it) *and* in a context in which it affects his own action. . . . When we say we trust someone or that someone is trustworthy, we implicitly mean that the probability that he will perform an action that is beneficial or at least not detrimental to us is high enough for us to consider engaging in some form of cooperation with him.[17]

The key point in Gambetta's definition, for our purposes, is that "trust" is relevant only when a person can make a choice about it. To say that the Williamite regime was concerned about trust in itself is also to say that its own subjects, its creditors, and foreign states might choose not to cooperate with it and take action accordingly. That was indeed possible or (more important) *believed* by the regime itself to be possible. Jacobitism (support for the exiled James II) was a distinct option, and it was suspected that some members of Parliament and even the king's Privy Council, perhaps even Queen Mary's sister Princess Anne, were secretly negotiating with James II's court in exile at St. Germain. Committed (or partial) Jacobitism, however, was only the extreme end of a spectrum of the mistrust that the government feared. Foreign allies and domestic subjects were faced with choices that required them to take the anticipated longevity of the new regime into their calculations. Paradoxically, the survival of the regime required that people trust it to survive.

An illustration of the paradox, and the most dramatic test of the government's credit, was the creation of the Bank of England and the Great Recoinage in 1695–96. The Bank was founded, literally, to provide the government with credit, but it in turn relied upon the belief of investors that the government was worthy of credit, or at the very least in the belief that the government would survive. As Carl Wennerlind has shown, the credit of the Bank in turn depended on the recoinage, an ambitious project to reconcile the face value of currency with the value of its silver metallic content (which had been in most cases severely diminished by clippers). Since notes issued by the Bank of England were backed by coins, restoring the currency was seen as necessary to establish the Bank's credit, that is, to making the paper notes issued by the Bank meaningful as currency. The recoinage was an even greater test of the trustworthiness of the government than was the establishment of the Bank itself. The government needed to persuade (or force) men and women to turn in the clipped coins which had been in circulation, as well as their silver plate, in return for which they were compensated with (the as yet unproven) paper notes from the Bank of England. The relative importance of persuasion and coercion in this process awaits a full historical investigation. It is clear, however, that in the short run, the recall of coins and plate generated anxiety. Moreover, as Wennerlind has emphasized, the eventual establishment of a reliable currency depended on violence in that it was accompanied by the extensive use of the death penalty against clippers, coiners, and forgers. In hindsight, we know that the recoinage succeeded and the Bank of England made possible England's victories against France and its eventual rise to world domination. In the 1690s, however, the Bank and recoinage were both scary experiments, meant to produce trust but paradoxically requiring trust to succeed.[18]

The vogue for defactoism in the 1690s also made painfully obvious the same paradox, that is, that the new regime's survival depended upon its ability to persuade people it would survive. Defactoism, a theory of allegiance often associated with Hobbes, was the belief that one owed allegiance to whatever government was currently in power, regardless of any other criteria for legitimacy, but that one owed it only as long as that government was able to retain power. When the government in 1689 required public officials, military officers, and clergymen to take an oath of allegiance to the new monarchs, it was widely feared that many subjects were taking the oaths on merely defactoist grounds; one clergyman, William Sherlock, created a scandal when he publicly advocated doing so! To any standing government, defactoism was a maddening compliment that was really a backhanded insult. A defactoist would be willing to swear allegiance but would consider himself absolved of allegiance the moment the survival of that government was seriously threatened. The attraction of defactoism, and the fear that people were attracted to it, was itself a sign of how much trust was an issue for both governors and governed in the 1690s. People wondered if they could trust the government to continue to exist; the government wondered if it could trust the people to help it survive; the two questions were mutually entwined, the answer to one affecting the answer to the other.[19]

Although they are not the primary focus of this book, theories of allegiance and the problem of reliable currency are connected to the story told here at many points. It is not, for example, entirely an accident that it was widely believed that Jacobites were responsible for the debasement of England's currency and that many coiners were thought to be Jacobites. The belief that the loyalty oath imposed in 1689 did not sufficiently separate real supporters from mere defactoists was what made plausible what would otherwise seem to be outlandish charges that persons holding office in the new government were secretly conspiring against it. This study of plot discoveries and informers is a piece of, not the whole of, a complete account of the struggle for political trust in the 1690s, but it is a critical and as yet unexamined piece.

It is fair to ask if it really is a critical piece of the story: In order to survive, did the Williamite regime need its subjects to believe in, say, the reality of the Assassination Plot with the same level of urgency that it needed them to believe that notes drawn on the Bank of England would be honored? My answer is "yes," because legitimacy mattered to this regime in a way that it had not mattered to its predecessor. Or, to put it another way, this regime could not rely as heavily as others had done on hereditary right and divine right for legitimacy, and so it had to rest its legitimacy at least partly on the consent of the people. That consent in turn was explained by way of a narrative about how the previous regime had both colluded with plotters and manipulated false accusations of plotting in order to squash political opposition and trample the liberties of the subject. If these abuses were the grounds upon which the people had cast off James II and invited William and Mary to take the throne, the new regime had to avoid the appearance of repeating the same abuses. It had to do so, moreover, under an unprecedented level of scrutiny. Even before the lapse of the Licensing Act in 1695 unleashed the press, rumors about plot discoveries and speculation about their truth ran rampant in manuscripts and in coffeehouses. Even more important, whereas Charles II and James II had shut down Parliaments, their continuing presence was guaranteed by the Triennial Act and by the expense of the war with France, which required that the king ask repeatedly for parliamentary subsidies. Members of Parliament had no inhibitions about commenting on the government's handling of plots, sometimes even intervening with their own investigations, all of which affected the progress of legislation vital to the government's survival: subsidy bills, bills pertaining to loyalty oaths treason trials, or even the Bank. And so, the allegation that the government mishandled plots, whether by inventing sham plots or failing to detect real ones, really did cut at the foundations of the new regime's legitimacy and really did threaten its existence.[20]

Historiographical Context

The Williamite regime's quest for credit in the financial sense has been the subject of excellent scholarship. Very few scholars, however, have considered the regime's credit in the sense discussed here—its capacity to attract trust, based in large part on how well it was perceived to keep promises of liberty while handling threats to its existence. Most recent books on the Revolution of 1688 barely cover the 1690s, especially in England (as opposed to Ireland and Scotland). Steve Pincus's *1688: The First Modern Revolution* does signal the importance of the early 1690s in that it argues that the revolution was not consolidated until 1696. As Pincus shows, crucial questions of political economy, the church, and foreign policy were unresolved by the events of 1688–89. The issues Pincus highlights, however, are not the ones discussed here: controversies over habeas corpus, treason trials, loyalty oaths, or plot discoveries.[21]

By focusing on such issues, this book reinforces the critique of the Whig-Burkeian historiographical tradition made by other recent scholars like Tim Harris, Edward Vallance, and Steven Pincus. Some explanation of the term "Whig-Burkeian" is in order here. As Herbert Butterfield memorably described it, Whig history is "the tendency in many historians to write on the side of Protestants and Whigs, to praise revolutions provided they have been successful, to emphasize certain principles of progress in the past and to produce a story which is the ratification if not the glorification of the present." Whig history is related to but not identical to the version of the Glorious Revolution presented in Edmund Burke's *Reflections on the Revolution in France* (1790). For Burke, the great virtue of the Glorious Revolution's framers was that they changed nothing: "Their whole care," he wrote, "was to secure the religion, laws and liberties that had been long possessed, and had been lately endangered." Whig historians, by contrast, celebrate 1688 as a move forward, a first step on the road to modern parliamentary democracy (and to all that is good about modern times). Still, as Edward Vallance and Steve Pincus have both emphasized, the Whig interpretation shares much with Burke in that it regards the Revolution of 1688 as orderly, controlled by elites, and nonviolent, a far cry from the bloody and more democratic revolutions of continental Europe. The Whig-Burkeian interpretation is still pervasive in popular history and in modern political discourse. Margaret Thatcher praised the Revolution of 1688 for having "saved us from the violent revolutions which shook our continental neighbors" and as "a first step on the road which . . . led to the establishment of universal suffrage and full parliamentary democracy." Similarly, the Whig narrative is perfectly encapsulated in the title of Michael Barone's *Our First Revolution: The Remarkable British Upheaval That Inspired America's Founding Fathers* (2007). Within the text, Barone celebrates the Revolution of 1688 as "mostly bloodless," "a giant step forward for representative government," "a bold step forward for guaranteed liberties," and "a step forward for religious liberty."[22]

While the Whig-Burkeian view thrives in political discourse and in popular history, key elements of it have been challenged by scholars. Most scholars would agree, for example, that the Revolution of 1688 looks "mostly bloodless" only if one ignores events in Scotland and Ireland, where, as Vallance puts it, the revolution was "marred by horrific violence." Steve Pincus likewise challenges the Whig view of the revolution as a model of (characteristically English) moderation and good sense, nonviolent and unrevolutionary, describing it instead as "popular, violent, and divisive."[23]

Historians are less united in challenging the Whig notion that 1688 was a step on the road to modern society and to the liberty that we value in modern society (that is, in Butterfield's terms, challenging the story "which is the ratification if not the glorification of the present"). Most scholars do agree with the Whig historians that the Revolution of 1688 greatly increased the power of Parliament in relation to the monarch (although given the narrow franchise by which Parliament was elected, that change should not be confused with democracy). Where scholars break with Whig historiography, and with one another, is about the significance of that change: Did it translate directly into, or was it accompanied by, greater liberty? How about modernity? Answering such questions becomes tricky because people have different understandings of what liberty and modernity mean.

As Edward Vallance points out, for example, almost all players in the Revolution of 1688 fought for "liberty" in some sense of the word: James II sought to give Catholics and dissenters religious liberty by royal fiat, and Irish Catholics sought liberty from English domination; liberty might mean the enjoyment of special privileges by members of Parliament or the liberty to trade slaves. Tim Harris, too, problematizes the notion that 1688 achieved "liberty":

> There would have been hundreds of thousands of people across Britain and Ireland who must have doubted whether the revolutions had done anything to secure the liberties that they particularly cherished: the Catholic majority in Ireland, of course (and the Catholic minorities in England and Scotland, too); the Episcopalians in Scotland (a sizeable minority, to say the least); many of those throughout the three kingdoms who found themselves liable to a much heavier tax burden; even the supposed victors in Scotland and Ireland who found their own political autonomy under threat from the metropolis.[24]

Steve Pincus, by contrast, retains elements of the Whiggish narrative of progress toward liberty, crediting the Revolution of 1688 with much of what today would be called "liberty": toleration, secularization, freedom from monopoly companies, limited monarchy, and the triumph of the idea that government is based on consent. He departs significantly from the Whig interpretation, however, in seeing the revolution not as a triumph of the "modern" over an ancien régime (represented by James II) but rather as a clash between two radically different versions of modernity. On Pincus's account, James II, who modeled his government closely on that of Louis XIV, should be seen as himself a modernizer. The revolution did not, as Whig historians would have it, produce modernity; rather, modernization in state and society was a precondition of the revolution, which simply determined whether modernity would take an absolutist or liberal form. Pincus's important revision of Whig historiography enables him to effectively challenge the Whig-Burkeian distinction between a moderate, sensible English non-revolution and the radical, bloody upheavals of continental Europe. Provocatively and controversially, Pincus insists that the Revolution of 1688 was the first of the modern revolutions, more similar to than different from the revolutions in France in 1789 or Russia in 1917 (both of which also took place in already modernizing societies).[25]

Pincus's insistence that the Revolution of 1688 can be compared to later "modern revolutions" is fruitful and enabling for the present study. The curtailments of liberty this book describes as occurring within the borders of England seem less surprising if we remember that many revolutions restrict liberty. This is not to say that the Revolution of 1688 in England was as bloody as the French Revolution. Pincus's claim that "the English endured a scale of violence against property and persons similar to that of the French Revolution at the end of the eighteenth century" has met with legitimate skepticism. In fact, compared to Ireland and Scotland, and to France in the Terror, the curtailments of liberty described in this book—the use of attainder, unreformed treason trials, restrictions on travel, the suspension of habeas corpus, detention even when the privilege of habeas corpus was operative—seem undramatic. That is no doubt why they are ignored. Still, such curtailments were an important part of the lived experience of the Revolution of 1688 and should not be written off for lack of dramatic appeal. At a time when the difficulties of reconciling liberty and security in a liberal polity are painfully obvious, they are of analytical significance. The Revolution of 1688 as it played out in England could be considered a best-case (or good-case) scenario for a revolution to establish liberty (in the sense that it had wide support, military backing, institutions that could manage transition).

The fact that even under such promising conditions the revolution failed to deliver on a promise of liberty is itself worth discussing.[26]

Informers

Pincus's suggestion that 1688 could be considered a "modern revolution" is also helpful in that it invites questions about the changing relationship of individuals to the state and points to ways in which the study of political informers might illuminate that relationship. Modern revolutions are generally associated with the transformation of obedient, passive subjects into engaged, active citizens (although whether that is due to their modernity or revolutionariness remains open to debate). In a modern revolutionary regime (let the French Revolution stand as the paradigmatic example here), the state becomes a focal point for a citizen's identity (as the citizen is now the state itself) and the object of supreme loyalty (trumping kin, party, or community). Although political informing is not exclusively modern or revolutionary (it was compulsory, for example, in early modern Muscovy), scholars have identified notions about informing characteristic of modern revolutionary contexts. French Jacobites and Russian Bolsheviks both attempted to distinguish conceptually and linguistically between the bad informing done by police spies in the old regime (*donos* in Russian, *délation* in French) from the virtuous revolutionary *signal* (the Russian term) or *dénonciation* (as the French called it), which was the duty of citizens and promoted as a sign of virtuous revolutionary citizenship.[27]

To an extent, the evidence of informing in Williamite England bears out Pincus's comparison of 1688 England to later revolutions. The rhetoric of 1690s informers can sound eerily like French Jacobites of the 1790s. Consider, for example, Joshua Bowes, who wrote to Secretary of State William Trumbull in 1696 to explain that he had discovered the author, printer, and publisher of a libel purely out of "zeal for the government" rather than hope of reward:

> Oh that my body were transparent that Sir William Trumbull might see what pure, sincere, unmixt love and duty lodges in my heart for King William: were it possible I would even make a chamber in my heart to secure him from all the malice and hatred, plots, and contrivances, gins and snares of his enemies; for my love to the King is like that of Jonathan's to

David, it passes the love of women. . . . I have a young wife that I dearly love, an only son that I am but too fond on, and a life that I am not a little careful to preserve, and yet I think I could freely part with all these to contribute to the King's welfare."[28]

In his yearning to be "transparent," his choice of duty to the state over love of family, his framing of political loyalty as a homosocial attachment, his sense of ubiquitous threat, Bowes conforms closely to an ideal of what would in the French Revolution come to be called *dénonciation* as opposed to *délation*. Still, while the similarities between some informers of the 1690s and later Jacobins are intriguing, and buttress the credentials of 1688 as a real revolution, there were nonetheless important differences. English and French revolutionaries had different notions about the nature of the enemy. They also had different senses of the past, which in turn had implications for their attitudes toward legal procedure and anonymity.

Williamite English and Jacobite French differed in how they imagined the threat facing them and how that affected their treatment of information. Colin Lucas notes that revolutionary authorities in France even before the Terror posited the existence of a unified, secret opposition and accordingly encouraged the reporting of all that was suspicious, so that (as Basire put it in 1791) "individual facts which are all connected with the great conspiracy" could be gathered in a central location. It has often been argued that Jacobite paranoia about treason within the revolution stemmed from the democratic ideology based on a concept of "general will," which had no way to explain internal dissent except as treason. For this reason, even the most ardent patriot might be unmasked as a conspirator.[29]

That epistemology of conspiracy seems absent in Williamite England. Needless to say, Rousseau had not written about the "general will" at the time of the Glorious Revolution, but that does not sufficiently explain the differences between 1690s England and 1790s France. One does not need a concept of the "general will" to look for treason within or to suspect wolves in sheep's clothing. England had a long tradition of conspiracy theorizing, which drew on Protestant notions about Catholicism's propensity for deceit and on a political tradition of framing criticism of royal policies in terms of saving the king from the evil counselors surrounding him. Nonetheless, the Revolution of 1688 cannot be said to have eaten its children in the way the French Revolution did in its Terror phase. It is true that some leaders of the revolution fell under suspicion: the Earl of Marlborough was confined to the Tower in 1692 on suspicion of negotiating with the court of St. Germain; the Duke of Shrewsbury was accused of secret Jacobitism several times in 1696 and 1697. But both men survived. There was no English equivalent of Danton or Robespierre.

Perhaps it was the very conspicuousness of ambivalence within the ranks of the elites that made it unnecessary for the English to imagine a hidden, secret enemy. As this book will show, the new regime chose not to purge the ambivalent and made loyalty oaths easy to take. Tories, whose loyalty to the revolution might be questioned, were to be found even among the secretaries of state. This was enough to occupy the attention of the most zealous Whig; there was no need to imagine yet more hidden enemies. To posit the existence of a large number of internal enemies would undermine the legitimacy of the new regime, which needed to present itself as having the support of the vast majority. Accordingly, Jacobite publicity was as much of a threat as Jacobite secrecy to the new regime, and was recognized as such.

English and French revolutionaries also had different attitudes to their own pasts and therefore to anonymity and procedure. In England, legal continuity was important to the legitimacy of the revolution, which had been largely justified as a restoration of the already extant laws. In this context, the all-important French distinction between *délacion* and *dénonciation* did not make sense. England had not had a secret police under Charles II and James II, and informing to the magistrates was a normal part of the English legal system. Although supporters of the Glorious Revolution often condemned the working of the justice system in the previous two reigns, they did not condemn informers of that period as informers per se (although they did condemn informers who promoted specifically hateful agendas, for example, the Hilton gang who persecuted religious dissenters or the witnesses who perjured themselves to convict the "Whig martyrs" of the Rye House Plot). Indeed, for many Whigs, the harsh punishment of the Popish Plot informer Titus Oates under James II constituted an abuse.[30]

If delation in England's old regime was not identified (initially) as a particular crime, denunciation in the new regime was not particularly glorified as a patriotic duty. The exception that proves the rule is the Societies for the Reformation of Manners, which emerged shortly after the revolution to encourage the prosecution of sin. Although they were more concerned with offenses to God than direct threats to the state, the Societies are of interest because their promoters did deploy a rough equivalent of the *délation/*

dénonciation distinction. Edward Stephens's 1695 pamphlet *Phinehas: or, The Common Duty of All Men* urged the "obligations of all, who have any knowledge of any offences against the laws, to give information thereof." Stephens assured his readers:

> It is true, the usual practice of informers, for malice or lucre, hath brought an evil name upon what is not only a thing indifferent in its own nature, but well used, both lawful, necessary and commendable. When men do it not out of malice or for lucre, but for the real good of the offender, of the community, and for the honor and service of God, this is an act of charity, and virtue, and truly honorable.

Nonetheless, no army of citizen informers appeared to denounce vice. As Faramerz Dabhoiwala has shown, the Societies for the Reformation of Manners relied upon a small number of full-time professional informers to bring offenders before magistrates. If the project of the Societies for the Reformation of Manners was to encourage patriotic denunciation, it failed.[31]

To an extent, it can be argued that French Jacobites had a very different attitude to legal continuity, and therefore to anonymity and legal procedure. In the French Revolution, according to Colin Lucas, the sharp break with the past was symbolized and guaranteed by the lack of anonymity for informers: in theory at least, in the early stages prior to the Terror, denunciation had to be public and ideally made in the press to distinguish it from the secret delation of the past. There was, however, a shift in the course of the French Revolution from the use of public, non-anonymous denunciation as a prelude to normal legal procedures to the use of secret denunciations during the Terror as "the first step in an *instruction* that led not to the due process of the regular law courts, but to the summary inquiry and trial of revolutionary justice."[32]

England, perhaps thanks to its reverence for legal tradition, looks different. There were certainly some instances in which normal legal procedures were laid aside, such as the suspensions of habeas corpus and the attainder of John Fenwick. Still, there was no equivalent to the procedures Lucas describes for the Terror: no one was convicted or attainted of treason without the identity of witnesses being revealed. Moreover, in 1690s England, the requirement that witnesses be publicly identified was not itself a marker of revolutionary change or participatory democracy but rather a normal aspect of legal procedure.

Still, the differences between 1690s England and regimes more familiarly defined as modern and revolutionary should not be overstated. As seen above, the French Jacobite attitudes to anonymity described by Lucas were themselves unstable. A sharp contrast with England is misleading. Although there was no dramatic about-face in 1690s English attitudes to informer anonymity (as there was in France), there was nonetheless a persistent ambivalence. On the one hand, no one was convicted in England on the testimony of anonymous witnesses. On the other, it was widely understood in the 1690s that the publicity was regrettable and problematic. Many informers and professional spies made it a condition of giving information that they would *not* have to testify as witness. Justices and government officials were willing to accept anonymous statements, many of which survive in the state papers and private papers of government officials. In 1691 justices of the peace in Middlesex, to discover which clergymen and other officials had yet to take the 1689 oath of allegiance, "agreed to a kind of balloting box to put in the names of all such persons as they think fitting to take the oaths, that it may not be known who are the informers." The reluctance to sign an information was not necessarily seen by informers as something that would reflect negatively on their patriotism but as the opposite. A woman who wrote to the Earl of Dorset in 1692 withheld her name, she explained, because "I desire to do what good I can to their Majesties and not to advantage myself only as too many do which is a great hindrance to the good of the whole nation." It seems, then, that although anonymous evidence was not usable in a court of law, government officials did not reject information on grounds of anonymity per se.[33]

It is important, then, not to confuse Williamite England with Jacobite France (or Stalinist Russia). Still, there may have been conditions common to all those polities that made informing attractive as a practice, even in the absence of compulsion or large cash rewards. The above-mentioned regimes all required something more than mere passive obedience from subjects; they encouraged citizens to make the state the locus of loyalty and identity, to actively and voluntarily support it. Yet in these regimes, the opportunities for individuals to have a meaningful voice in government were limited. In such a context, as Sheila Fitzpatrick argues for Stalinist Russia, informing becomes "one of the few available forms of agency."[34]

Of course, the conditions that make informing one of the "few available forms of agency" might occur even when no revolution is immediately on the horizon. Joanna Innes, in her study of the mid-eighteenth-century master carpenter and constable William Payne, finds that Payne used informing to impact a world in which political authorities would not otherwise take seriously the needs of persons of lower status such as himself. He took meaningful action on issues that mattered to him, such as the Catholic threat, prostitution, and the price manipulations of forestallers; informing may also have enhanced his standing among his peers and reinforced his self-perception as a righteous man. In many respects, he resembles the writers of letters of denunciation studied by Sheila Fitzpatrick. A plausible hypothesis, then, is that in a range of polities which demand active support from subjects while providing few outlets for genuine political participation, informing becomes attractive as a means for the individual to be heard and to establish personal standing and credibility.[35]

Perhaps, then, the study of informers is important not so much as a litmus test of whether 1688 counts as a modern revolution, but rather as a means of exploring questions about the nature of politics from below that interest historians of revolution, totalitarianism, and popular politics alike. Informing is, as Sheila Fitzpatrick and Robert Gellately note, "an important but unstudied point of contact between the individual and the state, one that embodies a whole set of inarticulated decisions about loyalties to the state on the one hand, and to family and fellow citizens on the other." My interest in informers is driven by a desire to put a human, nonelite face on what is often an impersonal story of regime change, consolidation, and legitimation. I look at informing as a two-way street, asking what the informer gets from the state as much as what the state gets from the informer; I ask how an informer's relationship with the state affects his or her relationship with other people ("family and fellow citizens") even as the informer affects what others think of the state. The stories of informers may let us see where and how the history of politics is also a history of human relationships. To the best of my ability, then, I will try to say who these people were and what they thought they were up to.[36]

Scope and Organization of This Book

It should be explained at the outset that there are some things this book does not do. First, it does not offer a complete picture of the intelligence "system" in William III's reign, of the sort that might be a sequel to Alan Marshall's thorough study of intelligence and espionage in Charles II's reign.

I do not try to cover every informer, spy, or plot. Nor do I try to evaluate the accuracy or military value of Williamite intelligence. Because my concern is with how intelligence shaped the relationship of the new regime to its English subjects, the focus is on intelligence about Jacobitism in England and how informers and authorities presented themselves to an English Parliament and public. This book, then, is less about intelligence than it is about intelligence in the political imagination.[37]

Second, this book focuses on England, only occasionally touching on Ireland and Scotland. Looking at how the practice of securing Their Majesties' persons and government played out in the other two kingdoms would probably make one even less sanguine about the problems of combining liberty and security than my study of England does. The negative consequences of Williamite victory for Irish Catholics are well-known. It is also worth pointing out that torture was legal in Scotland and was used to extract information from the Jacobite Neville Payne in the 1690s. The Irish and Scottish stories need to be told, but the profound differences between legal systems and political conditions in the three kingdoms make it hard to do justice to all of them within one book.[38]

Third, I make little effort in this book to decide if alleged Jacobite plots were real. I will certainly speculate about how aspects of a given allegation might seem credible or not to a contemporary audience. But I am not a historian of Jacobite plotting, nor am I a detective. If the reader feels uncertain as to which plot was real, she can console herself that men and women in the 1690s felt the same way.

This book covers roughly the period from 1689 through 1697 (the end of the Nine Years' War with France). The end point of the book is in some sense arbitrary: it would be foolish to say that in 1697 the regime had established itself as unequivocally trustworthy in the eyes of all subjects, never mind that it had resolved the tensions between liberty and security. Nonetheless, 1697 was an important turning point. The peace, which made the new regime's survival seem much more certain, coincided with the successful completion of the recoinage. In addition, the discovery of the Assassination Plot in 1696, and the government's astute response to it, enhanced the credit of the government. It also settled disputes over the conduct of trials, the status of Parliament, and the means of identifying loyalty or disloyalty, which had plagued the government since 1689 in a direction that Whigs found satisfying and that Tories were temporarily unable to disrupt.

The three sections of this book explore the Williamite regime's struggles with credit from three angles. The first section considers state policy, bureaucratic institutions, and the practices of government officials. The second section focuses on informers, their possible motives, and their narratives about themselves. The third section comprises case studies of two (alleged) plots—the Lancashire Plot of 1694 and the Assassination Plot of 1696—and their respective (and very different) impacts on the credit of the regime.

CHAPTER I

Debates on National Security

To be trusted was itself a complicated project: the new regime had to prove both that it could survive threats to its security and that it could make good on the story it told to justify its existence, that is, that it had restored law and liberty. There were obvious tensions between those two goals and, as this chapter will show, significant disagreement among contemporaries as to how to achieve them, which emerged during parliamentary debates on a range of subjects. The two chapters that follow this one consider other dimensions of the Williamite regime's quest for trust. Chapter 2 examines national and local institutions responsible for the security of the new regime, asking how these might enhance or undermine trust in the government (or do both at once). Chapter 3 focuses on the political informers who were necessary to the survival of the regime but who might undermine trust in it. The challenge the government faced in attracting trust was intertwined with the related challenge of deciding which subjects were trustworthy: building political trust was a two-way street.

"The head of Thomas Armstrong, executed for Rye House Plot, is taken down from Westminster Hall," wrote Narcissus Luttrell in his diary entry of 5 April 1689. Armstrong's head (along with his quarters) had been publicly displayed since 1684, when he had been condemned to a traitor's death by George Jeffreys, the judge later notorious for his savage punishment of Monmouth's rebels. Armstrong had been a suspect in the Rye House Plot, an alleged conspiracy by Whigs to kill Charles II and raise an insurrection. He had fled the country to escape prosecution, been outlawed, and then recaptured within the year. Armstrong then tried to take advantage of an Edwardian statute which gave outlawed persons the right to request a trial within a year of being outlawed but had been denied.[1]

The spectacular, public redress of what were perceived to be legal abuses of the old regime so quickly after the new one took power attests to the centrality of narratives about law to the Revolution of 1688. William of Orange had opened his 1689 *Declaration*, explaining in advance the reasons for his invasion with a ringing affirmation:

> It is both certain and evident to all men, that the public peace and happiness of any state or kingdom cannot be preserved, where the laws, liberties and customs established by the lawful authority in it, are openly transgressed and annulled.[2]

Accordingly, in the first few months of the new regime's existence several legal decisions of the old regime came under hostile scrutiny in Parliament and the press. The attainder of the Whig martyr Lord William Russell was reversed and his property restored to his widow. Inquiries were made into the death in the Tower of the Earl of Essex, another Rye House Plot defendant whose suicide while awaiting trial was suspected by many to have been murder. Parliament reviewed the past behavior of individual judges, asking who was to blame for allowing the previous two kings to murder judicial opponents, dispense with the laws, and conduct the notorious quo warranto campaigns against town corporations. Armstrong's case, for example, loomed large in Parliament's discussion of George Jeffreys, who, as Robert Howard put it, had "committed murder, and without the help of a jury."[3]

If the legitimacy of the new regime was connected to the appearance of upholding the law, that goal in turn might conflict with security. The many threats to the new government, both real and imagined, created an acute dilemma with respect to reconciling liberty and security. William of Orange had promised to restore the liberties of Englishmen. But the access of prisoners to the writ of habeas corpus was suspended for seven months in 1689 and then again in 1696. New legislation by Parliament banished Catholics from London and enabled the search and disarming of Catholics and other allegedly disaffected persons. Freedom of movement in and out of England was severely restricted. Books were burned, and the government conducted energetic searches for the writers and publishers of seditious material. The reform of treason trials to make them fairer to the defendant, which had been promised at the outset of the revolution, was repeatedly postponed by Parliaments that refused to pass a bill until 1696. Also during

Portrait of Whig martyrs, engraved and sold by John Savage, c. 1688–90. Thomas Armstrong, Lord William Russell, Algernon Sidney, and Alderman Cornish were widely considered victims of judicial murder. From Richard Bull's extra-illustrated copy of *Bishop Burnet's History of His Own Time* (London: Thomas Ward, 1723–34), 3:578. Reproduced by permission of The Huntington Library, San Marino, California.

Stephen College, executed for treason in 1681, was another Whig martyr whose trial was thought to exemplify the legal abuses of the Restoration regime. From Richard Bull's extra-illustrated copy of *Bishop Burnet's History of His Own Time* (London: Thomas Ward, 1723–34), 3:504. Reproduced by permission of The Huntington Library, San Marino, California.

the early years of the revolution, Parliament considered (but did not enact) legislation that expanded the definition of treason to include printing and speaking.[4]

For contemporary commentators who supported the exiled James II, the policies described above completely discredited the revolution: William III was held to be as bad as or worse than his predecessor. This point was made repeatedly in the pamphlets of the Whig-turned-Jacobite Robert Ferguson, who compared William's reign to that of Tiberius and lamented that "England under pretence of having its rights and liberties secured and vindicated, should be reduced to this worse than Turkish bondage and slavery." At the other extreme, the measures taken in the 1690s to secure the new government could be viewed as a temporary and understandable delay in a teleology of greater liberty. I reject both approaches: the compromises to civil liberty in the 1690s should be neither trivialized nor magnified to the point of indicting the revolution as a whole. My goal instead is to explore the controversies around the handling of threats to the regime as a window into the experience and process of regime change after 1688.[5]

This chapter looks at parliamentary debates on indemnity, loyalty oaths, habeas corpus, the reform of treason trials, the reversal of the conviction of Titus Oates, and the use of attainder. These debates reveal many kinds of divisions. Members of Parliament argued about the relative value of liberty and security, as well as about the relative importance of different institutions in upholding the revolution. Most important, however, these debates reveal the importance of ideology.

Whig and Tory Narratives

Whigs and Tories had very different experiences in the old regime, which in turn gave them very different approaches to justifying and preserving the revolution. A brief overview of the Whig and Tory parties in the late seventeenth century will help to clarify these differences.

The Whigs' relationship to the old regime and the revolution was formed in the matrix of the Popish Plot and Exclusion Crisis, in which, under the aegis of anti-Catholicism, they sought to circumscribe the power of the Crown and elevate that of Parliament. Given the prominence of the Popish Plot in later discussions of conspiracy, informers, and credibility, it is worth briefly recalling what it was (or was alleged to be).

In 1678, Titus Oates appeared at the office of the London magistrate Edmundbury Godfrey. He told Godfrey that Catholics were planning to kill the king, set fire to London, support a French invasion, and destroy the Protestant religion in England. The plotters, he alleged, were in the government, close to the king: his wife, his mistresses, his closest advisors, and his Catholic brother, the future James II.

Shortly after Oates made these revelations, Edmundbury Godfrey's body was found in a ditch, strangled. The murder gave Oates's story credibility.

Despite the air of sleaze hanging about Oates—he was rumored to be homosexual, his father was an Anabaptist, he had converted to and from Catholicism several times, and he was ignorant of Latin, despite his claims of having been in a Jesuit seminary—his allegations resulted in the execution of around twenty-five Catholics. Oates's revelations spurred Whigs in Parliament to press for an "exclusion bill" barring Catholics from inheriting the throne. Their immediate target was James, brother of Charles II and heir apparent to the throne, who had converted to Catholicism. But more broadly, Exclusionists were driven by a fear that Charles II would magnify royal power. By asserting a right to control royal succession, they made a radical claim about the superiority of law and Parliament over the king. Allegations about Catholics in positions of influence at court spilled over into a wider attack on powerful courtiers of any religion (like the Earl of Danby, the king's close advisor) who encouraged the king to ignore or manipulate his Parliament.

The Whig party that emerged in the Popish Plot and Exclusion Crisis was, then, not only anti-Catholic but also (as its enemies would allege) proto-republican or (as Whigs themselves would more likely put it) in favor of maintaining the structure of the ancient constitution in which kings were bound by law and ruled in conjunction with their Parliaments. The Whigs also emerged from the Exclusion Crisis as the party more sympathetic to the rights of Protestant dissenters (Presbyterians, Congregationalists, Baptists, Quakers), who suffered political disabilities and at times severe persecution because they defied the religious and political monopoly of the Church of England. This tie between dissenters and Whigs was cemented in part through the notion that *all* Protestants needed to unite against Catholics and in part because of deep historic links between Puritanism (from which Protestant dissent had emerged) and parliamentarianism/republicanism dating back to the first of the English revolutions.

The revelation of a Popish Plot gave Whigs a temporary upper hand in their struggles with the king, but eventually a backlash set in. Titus Oates

Flattering and unflattering images of Titus Oates. At left, Oates instructed by wisdom, from *A Prophecy of England's Future Happiness, after the Time That the Contrivers of This Popish Plot Are Cut Off. The Second Impression of Dr. Otes His Vindication: Shewing, His Evidence Is Not yet to Be Baffled by the Papists* (London: Thomas Dawks, [1680]). At right, Oates in the pillory, from *Titus Oates, Anagr[ram]. Testis Ovat* (London: Joseph Hindmarsh, 1685). Reproduced by permission of The Huntington Library, San Marino, California.

became less credible as his story grew and changed. He was convicted of perjury and sentenced to be pilloried and whipped with unusual brutality. Meanwhile, the government took advantage of the backlash against Oates to "discover" (scare quotes deliberate) the Rye House Plot in 1683, which allegedly involved prominent Whig opponents of the government (such as Algernon Sidney, the Earl of Shaftesbury, and Lord William Russell) in a scheme to assassinate King Charles II. The king also exploited fears of republicanism that had been raised by the Whig assault on his prerogative. Royal propagandists revived memories of the English Civil War, when a combination of religious radicals and anti-monarchical republicans had used the specter of popery in high places to plunge the country into horrific violence and, worse yet, chop off the head of their king. This royalist narrative now came to lay the groundwork for Tory identity. Casting themselves as supporters of the twin pillars of the monarchy and Anglican Church, the Tories (also known as "High Churchmen") preached that passive obedience to the monarch was a core doctrine of the Church of England, that dissenters threatened not only to the Church of England but also to the monarchy, and that consequently the king owed it to himself and the Church of England to stamp out Protestant dissent—or at the very least prevent dissenters from gaining any political power.

The Tories cast their lot so firmly with the monarchy that, despite their own anti-Catholicism, they opposed the Whigs' Exclusion Bill. They also supported Charles in a series of measures designed to curb the power of the Whigs by constitutionally dubious means. In the infamous quo warranto campaign of 1684, for example, Charles revoked and then rewrote the charters of a number of boroughs and corporations that sent members to Parliament in order to ensure that access to voting rights would be organized in a way that made it likelier that Tories would be elected as MPs. When Charles died in 1685, the Tories enthusiastically proclaimed allegiance to James II, in spite of his Catholic faith, in the belief that his reliance upon them as the pro-monarchical party would lead him to respect the rights of the Church of England and the Anglican monopoly on all political and military offices.

But over the next three years, James alienated his Tory supporters. He put Catholics into offices from which all non-Anglicans were by law excluded, claiming that as king he had power to dispense with such laws. He appointed Catholics to the governing board of Magdalen College, Oxford, which violated the college's charter and defeated its purpose as an Anglican seminary.

Moreover, James tried to win support for his pro-Catholic policies from Protestant dissenters by promising that both groups would get the benefit of religious toleration. To this end, he issued a Declaration of Indulgence, establishing toleration for Catholics and dissenters by royal fiat, without the consent of Parliament. To add insult to injury, James ordered the clergy of the Church of England to read the Declaration of Indulgence from their pulpits. Many clergymen refused, and seven Anglican bishops who had spearheaded the resistance were thrown in the Tower and tried for sedition. So it was that the High Church Tories who had brought James II to the throne united with their Whig opponents to overthrow him.

Although Whigs and Tories had joined to bring William of Orange to the throne, each group had a different relationship to the revolution and to the new king. Tories wrestled with ambivalence about the act of deposing a sovereign after having spent the previous thirty years preaching the doctrine of passive obedience. Their allegiance to William was thus in some doubt, and there was reason to wonder if, in a paroxysm of conscience, the High Churchmen would revert to their former support for James. But the Tories also had a claim on William's favor because they despised republican or commonwealth notions of the people being able to dictate to a king and were committed to upholding the powers and prerogatives of the Crown in relation to Parliament. Moreover, the very ambivalence of the Tories about the revolution meant that William had to placate them. At the beginning of his reign, then, William found reasons to trust and to distrust both Whigs and Tories, and he strove to balance places on his council and important offices of state between members of both parties. As a result, some of his influential advisors were Tories who had held high office in previous reigns. These included the Marquis of Halifax and the Earl of Danby (now elevated to Marquis of Carmarthen), who as noted above had been attacked by Whigs in the Exclusion Crisis.

Loyalty Oaths and Indemnity

Divisions between Whigs and Tories emerged most clearly in the debates about loyalty oaths and about indemnity for persons who actively supported the previous regime. These two debates hinged on the same question: Should the new government include or exclude those with a checkered political past or suspect political loyalties? How members of Parliament responded to that question was related to their own historical relationships to the governments of Charles II and James II and the paths by and terms upon which they had come to support the revolution. Not surprisingly, there were crass partisan stakes in these debates. Both Whigs and Tories tried to manipulate legislation on loyalty oaths and indemnity in such a way as to preserve their friends and disable their enemies. But alongside these strategic considerations there existed very different notions held by Whigs and Tories of what the revolution meant and how to legitimate and secure it.

Whigs felt that the Revolution of 1688 needed to be continually reaffirmed and vindicated. Parliament had to be seen to be active in defense of the regime not only financially and militarily but ideologically, promoting a narrative that established the unquestionable rightness of its actions and the legitimacy of the current order. To truly support the revolution, individuals were required to embrace that narrative. The Tories, following the fine Elizabethan tradition of "not making windows into men's souls," preferred to let people reconcile themselves to the revolution on their own terms; it was enough that subjects behave as if they accepted William's authority, and in return the government would treat its subjects as if they were (now) loyal. These two approaches to revolution did not coexist easily. To Tories, Whigs were ripping open wounds, creating unnecessary fears and divisions. To Whigs, Tories were probably crypto-Jacobites.

Loyalty Oaths

Loyalty oaths were fraught because they called to mind a history of infidelity and insincerity. During a discussion of a proposed oath to abjure James II, MP Robert Harley offered a scathing historical reflection:

> In the late times, how many oaths were taken? And yet when King Charles II returned, they took them again to him—nay, when the oath of abjuration of the royal family was taken some of those very men were at that time contriving to restore him. So that I think multitudes of oaths no great security; they serve but as a snare to some men and will not hold such as are your enemies.[6]

But if oaths had been broken, members of Parliament found them essential for distinguishing the loyal from the disloyal. Oaths were further intended to vindicate the new regime by teaching members of the public the true grounds of their obedience to it. Unfortunately, there was no consensus on those grounds for obedience. As noted above, overthrowing one king (to whom one had taken oaths of allegiance) and then taking oaths of allegiance to another presented many High Church Tories with a moral conundrum. Because Parliament was sensitive to this problem, the new oath of allegiance it imposed in 1689 was mild. The 1689 oath was largely modeled on the 1606 Jacobean oath of allegiance, which had been designed to distinguish loyal from disloyal Catholics. Like the 1606 oath, the 1689 oath required takers to repudiate the "impious and heretical doctrine" that the pope had the power to depose princes and to swear to obey the English monarch. There was, however, a crucial difference. The 1689 oath of allegiance did not (as the 1606 oath had done) require takers to acknowledge their monarch as a "rightful and lawful" monarch. This very deliberate omission was thought by contemporaries to substantially lower the degree of loyalty a person would need to feel in order to take the 1689 oath. Its wording made it possible for conscience-stricken Anglicans to justify swearing allegiance to the new regime in a defactoist spirit, continuing to regard James as their king de jure (by law) while accepting William as monarch in fact. While the defactoist oath may have enabled many High Church Anglicans to take the new oath now required of officeholders and clergy, it also cast doubt on what the oath was worth and whether those who took it could really be trusted to support the regime. If James invaded, if there were a military contest on English soil between James and William, if there were any doubt about William's continuing control, then those who had sworn allegiance to William in a defactoist spirit might switch their allegiance back to James. How many takers of the 1689 oath of allegiance contemplated such a switch is unknowable. The point for our purposes is that Whigs used the possibility of that switch to raise doubts about Tory allegiance. Tories in response argued that the voicing of such doubts was itself divisive and seditious.

On the nervous-making occasion of William's journey to Ireland, Whigs in Parliament proposed that a new oath to abjure and renounce King James be administered to all officeholders, with a proviso that justices of the peace have the power to imprison refusers of this new abjuration oath without bail. As the Whig Master of the Rolls Powle made clear, the wording of the new abjuration oath was intended to close the defactoist loophole in the existing oaths of allegiance, for "to obey the King de facto, is no other than to obey till I have power to rebel." Supporters of the abjuration oath suggested not only that loopholes existed but that many potential traitors had already slipped through. Thomas Lee thought the oaths especially necessary "when I am told, that men in employment drink King James's health." John Mainwaring staged a dramatic demonstration of the need for better oaths by accusing his fellow MP from Cheshire, Thomas Grosvenor, of wishing for King James's return. Despite (Whig) Controller Wharton's assertion that "this bill is not against the Church of England," Whigs directed much innuendo about oath takers who were secretly disloyal at the Anglican clergy. A jab at clergymen's skill in casuistry seems to lie behind John Thompson's quip, "One thing is missing in the bill, that all the lawyers in England swear to it; and then the divines will not scruple it." Thomas Littleton more directly cast doubt upon High Churchmen's loyalty and the motives for it: "The government was never asserted by the churchmen, till Magdalen-College was touched. They have a notion in their heads of the Great Turk, that if they may be bashaws, they will swear allegiance to the Great Turk."[7]

Not surprisingly, Tories opposed the bill on grounds that it was a partisan measure designed to marginalize, divide, or as Henry Goodrick colorfully put it, "garble the Nation." Other Tories cautioned, without mentioning names, that the bill would fail to distinguish friends from enemies and instead make more enemies than friends. Simon Harcourt predicted it would foment "jealosies."

> Such an unprecedented oath will give occasion to think there is some defect in the government, when such an oath was never required in this government to support it. Can we gain more friends? Those who quietly obey it, naturally, if they suffer by it, will find means to redress themselves. You will make no friends by it; you will make enemies.[8]

The very expression of a need for a better loyalty oath, it was suggested, would make England's vulnerability more obvious. As the Tory Thomas Clarges put it, "Where you put a buttress, there the building is weak." Lord Falkland, likewise, advocated the wisdom of overlooking possible disloyalty for the sake of winning friends, reminding his listeners that "when Augustus Cæsar had a list given him of those who conspired against him, he burnt that list; which made those and their families his friends."[9]

The new abjuration oath was voted down, but the controversy continued in the furor erupting around the publication of *A Modest Enquiry into the Causes of the Present Disasters in England*, a broad attack on the loyalty of

Anglican Tories. The author suggested that Anglicans were so driven by malice toward dissenters that, as they had in James II's reign, they would ally with Catholics to crush them. The pamphlet reasserted the veracity of the Popish Plot, the falsity of the Rye House Plot, and the existence of a third plot in which High Church Anglican Tories collaborated with Catholics to invite Louis XIV to invade England and restore James II. To make his claims plausible, the author asserted that since few of the disaffected clergy "had the courage to lay down their places," they had decided "to cheat the World and their own consciences with a ridiculous and foolish distinction of taking the oaths to a King *de facto*, but not *de jure*."

> And indeed what could be more efficacious to alienate the hearts of the people from their Majesties, than either to suppose them King and Queen *de facto* only, or to buzz into people's ears, that in swearing allegiance to them, they thereby acknowledge no lawful right to the crown to be in their persons.[10]

The Tory secretary of state, the Earl of Nottingham, promptly had the pamphlet's publisher Richard Baldwin committed to Newgate. For this Nottingham was warmly thanked by the Scottish Anglican politician George Mackenzie of Rosehaugh, who remarked that the pamphlet was read in (dissenting) conventicles and admired in Scotland and that he wished "you would further punish them [the authors] in order to free the churchmen of jealousies."[11]

Loyalty and Catholicism

The politics of loyalty oaths had an indirect but significant impact on the treatment of Catholics and on the question of whether loyalty was to be deemed a purely secular matter or equated with Protestantism. There were no obvious partisan differences concerning the treatment of Catholics. Important pieces of legislation like the "Act for the Amoving Papists and Reputed Papists from the Cities of London and Westminster and Ten Miles Distance from the Same" and the "Act for the Better Securing the Government by Disarming Papists and Reputed Papists" seem to have been entirely uncontroversial, enacted with no recorded debate in Parliament. Nonetheless, Tories had a particular interest in promoting the idea that Catholics were by definition disloyal and, conversely, that Protestants were loyal. Until 1696, they succeeded in using loyalty oaths to keep alive the association of

Catholicism and disloyalty in the face of mounting evidence that Protestants, too, could be disloyal. This strategy in turn helped to ameliorate the scandal of Anglican disloyalty, which had made the Tories vulnerable to having questions raised about their own allegiance to the revolution.

The credibility of the Tories as reliable supporters of the new regime was threatened by the existence of non-jurors, Tory Anglicans who refused to take the 1689 oath of allegiance. Although non-jurors were a minority of the Tory party, they were prestigious. They included, for example, William Sancroft, the archbishop of Canterbury, who had impeccable anti-Catholic credentials for leading the famous Seven Bishops in challenging the Declaration of Indulgence. When King William deprived the non-juring bishops and clergy of their offices and appointed new ones, the non-jurors proclaimed themselves to be the "True Church of England." They refused to recognize the new bishops that William appointed, continued to hold services, and printed a liturgy for use by their adherents. Their status as the "True Church" rested on a principle of episcopal succession stretching back to St. Augustine of Canterbury, the first English archbishop. Putting forth a strongly clericalist, anti-Erastian position, they maintained that William had no right to deprive bishops of their sees. The claim to be the "True Church of England" was also a reference to ideological consistency, their adherence to the essential doctrines of passive obedience and nonresistance.

Non-jurors were disturbing in disproportion to their numbers. Their existence called attention to the awkwardness in the position of Anglicans who did take the 1689 oath (continuing to claim passive obedience was their core doctrine even as they abandoned James II) and gave reason to question how sincere these juring Anglicans were in their support for the new regime. The existence of non-jurors also undermined the equation Anglicanism and loyalty, Catholicism and disloyalty, which had justified the Anglican monopoly on legal worship (until 1689) and still justified the continuing Anglican monopoly on political officeholding.

The sharp line between Anglican and Catholic, however, was reasserted forcefully in the way that loyalty oaths were administered. The 1689 oath of allegiance caught Anglicans as well as Catholics in its net, but penalties for refusing it were relatively light. Catholic and Protestant refusers alike faced fines of not more than £10, sureties for good behavior, and exclusion from political office. By contrast, refusers of the 1606 oath of allegiance, all of whom were Catholic, faced imprisonment and penalties of praemunire.

Nonetheless, Catholic non-jurors were punished more harshly than their Protestant counterparts, thanks to a new legal requirement that refusers of the oath of allegiance be tendered the Catholic-detecting Declaration against Transubstantiation, wherein the taker had to affirm that the invocation of the Virgin and saints and the sacrament of the Mass, "as they are now used in the Church of Rome, are superstitious and idolatrous." Refusers of the Declaration against Transubstantiation, having presumably outed themselves as Catholic, would then be subject to the penal laws affecting Catholic recusants. Thus instead of creating, as the 1606 oath did, a distinction between loyal and disloyal Catholics, the 1689 oath used in combination with the Declaration against Transubstantiation created a distinction between disloyal Protestants and disloyal Catholics, with Protestants given lesser penalties and a privileged status in relation to Catholics. The line between Protestant and Catholic was thus maintained and accentuated even when the oaths demonstrated that Protestants could be disloyal.[12]

The line between Protestant and Catholic disloyalty was insisted upon, in the early 1690s, even at moments when one would think secularism would triumph. A fascinating example of how the line between Catholic and Protestant could be sharpened even at a moment when a religion-neutral definition of loyalty was recognized was the abortive "Papist Toleration Bill," or "Act for Exempting Their Majesties' Popish Subjects from the Penalties of Certain Laws," which was drafted in a committee of the House of Lords in December 1689 but never came to a vote. The Papist Toleration Bill created an oath of allegiance in which (like the normal 1689 oath) the taker promised "to be faithful and bear true allegiance" to William and Mary and denied papal deposing power, but it dropped the reference (present in both 1606 and 1689 oaths) to papal deposing power as an "impious and heretical" doctrine. It thus was meant to pose no religious obstacles for Roman Catholics (and paralleled similar legislation for Quakers). Those Catholics who took the oath would be freed from the stiff financial penalties (£20 fine per week and the possibility of seizure of property), which had been imposed on recusants, and allowed to reside within London and its environs. They would have the same freedom of worship as dissenters under the Toleration Act, but this would not extend to the *public* exercise of the popish religion.

John Bossy has discussed the draft Papist Toleration Bill as evidence of the king's tolerationist intentions. And indeed, the draft bill does seem (except for the restriction of public worship) to make loyalty religiously neutral at last. However, even had the bill passed, it would still have treated Catholics very differently from Protestants. Those who did take the new oath would have been allowed to live in London, but the bill neglected to exempt them from the laws preventing Catholics from possessing weapons and horses. Such an omission could not have been mere oversight. Moreover, the bill, which made oath taking mandatory for all recusants, created penalties for Catholics who did not take it—a £100 fine and six months' imprisonment—that were far harsher than the penalties imposed on Protestant non-jurors. The importance of the Protestant/Catholic distinction was, moreover, underscored by the provision that a person could avoid these stiff penalties by taking instead the Declaration against Transubstantiation: that option was intended to let Protestants who could not swear "true allegiance" to William and Mary nonetheless prove they were not Catholics. Had the Papist Toleration Bill become law, then, it would have maintained and even sharpened the distinction between disloyal Protestants and disloyal Catholics and (if laws about refusers of the Declaration against Transubstantiation remained unchanged) also put loyal Catholics in a different category from loyal Protestants. In any case, the bill died in committee, which suggests that the idea of a religiously neutral loyalty test had little support.[13]

This maintenance of a Catholic/Protestant distinction was driven by the desire of High Church Tories to occlude the existence of Anglican Jacobitism, or rather (since one could not hide its existence completely), to give Protestant non-jurors a privileged status in relation to Catholics. What was being protected was not just non-jurors as individuals but the principle that Protestantism was by definition loyal (and hence that the loyalty of Protestants need not be questioned).

Indemnity

Partisan differences emerged strongly in debates on indemnity. Whigs and Tories alike agreed in principle that it would be wise to offer pardon or immunity from prosecution to most people who had acted in the service of the previous regime and might therefore now be accused of political crimes, as "no government can be so secure, as when satisfied that they have a gracious merciful king." Likewise, both agreed in principle that some exceptions had to be made in this general pardon for people who were particularly bad, so that the government was seen to do justice.[14]

Despite this general agreement, the debates about a proposed "Act for the King and Queen's Most Gracious General and Free Pardon" dragged on interminably, stalling over the question of whom to except from the general pardon and how to define their crimes. Not surprisingly, Whigs and Tories argued over what or whom to condemn in ways reflecting not only different experiences of the past but different agendas for the present.

The different pasts of Whigs and Tories affected their respective choices of emphasis. Tories tried to identify those responsible for the assaults on the Church of England during the reign of James II, such as the intrusion of Roman Catholics into the government of Magdalen College and the imprisonment of the Seven Bishops—in short, the acts that had turned them from supporters to opponents of the regime. Whigs brushed off their concerns. As John Hawles put it, "The case of Magdalen College is but a trifle to what they have done in other things." His fellow Whig Jack Howe pointedly asked, "Was there no property in England till Magdalen College? Nor any liberty till the Bishops were sent to the Tower?" The crimes against liberty and property on which Howe wished to focus lay not only in James's reign, but in that of Charles II, and they involved not only popish crimes against the Church of England but also Tory crimes against Whigs. The alteration of borough charters (quo warranto campaign) during Charles II's reign to ensure a Tory majority in Parliament, for example, was considered by the Whig Henry Capel to be "certainly the greatest of treasons." The Tory Joseph Tredenham, by contrast, while not endorsing the alteration of charters, warned against looking too closely into who was guilty on that score:

> You have been told of taking away charters of corporations; consider what a great number will be involved on that head, and how safe the government will be when so many are unsafe under it. . . . All sorts of persons have contributed to it; and people will rather upon severity cover past faults with greater, than be reformed.[15]

Whigs were also more prone to demand that the guilt be ascribed not only to immediate perpetrators of the old regime's crimes but to the councilors and ministers who lay behind them. The judges who had granted James II the power to dispense with laws in the notorious case of *Godden v. Hales* were not, argued some Whigs, the most culpable perpetrators of the attack

The Lord Chancellor Taken Disguis'd in Wapping [1688]. Reviled for his prosecution of Whigs and harsh punishment of Monmouth's rebels, Lord Chancellor George Jeffreys was captured trying to escape in disguise during the revolution. Even after his death in April 1689 he was hanged in effigy and excepted from Parliament's Act of Indemnity. The engraver's depiction of the devil and the bloodthirsty crowd, however, may express anxiety about mob justice as much as it recalls Jeffreys's crimes. City of London, London Metropolitan Archives.

on English liberty, for they had been pressured and set to it by ministers close to the king. The Whig Robert Cotton (of Cheshire) affirmed that the judges "were set on by greater persons, and those are fitter for our justice." Likewise, Jack Howe asked, "Which is the greater crime; they that went a fishing for a knave to do it, or the poor knave that did it."[16]

There were obvious practical stakes in the debate between Whigs and Tories about how to define the guilty. Whigs insisted on punishing high-ranking ministers from past reigns because some of those same ministers (Halifax and Carmarthen) were currently in William's councils and were identified with the Tories. The proposal to except such people from an act of indemnity was thus tied to efforts, in other contexts, to get the king to dismiss anyone who had served James II. Similarly, the lengthy discussions during the indemnity debates about who was to blame for the revocation of London's charter might be seen as a prelude to an unsuccessful Whig effort, six months later, to tack on to the "Act to Restore Corporations to Their Ancient Rights and Privileges" a proviso known as the "Sacheverell Clause," which would have politically disabled any officeholder who had cooperated in the quo warranto campaigns. Predictably, Tories opposed such efforts, recognizing themselves as the political target thereof.[17]

However, Whig-Tory differences on indemnity were not just driven by the immediate goal of disabling enemies. They reflected very different attitudes about how to best secure the revolution. Tories tended in the indemnity debates, as they had done in discussions of the abjuration oath, to speak of the need for unity and bad effects of division. The Tory Robert Cotton of Cambridgeshire warned against conducting inquiries that would "alarm the nation" and pleaded for a "quiet peaceable spirit amongst ourselves" which would lead to "moderation and unity." His fellow Tory William Ettrick declared himself in favor of "making as many friends as we can; so many as you except [from indemnity], so many enemies you make to the government." And Sir Joseph Tredenham stressed the need to limit the number of those excepted: the purpose of the Indemnity Bill, he argued, was to "reconcile men's minds to the government," and he thought it best to follow the example of Henry IV of France, who when France was "in combustion" took "great care to punish some, and leave the rest in some degree of favor."[18]

Whigs, by contrast, thought that what was at stake was the vindication of the revolution. As Thomas Papillon put it, punishments were required "not for revenge, but to vindicate the nation." At times, to punish the guilty was represented as a purification, a purging of blood. Thus, when arguing that the House of Commons should expel one of its members, Robert Sawyer (who had collaborated with the alleged judicial murder of Sir Thomas Armstrong), the Whig Robert Rich voiced an intention "to wipe blood off from this House." Colonel Robert Austen, also a Whig, insisted in the indemnity debates that Parliament could not "justice to the nation, nor is the cry of blood answered, if you do not your duty."[19]

Moreover, many Whigs linked punishment to public self-justification: to fail to exercise justice for the crimes of the old regime would make it look as if James had done nothing wrong and that the revolution was therefore groundless. Robert Rich thought that "to pass by all bloodshed and violation of our Laws, is the way to bring in King James." For Robert Howard, to pardon judges who had done James's dirty work was to "say King William has done all the wrong, and they none." One Whig MP, Anthony Rowe, brought similar arguments outside the doors of Parliament with a campaign pamphlet arguing that only the punishment of evil councilors would "vindicate his [William's] descent in England from being an unrighteous invasion." Not to identify such councilors, Rowe asserted, would make the reasons for giving William the crown "exposed and ridiculed," for William "must needs look upon all that was alleged, concerning the late King's violation of the original contract, and his subverting the laws of the constitution, as fiction and dream, while there were none to be found, that counseled him unto, or elicited him in it."[20]

The desire to vindicate the revolution dictated the approach some Whigs took to the process of drawing up the Indemnity Bill. The House of Commons had to decide whether to define exceptions to the Act of Pardon in terms of "things" or "persons," that is, to identify the crimes for which people would not be forgiven or to simply list the people who would be excepted from a pardon. The decision was considered at least twice. In May 1689 the Commons resolved to identify the crimes for which persons could not be pardoned and then name the persons guilty of those crimes. But after seemingly interminable debates with little progress toward writing the bill, they reconsidered their procedure. In the end, the king grew so impatient that he himself provided a list of persons to be excepted from the pardon![21]

The views of MPs on whether to define exceptions to the indemnity in terms of things or persons divided largely though not exclusively on party lines. The speakers who advocated identifying unpardonable "things" included the Whigs Robert Howard, Colonel Robert Austen, Henry Capel, John Wildman, and Richard Hampden. Such an approach made sense, they argued, because it was most in accordance with legality. "Were it not more clear to name your crimes?" asked Richard Hampden,

> And then we may the more impartially give judgment. In all courts, in all judicatures, they say, "Here is the law, and here is the fact, and then try if the persons be guilty of this fact." A man to be tried, and to be guilty of a crime which is not defined!

The Whig solicitor John Somers linked the identification of offenders' crimes with the vindication of the revolution itself, advising them to start with "heads" in order to "have the world see the crimes you have punished."[22]

A number of Tory MPs, by contrast, argued that to express the exceptions to indemnity in terms of crimes or things would threaten too many people. As Richard Temple put it, "to name the crime, you may involve more than you think" and "[if we name] things, we are in a wood, and shall never get out of it. . . . I would put men's minds in peace, and make examples only of notorious instruments." His concerns were echoed by Robert Cotton, who opined, "If you proceed that way, of enquiring into things before persons, you will leave such jealousies in people, as that they will not think themselves safe; it will go so large, I fear it will hazard the peace and safety of the nation."[23]

The divisions on this question of "things versus persons" were not entirely partisan: some Whigs, like John Hawles and Colonel Birch, thought that proceeding according to "things" would cause too much delay and so discredit the revolution by postponing the identification of the perpetrators of abuses in previous reigns. Nonetheless, differences over whether to proceed by things or persons did to a large extent reflect the Whigs' desire to be seen to act in accordance with law and to publicly name the offenses of the old regime while at the same time demonstrating the Tory preference for reconciliation and unity.[24]

The Nature of Law

The discussions of indemnity pointed to a conundrum concerning the law. The very idea of giving a pardon and then making exceptions to it for heinous perpetrators or heinous crimes implicitly relied on the notion that laws had been broken in the previous reigns. But given that English common law was understood to be based on precedent, and given that many of the proposed exceptions to indemnity concerned judges and the rulings they had handed down in the recent past, how was one to know the law? Could decisions made by judges be called "illegal"? And if so, by what standard?

The largely Tory group that wanted to define exceptions to the Indemnity Bill "according to persons" was able to dodge this question of what the law was. They adopted an I-know-it-when-I-see-it approach to assigning guilt. As the Tory Gilbert Dolben put it, "Some [unpardonable persons], like Cain, bear their brands about them. You will find enough to satisfy the justice of the nation."[25]

The largely Whig group that wanted to proceed "according to things" faced a harder challenge. They had to define the crimes that had been committed, which in turn meant specifying what laws had been broken. The stakes for Whigs went beyond the punishing of enemies. Their insistence that the most fundamental crimes of the former regime could be named allowed them to assert the existence of that law, independently of any decisions made by the courts.

The uncertainties about the law implicit in the indemnity debates surfaced in other contexts. Given William's promise, in his *Declaration*, to defend the "laws, liberties, and customs established by the lawful authority," it is striking to find a wide range of attitudes to the sanctity and effectiveness of law expressed in parliamentary debates. Members of Parliament differed on how the law was to be known, which institutions were best suited to define and secure it, whether English law needed to be restored or reformed, whether good or bad laws actually mattered, and, most painfully, what to do if the law clashed with the need for security. Such questions, especially the last, suffused parliamentary debates about the suspension of habeas corpus, the reform of treason trials, the use of attainder, and the reversal of Titus Oates's conviction for perjury.

Habeas Corpus

The most agonizing issue facing the new government was how far it could go in detaining suspected traitors when there was little evidence against them. According to the Habeas Corpus Act of 1679, a person arrested had the right to ask his jailor for a copy of the warrant and to take it before a judge, who would then review the evidence to see if the prisoner should be released, bailed, or remanded for trial. Although the Habeas Corpus Act itself was young in 1688, the judicial practice of issuing writs to ensure that jailors did not abuse their power was longstanding and, as Paul Halliday and G. Edward White have shown, done with impressive frequency in the late seventeenth century. By 1688, as the debates about its suspension were to show, the right (or privilege) of obtaining habeas writs was widely deemed a safeguard of the subject's liberties, which the revolution had been meant to protect. The suspension of habeas corpus for several months in 1689 did not occur without painful debate.[26]

Before turning to the debates, it is helpful to consider how English men and women in the late seventeenth century experienced the possibility of detention in various contexts. How effective writs of habeas corpus were in protecting men and women from arbitrary imprisonment is an open question. There is some evidence that secretaries of state scrupulously respected the rights associated with habeas corpus, even when it did not seem in the state's interest to do so. The Earl of Nottingham was frustrated when sworn depositions providing evidence against suspected conspirators John Cockeram and Robert Ferguson failed to arrive from Scotland, for "without some proof upon oath, they cannot be detained." Although King William commented to Nottingham that the law requiring him to grant bail to these suspects was a "great defect in the government," they were indeed bailed.[27]

Secretary of State Shrewsbury, too, made sure that habeas rights were enforced. On 26 December 1689, he wrote sternly to remind the mayor of Bristol to follow the law when, after several prisoners exercised their right to demand a written copy of their commitment, it was found that the jailor had received them in prison on verbal orders only.[28]

However, the power of habeas corpus to protect the liberty of the subject was somewhat limited. It is important to note, for example, that although the Habeas Corpus Act guaranteed that a judge would review a case, it did not tell judges how to behave nor did it punish them for improperly refusing to admit a person to bail.[29]

Moreover, the right of habeas corpus did not affect persons committed to prison by Parliament in its capacity as a court. Thus, when habeas corpus was restored in October 1689, some people found that upon being admitted to bail by the Court of King's Bench they were promptly impeached by the House of Commons and recommitted to prison. The issuing of blank warrants and blanket instructions to round up categories of people continued even after habeas corpus had been restored. Lord lieutenants of the counties, such as Lord Brandon in Lancashire, exercised broad powers of detention. In May 1690, for example, he was ordered to "disarm and seize all disaffected persons in Lancashire." Vague orders, such as that from Secretary of State Nottingham to one Mr. Taylor, to "detain all people you suspect of designs against the government," appear frequently in the state papers.[30]

Although these detentions may have been brief, they were nonetheless distressing and destructive. John Farmer's irate letter to Nottingham about his imprisonment in Beaumoris, without accusation or warrant, no doubt expressed the feelings of many; although in fact held only two days before being brought to the mayor and released, he was "damnified in business and health."[31]

The most intriguing evidence that people were sometimes detained on slender grounds comes from a moment when many of them were released. In mid-August 1690, after the threat of a French invasion had evaporated, Luttrell recorded in his diary:

> It has been lately ordered in council upon the petition of several persons in custody, that those against whom there was no positive proof should be admitted their liberty upon bail, and accordingly several are bailed out; those charged upon oath are continued in custody.[32]

We can deduce from this that people had been detained without bail even when there was no positive proof against them. The argument that many persons committed on charges of treason had, it turned out, little evidence against them was stated powerfully by the anonymous author of *Reasons for a New Bill of Rights*, who wrote that since the passage of the Habeas Corpus Act in 1679,

> five hundred persons to one have been committed more than ever were tried, or so much as indicted: it is observable that every year or two, a dozen or twenty Lords are usually shopt together with incredible numbers of the greatest commoners, over and besides the small fry of &c. Halls and churches have been turned into prisons when the common gaols were crowded even to the danger of infection; and I am apt to believe that hundreds have been committed without oath; and consequently without just cause of suspicion, for there ought to be oath of that fact or circumstance which rendered the party suspected.

As we will see in chapter 7, there were ways to detain people in prison without trial: John Bernardi, a suspected Assassination Plot conspirator, spent thirty-three years in Newgate.[33]

Nonetheless, while the existence of habeas corpus did not fully protect subjects from arbitrary detention, the prospect of holding suspects without bail on dubious charges occasioned fierce debate in Parliament. The first of these occurred even before William and Mary were crowned. In February 1689, London Tory alderman James Smith was brought to the bar of the House of Commons to explain why he had granted bail to Robert Brent, a well-known Catholic supporter of James II who had subsequently absconded. Smith replied, simply, "I bailed him, because there was not any information against him, but that he was a papist." Smith went on to explain that he had issued a warrant to commit Brent to the Compter at the request of the sheriff of London, William Waller, who had informed him that Brent was "a great criminal." When Waller failed to bring a charge against Brent, however, Smith turned to the recorder of London, the jurist and MP George Treby, for advice on "what he should do with Brent. . . . There was a great complaint against him, but no evidence: whether he should bail him or no, and what bail he should take?" Treby advised him to keep Brent in prison for a reasonable time and give notice to the prosecutor to bring evidence but not to detain him longer, for "if he be kept a reasonable time, and no prosecutor appears, it is reasonable to bail him."[34]

Smith's explanation did not, however, satisfy the House of Commons. Members who condemned Smith's actions pointed to the obviousness of Brent's guilt and the smallness of the bail Smith had asked (£1,500) in comparison to the amount of bail required of prominent opponents of the previous regime (like Lord Delamere, who had to come up with £20,000). They further suggested that some "great persons" (including the infamous Earl of Danby) might have influenced Smith on Brent's behalf. In the end, Parliament decided that James Smith had to be punished and had him committed.[35]

Shortly thereafter, Parliament found itself more systematically considering the government's powers to detain suspects. In March 1689, William informed Parliament that a number of people conspiring against the government had been seized, on "suspicion of treason only" (meaning, without proof), and that it would be dangerous to the government should these people obtain liberty through means of habeas corpus. He told Parliament he was loath to do anything against the law and asked their advice. Members of Parliament were pleasantly shocked by this request. Tellingly, the only thing they could quickly agree on was that they should thank the king for having asked their advice![36]

Parliament, after long debate, did pass an "An Act for Impowering His Majestie to Apprehend and Detaine Such Persons as He Shall Finde Just Cause to Suspect Are Conspireing against the Government" on 6 March 1689. The act in effect suspended habeas corpus in cases of treason or suspected treason, but only for one month. It stipulated that on a set date, 17 April, everyone detained would have the right of habeas corpus restored. Unfortunately, when that day rolled around, England was if anything in more danger, and habeas corpus was suspended for another month by an apparently unanimous vote, until May. And in May, faced with continuing threats, Parliament voted to suspend again, though with much more debate. Since summer recess was coming, they suspended until October. All in all, habeas corpus was suspended for a total of seven months, after which it was restored, until the discovery of a plot to assassinate William in 1696 again led to its suspension. Subsequent suspensions occurred in 1708, 1715, 1722, 1745, 1794–95, 1798–1801, and 1817.[37]

In addition to the suspension of habeas corpus, Parliament seriously considered two proposals that would have increased the government's power to detain suspects. As noted above, a provision of the rejected Abjuration Bill in April 1690 was that justices of the peace would have the power to imprison without bail anyone refusing to take the new abjuration oath. Very shortly thereafter, Parliament considered a bill to secure the government during the king's absence in Ireland, which included a proviso that members of the Privy Council have the right to commit persons suspected of treasonable correspondence, without a chance of bail. Neither proposal was adopted. However, two acts of Parliament indemnified persons who acted in the interest of the new government, protecting them from lawsuits even if they had broken the law. Such measures significantly limited the scope of the right of habeas corpus since persons who had been detained without cause had no legal recourse against those who detained them.[38]

The central question raised in debates on the above-mentioned measures was whether the security of the government lay in having wider powers or in adhering to the principles that legitimated its existence. The former position was well expressed by the Whig Colonel Birch:

> We are in a state of war, and worse than war. There is a great man on one side the water, and King James on the other, and a popish party, and another, in the midst of us; and this is a state of war, sure. If this be our

condition, and disaffected persons in every corner, I would know of any man how this Habeas Corpus Act is now practicable.

The latter was as eloquently stated by Sir William Ettrick, who asserted that "the security of all governments is the good-will of the people; and I fear this may take their good-will from you."[39]

Treason Trials

The several iterations of a bill for regulating treason trials proposed in the early 1690s brought out exactly the same conflict of views as did the debate over suspending habeas corpus. The proposals were meant to give defendants in treason trials a fairer chance of acquittal. Two sworn witnesses would be required to convict. Defendants would be shown a copy of the indictment and a list of prospective jurors prior to the trial; they would be able to put their own witnesses under oath and to have the benefit of legal counsel. Such reforms were popular at the outset of the revolution. It was widely believed that the lack of such protections for defendants had made possible the judicial murders of Algernon Sidney, Lord William Russell, and other opponents of the previous regime. Thus, as Alexander Shapiro puts it, "trial reform became a plank of the revolutionary platform of the Prince of Orange."[40]

Versions of a bill to reform treason trials came before the House of Commons seven times before finally being passed in 1696. The difference of views that emerged in the debates over habeas corpus was echoed in arguments about the treason trial reform. Speaking in November 1692 in favor of an amendment that would have delayed the start of the proposed reforms until after the end of the war with France, Solicitor Trevor rhetorically asked whether the greatest danger was "from your enemies, or an imaginary one of injustice from Westminster-Hall?" To which Robert Harley responded much like the speakers who opposed the suspension of habeas corpus, asking, "Will putting off this Bill secure you? The best way to secure the government is to set men at ease."[41]

Party differences were often significant in the debates. Colonel Birch, quoted above speaking so strongly in favor of suspending habeas corpus, was a Whig, and William Ettrick and a number of other opponents of suspension—Robert Napier, Robert Sawyer, Thomas Clarges, and William Whitelocke—were Tories. Samuel Rezneck has pointed out that treason trial reform after 1688 ironically became a Tory cause and was only "reluctantly accepted by Whigs." To what can we attribute this apparently stronger civil libertarianism of the Tories in these debates? Rezneck speculates that the civil liberties, especially for defendants in treason trials, were typically a cause embraced by an "out" group that feared coming under suspicion.[42]

Another possible explanation of Whig-Tory divisions over treason trial reform might be that the narrative embraced by Whigs about the illegality of the previous regime made Whigs more resistant than Tories were to legal change. As discussed above, during the debate about the Indemnity Bill many Whigs insisted that the most fundamental crimes of the former regime could be named, even when those crimes took the form of legal decision by judges. The logical implication was that the law existed independently of decisions made by bad judges appointed by bad kings. Now that England had good government, legal reform would not be necessary. John Lowther expressed this logic, holding existing laws sufficient "especially as we have so good a government as this now is wherein this law [the Treason Trials Bill] is needless. And if a bad one [government] come I am sure this law will signify little and be no protection to the innocent."[43]

The notion that bad men, not bad laws, were responsible for the judicial murders of the previous regime might have found some support from the work of the Whig lawyer John Hawles, who in 1689 penned an extensive analysis of what he deemed to be legal irregularities in the Crown's proceedings during the Restoration against Algernon Sidney, Stephen College, William Russell, Alderman Cornish, and other Whigs. Hawles argued that the judges and lawyers acting on behalf of the two late kings, Charles II and James II, had violated the *existing* law. Although Hawles called attention to the many unfair disadvantages under which defendants had labored in these trials, he insisted that such disadvantages were not actually part of English law at the time but the result of recent tyrannical practice. Members of Parliament echoed his views. As George Treby put it, "The fault was not in the law, but in the men." The notion that the two previous Stuart monarchs had broken the law *as it existed at the time* may, then, have been a deterrent to legal reform (or an excuse to avoid legal reform), especially for Whigs with a long-term record of opposition to Charles II and James II.[44]

Ironically, Tories who had supported Charles II and (initially) James II, and who had a stake in believing in the lawfulness of what was done by those monarchs, were more open to the idea that it was the law itself that now needed reform. This might help explain one of the most ironic turnabouts of the period: the Tory lawyer Bartholemew Shower, who in 1683 vehemently asserted the guilt of the Whig martyr Lord Russell, penned an eloquent plea for the reform of treason trials in 1692.[45]

While party differences mattered, they should not be overstated. In the debates on habeas corpus many MPs fell somewhere between the Whig hardliner Colonel Birch and the liberty-conscious Tory William Ettrick. The Tory MP Mr. Finch acknowledged both sides of the issue, saying, "Tis of absolute necessity, that those persons be secured for tampering with the government, and of as absolute necessity that the laws be secured too." The Whig Robert Clayton showed a similar sense of balance. He supported the suspension of habeas corpus but nonetheless admitted that "had it not been for the Habeas Corpus Act, there had not been many of us here now; we had been dead and rotten in prison." The recorder of London George Treby was usually classed as a Whig, yet as noted above he encouraged James Smith to grant bail to Robert Brent. There seems to have been broad bipartisan consensus that the suspension of habeas corpus in a moment of crisis should be for a limited time and that it should not be turned into a precedent for the future.[46]

But although there was broad consensus among members of Parliament that liberty and security were both desirable, there were still significant ideological differences about which institutions could best be trusted to preserve both. The divides can sometimes be described in terms of Whig or Tory, sometimes as court or country, and sometimes in terms of Lords and Commons. Perceptions of institutions in turn were closely linked to narratives about the purpose of the revolution and of the wider constitution.

The closely related debates in 1690 about a proposed Abjuration Bill and a proposed Bill for Securing the Government show the importance of divisions around the institutional aspects of detaining suspects; the most important fights were about who was able to detain suspects, and why, rather than about detention per se. As noted above, the Abjuration Bill contained a proviso that persons refusing the new abjuration oath could be imprisoned without bail by a justice of the peace, and the Bill for Securing the Government allowed privy councilors to imprison treason suspects without bail. Both bills thus involved the denial of bail. The Tories Joseph Williamson and Henry Goodrick resisted the Abjuration Bill, but in the debate over the Bill for Securing the Government they favored allowing privy councilors to detain suspects. The Whig John Thompson, conversely, seemed to support an Abjuration Bill but not the increase in the power of privy councilors allowed in the Bill for Securing the Government. The differences in Whig and Tory views stemmed from, first, the nature of the offense to be punished (that is, Tories did not want to impose the abjuration oath) and, second, in where the power to detain would lie. Thus Whigs resisted increasing the powers of the Privy Council because it enhanced royal power over and against Parliament and also because it was dominated by Tories.[47]

In these debates, then, the question on which many Whigs and Tories divided was not whether to suspend habeas corpus but where to put the power to do so and for what reasons it could be suspended. Indeed, it was the fact that Parliament and not the king or council had suspended habeas corpus in the first place that had made it palatable to some Whigs. As the Whig Robert Howard put it, "I think it gives great veneration to the Habeas Corpus Act, that it cannot be suspended but by act of Parliament."[48]

Discussions of proposed bills to indemnify officials who might have violated the law to bring in or secure the new regime similarly reveal a concern with what sort of person should be entrusted with the power to violate subjects' liberties in times of emergency. For example, the country Tory MP Roger Kenyon responded to such a proposal in 1689 with an impassioned attack on privy councilors. Acting for the safety of the kingdom, he said, should not require a pardon, so he deduced that privy councilors must be masking more sinister plans (to introduce "something else that could not come in if this did not open the door"). Distrust of the Privy Council in particular was also expressed by many opponents of the proposed "Act for Preventing Vexatious Suits against Such as Acted for Their Majesties Service in Defense of the Kingdom" in 1692. Paul Foley, for example, distinguished between local authorities and the Privy Council. He would consent to committing the bill only if it indemnified "such as had acted in the country, and not our privy councilors here."[49]

Debates on the reform of treason trials also revolved around the privileges and powers of different institutions. In this case, however, the members of the House of Commons directed their distrust not at the Privy Council but at the House of Lords. Two features of treason trials bills approved by the Lords in 1691 raised so much opposition in the Commons that the bills were abandoned. The first of these was a provision abolishing the Court of the Lord High Steward, thereby ensuring that noblemen were tried by a full House of Lords. Such a change, the Lords explained, would protect aristocratic defendants from being victimized by the king. Peers were, they argued, more vulnerable than the meanest subjects to rigged treason trials because through the Court of the Lord High Steward the king could handpick the jury.

Reactions to the proposed abolition of the Court of the Lord High Steward revealed wildly varying ideas about the role of aristocrats in government. Defenders of the provision invoked an image of honorable noblemen standing up against tyranny. Sir Thomas Clarges thought that the clause "will make the peers honest, and not be influenced by the court, but on all occasions they will be ready to stand up in defense of the English liberties." But the peers' commitment to English liberties and to the new regime was called into question. The Whig Henry Capel reminded his colleagues in the Commons that a proposal for a regency (a conservative scheme that would have kept James II nominally on the throne) was narrowly defeated in the House of Lords during the convention in 1688, implying that most peers opposed the revolution settlement. Abolishing the Lord High Steward's Court, opined George Treby, would be a "temptation to the lords to plot and conspire against the government." It was, moreover, especially likely (opponents thought) that aristocrats would protect one another. Should all members of the House of Lords be invited to sit in judgment on their peers, "the care for a friend will not fail to bring friends to the trial; the concern to preserve their family from that stain [of treason] will bring relations; and if there be any accomplices, they must be ready, for their own sakes, to acquit the accused."[50]

Those who opposed abolishing the Court of the Lord High Steward repeatedly invoked a nightmare scenario in which the Lords would "instead of a monarchy, set up an aristocracy." Mr. Dolben opined that the clause "will give the Lords such power to endanger the government, that I cannot agree to it. They have a power of over-ruling the courts of Westminster; and you, by this clause, will complete the work, to overthrow the King's prerogative, and establish their own." In this way, the Commoners depicted themselves as the upholders of legitimate royal power. It was the king's "necessary prerogative" to appoint officers of justice, and therefore it was his right to set up a Lord High Steward's Court; any attempt to abolish that court and put justice into the hands of House of Lords would "erect a judicature independent of the crown" and alter the government of England, which was, the Lords were reminded, "monarchical."[51]

The status of the House of Commons was thought to be threatened by another amendment that the House of Lords proposed to the Treason Trials Bill that would give defendants in parliamentary attainders and impeachments the same rights as defendants in trials at common law. On the face of it, this leveling of the playing field might seem fair. But John Somers admonished his colleagues in the House of Commons not to "go from their dignity, and lessen themselves":

> The power of impeachment ought to be, like Goliath's sword, kept in the Temple, and not used but on great occasions. The security of your constitution is lost, when you lose this Power.[52]

The enthusiasm expressed by many members of the House of Commons for impeachment and attainder, the mechanisms whereby Parliament acted as a criminal court, requires some explanation. Parliament's right to take upon itself the investigation and prosecution of treason was rooted in its standing as the highest court in the land. That right was thought to be further affirmed in the Statute of Treasons of 25 Edward III, which had stated that as cases might arise which the law did not cover, it was up to Parliament to decide what constituted treason.[53]

Moreover, in recent memory the common law courts, where judges had served at the king's pleasure, had proved subject to manipulation, allegedly murdering Sidney, Russell, College, Armstrong, and the other Whig martyrs at the king's behest. The case of Edward Fitzharris was an especially vexed memory. Many MPs believed that Fitzharris had been hired by Catholic courtiers during the Exclusion Crisis to plant incriminating evidence on the persons of prominent Whigs in order to frame them for treason. In hopes of persuading Fitzharris to reveal which courtiers had set him onto this devilish task, Parliament impeached him. However, attorneys for the government of Charles II succeeded in having Fitzharris's trial moved to an ordinary common law court, where he was quickly convicted of treason and executed, all for the purpose (so angry members of Parliament thought) of stifling the revelations he would have made.[54]

Impeachment and attainder, then, were seen as Parliament's weapons against a tyrannical regime. In the aftermath of the Revolution of 1688, they also offered a stage upon which Parliament could show itself as the reliable guardian of the new government. Such an opportunity presented itself when Parliament considered the best way to proceed against the printers and publishers who had distributed copies of King James's *Declaration* throughout England. This *Declaration*, in which the exiled king promised to rectify his previous mistakes and encouraged his subjects to reinstate him, was considered a particularly dangerous piece of sedition. Many members of Parliament argued that rather than allow its publishers to be indicted in common law courts, Parliament should proceed with a bill of attainder against them. One conspicuous disadvantage of the common law in dealing with these publishers was that it did not recognize the dispersing of King James's *Declaration* as a serious crime. But another reason to prefer attainder to a common law indictment was that attainder gave the House of Commons a chance to demonstrate its solidarity with the new rulers. To impeach the offenders "in the name of all the Commons of England," opined Sir William Williams, "gives a dignity and honour to the King." Or as Mr. Garroway put it,

> You see many people abroad in the nation, who refuse to own the government. We cannot give too much assistance to support it. I desire this prosecution may be by impeachment, and not by indictment, that the world may see you stand by your government.[55]

What was at stake in debates over habeas corpus and the conduct of treason trials was not *just* the relative value of liberty and security but also the prestige and powers of particular institutions and the claims of different groups to be the true guardians of the revolution. The many kinds of divisions tracked in this chapter—over the nature of law, the institution best suited to guard the subject's liberties, the correct narrative about the revolution, and the means of justifying it—were all on full display in Parliament's disputes about reversing the conviction of Titus Oates.

The Return of Titus Oates

Titus Oates had been convicted in May 1685 for two perjuries committed at the 1678 trial of the Jesuits William Ireland, John Grove, and Thomas Pickering. First, Oates had claimed to have been present at a consult of Jesuits at the White Horse tavern on 24 April 1678, whereas witnesses from St. Omers, the Jesuit seminary, said he had been at St. Omers on that date. Second, Oates had claimed to have seen one of the defendants, William Ireland, at a second meeting of Jesuits in London in August, whereas other witnesses established that Ireland was out of town. The punishment for these perjuries was harsh: Oates was fined 2,000 marks, divested of his canonical habit, whipped, pilloried, and imprisoned for life. In his addresses to Parliament and the public, Oates emphasized the physical brutality of his punishment, which was

> executed with all barbarity, upon the petitioner; lying ten weeks under the surgeon's hands: But that some of them afterwards got into his chamber, whilst weak in bed; and attempted the pulling the plaisters applied for the cure of his back; and threatened to destroy him; procuring him to be loaded with irons of excessive weight for a whole year, even when his legs were swollen with the gout; and to be shut up in the dungeon; whereby he became impaired in his limbs, and contracted convulsion fits, and other distempers, to the hazard of his life.[56]

In May 1689 Oates petitioned the Commons to take action on his behalf while simultaneously filing writs of error in the House of Lords (which, as the highest court, had the power to review the decisions in King's Bench). His allegation of "error" hinged in part upon a very narrow definition of perjury. Oates's lawyers, Sergeant Lovell and Sergeant Thompson, told the House of Lords that even if Oates had lied about the consult of Jesuits and about William Ireland's presence in London, these particulars had not been cited in the indictment against Grove, Pickering, and Ireland and hence were not pertinent to the judgment against the three men. However, the core of Oates's case was that the punishments were "arbitrary and excessive, severe, cruel, inhuman and horrible, and such as by the law of England in this or any other case upon an indictment against a clergyman or any other freeman of England ought not to be given, nor ever heretofore was given."[57]

The Lords, accordingly, brought in the two surviving King's Bench judges who had presided over the perjury case, Sir Francis Withins and Sir Richard Holloway, to explain their reasons for the sentence passed on Oates, and then heard from current Lord Chief Justice John Holt and eight other judges as to its legality. Precedents were cited on both sides of the question. Withins emphasized the egregiousness of Oates's perjury. He had found precedents for punishing perjury by cutting out the tongue and by death in Coke, and for imprisonment for life, beatings, and whippings in Bracton. He had further considered Peter Cary's case, reported by Croke as a precedent for life imprisonment, as well as "the law of God in the case of Nabal, who lost his life by a false oath." In short, Oates deserved what he got.[58]

On the other side, Holt and others concurred with Oates's lawyers. Bracton was dismissed as an authority by Justice Eyre, who dubbed Oates's sentence "a villainous judgment, let Bracton say what he pleased." As for Croke's report on the sentence of perpetual imprisonment in Peter Cary's case, said Holt, "I take this book not to be law." Whipping, in itself or in conjunction with other punishments, was described as "inhuman, unjust," "barbarous," permitted by common law only in cases of petty sacrilege and "not allowed amongst the Romans." Although some commentators acknowledged that precedents existed in the now defunct and much-maligned Court of Star Chamber, that fact only confirmed their barbarity. Finally, all the judges (except Withins and Holloway) agreed that the temporal court in divesting Oates of canonical habit had overstepped the boundaries between secular and ecclesiastical authority.[59]

The House of Lords responded with obvious ambivalence to Oates's case. On the one hand, they asked the king and queen to discharge Oates from "the remaining part of those punishments, which he will otherwise be liable to undergo" on grounds that he had "already received a severe punishment for the perjury whereof he hath been formerly convicted." But despite the fact that Withins and Holloway were soon to be among those excepted in the Indemnity Bill for being especially heinous collaborators with the previous regime, the House of Lords accepted their arguments and voted 35 to 23 to uphold the 1685 judgment of the King's Bench.[60]

The Commons, however, having also received a petition from Oates, resolved that Oates's indictments were "a design to stifle the Popish Plot: and that the verdicts given thereupon were corrupt: And that the judgments given thereupon were cruel and illegal." They quickly drew up a bill to this effect, condemning not only the 1685 verdicts in King's Bench but also, significantly, the Lords' decision to uphold them.[61]

The Lords voted to accept the Commons' bill, but with extensive amendments that vitiated its meaning. First, not surprisingly, they removed any condemnation of their own decision to reject the writs of error and uphold the judgment in King's Bench. Second, they softened the language in which the 1685 verdict in King's Bench was condemned, changing the phrase in the Commons' bill condemning the judgment as "erroneous, illegal, cruel, and of evil Example to future Ages" to read "erroneous, unprecedented; so that the practice thereof ought to be prevented for the time to come" and adding that "it is hereby further enacted, by the authority aforesaid, that it shall not be lawful, at any time hereafter, to inflict the like excessive punishments again on any person whatsoever." In making this change, they acknowledged that the King's Bench judgment was bad but avoided describing it, as the Commons had done, as "illegal." Finally, the Lords signaled their continuing skepticism about Oates's innocence by adding a proviso that "until the said matters for which the said Titus Oates was convicted, as aforesaid, for perjury, be heard and determined in Parliament, that the said Titus Oates shall not be received, in any court, matter, or cause whatsoever, to be a witness, or give any evidence." Not surprisingly, these very heavy alterations made it impossible for the two Houses to agree, although Oates was pardoned by the king and given a small pension.[62]

The debate over reversing Oates's conviction raised institutional and ideological issues about the nature of law, its relation to Parliament, the vindication of the revolution, and the protection of the subject's liberties. The conflict over Oates was to an extent one between the two Houses. The Lords, for example, took umbrage at the fact that Oates petitioned the Commons to come to his aid before the Lords had finished considering his writs of error and had Oates committed for a breach of their privileges. The more significant division, however, was between Whigs and Tories. Oates's petitions found supporters not only in the Whig-dominated House of Commons but among a large number of Whigs in the House of Lords.[63]

A central point of disagreement between the Whigs and Tories was about whether to describe the 1685 judgments against Oates as "illegal." The Tory majority in the House of Lords, consistent with what has been described above as the Tory understanding of the previous regime as being law-abiding, resisted using the word "illegal." They had found "no viciousness nor defect in the judgment" against Oates. Moreover, the committee appointed by the Lords to explain their reasons for adhering to their amendments expressed concern that overturning Oates's conviction would "reverse so many judgments given in the course of so many years." It was not "for the honour of the nation and religion" that "a conviction passed in the form of law be set aside."[64]

Oates's supporters in both Houses, by contrast, insisted that the conviction "ought plainly to be declared positively against law, justice and the undoubted rights of the subjects." They argued that the House of Lords' wording, even if it promised that judgments like the one against Oates would not be given in the future, still implied that the past judgment was lawful, "which may be of pernicious consequence." The Declaration of Rights, which had been affirmed by William and Mary at their coronation in February, lent weight to the claim that Oates's punishment was already illegal: it had asserted that "excessive bail ought not to be required, nor excessive fines imposed, nor cruel and unusual punishment inflicted." Oates's supporters, therefore, were able to depict the House of Lords as undermining the Declaration of Rights and thus the revolution itself. The Lords' amendments to the Commons' bill, opined the Lords who dissented from them, were "the greatest blow that ever the English liberties received, and puts them under a greater disadvantage than if they had not so lately been declared."[65]

Paradoxically, then, despite the Lords' reluctance to overturn an existing judicial decision, Oates's supporters could accuse the members of the House of Lords who wanted to uphold the court's decision of making new law. Responding to the Lords' final refusal to alter their proposed amendments, the Commons angrily admonished the House of Lords:

> It is recorded, to the honour of your noble ancestors, that they declared they would not change the laws: and the Commons hope you will pursue their steps; and not, by affirming erroneous judgments, go about to make that law, which was not so before . . . which is, not only to change the law, but to subvert the constitution of the government.[66]

English law, as understood by Oates's supporters, was not made by judicial precedent. Rather, it was eternal, albeit only recently declared. The role of Parliament in that process of declaring law was critical. Oates's supporters consistently elevated Parliament over the corrupt courts, casting it as the ultimate protector of the liberty of the subject. Hence the Commons was enraged by the failure of the Lords to agree with them over the bill reversing Oates's conviction: "When the Commons send up a Bill to your Lordships, in order to prevent the mischiefs of such destructive precedents, for your Lordships to refuse to reverse these judgments (though confessed to be erroneous) . . . is to leave the Kingdom without redress against acknowledged wrongs."[67]

That Parliament should have such large powers was, in the eyes of Oates's supporters, proven by Oates's narrative. Oates brilliantly brought together the vindication of himself, of the truth of the Popish Plot, of the revolution, and of the Parliament in one package. "The papists," Oates wrote in his petition, "themselves have verified and confirmed his evidence by their late open and avowed violations of our religion, laws and liberties." Predictably, insistence on the truth of the Popish Plot, and perhaps especially the insistence that supporters of the revolution were now obligated to believe in it, sat badly with Tories who remembered how well Whigs had exploited the story and who were still vulnerable to it. Halifax was said to have been "very warm in opposition to the bill." Oates himself, moreover, played to Whig partisanship, alluding in one of his printed papers to "the under-hand dealing of a great minister of state" under Charles II "to procure a great sum of money, to put off the Parliament." That statement was widely read as a thinly veiled reference to Danby (now Carmarthen). Not surprisingly, Carmarthen retaliated, telling the House of Lords that "there could only be one way of reversing Oates' sentence; as he had been whipped from Aldgate to Tyburn, let him be whipped back again."[68]

In contrast, Whigs in both houses of Parliament thought that the reversal of Oates's conviction would vindicate both the truth of the Popish Plot and the rightness of the revolution. In the Commons, John Hawles opined that it was entirely unsurprising to find people disowning the government and dispersing pamphlets when the House of Lords was seen to affirm "the worst judgment that was ever given in law." Sir Robert Howard feared that affirming the perjury judgment against Oates "condemns all we have done, and whatever the Papists have done is justified, and the Protestants condemned." Oates's supporters in the House of Lords likewise thought that what was at stake was the "credit of the Popish Plot." They pointed to the pernicious effect that barring Oates from testifying again would have on the public image of the government. For William to accept the bill with the Lords' proviso barring Oates's testimony would promote the interest of the king's enemies, "who always did and do think themselves concerned to discredit the opinion of the Popish Plot, to which this seems to have a great tendency." Indeed, upholding the perjury conviction would make people think that members of the new Parliament had something to hide. The Whig Jack Howe, in the Commons, darkly hinted that "possibly it is in the interest of some persons that no witnesses be believed."[69]

For Whigs, moreover, the affirmation of the Popish Plot was not simply a condemnation of Catholicism. It involved a more wide-ranging narrative about attempts under both Charles II and James II to subvert the law, the constitution and especially the Parliament. That Parliament in the reign of

Charles II had protected Oates was a point stressed by both Oates and his supporters. For example, Oates invited the Commons to "vindicate the proceedings of former parliaments" and said that his conviction cast "a reproach upon the wisdom and honour of four successive parliaments who had given him credit." Oates's supporters in the House of Lords pointed out that the proviso barring Oates from further testimony "gives the jury preference, in point of justice, above four successive Parliaments." They contrasted the rightness of these parliaments with the wrongness of the common law courts, pointing out that Oates had been convicted "at a time when the whole administration of justice was corrupted." Accordingly, they refused to endorse "the judgments of profligate wretches set up for judges in Westminster Hall."[70]

Whigs in the House of Commons linked the quo warranto campaign to Oates's conviction, noting, "The juries, who passed upon those trials, were returned by officers unduly chosen, after the unjust seizure of the liberties of the City of London." The Whig MP Robert Howard tied together "the rise of a popish successor, the violation of the choice of sheriffs, corruption of judges." Howard's colleague Henry Capel invoked the bitter memory of how Charles II had aborted Parliament's attainder of Edward Fitzharris to prevent it from discovering the machinations of Catholic courtiers. What was at stake in the debate on Oates was the prestige of Parliament as an arbiter of justice.[71]

Oates's Whig supporters in both Houses held a view of English law that was both conservative and revolutionary. On one hand, they insisted that English law was eternal; the revolution had not changed anything. On the other, they recognized themselves as occupying a new, revolutionary moment in which that law could finally be proclaimed, and in which it was Parliament that had the undisputed right to proclaim it. At the same time, the legitimacy of that Parliament hinged on its support for the revolution, which was identified with the new king.

There were some obvious contradictions in the attempt to simultaneously glorify law, Parliament, the revolution, and the new king. What if Parliament changed the law? What if the king and Parliament clashed? In the early years of the revolution, in the debates discussed here, members of Parliament seemed oblivious to these possibilities. The contradictions would emerge later as fissures between court and country.

Conclusion

The old Whig narrative in which Whigs were credited for the advance of civil liberty has of late taken a beating. Recently, for example, Mark Goldie and Clare Jackson have called attention to the existence of Whig-Jacobites, former Whigs who came to think that liberty resided not with William but with Jacobites. This chapter has given some support to the critique of Whig complacency. Certainly, vindicating Titus Oates, suspending habeas corpus, and resisting the reform of treason trials are not activities that can be described as "civil libertarian."[72]

However, my purpose in this chapter is not to give out grades for who was more committed to liberty but to call attention to the matrix of issues in which differences over national security emerged. The question facing members of Parliament was not whether to choose liberty or security but rather how to ensure both. To this question, Whigs and Tories had radically different answers, which accorded with their past experience and their respective understandings of the revolution.

Tories combined a narrow view of the new regime's raison d'être with a generous definition of who (among Protestants, at least) should be numbered among its supporters. The justification for the revolution, for Tories, lay in a relatively small number of offenses committed in the late reign by Catholics against the Church of England. They were therefore more tolerant than Whigs of continuities in court or Privy Council personnel, in judicial precedent, and in systems of local governance left over from the previous reign. The survival of the revolution, they thought, would be assured by obtaining support even from those who might be ambivalent. Ironically, such tolerance for ambivalence sometimes made some Tories into better defenders of the rights of political minorities than Whigs, as appeared for example in the debates over habeas corpus. One might of course write off the Tory tenderness for the rights of suspected persons as mere crypto-Jacobitism, a desire to make life easier for Jacobite plotters. That was precisely the charge made by their opponents. It was also and more likely, however, the logical outcome of their need to find a way to accept the revolution without entirely repudiating their own past as supporters of the late Stuart court.

In contrast to the Tories, the Whigs' account of the grievances that justified the revolution was more wide-ranging, encompassing a range of legal and constitutional as well as religious crimes committed by previous regimes.

Meanwhile, their definition of who could be counted as a supporter of the new government was narrower, and they pushed for more rigorous loyalty oaths that would have excluded many people. In comparison to the Tories, the Whigs could be (and have been) described as intolerant, even vengeful, and possibly already displaying a tendency toward absolutism. Certainly, the Whigs could be accused of ignoring the civil liberties of their opponents: they showed little sympathy for the rights of Titus Oates's victims, for example, and they resisted treason trial reform.

Yet what drove Whigs was not (as opponents like Robert Ferguson would have it) a secret fondness for absolute monarchy but rather a sense that the revolution needed to be not merely accepted but "vindicated." That meant that the founders of the new government, the people, and their representatives in Parliament (especially the Commons) had to be continually seen to affirm their loyalty to the revolution and the narrative that justified that loyalty. If Whigs did seem to betray the cause of liberty, it was, ironically, a function of their belief that the Glorious Revolution was, truly, a revolution.

CHAPTER 2

A Trusted Government?

The two major goals of the new regime, securing itself against enemies and winning the trust of subjects, were mutually interdependent but sometimes contradictory (as in the dilemma over suspending habeas corpus). In the previous chapter I showed how this tension was expressed in parliamentary debates. In this chapter I will look at how it affected the institutions of government at national and local levels. Responsibility for guarding the new regime against its enemies was distributed among a variety of officeholders: postmasters, mayors, justices of the peace, customs and excise officers, and military and militia commanders. Such persons were called upon to discipline the public. But they were themselves objects of scrutiny, by the public and by one another. Whether this eclectic collection of officeholders themselves could be trusted was an open question in the 1690s.

Trust and Modernity: The Williamite State in Historical Perspective

Most historical accounts of the state begin with the question of "modernization." The term suggests two interrelated developments. First, the creation of a professional bureaucracy loyal to the central government and clearly demarcated from "society," enabling the central government to impose its will on localities. Second, an increased ability on the part of the state to monitor and penetrate into the lives of subjects, whether to extract resources, suppress dissent, or enhance well-being.

The English state can be said to have modernized in many important respects during the late seventeenth century. The excise service in the Restoration might stand as a microcosm and epitome of such modernization. Under the leadership of Charles Davenant during the reign of Charles II, the Excise pioneered techniques for separating state officials from the population with whom they interacted. To discourage corruption, officers were paid sufficient salaries and frequently rotated between posts. Excise officers were also subjected to constant surveillance from superiors. Irregularities in record keeping were severely punished. As Steve Pincus has emphasized, James II further extended the modernization of the state along lines theorized by Hobbes and pioneered by Louis XIV, building a state with an efficient bureaucracy, an extensive reach into the lives of its people, an insistence on ideological purity, and mechanisms of propaganda and surveillance that enforced such ideological purity. In James II's reign, mail was examined, the press was censored, and spies were placed in churches to listen to sermons. Troops were quartered in communities to intimidate the population. By using royal fiat to dispense with laws that prevented Catholics from holding public or military office, James created a class of officials who owed allegiance exclusively to him. Modernization, according to Pincus, predated the Glorious Revolution.[1]

The question to answer here, however, is not "when did the state become modern?" but "what were the conditions of possibility for trust or mistrust between the Williamite state and its subjects?" Although modernity may have a bearing on trust, the two are not identical. A thoroughly modern state may attract trust on grounds that it is capable of protecting itself, and of doing so at the least possible cost to subjects. Yet modern states stand apart from and impose their will on local society in ways that may erode people's trust in their government. English men and women in the late seventeenth century would have known that Louis XIV's France, and James II's efforts to imitate it, required absolutism and brutality.

Thus, for the new Williamite regime, modernization was not in itself a sufficient solution to the problem of how to secure trust. Following the footsteps of James II could backfire. And yet the pressures of war and fears of Jacobite subversion sometimes pushed the Williamite regime to extract from and impose on subjects in ways that seemed a continuation of the policies of James II.

Assessing the new regime's ability to win the trust of its subjects, then, requires recognizing the complicated and sometimes contradictory factors shaping the way William's government interacted with subjects, particularly in pursuit of domestic security. In some ways the new regime continued on the modernizing path of the two previous monarchs, with potentially alienating results. Yet modernization was never complete. Offices were held as sinecures and auctioned to the highest bidder. Many public functions were in private hands. The loyalties of officeholders were divided between the central authorities and local communities. Salaries were insufficient, leading inevitably to corruption that sometimes entailed complicity with enemies of the new regime.

Insofar as James II had successfully modernized the English state, moreover, that achievement posed problems for the new Williamite regime. Many public servants appointed by James had retained their office under William, and the quo warranto campaigns of Charles and James left town governments in the hands of people whose loyalty to William was dubious. In addition, even if modernization had worked for James, it would not work in the same way for William. Ideology affected the way that modernization interacted with the government's credit. The Glorious Revolution had promised freer subjects, not a more intrusive and powerful central government. In short, a different ambition—an engaged citizenry—might be in tension with the creation of an efficient state.

Moreover, insofar as the security of the new regime depended on intelligence acquired through methods requiring secrecy, agents of the government might inevitably deceive not only subjects but also one another. A side effect of such deception was that to the public the state often appeared internally divided and that officials themselves crossed the line between legality and illegality. What was conducive to the state's security might not be conducive to the state's credit, in the sense of its appearance of trustworthiness.

This chapter considers the trustworthiness of the state officials most closely involved in securing the Williamite regime from invasion or subversion. It considers members of central bureaucracies, like the Customs and the Post Office, along with local officeholders, such as mayors, lord lieutenants of the county militia, constables, and justices of the peace. Central and local officials differed from one another in terms of how they were appointed and, to an extent, how closely they were tied to the communities in which they operated. For this reason, they are discussed separately here. Such distinctions, though, were in part artificial. There was considerable overlap in the responsibilities of central and local officeholders. Mayors, customs officers, or specially appointed "riding officers" were all called upon to check the passes of travelers. Local officeholders might conspire with local smugglers. But so too might customs officials.[2]

Just as distinctions between local and central officeholders can be hazy, so too can the distinction between state officials and society outside the state. Customs officers, for example, might (despite regulations prohibiting it) also be employed by or own businesses in the local community. Postmasters almost always had a second source of income as innkeepers. Moreover, some persons undertook service to the state without any official position or guarantee of reward, though in the hope of future reward. Political informers too straddled the line between state and society.

Persons who served the new regime outside the boundaries of an official position presented a paradox. In one way they fit more harmoniously than did state officials with the new regime's promise to govern in accordance with the needs and liberties of its subjects. Yet their services might be suspect and damaging to the credibility of the regime.

It is impossible here to produce any quantitative measure of the state's effectiveness, either in establishing security or in winning trust. It will be sufficient to show that the general public and highly placed members of the government alike had reasons to be suspicious and dissatisfied with institutions meant to protect them. Such dissatisfaction and distrust in turn explains how informers, who are the subject of much of the rest of this book, gained so much traction.

Central Government

Jacobite propagandists repeatedly claimed that the Glorious Revolution had substituted one overweening central government for another. One need not be a Jacobite, however, to see that the demands of war in some respects pushed the Williamite state to restrict local liberties and intrude into the lives of subjects. Government officials saw the need for a loyal, efficient bureaucracy to discipline and spy on a not entirely cooperative population.

A set of "suggestions for an intelligence service" by an anonymous author that the Earl of Portland forwarded to Secretary of State Nottingham in 1692 shows what some government officials thought should and could be accomplished to secure the new regime from enemies. The paper proposed a comprehensive program of surveillance and propaganda. Significantly, the author appears to have been influenced by developments in the Excise bureaucracy during previous reigns. He identified "the several officers employed in his Majesties revenue" as likely candidates to carry out his plan. He recommended that a record be kept "in an alphabetical manner" of all streets within ten miles of London; that gatherings of persons refusing to swear allegiance be closely watched; that agents be employed to keep track of all inns and report to the secretary of state about who lodged there and what horses they kept; that a regular correspondence be established with well-affected justices of the peace in each county; that watches be placed along roads, especially to Scotland and the seacoasts nearest to France; that an account be kept of persons riding post; that someone attend Smithfield market and provincial markets, weekly, to observe the buying and selling of horses; that constant inquiries be made among gunsmiths; that the government take an aggressive approach to public relations, employing "a good pen" to obviate malignant objections and maintain truth; and finally, that repeated transgressors be punished according to law, "the omission of which hath emboldened [them] to so great a degree."[3]

The security operations of the new regime fell short of what was envisioned in this paper, and there is no evidence that the anonymous author's advice was followed. If the Williamite state looked like an imposing juggernaut to its critics, it sometimes reminds the modern historian of the Keystone Cops. The constable who was found hiding two French privateers under his bed may have been unusual, but escapes by prisoners from the royal messengers, the Tower of London, or local jails were alarmingly common. The Dungeness lighthouse, at the edge of Romney Marsh, was entrusted to keepers who let French sloops land Jacobites and contraband with impunity.[4]

Some of the regime's failures stemmed more from incompetence than treason, but the line between incompetence and treason was hard to draw. And in a military context, either was terrifying. The loyalty and competence of the army and navy in the early years of William's reign were subjects of anxiety. In his diary entry of 23 February 1689, Narcissus Luttrell took note of reports "that several of the late army are much disaffected" and estimated that 10,000 remained of the original 35,000 men. On 15 March of the same year, the House of Commons learned that the regiment of the Earl of Dunbarton, en route to Holland, had mutinied and then declared for James II. John Morgan, the governor of Chester Castle, expressed fears to Shrewsbury that Catholic prisoners might be set free by the soldiers sent to guard them: "For really there are so many Roman Catholics that thrust themselves into regiments that if it should happen that some disaffected officer should allot me such a guard, they may easily betray me and set the prisoners at liberty." In

September 1689, the government heard from multiple witnesses that Robert Minors, the governor of Upnor Castle who was supposed to be guarding the coast of Kent, was harboring Jacobites and helping them escape to France. He drank healths to King James and damnation to King William.[5]

Beyond open disloyalty, there were cases of incompetence that were understood by some to be treasonous. Until William's victory at the Battle of the Boyne in July 1690 gave the English new hope of victory, the war in Ireland went badly. Attempts to relieve Irish Protestants in the besieged town of Londonderry were confounded when the convoys carrying supplies were mysteriously turned away. Commissary John Shales, who had been appointed to office by James II, failed to get enough supplies to troops in Ireland, leading some in Parliament to suggest he was secretly a Jacobite. Meanwhile, sailors in the navy had been given victuals so loathsome that many thought they were deliberately being poisoned. And the ignominious failure of Admiral Torrington to assist the Dutch fleet off Beachy Head when it was fighting the French only exacerbated the sense that many of those in charge of the war were helping to lose it.[6]

The military was not the only branch of the central government to raise suspicions about disloyalty in high places. Given that the paper on intelligence described above had singled out revenue officers as being especially well suited to carry out the work of surveillance, it is noteworthy that some high-ranking officials in both Customs and Excise attracted suspicion. In 1694, members of the Privy Council recommended to William that several commissioners of both Customs and Excise be dismissed. Secretary of State Shrewsbury, writing to the king, explained that he had readily come to agreement with his fellow councilors Somers, Trenchard, and Lord Godolphin that Sir Richard Temple of the Customs should be removed for "corruption, disaffection, neglect and in short being good for nothing"; Mr. Aram of the Excise, too, was "suspected to be ill-inclined to the government"; and Mr. Hornby was "an avowed Jacobite." The only significant disagreement among Shrewsbury, Somers, Trenchard, and Godolphin concerned John Werden, a customs commissioner. Somers, Trenchard, and Shrewsbury believed Werden "had a bias towards employing under-officers disaffected to your government," but Godolphin defended him as experienced and uncorrupted. That men alleged to be conspicuously Jacobite or corrupt had been employed as customs and excise commissioners as late as June 1694 suggests an inability of the central government to ensure loyalty and competence among high-ranking officials. It is especially significant that even Lord Godolphin, the political outlier in the group who grumbled to William about the overly partisan "manner and motive" of the changes, agreed with the others about the alleged Jacobitism of all but one of the commissioners removed and remarked tellingly, "The Commission of the Customs cannot be made worse than it is at present."[7]

If the highest officers in the customs and excise services could be accused of Jacobitism and incompetence, it is not surprising to find lower-ranking officials accused as well. An excise officer at Dartford, hearing a rumor that the king was killed, gathered a mob to celebrate the rumored death of William III in Flanders. Worse, the general surveyor of the London Brewery, knowing this, had shrugged it off, saying the officer was "not a rogue, but a fool for making such a noise."[8]

The customs service, especially on the coasts of Kent and Sussex, elicited even greater concern. Customs officers were expected to guard the coasts, preventing the smuggling not only of goods but of Jacobites and Jacobite correspondence. The task was challenging. The creeks and hidden landing places on the southern coast of England were so numerous that it would have taken far more people to police them than were actually available for the job, and the occasional addition of riding officers or sloops to patrol the coast did not solve the problem. The tidewaiters, customs officers who rode with vessels down the Thames in order to prevent people or goods from being taken aboard or offloaded en route, were physically unable to watch all parts of the vessel at once, and in addition they were often subject to harassment by the crew. Moreover, the customs service had not been reformed in the way Excise had been in the Restoration. Unlike excise men, most customs officers were not paid a regular salary but depended on fees that in turn were affected by the volume of trade. In wartime, with trade down, corruption was tempting. Schemes to institute systems of surveillance among customs employees had been proposed but mostly rejected. In 1689, for example, the customs commissioners angrily rebuffed a set of proposals for preventing frauds, including the hierarchy-overturning idea that officers who discovered corruption on the part of their superiors be rewarded by being given their jobs![9]

Customs thus seemed a weak link in England's defense against Jacobite infiltration. Secretary of State Shrewsbury was indignant that customs officers

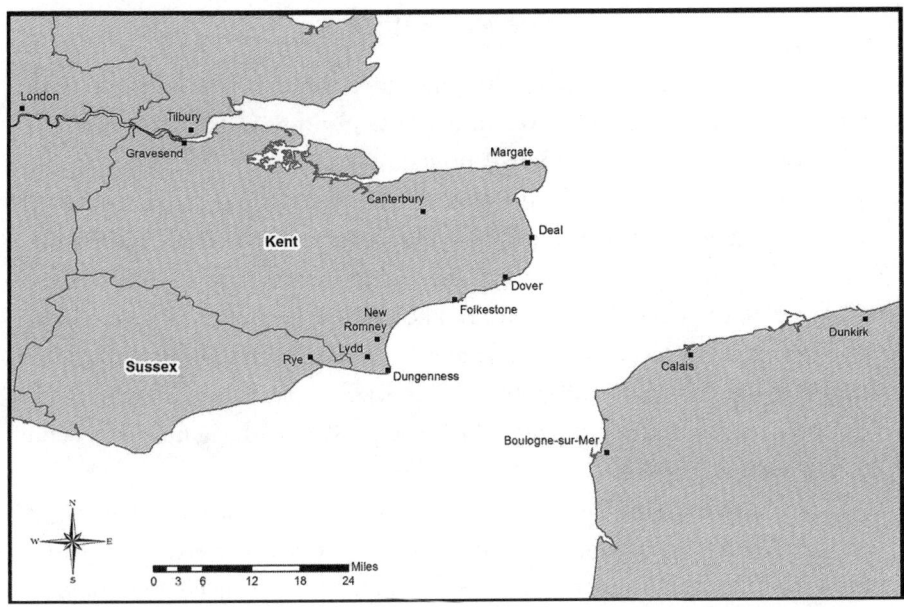

Map of Kent and Sussex, showing locations mentioned in this book. Map of Kent and Sussex. 1:1043,897. ESRI Data and Maps: World and Europe 2001 CD-ROM. Redlands, CA: ESRI © 2001. Ithaca, NY: Cornell University Library Map Collection, 2012. Generated by Boris Michev and Johannes Plambeck using ArcGIS 10 (Redlands, CA: Environmental Systems Research Institute, 1992–2012).

at Dover had refused to cooperate with the mayor's request to search all passengers for letters going to or coming from France, claiming to await orders from a higher up. Too many officers on the Kentish coast, Shrewsbury scolded Commissioner Jephson, "willfully or negligently give opportunities for conveying intelligence and persons beyond the sea." The next month Shrewsbury alleged that Mr. Chiffinch, the searcher at Gravesend, connived with the Quaker Jenner to convey disaffected persons abroad, "knowing them to be such, and that they were designed for the late King James's service." William Trumbull, Shrewsbury's colleague, made similar complaints. Perhaps the most spectacular case of disloyalty in the upper ranks of the customs service was that of Thomas Noel, the collector at Dover, who abetted smugglers, assisted in the escape of Jacobite Paul Pepper, and was eventually (after his dismissal) engaged in coining.[10]

The Post Office

The Post Office occupied an intermediate position between central government and local society. It was a national institution: by 1689 even the previously independent London Penny Post had been integrated into the General Post Office system. At the same time, postmasters and postmistresses were rooted in local communities, deriving income not just from a salary but from running inns and stables that generated greater profits because they were also nodes in the postal network. The Post Office impacted the credit of the government in several different ways. It was an institution through which the new regime hoped to attract trust by providing a service to its subjects; it was also a mechanism for spying, which had positive and negative effects on the new regime's credit.

The Post Office in William's reign not only grew in size but changed in purpose. As Howard Robinson has pointed out, the raison d'être of the institution from its establishment was to enhance the power of the government. Originating under the Tudors as a way to transmit important messages among the king and his ministers, it evolved into a means of spying on the population. Revenues generated by the Post Office flowed into royal coffers, financing pensions to favorites, like the Duchess of Cleveland, and to James II himself when he had been Duke of York. It was for all these reasons, of course, that the Post Office was made a monopoly, and the carrying of unauthorized mail was severely punished.[11]

The Revolution of 1688, however, coincided with an expansion of the Post Office and its redefinition as an institution that existed primarily for the benefit of the public rather than the state. As such, it was an important point of contact and potentially bonding of subjects with the Williamite government. In providing a service on which ever greater numbers of subjects depended, the Post Office subtly drew the nation into an investment in the stability of the new regime. Every person who sent a letter was implicitly acting on the assumption that the state could be trusted, and frequent use of the service made such trust a matter of routine.

But the Post Office could drag down the credit of the government as well as enhance it. In 1690, Postmaster General John Wildman was forced to publish a broadside asking the public to help discover the authors and inventors of "divers infamous scandals" dispersed in coffeehouses by "ill-minded persons, for some wicked designs against the government" to the effect that "letters are stopped, broke open, and destroyed at pleasure" and that "great numbers of letters about elections to members for the next Parliament, have been burnt." These insinuations, Wildman complained, "reflect on their Majesties just and gracious government and lessen their revenue from the said [post] office."[12]

The outcome of Wildman's public relations efforts is unknown, but the stakes were clear. The new regime could not flourish unless subjects trusted the Post Office. At the same time, the ability of the Post Office to attract trust was complicated by the other uses to which it was put. Its intelligence functions, as well as its monopolistic privilege, remained in place. The Post Office was a means for the government to distribute propaganda and for officeholders to make a profit. The Post Office in William's reign was thus an arm of the state and a servant of the people. Moreover, it was itself subject to internal division. No wonder, then, that its capacity to garner trust was uncertain.

The Post Office (which comprised a national postal service and the London Penny Post) could be described, like the customs or excise services, as a national bureaucracy run from London. However, its pattern of hiring was different. The work of sorting and carrying mail required fewer specialized skills than the measuring and calculating involved in the revenue services. Moreover, people employed by the Post Office do not seem to have been "career" postal workers. Compared to other paid employees of government bureaucracies, they were more integrated into local society. The job of foot carrier in the penny post was sometimes given to the needy. Provincial post-masters and -mistresses were almost always innkeepers, already substantial enough to keep the supply of ready horses that the position required.

Working for the Post Office offered advantages that went beyond salary. It could be combined in a synergistic way with other occupations. Packet boat operators, for example, could take paying passengers along with them on mail routes. Many postmasters, taking advantage of their ability to send letters for free, ran a side business in newsletter writing (see below). For men and women who kept inns, stables, and public houses, appointment as a postmaster would mean a greater flow of customers, since travelers and locals alike would come to send or retrieve mail.

The very appointment of a person as postmistress, moreover, indicated that the appointee was trusted by the government and therefore worth trusting. The combination of loyalty and local prestige connoted by the office is captured on a recommendation that Margaret Bowles be appointed to manage the Post Office at Deale, signed by nineteen male citizens. Not only did the signatories "very well know" the candidate to be a "loyal person to the present government," but they knew the house she lived in to be "a very fitting house to make a post house," for "a great many of the noble men of the nation when they come to Deale do take up their lodgings at her house" and the governor of Dover Castle took it "as quarter for his horse and men." On the back of this paper, as if to underscore local consensus about her worthiness, Margaret Bowles herself noted, "Sir, if you think more hands are requisite I can have a hundred more."[13]

Margaret Bowles's promise of "a hundred more" signatures suggests that the aura of trust surrounding a postmaster or postmistress could not just be conferred from above by the government. The appropriateness of an appointment, the deportment of an officer in his job, became the occasion for a conversation between communities and the government about trust. Petitions to Wildman and his successors frequently alluded to public sentiment and carried signatures from concerned community members. Two disgruntled denizens of Yeovill, complaining of "a very bad man in the post office," asserted in a letter to Wildman that "it is desired by most of this town that he be removed." When John Marshall, who had been dismissed from his post as a letter carrier in Fenchurch Street, asked to be reinstated in the job, being sixty years old with a sickly wife and child to provide for, he presented the signatures of about thirty-three residents attesting that he "behaved very honestly and carefully." Catherine Woodward found thirty-six men to endorse her application to be postmistress of Sherbourne in Dorset. Roger Hermon obtained thirteen signatures from burgesses and inhabitants of Bristol in support of his bid to be postmaster. Elizabeth Gaylord of Totnes, threatened with dismissal as postmistress for allegedly losing a package, promised Wildman a "testimonial from the principal merchants and other inhabitants of this town."[14]

Accusations made against postmistress Elizabeth Watts sparked a widespread debate in the community about whom to trust. According to one of Watts's supporters, Julius Deedes, Watts had been slandered by George Hulke, a plumber and a man of loose life and ill conversation, who gave "strange informations" in order to supplant her in her employment. Mrs. Watts provided not only the predictable positive testimonial as to her "care and industry" but also damning information about her accuser. According to the thirteen signatories of a certificate in her favor, George Hulke was not only a person of a scandalous life but also litigious, having already pursued and lost a vexatious suit against Mrs. Watts's late husband, the grazier John Watts. Those willing to dish dirt on George Hulke ranged widely in social status: the certificate against Hulke was signed by a justice of the peace, Jeffrey Welles, and also by one Henry Parsons, who signed with a mark.[15]

Appointments to the Post Office could be a mechanism whereby the new government strengthened its bonds with subjects. These appointments gave the new regime an opportunity to place trusted supporters in positions of local power and to reward those who had supported it. Conversely, communities, by actively intervening in the choice of postmasters, sought to force the government to listen to their views of trustworthiness, and perhaps the government had an interest in understanding their views—if people did not trust the postmaster, they would not use the system, to the detriment of government security and credit. A postal service employing persons known for loyalty and trusted by their neighbors could create a strong bond between the government and people, give people a stake in stability, and give government authorities a trusted local ally. Of course, the converse of this potential was anxiety. Bad postmasters destroyed trust in all directions. Not surprisingly, postal officers were subject to scrutiny from above and below. The very desirability of Post Office jobs created competition and jealousy.

One reason that Post Office employees might become the object of anxiety was that they were especially well-placed to do damage to the new regime. Packet boat operators, it was feared, would for a price carry Jacobites and Jacobite correspondence between Dover and Calais. The privilege of sending mail for free (franking), enjoyed by all postal employees, also left room for abuse. Many postmasters took advantage of their franking rights to run a profitable side business in writing newsletters. So large did this business become that in 1696 Secretary of State William Trumbull complained that £14,000 in revenue was lost every year because of the free transmission of gazettes and newsletters. William Murcott complained to Wildman that letters in the London Penny Post lay undelivered because messengers were taken off their duty to write newsletters.[16]

The exploitation of franking privileges by Post Office employees not only impeded the delivery of the mail but also, it was feared, allowed for the dissemination of negative information. Robert Mason, the Dublin postmaster, suspected as much when he refused to share news with Edward Sawtell, the clerk of the Irish and Chester Roads, on grounds that he thought Sawtell was hostile to the government. Mason's suspicions seem to have been confirmed in 1696, when Sawtell was accused of writing negative newsletters.[17]

The Post Office, in short, could harm as well as help the new regime. Not surprisingly, the loyalty of postal employees to the government was a matter of concern. Wildman, an ardent Whig, received many applications and recommendations for positions that emphasized the candidate's political allegiance. A number of these petitioners were former postmasters who had been turned out under James II, they claimed, on political or religious grounds. Joseph Wartman, for example, wrote Wildman that he had been postmaster of the stage between Ashburton and Plymouth in Devon for fourteen years, "until he was put out at the instance of the late regulators because he would not give or declare his consent to the taking off the Test and Penal laws against Popery." Many of the requests to obtain, keep, or be restored to a position that Wildman received during his first months in office cited the candidate's well-affectedness to the present government, zealous Protestantism, and/or sufferings in the previous reign. Some applicants could boast recommendations from committed Whigs like Jack Arnold, Basil Dixwell, Thomas Papillon, Robert Ferguson (before he became a Jacobite), and Charles Brandon (later Earl of Macclesfield).[18]

Not all Post Office employees, however, were persons of unquestioned loyalty and honesty. One anonymous informant complained to Wildman about Mr. Prince, postmaster of Bridgewater in Somerset, who was "haughty, proud and disaffected to the present government," and another reported that Pennington, postmaster in Pentworth, Sussex, was a papist and a Jacobite. In 1696 a printed paper publicized more serious charges against more dangerously placed officials. It alleged that William Brockett, the controller of the Outland Office (handling overseas correspondence), opened or confiscated mail from Holland, including that of the king and other high-ranking officials; that William Gosling, clerk of the Outland office, conveyed letters from France to the Jacobite Earl of Clancarty when he was imprisoned in the Tower; that the Transylvanian immigrant Adam Francko, another clerk of the Outland Office (who himself gave testimony against Brockett) was a Socinian, an agent of the Dutch East India Company, a favorer of the Jews, and a spy; and that Edmund Sawtell, clerk of the Chester and Irish Roads, broke open the mail, wrote disloyal newsletters, and refused to drink King William's health. The investigation of these charges by the Lords Justices was itself was a violent affair, in which witnesses were threatened.[19]

The London Penny Post was also riven by scandal and accusations of disloyalty. In 1689 William Murcott launched a sustained campaign against Francis Golling and Nathaniel Castleton, respectively, the collector and comptroller of the London Penny Post, as well as against several sorters employed in offices at Cornhill, St. Martin's Lane, and the Temple. He accused these men of offenses ranging from drinking, swearing, and irreligion to the open expression of Jacobite sympathies to financial manipulation. To support the last charge, Murcott enlisted in his campaign one J. Farmer, a dismissed employee, who "looking upon my dismission as unkind" undertook to inspect the account books to discover irregularities. Murcott also obtained information from Isaac Ward, former letter carrier in Epping Walk, who said that Francis Golling had bribed him to cover up evidence of embezzling. Murcott's charges were amplified by another complainant to Wildman, a Mr. Lunn, who wrote in September to say that most people in the penny post office were disaffected to the present government, that "such persons may do mischief by opening letters, it having formerly been and is still too much practiced by them," and that at most penny post offices "there is a subtle trade in writing newsletters and votes of parliament . . . being a great detriment to the concern, several persons being taken off their duty of delivering letters, to write copies of the said votes etc., and the letters lie undelivered." He specifically cited Watkinson, Howell, and Kempton, sorters in post offices around London who had also been targeted by Murcott. Further negative information about one of Lunn's targets came from Meredeth Bromhead and Robert Mason, who wrote to Wildman in November to say that Mr. Howell was often absent from work and was "a disaffected person to the present government; and keeps company daily with those who are likewise so; and frequently drinks healths to King James."[20]

The truth of these charges is unclear at this distance, but the documents convey a strong impression that many of the parties involved were engaged in a bitter struggle over jobs and patronage. Mr. Lunn's letter ended with a note that sheds light on the sources of resentment: "Many persons who were receivers of penny post letters, whose houses stood very commodiously, have been discarded, there being little or no cause at all, only to fulfill the bitter and [impious?] passion of him who collects the money [Golling]."[21]

That professional ambition lurked behind accusations was also suggested by a letter from Mr. Farmer, explaining that Murcott, who had launched the accusations against Golling and Castleton, was himself a tool of Mr. [Henry] Oxenbridge, who had "great pretensions to the management" of the London

Penny Post. Farmer further admitted that his own behavior was driven by ambition. Resentment at his dismissal had brought him into the camp of Murcott and his friends, but he became dissatisfied with their promises of recompense and came to believe that John Wildman was "too subtle to be imposed upon" by their accusations. For that reason, he explained, he had switched sides and informed Francis Golling of the plot against him.[22]

Another ally of Murcott, the accountant Mr. Law, proved equally fickle. According to Murcott, Law had often said that he believed the controller (Castleton) was a papist and a devilish Tory and that Golling had the pox. Somehow, though, Law had reached an agreement with Golling, and, as a result (Murcott complained) "the intimacy between Law and this writer [Murcott] is vanished." Alliances made to further ambitions were apparently unstable. The London Penny Post, it seemed, was a hotbed of intrigue and betrayal.[23]

The case of Francis Bastinck, manager of packet boats at Dover, further illustrates the way that accusations of Jacobitism ran rampant in the Post Office and how difficult it is to parse the accuracy of the charges. As with the accused penny post officials, the historian can find repeated indications that Bastinck was a Jacobite but also reasons to question the motives of the accusers. Bastinck was suspected of Jacobite sympathies early on. Secretary of State Shrewsbury wrote to Wildman on 12 December 1689 to say he had heard from a reliable source that the master of the packet boat at Dover had "a very bad character" and allowed all manner of persons to travel to and from Calais. A paper in the possession of Whig MP Thomas Papillon contained a number of allegations: Bastinck had boasted at the time of the Popish Plot that he helped George Wakemen flee the realm, had expressed a willingness to do away with the Test and Penal laws, and had corresponded with Catholics abroad. At the time of the revolution he spoke of the new king with contempt and had deliberately had the lighthouse at Dungeness turned off when the fleet went by in the hope of making it miscarry. He was said to belong to a secret organization, the Knights of Montgomery, dedicated (according to the paper's author) to serving "some interest contrary to the nation's welfare." Papillon also preserved in his papers a hard-to-understand but clearly hostile complaint about Bastinck from one James Lingo, whom Bastinck had apparently dismissed from the packet boat service.[24]

Despite such negative buzz, Shrewsbury at times appeared to trust Bastinck. He took seriously Bastinck's claim that the mayor of Dover was lax in searching people coming from France. Bastinck, moreover, provided Shrewsbury with information about the seditious speech of Francis Williamson, who was alleged to be helping Jacobites cross the Channel. As late as September 1690, Bastinck was receiving instructions from Secretary of State Nottingham to search for suspected persons.[25]

It is plausible, then, that Bastinck was not so much a Jacobite as a victim of factional struggle. Such a hypothesis is strengthened by the fact that James Lingo, whose complaint about Bastinck was preserved by Papillon, was himself the subject of a complaint by Ralph Bell, who alleged Lingo was involved in the smuggling of people and correspondence to France. It is further supported by the fact Francis Williamson, against whom Bastinck provided evidence, had been given a pass by Wildman to go to France. Wildman's assistance to Williamson fueled suspicions that Wildman was involved in the Jacobite Montgomery Plot.[26]

One might argue, then, that Papillon, a close Whig associate of Wildman, attacked Bastinck to protect Wildman. Yet Bastinck continued to be the object of suspicion long after Wildman's dismissal—and from Tories as well as Whigs. Abraham Stock, writing to Secretary of State Nottingham, said that he distrusted another man on grounds that the man kept company with Bastinck. Moreover, Bastinck's name appeared on a list of people that Treasury solicitor Aaron Smith intended to prosecute "for trading with France" in 1694. The experienced spy Richard Kingston named him as a "professed enemy to the King" in his 1695 account of his travels on the coast.[27]

In the case of Bastinck, as in the other cases of accusations against postal officials discussed above, it would be foolish to pass judgment on the accuracy of the charges. Whatever way one judges Bastinck, the case shows that the trustworthiness of the Post Office could not be taken for granted. If Bastinck was a Jacobite, then it is striking that he kept his job as long as he did and that he had the occasional ear of a secretary of state. If he was not a Jacobite, then it is striking that a loyal man in a position of trust would be such a frequent target of malicious accusation from his own colleagues.

Obviously, in the wrong hands the Post Office was a threat to the security of the regime. But even in the hands of people who honestly supported the revolution, the Post Office could still provoke anxiety, for an entirely different set of reasons.

The potential of the Post Office to cement trust between government and people was complicated or undermined by its intelligence functions, which were already well established prior to the Glorious Revolution. John Thurloe, secretary of state in the interregnum, had taken over the postal monopoly precisely in order to "have the best means of discovering and preventing many dangerous and wicked designs . . . the intelligence whereof cannot well be communicated but by letter." William's first appointment as postmaster general, the republican John Wildman, personally symbolized the continuity of the Post Office as a tool of surveillance throughout the later seventeenth century. As Maurice Ashley points out, Wildman himself had tutored the new Restoration government in Thurloe's techniques of intercepting and copying mail. The Williamite regime also retained the services of the mathematician and cryptographer John Wallis, who had served Charles II.[28]

The practice of opening mail continued after 1688. Queen Mary ordered that the postmaster at Plymouth be instructed "not to send away any letter that has not first been perused." Messengers, clerks, and sorters were expected to recognize handwriting and to be familiar with the false addresses that Jacobites used to disguise the real destinations of their letters. James Lawrence, clerk in the General Letter Office, received a warrant in 1693 to watch the house of one Smith, a bookseller in Covent Garden, "and to observe all letters delivered there to be conveyed into the country or abroad." Lawrence was sent a handwriting sample with the warrant and told that anyone bringing a letter with that handwriting should be arrested. Similarly, when Peter Colter and Edward Hampson, two messengers of the penny post office for Westminster, thought that a packet sent to "Douglas a periwig maker in Wilde Street" was addressed in the handwriting of the Jacobite astrologer John Gadbury, they brought this suspected "roguery" to the attention of their superior, who upon opening the package found it to contain seditious literature addressed to Sir John Curzon in Oxfordshire. The identity of the sender was confirmed when Gadbury himself turned up to complain about the non-delivery of this packet to Mr. Douglas, at which point the postmaster pretended that the packet had never come to the post office.[29]

The continuation of older practices seems, however, to have produced some ambivalence among Williamite political elites. An intriguing sign of such ambivalence is the treatment inventor Samuel Morland received at the hands of the new government. In the Restoration, Morland had provided King Charles II with methods of opening and copying intercepted mail. His machines, however, were destroyed in 1666 in the Great Fire of London. In June 1689 Morland proposed to the king that he would oversee the construction of "engines and utensils" for opening letters, counterfeiting hands and seals, and quickly copying long dispatches, and that he would instruct others at the General Post Office in their use. A surviving copy of the proposal, which Morland had submitted to the king by way of Secretary of State Shrewsbury, is endorsed with a notation in the latter's hand indicating that the king refused the offer, thinking "the secret ought to die with him [Morland], as too dangerous to be encouraged."[30]

Even so, Morland's machines were apparently used by the new regime. In 1690, Morland complained that John Wildman had promised him reimbursement for all his charges as well as the payment of arrears on his pension if he would "discover to him the true art of opening and sealing up letters, counterfeiting of hands and seals, copying out any number of whole sheets of paper, written on all sides, in as many minutes, washing out ink, etc." Morland had accordingly spent £300 to employ "near 60 workmen in preparing engines and utensils for that service" and had found Wildman to be "industrious and curious in observing all operations," but he had not received his promised reward. Further evidence that Wildman made use of Morland's talents comes from Morland's erstwhile partner, Dr. Robert Gorge, who in 1695 tried to interest Secretary of State William Trumbull in a project to recreate Morland's "machines of intelligence." According to Gorge, Morland had built the machines for Wildman, but Wildman had "embezzled and spoilt" them upon leaving his office as postmaster general rather than let his successors make use of them.[31]

It is intriguing that the king (or at least Shrewsbury) rejected Morland's machines and even more intriguing that Wildman may have flouted his wishes and used them anyway. The mixed signals might have reflected the desire of some members of the new government to break with the tyrannical practices of the previous monarchs or at least to *appear* to break with them. (Recall here the indignant protestations in Wildman's 1689 broadside lamenting the "false" belief that mail was opened!)

The equivocal, ambivalent reception of Morland's offer also reflected anxieties among high-ranking politicians that the power to forge handwriting, imitate seals, and open letters might be turned against them. Wildman's history as a republican and a plotter made him already an object of distrust, and Morland's technology in his hands made him more so. Lord Carmarthen, noting Wildman's ties with Morland, dubbed Wildman "a most dangerous man to the government" and warned the king that his own and Queen Mary's letters might not "escape his search if he can get to them." Queen Mary herself came to suspect that Wildman's capacity to imitate handwriting and seals was being used against political rivals. When Wildman's associate the Earl of Monmouth claimed to have intercepted letters written in white ink that conveyed information known only to members of the Council of Nine, Mary concluded that the letters were in fact forgeries invented to implicate members of the council in a sham plot. She was supported in that view not only by the Tory Carmarthen but by the Whig Edward Russell, who told her (as she reported to William) that "they were certainly writ by Wildman" in order to "give suspicion that some of the company betrayed us; for, he said, Wildman was of the Commonwealth party, and his whole design was to make stirs, in hopes by that means to bring it about." Wildman was distrusted by Marlborough as well, enough so that he resolved to "write only by expresses since he had reason to believe that Major Wildman had exact impressions of most people's seals, and that he makes use of his art." The anxiety that Wildman inspired in Whigs, Tories, and the queen may well explain his dismissal in February 1691. The Post Office, it was feared, was a tool that could turn against its user.[32]

Local Government

Mayors and justices of the peace also did work vital to the security of the new regime. It is tempting to think of such officials as representatives of "society" rather than "the state." They owed their power in part to local prestige, and they were affected in the same way as their neighbors by policies of the central government that sometimes prioritized national security at the expense of local peace and prosperity. But it would be a mistake to exaggerate the opposition between the central state and local government. First, there was no clear division of labor between emissaries of the center and local officeholders. The responsibility of guarding of the coasts and the inspection of travelers' passes fell to mayors, JPs, and customs officers alike. Moreover, in the reigns of Charles II and James II the central government had reached deeply into local politics, remodeling town corporations and placing supporters in the lord lieutenancies and judicial benches. Local power, then, was affected by national politics.

The practice of intervening in local government did not end with the Glorious Revolution. Williamite authorities, for example, arrested Thomas Hawkins, the mayor of Stamford, for "dangerous practices" after he tried to stop townspeople from ringing bells to celebrate William and Mary's coronation. The Earl of Shrewsbury intervened with the Corporation of Exeter when he learned that George Saffin, a member of the chamber who had refused oaths of allegiance, was acting in his former capacity. He was quickly reassured that Saffin had appeared in the chamber only briefly on business, was no longer a member, and "will never act there even in a low and mean capacity." Participants in local political contests sometimes attempted to draw secretaries of state in to prevent the "disaffected" from getting elected to office. Such was the plea made by the mayor of Bristol to Shrewsbury in 1689. Conversely, when a new Whig sheriff dismissed William Tomlinson, the governor of the Preston House of Correction, on grounds of alleged Jacobitism, local Tories appealed to and received the help of Secretary of State Nottingham to restore Tomlinson to his post.[33]

It would be a mistake, however, to think that the new regime exercised thorough control over local affairs. In many cases, local authorities acted against the representatives of the central government, sometimes for ideological reasons and sometimes for local and economic ones. If one prefers to consider local government as part of "the state," then the Williamite state could be found divided against itself.

The new regime's lack of control stemmed in part from its reluctance, on ideological and pragmatic grounds, to repeat the systematic intervention in local government undertaken by the two previous monarchs. As Lionel Glassey has shown, there was surprisingly little turnover among justices of the peace at the time of the revolution, especially in counties where the lieutenancy of the county militia remained in Tory hands. As a result, despite some half-hearted efforts to purge the disaffected from the judiciary, justices of the peace who had not taken the oaths of allegiance remained on the bench until at least 1694. Town governments tell a similar story. Parliament in 1690 had considered the infamous "Sacheverell Clause," which would have barred persons who had been appointed to office as the result of the quo warranto campaigns of the two previous reigns from holding office for another seven years. The Sacheverell Clause was, however, rejected.[34]

Thus, a number of Jacobite mayors and town corporations plagued the new regime. Having been informed that one Tootell kept a coffeehouse in

Wigan furnished with "letters and false news defaming the government," the mayor of Wigan failed to take action. Walter Nynn, the mayor of Gravesend, was said to protect the openly disaffected, and the mayor of Maidstone allegedly encouraged a mutiny. The Corporation of Chichester was reported to be openly disaffected. According to a scathing account, few of its members had signed the Association oath in 1696, nor did any drink the king's health after peace was proclaimed in 1697. A newly chosen burgess, one Captain Carr, "was a long time in prison with the papists for not taking the oaths." Ironically, the only solution the writer could find was to bring a quo warranto action against the city charter.[35]

Not every local official who ran afoul of the central government, however, was a Jacobite. Resistance by local officials to orders from the center might reflect the stress that war with France placed on some communities. The quartering of troops caused hardship and sometimes led to violence. The mayor and aldermen of Canterbury petitioned the Treasury on behalf of the innkeepers and victuallers who faced imminent ruin "for want of trade and soldiers being quartered there." Significantly, the petitioners suggested that Canterbury was unusual in having thus far provided supplies "out of a sense of duty and loyalty to their Majesties": the eight companies of marine soldiers that the town quartered and had provisioned had been "kept in good condition without deserting which has happened *in other places where the like care has not been taken*" (italics mine). That other communities were less friendly to soldiers is evident from the published *Complaint of the Inhabitants of the Island of Guernzey*, which claimed that soldiers and officers alike stole with impunity from residents and used the threat of violence to extort money and supplies.[36]

Restrictions on trade and travel also put strain on the relationship of local communities to the central government, with local officeholders often siding with their neighbors. A small but telling example is the reaction of William Stokes, mayor of Dover, to an order he received from Secretary of State Shrewsbury to prevent all persons not having passes from crossing the seas. Stokes tried to explain that doing so was impracticable and would cause a loss of revenue to the town. Merchants who crossed the seas regularly were accustomed to passing through Dover without hindrance, in return for which they paid the town a fee; harassing them might cause them to embark from some other port and deprive the town of the many economic benefits of their presence. It is perhaps not surprising, then, to find Shrewsbury several months later scolding the mayor for laxity in enforcing what must have been, for the people of Dover, an even more unwelcome order to stop and search *everyone* coming from overseas, pass-holders and non-pass-holders alike.[37]

Many clashes between local society and central authorities concerned trade and smuggling. People on the coasts of Kent and Sussex had profited from "owling," the smuggling of raw wool to France, a practice which although illegal often had the support of local authorities. The owler hunter William Carter described, for example, how one of his men was threatened at Lydd by the bailiff's son, sent, he said, by his father. The mayor of New Romney allowed several owlers that Carter had committed to be bailed out of jail, and, Carter reported, "himself is since discovered to be an owler." A barn full of raw wool ready for smuggling that customs officers raided in a deadly clash with local men turned out to belong to the mayor of Hythe, Julius Deedes. At least one of the men recruited or dragooned by customs officers into helping with the raid on Deedes's wool expressed regret about the job, in a way that suggests it was Deedes, not the customs agents, who commanded local respect. Thomas Coxhall of Lydd, husbandman, told the customs officer John Ellesdon that "Mr. Deedes was a gentleman he had earned a great deal of money of and by this [assisting in the raid] he might lose his work and incur his displeasure."[38]

The prohibition of trade with France was especially damaging to the livelihoods of the Channel Islands. Residents of Jersey, who had historically been permitted to trade with France even during wartime, were angered to find that privilege revoked in 1689. Apparently they resisted. In 1690 Shrewsbury complained that Jersey islanders were shipping lead and ammunition to St. Malô simply because it fetched a much higher price there than it did in England. In 1691 Charles LeHardy, former constable of the island, came with witnesses before the Privy Council to give evidence that some of the highest-ranking officials in Jersey colluded in trade with France. Those accused included the island's lieutenant governor, Edward Harris, and the collector of customs, William Hely, as well as the king's advocate on the island, several jurats of the royal court, and the sheriff. If LeHardy can be believed, officials openly inverted the policies of the central government: Governor Harris publicly proclaimed that he had an order to allow a trade with France, persons who tried to report on lead being exported were ignored by magistrates, and LeHardy himself was called a dog and rogue by the governor when he tried to stop a shipment of lead. Although the complaints were brought to the attention of Parliament, Harris and Hely were apparently still employed and the objects of similar complaints as late as 1693.[39]

The case of the Jersey smuggling conspiracy demonstrates that the Williamite regime's struggles with smuggling and sedition cannot be described solely in terms of the opposition between central and local. True, the trade in lead and other commodities with France was in the interest of Jersey islanders, and thus their smuggling represented a classic case of community resistance to the central state. At the same time, the conspiracy was supported by representatives of the central state, like Governor Harris and Customer Hely, while some local residents, like LeHardy and his witnesses, tried to stop it. The corrupt customs officer Thomas Noel of Dover also defied easy classification in terms of having national versus local allegiances. Noel justified the establishment of a smuggling trade with Flanders by saying its founders "were very honest men and merchant smugglers only" and that the business "would employ all the poor people on the coast." Not all conflicts took a local versus national form, nor did agents of the central bureaucracies inevitably support the new regime's agenda or local officials oppose it.[40]

The Jersey smuggling case contains a further layer of complexity. Sometimes knowing what actions constituted support of the new regime's agenda was difficult in itself. As noted above, Charles LeHardy complained that Governor Harris publicly proclaimed that he had an order to allow trade with France. Harris, it appears, actually did receive instruction to permit some smuggling! On 21 August 1690 Nottingham had asked Harris to help one of his spies in France to send letters home. "If you can find any persons that you can trust, who use the trade of France, as 'tis certain there are too many at Jersey notwithstanding all the care you can take to prevent it," he wrote, "you may connive at the going and coming of such a boat, if the master will undertake to bring such letters as shall be put in his hands." Nottingham's reference to the care Harris took to prevent trade with France might be taken with several grains of salt. It is entirely likely that Harris made more of the very limited permission to connive with smuggling than Nottingham intended. Still, this case alerts us to the murkiness of the line between sanctioned and unsanctioned activity.[41]

In some cases, the distinction between working on behalf of the government and working against it was hard to make because central authorities might permit illegality for the sake of national security. In December 1693, for example, the shipmaster William Cotton petitioned authorities to explain that he had been employed to procure intelligence about enemies overseas and to that end had transported prohibited goods. In 1698 one Captain Gibson, employed by Secretary of State James Vernon, took Jacobites across the Channel, presumably for the purpose of spying on them. Although Vernon expressed great annoyance when Gibson made "use of my name as a a conniver at Jacobites provided they take their passage with him," Vernon was clearly doing just what Gibson said he was doing.[42]

Another activity that straddled the boundary of legality and illegality was privateering. Privateers held licenses from the government to attack enemy shipping and were rewarded with proceeds from the sale of the prizes. However, privateering often merged into smuggling through the practice of "collusive capture," whereby a French merchant might allow himself to be captured by a privateer so that the privateer could sell the captured cargo and share the profits with him. Persons who in one context were part of the "state" might in other contexts act in opposition to it—or appear to act in opposition to it. Awareness of this point complicates any simple model of a unified government imposing its will on unruly society.[43]

An especially intriguing case that illustrates how hard it was to tell who was acting on behalf of the state and who was acting against it concerns the merchant-spy John Letherhead. Letherhead was closely connected to William Carter, whose activities will be examined later in this chapter, and for whom the relationship with Letherhead proved problematic. For purposes of the present discussion, however, it is enough to know that in April 1691 John Letherhead obtained, through Secretary of State Nottingham, a very unusual privilege, a pass to travel freely to the coast of France, presumably for the purpose of spying on French military preparations. But to cover his spying, Letherhead purchased goods in Dunkirk. Predictably, his possession of French goods got him into some trouble. "The customs house officers have been a little hard with him," Admiral Russell reported after Letherhead's first voyage.[44]

The second voyage was more fraught. Word that Letherhead was a spy had leaked out in his home port of Margate, making it difficult for him to gather a crew. He was able to sail only after John Watkins, described as a "messenger for preventing the exportation of wool," agreed to come on the voyage to encourage other seamen to join. But when Letherhead arrived in Calais he was, alas, arrested. Meanwhile, back in Margate, the "mobily," as Letherhead later called them, attacked his wife, "rent her cloths from off her, and her flesh in several parts, in the most lamentable manner, telling her, her husband was a rogue, and that he was gone to France to sell us." Meanwhile, French merchants helped to obtain Letherhead's release in Calais and "to color the matter better he was obliged to buy goods, which he brought to Margate."[45]

Once again, customs officers swooped in. This time a conflict erupted among the officers themselves. The first to seize Letherhead's goods was John Watkins, the friendly officer who had helped Letherhead recruit a crew. His action might have been intended to quell suspicions that Letherhead was a spy and to preempt any attempt by other customs officials to confiscate the goods. But they were promptly confiscated by another officer, Abraham Hough. Fearing that his goods "by stress of weather . . . will be much damnified if they lie long," Letherhead begged Nottingham to let his friend John Watkins bring the goods to London to be sold. He later launched a lengthy complaint against Hough with the Treasury. In addition to protesting the seizure of his goods, Letherhead accused Hough of having "discovered and making known" his spy mission, "to the great hazard of his life on his arrival in Calais."[46]

Letherhead's complaints were referred to John Lowther and commissioners of customs for an investigation. Hough, in his defense, produced testimony from one Mr. Wells, the collector and deputy controller at Sandwich, that Hough was innocent of divulging Letherhead's pass and "well-affected to the present government." He further provided "certificates under the hands of most of the chief inhabitants of Margate" to the same effect. Letherhead offered to show "by affidavits from most of the substantial and well-affected persons in and about Margate" that the men who signed the certificates in Hough's favor were "criminals in this affair" and "true French and self-interested persons." Faced with conflicting testimony, the customs commissioners tried to satisfy both parties. They cleared Hough of the charges against him and upheld his right to seize the goods and prosecute them in the Exchequer, but they recommended that Letherhead and Watkins be recompensed with a share of the takings "as a further reward and encouragement to them for their diligence in the public service." Later on, however, Letherhead was again caught colluding in the illegal importation of French silk.[47]

Many elements of this story should by now be familiar: resentments sparked by the stoppage of trade and policing of travel, state authorities at odds, the circulation of charges that customs officers (agents of the state) were themselves corrupt and Jacobite, and conflicting testimony about who was a patriot and who was a scoundrel. Several unanswered questions remain: Was Letherhead spying under cover of trading, or trading under cover of spying? Did the popular rage against Letherhead at Margate stem from the belief that he was a Jacobite or from resentment that in a time of trade embargo which hurt the local economy Letherhead alone was allowed to travel? Were the citizens who testified to Hough's honesty themselves honest? As we saw, the Treasury commissioners themselves were uncertain as to what to believe. These very uncertainties can tell us much about the problematic credibility of state institutions (responsible for security) and of enterprising patriots (who sometimes flouted those institutions). Both sides in the dispute, Hough and Letherhead, claimed to be performing a service for the state but could be accused of self-interest.

Patriotic Entrepreneurs

Up to this point I have considered persons acting in an official capacity. Some did their jobs; the performance of others was compromised by corruption, ambition, or perhaps treasonous intent. Occasionally, however, the records provide a glimpse of people who showed a zeal for the preservation of the new regime that went far beyond any job requirement. If they obtained salaried positions in the government, it was after they had already performed significant service. These "patriotic entrepreneurs," as I call them, can be distinguished from other bureaucrats and government officials. They acted outside the restrictions of any one job description; they took financial risks without the guarantee of a reward. Patriotic entrepreneurs offered the kind of service to the government that was most compatible with the new regime's ideology. They were native, not foreign, and they stood as examples of an engaged citizenry acting in its own defense. At the same time, the line between patriotic entrepreneurs and political informers might be thin. Both, after all, portrayed themselves as patriots and sought profit.

One example of patriotic entrepreneurship undertaken at the group level was the Commissions to Discover Lands given to Superstitious Uses (known for short as the "Superstitious Lands Commissions"). The commissions were composed of private investors who obtained licenses from the Crown to seek out property intended by its Catholic owners to be used for the benefit of the Catholic Church. According to statutes from the reigns of Edward VI and Elizabeth I, such lands would be forfeit to the Crown. The Superstitious

Lands commissioners held inquests in the relevant counties before local juries, who in turn, if they found cause, would then permit the commissioners to pursue cases against the landholders in the Exchequer. If the lands were forfeited, the commissioners would divide the proceeds with the government.[48]

The private individuals who stood to profit from the work of the commissions represented a wide slice of English society. At the top were the courtiers who nominally headed the commissions and who used their influence at court to obtain the license to hunt for superstitious lands: the Marquis of Winchester, Lord Delamere (later Earl of Warrington), the Earl of Monmouth, Sir Scroop Howe, and Sir John Guise. The work of the commissions was handled by full-time managers, many of whom (according to Paul Hopkins) had colorful and shady careers with a distinct Whig tinge. They included Peter Stepkin (whom Hopkins calls an "impoverished gentleman-swindler") and Henry Baker (a "Whig debauchee," according to Hopkins, closely associated with Ralph Montagu and the Green Ribbon Club during the Exclusion Crisis). Also standing to profit from the work of the commission were the witnesses, many of them ex-Catholics, like ex-priests John Taaffe and Peter Bérault or the Lancashire convert Agnes Barker of Warrington (see chapter 4). The Superstitious Lands Commissions were notorious for dishonesty. Some of the witnesses for the Lancashire commission, for example, including Taaffe and his brother-in-law John Lunt (as well as Agnes Barker), became "discoverers" of the discredited Lancashire Plot. Hopkins points out, moreover, that the financial hopes of the government in the commissions never came to fruition as their suits foundered in the Exchequer.[49]

Other patriotic entrepreneurs acted in an individual capacity. Although most seem less sleazy than the Superstitious Lands commissioners, their reputations and motives could be questioned. Joseph Beverton is one example of a patriotic entrepreneur. In 1693 or 1694, while living in Canterbury, he "having never been an offender in owling or smuggling himself but purely out of a zeal for his Majesty and the good of the Kingdom, took upon him to discover and prevent those so pernicious practices." On his own account, his services to the government were varied and significant. He stopped the smuggling of wool and horses to France, as well as the illegal importation of French silk and lace into England. He also gave intelligence of an intended invasion from Calais; persuaded the owler John Writtell to turn informant; and helped to turn the owler James Hunt, who transported Jacobites abroad, into a witness for the government. As he insisted in a string of petitions to

John Somers, William Trumbull, and the Lords Justices, Beverton took financial risks in performing these services, which "brought the King a considerable amount of money, and but a small advantage to myself." Although Beverton at one point described himself as "one of the riding officers of the Customs at Canterbury," he also said that he acted "only by deputation at large and without salary." Beverton borrowed from the Royal Lutestring Company (which had a monopoly on the production of a certain kind of silk cloth and therefore a motive to support his efforts to prevent smuggling). But, as he complained, the Lords of the Council had not come through with funds that would allow him to pay back the loan. To make matters worse, Beverton was robbed of the profits that he would have made from prosecuting the notorious owlers James Hunt and Thomas Lad in the Exchequer because in return for their confessions "they were promised a pardon, and all my proceedings against them are stopped, and charges wholly lost to me, so that it had been better as to my private interest that I had never taken the said Hunt." In the end, however, perhaps Beverton did receive more satisfactory compensation. In 1698 Sir Rowland Gwynne commended him to Secretary of State James Vernon as a person who had "done service," and Vernon and the Lords Justices recommended he be advanced to more beneficial employment.[50]

The intrepid John Macky is another example of someone whose service to the state was wide-ranging and performed outside the bounds of an already held office. Macky, who later became important as an organizer of spy networks in the War of the Spanish Succession, warned of French invasion plans in 1692. Although he stated in his *Memoirs* that he was already in King William's service, it is not clear how he was employed, and his information met with a cold shoulder from Secretary of State Nottingham. It was only after his information proved right that he was given a job as a "riding surveyor" of the coast around Harwich, directly under the authority of the secretary of state, with broad powers to apprehend smugglers and suspected persons and a general responsibility for keeping track of persons going to or coming from Holland. He was also eventually given charge of the Dover packet boats in 1697.[51]

The most energetic and best documented of individual patriotic entrepreneurs was William Carter. He was a shining example of the individual patriot selflessly promoting national interest, sometimes at great risk to person and fortune. Yet his relationship to the government was complicated. His very zeal tended to delegitimate the state officials whose failures made his work necessary. His writings are in themselves a great source of evidence about the corruption of customs officers or the collusion of town governments in smuggling. At the same time, Carter's status as an independent operator meant that he inevitably sought ways of making his work profitable to himself (or at least of making up the costs of it), which in turn compromised his claims to selfless patriotism. Carter himself was not immune from suspicion, and on one occasion he was publicly criticized by clothiers (or someone purporting to speak for them). Although he did not inform about plots, Carter had something in common with political informers. The sources of his legitimacy were unstable; his work was carried out on behalf of the government yet cast suspicion on it.

Carter's career as a patriotic entrepreneur predated the Glorious Revolution. He was by trade a clothier, who once apologized to his readers for his "shortness as to parts, education, time and authors." He was thrust into his multipronged activism by bitter personal experience. In October 1667, he recounted in one of his earlier tracts, 1,500 packs of raw wool that he had purchased at Romney Marsh were stolen and, he later learned, put aboard shallops bound for France. He quickly came to London, "leaving my own private concerns, to acquaint Parliament what danger the trade was in." The threats went beyond smuggling. Especially irksome to Carter, as a would-be exporter, was the high tariff Louis XIV placed upon English wool cloth. He presented a petition to Parliament for legislation to correct the trade imbalance, urging among other things that a tax be levied on imported French linens to "encourage the wearing of the English manufactures." He further successfully petitioned King Charles II for a party of horses and some frigates to patrol the coast of Kent and boasted that he had thereby prevented the export of a thousand packs of raw wool in a summer.[52]

During the next two decades, Carter kept up a rush of activity. He financed his own armed expeditions against wool smugglers; he lobbied in Parliament for legislation to better prevent the exportation of raw wool and to protect clothiers from abuse by aulnagers (farmers of the tax on cloth); he set up a network of correspondents in Irish and foreign ports; he campaigned against a bill to enable limited export of wool from Ireland; and he published numerous pamphlets arguing that it was in England's interest to promote domestic woolen manufacture by preventing foreigners access to English wool and erecting barriers to the import of French luxury goods.

The challenges facing Carter concerned both his physical and financial survival and his legitimacy and credibility. First, his work entailed violence. There were complaints that Carter used a "military power." On Carter's account, it was indeed a war. Twenty inhabitants at Hythe "rose in the night with weapons" to wound Carter's men and carry off wool that had been seized. The women of Folkstone threw rocks at him on the beach, forcing him to relinquish a prisoner. His witnesses were "forced to fly from their habitations for the threats of the owlers." The most spectacular attack on Carter and his men occurred in and near Lydd in December 1688 when Carter's men were violently assaulted, chased by riders on horseback, and warned off with death threats. Wool smugglers also, according to Carter, used law as a weapon. When Thomas Petley, a poor wool comber, gave evidence against his former employer, Mark Gabree, Gabree in turn had Petley arrested on a perjury charge "out of revenge, and to undo him." One of Carter's men was imprisoned in Dover Castle in 1685 on a sham complaint about a debt trumped up by exporters.[53]

Little help was forthcoming from the legal system or the customs officers. Attempting to prosecute two exporters of wool at the Maidstone Assizes on the king's instruction, Carter found on his arrival that the accused had bribed his accusers and "taken off the witnesses." Customs officers routinely thwarted Carter's attempts to have illegal shipments condemned in London by allowing the exporters to compound for them (pay a fine to get the shipments back). In doing so, they robbed Carter of the moiety to which he would have been entitled had the shipment been condemned in the Court of Exchequer, and the wool was exported anyway.[54]

The inability to prosecute suits added to Carter's already serious financial problems. Carter occasionally persuaded the monarchs to pay for men, horses, and vessels for the policing of owlers. He obtained a commission from James II to stop the illegal transport of wool, but it was granted so close to the end of James's reign that Carter was never able to profit from it. He tried creative ways to find backers, but those too failed. In 1668, for example, he lobbied the Council of Trade and the king "at my own cost and charge" to grant the governors of Christ's Hospital a commission to see that the laws against wool export were put into execution (the plan being, one presumes, that if the governors of Christ's Hospital got the commission they would hire Carter to carry it out). Although the commission was granted, the governors of the hospital, to Carter's disgust, declined the task, "upon some frivolous objections, without allowing me one penny for the money expended, which was not less than £40, besides my own labor and attendance."⁵⁵

William's accession did not bring Carter financial security. He was given a job as a visiting surveyor of landwaiters in the western outports, but for reasons unknown it was taken away from him (much to the annoyance of the customs commissioners). He petitioned the Treasury for financial support, stressing that he had at his "voluntary cost" succeeded in preventing the exportation of much wool, "though to his own private loss and to the hazard oft times of his life." He was now "threatened to be sued" for money he had borrowed to outfit ships and hire men; the captains of his vessels were "arrested and prosecuted for money for victualling the said vessels and for the wages of seamen, and are exposed to ruin thereby, and some of them threatening the said Carter for the same; for that he put them upon the said service."⁵⁶

Carter did manage to extract £300 from the Treasury in November 1689 and another £200 in April 1690, thanks to a favorable report by Treasury solicitor Aaron Smith praising his past effectiveness and honesty. His compensation, however, seemed to lag behind expenses. Once again he was threatened by former employees and persons who had loaned him money. Carter was eventually promised some horsemen, a frigate, immunity from prosecution, and a payment of £249, but within a month he complained to the Treasury that promises were unfulfilled and that he "never received any recompense, but still spending my money daily in this affair." In May 1691 he lamented that he was unable to proceed at law against owlers "for want of supplies, he having found himself in considerable debt in the said service."⁵⁷

Perhaps Carter's biggest challenge was legitimacy. His moral code hinged on a dichotomy between private interest and public good, and he consistently presented himself as eschewing the former for the sake of the latter. In his 1671 pamphlet *England's Interest by Trade Asserted*, he lamented "the want of public spirits" among the otherwise happy English. The many subjects who carried on trade with the French king, he warned William in 1691, "prefer their own private gain before the public good." In a 1694 pamphlet he printed a letter from a former aulnager, whom he had put out of business, vouching that Carter preferred "the public before his private interest." In his 1695 *Usurpations of France*, he recounted the fall of Constantinople, blaming the inhabitants: "Every man (as now here) was careful how to increase his own private wealth, few or none regarding the public state."⁵⁸

Given that much of the public resented Carter's efforts to stop wool smuggling, and given that his relations with political authorities were mixed, Carter's claims to represent "the public" were problematic. Not surprisingly, then, Carter worked hard to define "public interest" in a way that coincided with his own projects. Through his frenzied round of pamphleteering, grassroots organizing, and parliamentary appearances, Carter created the "public" on whose behalf he could be seen to act. His pamphlets simultaneously identified a common interest among clothiers and merchants and made their interests identical to the interests of the nation. Having defined that interest, Carter visibly lobbied for it. Moreover, he initiated letter-writing campaigns and petition drives that helped members of the trade see themselves as having a corporate interest. These campaigns allowed Carter to appear to reflect sentiments that he in fact had helped to create. In providing the text for letters and petitions to be signed and presented by individual clothiers, towns, and corporate groups to Parliament, Carter acted like a ventriloquist, putting his own words into the mouths of others and then presenting himself as a spokesperson for those others. In the early 1690s, for example, when opposing legislation that would have transferred the collection of taxes on wool from the aulnage to the Customs, Carter "sent down printed forms of letters to a great many corporations, for them to transcribe and subscribe, and direct to their parliament men."[59]

The mutually supporting activities of writing, lobbying at Whitehall, and grassroots organizing allowed Carter to create a sense that there was a public, independent of the state, in whose interest he acted. The very act of organizing, moreover, gave Carter a network of support among merchants and clothiers, which he could then mobilize to give weight to the claim that he did indeed represent the interest of the group.

Carter's powers of mobilization and ventriloquism were on full display in his campaign to defeat a rival, Francis Monk. Monk claimed, like Carter, to act on behalf of the ruined clothiers of England and had made several attempts (between 1677 and 1684) to get a commission to execute laws against the exportation of wool. Carter thwarted him. When some gentlemen who were to be Monk's collaborators and contributors asked Carter's advice in 1682, Carter "advised them to spare their money." When in 1684 the Treasury asked the Company of Merchant Adventurers and other trading companies for advice on yet another of Monk's proposals, the companies solicited Carter's advice and later told the Treasury that Monk and his fellow undertakers "designed their own private profit, more than the effectual carrying out of their intended work" and that the clothiers who did support Monk's proposal were "generally mean persons, not to be credited in a thing of that nature and consequence."[60]

Carter also orchestrated a display of public sentiment to fight Monk. In 1684 he arranged for "a petition drawn up by me" to be presented to the Treasury Lords by "several clothiers and factors of the woolen manufacture within the counties of Worcester, Glo[u]cester, Somerset and Wiltshire." The petitioners urged the Treasury to allow members of the "Hamburgh, Turkey, and other companies" (that is, companies of merchants selling English wool cloth abroad) to propose methods to prevent illegal exportation of raw wool. Carter then energetically lobbied each company concerned to establish a subscription among clothiers and merchants to pay the charges of enforcing the laws; he himself wrote an uncharacteristically short pamphlet urging all woolen manufacturers to support the undertaking. In it, he reminded his readers that Monk and his associates had been found unfit to undertake such a project. The distinction between himself and Monk was, for Carter, that between the pursuit of public good and the pursuit of private good. Public good, in turn, was defined by the good of the community of merchants and clothiers (and by extension England) who backed Carter.

> And the said prohibition [on the export of wool] can never be managed with that candor and uprightness, by private and particular persons. Who, as they declare, undertake it to get money by it; Whereas these companies do propose to spend both their time and money without any manner of design of private benefit to themselves, but with a constant annual charge, freely contributed for the public good.[61]

We can better understand now how Carter, a private individual, was able to define himself as acting in the public interest, even when he sought compensation and even when neither the state nor the majority of people necessarily supported him. The claim that his work was for the "public good" was backed up by the fact that merchants and clothiers had collectively chosen to fund him. He was himself, of course, largely responsible for guiding their choice.

Although Carter had begun his owler hunting long before 1688, and had found ways to legitimate it, the revolution gave him a further layer of legitimacy and expanded the scope and meaning of his work. The new regime was more ideologically congenial to his concerns. Carter's published pamphlets argued passionately for what Steve Pincus has identified as a "Whig" version of political economy espoused by so many of William's supporters: that is, the notion that national wealth would be increased by manufacturing. His strong antipathy to Louis XIV was also well in harmony with the new regime's policies. Not surprisingly, he chose in 1689 to republish his earlier pamphlets in omnibus editions with a dedication to the new king and a long narrative of his services up to that point. In his post-1689 writings, he predictably spoke more negatively about the two previous monarchs than he had in the work he published during the Restoration. It was only in 1694, for example, that he told his audience that in 1671 he had been imprisoned in the Gatehouse when he neglected to bring his pamphlets to a licenser. He spoke darkly of the "cunning artifices and secret contrivances of French agents," and of "all the interest they had in our court the two last reigns."[62]

War with France and the threat of Jacobite conspiracy also helped Carter to make his case against wool smuggling and more closely aligned his cause with that of the new regime. By French sloops landing on English shore to deliver commodities and carry away wool, Carter pointed out to the king, "a constant and secret correspondence is kept with your majesties enemies, and the French made acquainted with all the creeks and convenient landing places on the Kentish shore."[63]

By the spring of 1691, accordingly, Carter had embarked on a new kind of service to the government, one which dovetailed nicely with his own concerns. He undertook with Secretary of State Nottingham to recruit and manage two men, William Gatley and John Letherhead, to spy on the condition of French ships and troops in French ports. Having the ear of the secretary of state allowed Carter to frame wool smuggling as a security issue. He used information he obtained, for example, to draw Nottingham's attention to the French shallops that carried wool and Jacobites across the channel and pushed him to take action against the lighthouse keeper at Dungeness who notoriously abetted owlers.[64]

The recruitment of Gatley and Letherhead, however, proved compromising for Carter's credibility. Gatley was obstructed by government officers on the eve of a voyage to Calais; when Carter complained, Nottingham informed him that he had learned Gatley had spoken indiscreetly in a public house of his mission to spy on the French. Letherhead proved even more problematic. As discussed above, he incurred the hostility of the crowd at

Margate and had his goods seized by the customs officer Abraham Hough. Moreover, his intelligence made a poor impression on Admiral Russell, who told Nottingham he did "not find his report very probable."[65]

Carter's support for Letherhead raises some questions. Carter could not have known, as we now know, that a few years later Letherhead would be caught by Joseph Beverton colluding in the illegal importation of French silk. But even at the time Carter hired him, Letherhead's trustworthiness would have been at best ambiguous. What do we make, then, of Carter's association with him? Did he naïvely trust Letherhead? Was he hoping to profit from Letherhead's ventures? How did it affect Carter's standing as the self-appointed guardian of the public interest?[66]

We have only fragmentary clues with which to address these questions. Carter certainly never repudiated Letherhead. Even after the troubled first voyage, Carter borrowed money to finance Letherhead's second voyage. Indeed, he tried to make arrangements to get Letherhead a pass for a third voyage. It does seem significant, however, that Carter placed his trusted associate John Watkins, a man described as a "messenger for preventing the exportation of wool," in close proximity to Letherhead. Watkins had traveled with Letherhead on his second voyage and was eventually awarded, with Letherhead, a share of the proceeds from the sale of the ship's cargo. It seems likely that Carter relied on Watkins not just to assist Letherhead but to control him—and perhaps to ensure that a share of the proceeds from any forfeiture ended up in Carter's hands. Carter was eager to assure Nottingham that Watkins would be engaged in Letherhead's proposed third voyage.[67]

Perhaps Carter's trust in Letherhead was not absolute. Such a hypothesis is strengthened by the fact that Carter, in his public writings, never mentioned Letherhead's name. He did boast in vague terms that "I was by order of the Queen directed to attempt another affair . . . the effect of which service ended in the method for a descent into France, in the beginning of the year 1692." But he was uncharacteristically scanty with details. His reticence might mean that Letherhead was still active as a spy and that Carter did not wish to blow his cover. It seems more likely, though, that he knew his association with Letherhead might put his reputation at risk.[68]

Carter's reputation was further stressed in the 1690s by conflicts among clothiers and merchants about controversial legislation affecting the aulnage, the excise tax on cloth. Throughout his career Carter had energetically campaigned against abuses by the collectors of the aulnage, who extorted money from hapless clothiers to the point of ruining them. Eventually Carter bought the aulnage farm himself, ostensibly as the best way to protect clothiers from further abuse. But when Carter campaigned against a parliamentary bill that would have shifted the collection of the excise on cloth from the aulnage to the customs house, he appeared to be acting in self-interest. He was stung to see himself derided in a broadside as "Wooll-Carter" who "was formerly a zealous solicitor against the Aulnage-Office, but now, by reason of yearly payment, is become their friend." He rushed into print to defend his position on the issue and to reiterate his long record. He even printed a letter from a former aulnager, whom he had put out of business, that praised Carter for "preferring the public before his private interest, and tho' an enemy, yet acting fairly and above board."[69]

The fact that William Carter had to defend his altruism underscores the fact that no patriotic entrepreneur could entirely evade suspicions of self-interest. The very fact that such men took financial risks in their service to the regime and inevitably sought recompense could compromise their credibility. The line between the patriotic entrepreneurs discussed here and the political informers who will be considered later in the book could be thin.

Patriotic entrepreneurs like William Carter should not be equated with unscrupulous witnesses for the Superstitious Lands Commissions, such as John Taaffe (see chapters 4 and 6). It is fair to say that the former was an energetic servant of the public who sought recompense only to be able to do his work, while the latter was a scoundrel profiting from perjury. But would the distinction have been clear to contemporaries? The foregoing discussion shows how hard it was to separate patriotism from profit seeking, the necessary business of security from exploitation, the formal state machinery and its concerns from the agendas of a host of local actors. The difficulty of making such distinctions, for contemporaries as well as historians, helps explain why the new regime might appear insecure, how political informers might seem legitimate, and how the credit of the government became a matter of fierce debate.

CHAPTER 3

"A Tool with so Devilish an Edge"

Government Officials and Political Informers in the 1690s

> For among the other disappointments we have met with under the late change, ... it is with extreme sorrow that we find that crime unknown to Turks and Heathens as well as all nations professing Christianity besides these. Namely, not only of countenancing mercenary and infamous rascals, to swear quiet and innocent men out of their lives. But of bringing, instructing and training them thereunto, still kept up with all the scandalous openness that it heretofore was, yea better encouraged and rewarded.
> —ROBERT FERGUSON, *A Letter to the Right-Hononrable* [sic] *My Lord Chief Justice Holt, Occasioned by the Noise of a Plot* (1694)

The challenges facing Williamite authorities when they sought information about threats to the security of the new regime were not unique. Espionage carries some perennial structural problems (at least in societies run in accordance with an Anglo-American system of law). There is, for example, the agonized choice to be made between prosecuting offenders (and in the process "outing" witnesses who had provided information while under cover) or preserving the cover of agents (but allowing offenders to keep offending). The fact that spies are by definition liars always complicates the ability of their employers to trust them.

Still, the particular political conditions of the 1690s affected the way intelligence was gathered. Officials in Williamite England operated in a context that made the question of what to believe, and how to appear believable themselves, especially vexed. Their perception that their actions would affect both their own credit and that of the regime had an impact on the way they acquired and assessed information. In turn, the public's anxiety about the regime's prospects for survival meant that successes and failures of intelligence when they became known had political consequences. In this chapter I examine the interplay of politics and intelligence in the 1690s, describing the structures and personalities relevant to the gathering of intelligence and showing how the conditions of this work were shaped by political circumstances.

The conduct and reception of intelligence in the 1690s was influenced by fears of treason within the regime. Many politicians were ready to believe that their opponents were involved in Jacobite plots, or at least to believe that accusations could effectively intimidate them. Such beliefs seemed more plausible because so many of William's advisors had also advised his predecessors. Given the small size of the early modern political elite, continuity in personnel was inevitable. The Marquis of Carmarthen (formerly Earl of Danby) and the Marquis of Halifax, important advisors to James II and Charles II, became members of William's Privy Council. In one of the more remarkable political comebacks of the century, James II's former henchman the Earl of Sunderland remade himself as a Williamite and member of the governing Whig Junto.[1]

Many members of William's government were suspected of Jacobitism, if only of what historians term the "fire-insurance" type (that is, keeping up Jacobite connections in case James II came back). The Earl of Marlborough, who had so crucially abandoned James in 1688, had Jacobite relations (by way of his wife Sarah's sister, the Countess of Tyrconnell). Suspected of conducting a secret correspondence with the court of St. Germain, he was deprived of his offices and briefly thrown into the Tower in 1692.[2]

The difficulty of keeping their work secret also affected how Williamite officials handled intelligence. There was much public speculation, sometimes though not always well-informed, surrounding accusations made by informers and the arrests, interrogation of, and negotiation with Jacobite suspects. When the indicted Jacobite conspirator John Fenwick tried to save his life by suggesting that some of the king's closest advisors were closet Jacobites, rumors spread about the identities of those he accused, and citizens at a London Common Council meeting delivered a petition demanding that Parliament make a thorough inquiry into the plot. Negotiations between authorities and Jacobite prisoners were watched intently.[3]

The easy flow of rumor ran in the other direction as well. Government officials had no trouble learning about Jacobitism—if anything, they learned too much. Many Jacobites were conspicuously indiscreet. Their openness sprang from a basic ideological assumption that most people gave allegiance to William III only grudgingly, as de facto conqueror, and that if they thought

James II could successfully retake his throne, they would flock to his standard. Given that assumption, toasting King James or bragging in public about an imminent invasion was a strategy meant to give courage to the mass of potential supporters.

One result of Jacobite braggery was that it was easy for a would-be political informer to find *something* to report. James Ormiston wrote to the secretary of state in 1695 with a fairly typical story. He had been approached by one Captain Clifford, who mistook him for a Catholic and then blabbed under the influence of alcohol. "After having gone into an ale house," Ormiston explained, "I begun and asked him what news. He told me there was very good news for the French would certainly relieve the Castle of Namur [which was under siege by William's forces] and have the town again." Clifford had gone on to say that "the business was going very well at home for in a short time we should have home our sovereign King James again." Pressed by Ormiston for more detail, Clifford demurred, pointing out that "their designs were so often frustrated by not keeping them secret that they would declare them to none but who there were sure would sign to assist." But Clifford hinted that an uprising was planned. Ormiston, optimistic that he could gain Clifford's further trust, asked Trumbull for money so that he could equip himself with the horse and arms necessary to join the secret Jacobite army being raised and so betray it to the authorities.[4]

What Ormiston told Trumbull was not false. Richard Kingston, the experienced agent to whom Trumbull often turned for advice, explained that "the general notice he [Ormiston] gives you is true, but not secret, being trumpeted in all their coffee houses." The problem for Trumbull, and officials like him, was that it was hard to tell on the basis of Ormiston's information whether Ormiston had taken a first step in penetrating a Jacobite network that was engaged in dangerous conspiracy, or if he was trying to sell the government information that could be had for free.[5]

The government's ability to gather intelligence was further hampered by a lack of centralization. No single office collected all information about suspected Jacobite activity, and no one coordinated or cross-referenced what was learned. As Paul Hopkins has observed, William and his ministers "had only fragmentary intelligence of significant Jacobite activity, gathered by scattered agents and not analyzed to form a coherent picture." It is therefore necessary to turn to several sources that, even collectively, give us only partial views of the work of several kinds of actors involved in the securing of

Their Majesties' persons and governments. The archives and the personnel are introduced here.[6]

The secretaries of state did most of the work of securing Their Majesties' persons and government. There were generally two secretaries of state, one responsible for the north and one for the south; sometimes there was a third responsible solely for Scottish affairs. Secretaries of state employed agents directly, and they also received occasional reports from local justices or mayors about suspicious activity. Some of their correspondence is preserved in the official "State Papers Domestic" of William's reign, housed in the National Archives. But some secretaries of state kept papers in private collections.

These private papers survive irregularly. Daniel Finch, the Earl of Nottingham, who served from 1689 to 1693, was a pack rat. John Trenchard, who served 1693–94, was not, or if he was his papers are lost. Henry Sidney, the Earl of Romney, left almost nothing to give insight into his brief term, whereas William Trumbull (served 1695–97) left volumes, including an extensive correspondence with the spy Richard Kingston. Relatively few letters written by the Duke of Shrewsbury (1695–97) survive. However, for much of his term his undersecretary James Vernon handled the business of the office on his behalf and reported to him regularly. Vernon himself later became secretary of state in his own right, as did Trumbull's undersecretary John Ellis (both in 1697), and each left private papers documenting his term.

Even when letters and papers survive, of course, it would be foolish to think that they represent the sum total of what happened. Much important business was probably conducted orally. This chapter, then, necessarily privileges some voices and conversations over others. The letters of James Vernon and Richard Kingston will loom large in this account, in part because each man was opinionated and quotable but also because their letters survive in large numbers.

The secretaries of state had no monopoly on intelligence gathering. Some members of the House of Commons, notably the Whig MPs John Arnold and Henry Colt, cultivated private spy networks. So too did the Earl of Monmouth, one of the Lords. Some informers chose to confide in powerful churchmen, like John Tillotson or Thomas Tenison. The aristocratic lords lieutenants of the counties (leaders of the county militia) might investigate or arrest suspects and report to any high-ranking politician with whom they had a personal connection.

The Treasury, too, was an important locus for the investigation of treason. Treasury solicitors (initially Aaron Smith, later Nicholas Baker) took responsibility for the management of prosecutions at the assizes because conviction for treasonable offenses caused the defendant's property to be forfeited to the government. In addition, the work of the Customs and Excise offices, the Post Office, and the Mint all touched on the detection of Jacobite activity.

The coordination of information coming through so many channels was difficult. Moreover, it was sometimes impossible for officials at the time (or historians now) to know if two separate sources were talking about the same person. Aliases were commonly used, photographs and fingerprinting technology did not exist, and names were spelled inconsistently. Officials sometimes made valiant efforts to compare notes. In 1695, one Mr. Wall had offered his services to the government as a privateer; he bore the same surname as an imposter who had some time before presented himself "as my Lady Oglethorpe's brother, and pretended to do service, by discovering intelligence that passed between England and France, by the way of Holland." The Earl of Portland undertook inquiries that eventually established that the two Walls were of different ages and had different first names and different handwriting. But evidence of such efforts is rare.[7]

The foregoing helps explain both why government officials found it hard to obtain reliable intelligence, and why the validity of intelligence might itself become an object of political struggle. The rest of this chapter explores in greater detail the relations between secretaries of state and particular informers and the way those relationships were affected by and in turn affected the wider political landscape.

The Politicization of Intelligence: William Fuller and Matthew Smith

The vulnerability of "great men" in government to suspicion, the willingness of politicians to accuse one another of plots, and the publicity surrounding trials and investigations allowed some political informers to achieve fame and wield a surprising amount of power. The career of William Fuller is a case in point. Fuller is now remembered as the most colorful con man of the period. But in 1690 the government had every reason to reward him.[8]

Fuller claimed to have been raised Catholic and to have been employed as a servant to James II's advisor Lord Melfort and as a page to the queen consort, Mary of Modena, during James's reign. He had, he claimed, already switched sides and been working as a Williamite agent when he went to St. Germain in 1688. It is hard to verify this account of his early life, but it is clear that, after having accompanied the Jacobite courier Matthew Crone back to England from St. Germain in March 1690, he helped to apprehend him and then testified at Crone's trial in June. Crone was found guilty. The next month Secretary of State Nottingham gave Fuller £100 to equip himself for William's service in Ireland. That may not have been the only payment Fuller received. When Fuller later submitted an account to Portland of money he had laid out in the king's service since 1689, he acknowledged a further £180 "received by his Majesty's commands" and £110 "received from the Earl of Shrewsbury." Such payments, which seem unusually large, did not make much dent in the whopping £879 that Fuller claimed to have laid out in the government's service.[9]

In May 1691 Fuller again proposed to serve the government. Using the archbishop of Canterbury, John Tillotson, as his intermediary, he offered his services to Queen Mary. This time Fuller's service involved the management of a Jacobite double agent, one Delaval, with whom Fuller claimed to maintain a correspondence in cipher. If Delaval were assured of being pardoned for his Jacobitism, Fuller told Tillotson and Mary, Delaval would reveal all the designs of the king's enemies. Since Fuller deemed it necessary to personally supervise Delaval's meeting with King William in Flanders, he asked for a vessel to conduct him speedily to Flanders "that this good occasion may not be lost."[10]

By now, however, Fuller had lost the trust of important members of the king's inner circle, including the queen. He complained of being "dissatisfied at the ill opinion I find her Majesty hath of me." He grew more defensive as his trip to Flanders was delayed and, as Queen Mary refused him access, lamented that "my adversaries have represented all my circumstances as worst than they are" to put "my honesty in dispute." Meanwhile, in June 1691 he was imprisoned for debt in the King's Bench prison.[11]

Nonetheless, Fuller was able to make another public appearance as an informer in December. His opportunity came largely as the result of political struggles in Westminster and Whitehall and attempts by politicians to use informers against their political enemies. Because Fuller's negotiations with Mary had been kept private, moreover, neither MPs nor the public had reason to distrust him. He was still remembered as the witness who convicted Matthew Crone.

Fuller was able to appear before Parliament because the Marquis of Carmarthen wished to use information extracted from Matthew Crone and Lord Preston (another convicted Jacobite) to attack his political enemies. Among the people named by Crone and Preston was the Tory MP Edward Seymour, a fierce opponent of the court. In February 1691 when Lord Preston had mentioned Seymour's name in a written confession, Carmarthen told William he hoped to use Preston's confession to "break the teeth, not only of Sir Edward Seymour, but of that whole party, from doing your business any harm in parliament." Carmarthen's chances improved after Matthew Crone named Seymour as a person he saw in the company of Jacobite James Grahame (Lord Preston's brother). The name of the Marquis of Halifax, another political enemy of Carmarthen, surfaced as well in a further confession made by Preston.[12]

Neither Seymour nor Halifax appeared as a major player in Crone's or Preston's confession and William's advisors agreed that there was little ground to proceed legally against them. Nonetheless, Parliament decided to have the linked confessions of Crone and Preston publicly read before them. That gave Fuller an opening. In November he wrote to the speaker of the House of Commons, saying he had "great discoveries to make in relation to the plot wherein Crone was concerned."[13]

Fuller appeared twice before the bar of the House of Commons to make statements. He named as Jacobites many people who were already widely known or suspected to be such. But some of what he said impinged on the credit of the government. He took a swipe at Tillotson for not bringing him before Lord Portland. He alleged that there were spies for the French king in the Privy Council and in the office of the secretaries of state. He mentioned the Lord Halifax and the Lord Treasurer Godolphin. All of his allegations, he promised, could be proven by two witnesses, currently abroad, who if given passes and protection would be willing to give evidence.[14]

The House of Commons accordingly voted to give Fuller (who was still a prisoner in King's Bench) a daily allowance for subsistence and another £50 to pay the charges of bringing his witnesses to London to testify before Parliament. Speculation as to the identity of these witnesses swirled around London in the next weeks while other would-be informers presented themselves as possible corroborators of Fuller's testimony. On 29 December 1691, the Tory MP Narcissus Luttrell recorded in his diary, "Wilcox, a non-swearing parson, offers to come in and make an additional discovery to Fuller's, relating to the conspiracy." On 7 January 1692 Luttrell wrote, "The late Lord Chief Justice Herbert is one of the persons that Fuller will send for out of Flanders to corroborate his evidence." By 28 January, however, he had heard the witnesses were to be "Mr. Halley and Mr. Ettrick, a Scotsman."[15]

It was finally revealed that Luttrell was wrong every time. Fuller identified his witnesses as James Hayes and Colonel Thomas Delaval, the latter presumably the same Delaval in whom Fuller had previously tried to interest Tillotson, Portland, and Queen Mary. But Hayes and Delaval did not appear. When the House sent for Fuller again, the marshal of the King's Bench who went to fetch him found him "very ill, with great vomiting and looseness." He claimed he had been poisoned. Apparently on the brink of death, he provided the small group of MPs who came to see him with a sworn statement and directed them to the house of Mr. Richardson, an apothecary in Holborn, where he said Hayes and Delaval lodged. But Hayes and Delaval were not there. Losing patience, Parliament gave Fuller one more chance to produce witnesses. When he failed, it was none other than Edward Seymour who proposed that the House declare Fuller an imposter. And so the House resolved that Fuller was an imposter, cheat, and false accuser who had "scandalized Their Majesties and the government and abused this House and falsely accused several persons of honor and quality."[16]

Why was the House of Commons strung along for so long? The gullibility of MPs is in part understandable as Fuller's unsuccessful negotiations with Mary had been kept private. Moreover, the very fact that his testimony against Crone had been gratefully accepted by a jury made it difficult for anyone to air doubts about Fuller without discrediting the state that had prosecuted Crone. When Fuller first asked to appear before the Commons, some MPs had already heard about the credit scams for which Fuller was to become legendary. John Guise described Fuller as a "rascal," reporting that he had been told by Peter Morisco, the messenger, that Fuller "impersonated people beyond the sea and cheated them of great sums of money." Fuller's allegations that Tillotson and Portland had ignored him, when countered by John Chadwick, MP and son-in-law of Tillotson, also cast doubt on Fuller's credit in the eyes of MPs like Jack Howe. John Thompson, too, was uncertain as to which side Fuller was on: "I find he has played with both hands here and in France; but in which he is most sincere, I know not." John Lowther, however, eloquently summed up the reasons why the House simply could not afford to ignore Fuller, especially after having agreed to have him appear in the first place:

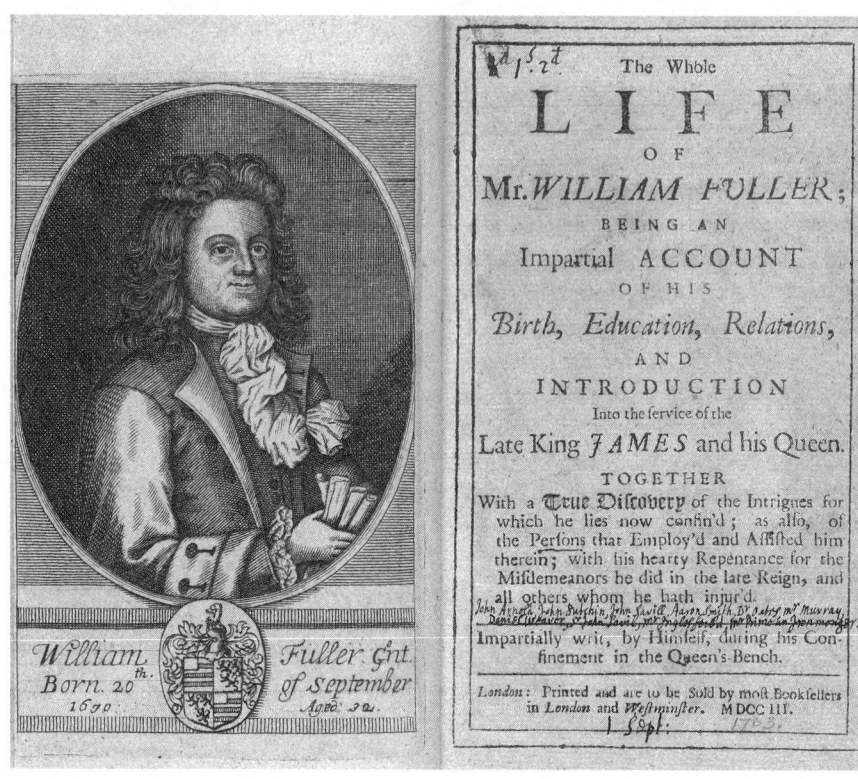

Frontispiece and title page of *The Whole Life of Mr. William Fuller* (1703), Fuller's memoir recanting many of his previous "discoveries." The book's owner has written into the title page the names of the persons who assisted Fuller in his frauds, including Titus Oates and the MP Jack Arnold. Courtesy of Beinecke Rare Book and Manuscript Library, Yale University.

> Whatever this man's credit is now, it appears it was not so inconsiderable when the Secretaries of State employed him to go to and from France. There are many great persons named in his information. It concerns you to have this matter cleared for their reputation, the government being concerned herein. And you can do no less than hear him since he offers so fair as to bring in others to confirm his testimony.[17]

Even after the House voted that Fuller was an imposter and Attorney General John Somers took steps to prosecute him, it was hard for government officials to dismiss Fuller completely. Strikingly, Nottingham still felt obligated to search for Hayes and Delaval when they were spotted in Yorkshire, though he doubted that they could be found. The other secretary of state, Shrewsbury, was willing to support Fuller to the extent of providing a certificate testifying to his previous good service to the government.[18]

Aside from the fact that he really had done service to the government, what enabled Fuller to survive was his ability to spin his previous failure into a new narrative that, however improbable, was impossible to falsify and dangerous to be seen to ignore. Hayes and Delaval had failed to appear, Fuller now explained, because they had been spirited away by Jacobites, precisely in order to discredit his testimony. Moreover, Fuller alleged in an inflammatory letter to the House of Commons that the plot to discredit him had been laid by persons (unnamed) deep in the inner circles of government.[19]

None of that saved Fuller from being sentenced to stand in the pillory and pay a fine of 200 marks. But his narratives continued to find an audience among government officials and the public. The story of Fuller illustrates how hard it was to tell a valuable servant of the state from a charlatan and how, even if one could tell the difference, the charlatans could find an audience that had to at least pretend to take them seriously.

The fears of treason within, which Fuller exploited, affected the conduct of the secretaries of state, many of whom found themselves vulnerable to accusations of being Jacobites or of "stifling" plots to protect plotters. In 1693 Richard Holland alerted Nottingham that a disgruntled informer, John Capel, had been recruited by two sons of the Earl of Wharton, a powerful Whig politician, to accuse Nottingham of "stifling" plots and ignoring informations. When William Trumbull assumed the secretaryship of state in 1695, he was cautioned by the experienced agent Richard Kingston that his Tory affiliation might give grounds for suspicion. Writing Trumbull from Dover,

Kingston warned of a troublesome Whig MP, William Brockman, who has "made very sad prognostications of ill things that are to happen upon the management of so great a Tory."[20]

It was perhaps his sense of vulnerability—and the memory of Nottingham's experiences—that caused Trumbull to tolerate James Ormiston as long as he did. As we saw above, Ormiston came to Trumbull with a story of an imminent Jacobite uprising, which Richard Kingston had characterized as common coffeehouse gossip. Even so, Kingston counseled Trumbull to deal with and even pay the would-be informer for political reasons. In Nottingham's time, Kingston explained, Ormiston had done some service, but when the secretary had cut off Ormiston's funding the informer had retaliated by drawing up an information against Nottingham for "stifling plots and discouraging informers." It was best for Trumbull to pay Ormiston something so as to avoid Nottingham's fate. "I am sure you are to be cheated of two guineas," Kingston quipped, "and yet dare not persuade you from giving them; to prevent the hideous clamor that will otherwise be made against you for stifling plots." And so, Trumbull, using Kingston as an intermediary, continued to receive reports from Ormiston about his efforts to join the secret Jacobite army, accompanied by requests for money and a place "as chamber-keeper in your office at Whitehall." The ominous "design" that Captain Clifford had hinted at to Ormiston in August seemed, however, to be continually postponed. Finally, after Ormiston complained in December 1695 about a lack of signs of favor, the correspondence dropped off. The striking thing is not that Ormiston was dropped, but that Trumbull went through so much effort to pacify him.[21]

Whig secretaries of state were not immune from accusations either. Three separate but linked sets of accusations—from Matthew Smith, John Fenwick, and Aubrey Price—drove the Duke of Shrewsbury into a dysfunctional slump in 1697. Shrewsbury was, like so many others, vulnerable because of his history: he had Catholic relations, and it is not unlikely that he had made contact with the court of St. Germain in the early 1690s. His troubles were exacerbated by the bad relationship that he and his undersecretary, James Vernon, had with the other secretary of state, William Trumbull. Trumbull's diary testifies to his belief that Shrewsbury and Vernon had shut him out of important investigations and monopolized patronage. In October 1696 Trumbull contemplated resigning from office, citing as a reason that "Mr. Vernon and others of ye Duke's officers threatened any one that brought me business with ye Duke's disfavor." Moreover, Trumbull came to suspect that Vernon, at least, was a Jacobite. In 1697 Trumbull made an unlikely alliance with Alexander Johnston, the sleazy brother of the secretary of state for Scotland James Johnston. Alexander told Trumbull "that in late plot, one Stow, an acquaintance of his, being examining before Vernon, he heard Vernon bid him fear nothing, but 1 witness against him." This was, Johnston has said, "but 1 instance of a 100."[22]

Trumbull's suspicion of Shrewsbury and Vernon lay behind his support for the campaign of Matthew Smith, a disgruntled informer, to persuade Parliament and the public that Shrewsbury had ignored his discovery of what came to be known as the Assassination Plot. Smith's story, like that of William Fuller, shows how suspicions of treason within the government gave some informers leverage and how informers could use the Parliament and the press to advance their claims.[23]

Captain Matthew Smith was nephew to Sir William Parkyns, a Jacobite gentleman executed in 1696 for his role in the Assassination Plot. Smith had held a commission in the Duke of Norfolk's regiment, but his commission was taken from him after 1688, he said, because he had Catholic relatives. His resentment led him to join the Jacobites, among whom "my disgrace and other circumstances brought me into a confidence and greatness." But, Smith continued, when he learned that his new friends were French-loving king-killers, he resolved "to disappoint such damnable designs."[24]

So in November 1694 Smith began to provide intelligence about the Jacobites to Shrewsbury and James Vernon. Some was generalized political information that would have been available elsewhere, such as the fact that the Jacobites were split into Melfordian and Middletonian factions. Other "discoveries" by Smith, such as the location of arms buried at William Parkyns's estate in Warwickshire, seem not to have been acted upon by authorities. Shrewsbury's response to Smith was lukewarm. Payments to Smith dribbled out in £20 chunks, but Shrewsbury was clearly holding back. In December 1694, for example, he told Smith that "though I shall be willing to give all reasonable encouragement to your endeavors; yet it being the King's money I am to dispose of, I cannot think myself discharged, if I advance any money before I see some service performed." Indeed, Shrewsbury even made efforts to break off the relationship, telling Smith, "You will upon my account put yourself to no further charge or trouble." He did enclose £20 with this note, which gave Smith a chance to declare himself in Shrewsbury's debt and hence to endeavor to repay him with more service. The relationship had its ups as well as downs. In December 1695 Shrewsbury seemed positively enthusiastic about the prospects of Smith cultivating an informant, Jack Hewett, who could find the private boats that carried letters to and from France.[25]

Smith soon had something even more interesting than letters from France. He told Shrewsbury of a plot to seize or kill the king, involving among others Jack Hewett's uncle, Mr. Holmes. As the details of this plot were not yet clear, Smith requested large cash advances from Shrewsbury in order to enhance his credit with the Jacobites and thus garner the information needed. The Jacobites would share details of the plot with him, Smith explained, only if he showed himself a willing participant, which in turn meant that he had to spend £50 to equip himself with a horse and weapons. Moreover, he had already run up huge debts working himself into the plotters' confidence. As he explained to Shrewsbury, Jacobites liked to drink,

> so that my expenses are very considerable, by reason I am necessitated to excuse some of the company from paying; and a man is also obliged to appear well in clothes, otherwise he is slighted: and it prevails upon people to be the more open and free when they see he has the appearance of a gentleman.

If Shrewsbury would pay his expenses, Smith promised he would soon be in a position to thwart the plot.[26]

As it turned out, there was a plot, but it was thwarted without Smith's help. Even as Smith pleaded for money, two conspirators, Prendergrass and De La Rue, betrayed what has come to be known as the Assassination Plot to the authorities. The revelation vindicated some of Smith's information, as people he had named (Holmes, William Parkyns, Robert Charnock, and John Friend) were indeed among the plotters. But, to Smith's disgust, Prendergrass and De La Rue got the credit for their discovery. Smith's services went unrewarded.

Smith expressed his frustration in public places like coffeehouses and taverns and claimed to be preparing a petition to Parliament. He also sought alternative patrons. Smith complained to his old commander, the Duke of Norfolk, who in turn introduced him to Shrewsbury's antagonist, William Trumbull. Smith also met with Charles Mordaunt, Earl of Monmouth, who was gentleman of the bedchamber to the king and the cousin of Norfolk's wife. Eventually Smith met with Portland and with King William himself. According to Smith, all of these people at least initially expressed appreciation for his services. For their benefit, Smith produced and circulated a manuscript containing copies of his correspondence with Shrewsbury and Vernon and minutes of his meetings with them. His complaints spread far enough that in May 1696 James Vernon threatened Smith, saying he heard rumors that Smith intended to accuse Shrewsbury of negligence for having never acquainted the king with Smith's discoveries.[27]

Shrewsbury, already the target of Smith's manuscript and tavern brags, became more vulnerable after September 1696 when the captured Jacobite conspirator John Fenwick, hoping to save his own neck, wrote a confidential letter to William offering "a sincere and ingenious confession of all I know of men who correspond with France, employed by him [William] in places of trust in the government, fleet and army." The men Fenwick named included Admiral Russell, Sidney Godolphin, Lord Marlborough, and the Duke of Shrewsbury. The revelation, in fact, made very little impression on William, who complained that Fenwick "only accuses those in my service, and not one of his own party." The names of those Fenwick accused were not immediately made public, but speculation ran wild. Shrewsbury repeatedly offered to resign, and even the friends who urged him to stay acknowledged the seriousness of the situation. "For although you are above suspicion," wrote Portland, "if it do not remain secret, everyone having enemies as well as friends, it will be impossible to prevent disagreeable conversation and reflections, as I know by experience."[28]

In the following weeks, Shrewsbury's political allies decided that it was better to bring the matter before Parliament than to ignore it. They hoped, moreover, that a rousing vote by Parliament vindicating the men Fenwick accused might facilitate the subsequent business of persuading members to vote in favor of a large government subsidy. They so effectively managed affairs in Parliament that the House of Commons not only voted to attaint Fenwick but also resolved that his informations were "false and scandalous, and a contrivance to undermine the government."[29]

The Fenwick affair mattered because it made Matthew Smith potentially more dangerous: his complaints, if known, would give more credibility to Fenwick. And so, as the bill to attaint Fenwick wound its way through the Commons and then the Lords, Shrewsbury's allies paid Smith off to keep him silent. The money came from Shrewsbury's and Vernon's office. Vernon, however, was careful to hide the genesis of the money from Smith, arranging instead for it to be paid to Smith by the Earl of Portland.[30]

Smith might well have been quiet were it not for the intervention of the Earl of Monmouth, to whom Smith had already appealed in his search for patrons. For reasons that have mystified both his contemporaries and historians, Monmouth tried to bring about a full investigation of Fenwick's allegations. He caused Smith to be questioned at the bar of the House of Lords, whereupon Smith reiterated his complaints about Shrewsbury's failure to reward him. That gave Shrewsbury and Vernon a chance to show Smith's worthlessness in public. Having been requested to provide copies of all his correspondence, Shrewsbury wrote to the House of Lords explaining that he had failed to keep copies of Smith's letters because they had been so useless, except for the very oldest ones, which he kept when "I had more value for his intelligence than I had afterwards." Smith was above all humiliated when John Hewett, his informant, explained to Parliament that all the information he gave Smith had been taken by him out of printed copies of the *Post-Boy!* Attorney General John Somers put another nail in the coffin of Smith's reputation: having learned that Smith had once tried to trick a widow into marriage to obtain her property, Somers took "care to acquaint such as I thought most proper" with that fact. The House of Lords voted both that there was no ground for Smith's complaint against Shrewsbury and that Smith deserved no further reward.[31]

Smith, according to himself, intended to petition the House of Commons for redress, and he found a member, Jack Arnold, willing to present his case. But he was distracted from that purpose by a mysterious benefactor bringing welcome news that King William would employ Smith to spy on Jacobite exiles in France. Smith went abroad, but the money supply dried up. Concluding that he had been deceived, he returned to England.[32]

In 1699, Smith finally went into print. His timing might have been inspired by other political scandals that tarnished the reputations of his opponents, such as recent revelations that Shrewsbury and other members of the Junto had invested in the now-notorious pirate voyage of Captain William Kidd. Darkly observing that "notorious truths must prevail at this time in my favour," Smith now gambled that the public was ready to believe the worst about the "great men."[33]

Smith's first book, *Memoirs of Secret Service* (1699), reproduced the correspondence with Shrewsbury that Smith had already presented in manuscript.

He followed up *Memoirs* with a much more combative piece, *Remarks upon the D—— of S——'s Letter to the House of Lords*. Because the latter tract printed a copy of Shrewsbury's letter to the Lords, the House found him guilty of a breach of their privilege. They ordered the book burnt by the common hangman, once again voting that Smith did not deserve any reward for his services. The task of cudgeling Smith in print was then taken up by Richard Kingston. Suffice it to say that in the ensuing pamphlet war both Smith and Kingston deployed a wide vocabulary of dishonor: Kingston charged Smith with cowardice, of not having written his own pamphlets, of being ignorant of Latin, and he likened his writing to a horse's fart; Smith claimed that Doctor Kingston had faked his clerical credentials and that he was a bigamist, adulterer, rapist, and sodomite.[34]

It was very hard to get rid of Smith. How widely his books circulated is unknown, but Vernon did take notice in February 1700 that "some poor refugee has been translating Smith's book, in hopes to get a penny by it." But if Smith continued to do battle in the press, he also tried to keep open the option of *not* using the press, of being once again paid to keep silent. He wrote to Vernon in June 1700, asking (as Vernon reported it) "to make a composition . . . to keep his other books from coming out in public." Smith returned sometime after William's death with a petition to the House of Commons, again asking compensation for his services.[35]

Exchange and Epistemology

One striking feature of the conflict between Matthew Smith and the Duke of Shrewsbury was their wildly differing views of the relationship of money to truth. Shrewsbury's friends and colleagues, responding to Smith's charges, contended that Smith's greed had damaged his credibility. As James Vernon put it, it was Smith's "sharping pretences of craving money" that "gave me such a jealousy and mean opinion of him, that I could never bring myself to believe one word he said of any kind." Smith, though, had a response, which is worth quoting at length:

> Men are undoubtedly bound in duty to contribute all that lies in their power to the public security. But the only natural reason that I can find for it, is, because as members of the public, they have their principal security and protection from it. But that consideration alone does not carry men very

far; self-preservation is a principle of more caution than action, and renders men more careful to give no offence, than to do any service. It is Hope only that animates 'em for action, and makes 'em forward in its service. They expect that what they do for the public, should redound in some proportion to their own particular benefit, and that themselves should be considered as instruments, for the advantages that may accrue to the public, and the fatigue or hazard they expose themselves to. This is so universally true, that I doubt some who pretend to have done the nation great service would abate of their zeal, if they did not find it as necessary and advantageous to their own private fortune. I say this not invidiously to lessen the services of any man, or to reproach him, for the just advantages he may make of 'em, but to obviate the objections of some of my unreasonable adversaries, who pretend my services lose their merit, when I appear to expect any reward.[36]

Smith's printed defense was unique but receiving something in exchange for information was not. Most of what government officials learned about crime and treason came at a price. People giving information vital to the security of the regime might get cash payments, government jobs, or reprieves from execution. The struggle between the Duke of Shrewsbury and Matthew Smith was in part a philosophical clash over whether information obtained by barter could be trusted. Shrewsbury's views were closely in line with what Steven Shapin has described as a "gentlemanly" model of credibility, according to which independence was a precondition for truth-telling and therefore only people of sufficient wealth and status (and masculinity) could be relied on to tell the truth. Smith's view, which we might dub the "market" model, was that information about conspiracy was, like any other product useful to society, produced by labor and had a price.[37]

The "gentlemanly" and "market" models described here, however, are unusually stark and cartoon-like. Neither really represented the more nuanced and ambivalent contemporary opinion. The ideal of the disinterested informer was implicitly rejected by the government, which had always offered rewards for information. By the late seventeenth century the "trade of informing" had expanded and diversified. The Second Conventicle Act of 1670, which allocated one-third of the hefty fines levied on religious dissenters to the informers who discovered them, inspired the notorious Hilton gang to spy on and prosecute religious nonconformists. The Societies for the Reformation of Manners took advantage of the 1695 "Act for the More

Effectual Suppressing Prophane Cursing and Swearing," which levied a fine of £5 on justices who failed to take action against swearers and cursers and granted a moiety to the informer. Rewards for convictions against a growing list of offenders were granted through the Crown. Charles II and James II ordered a payment of £10 to anyone who helped convict burglars. William issued proclamations offering rewards of £40 or more for information about highwaymen, the forgers of the Earl of Nottingham's seal, printers of King James's *Declaration* and other specified texts, and coiners and clippers. In the aftermath of the Assassination Plot, £1,000 was offered for the apprehension of anyone named on a long list of accused plotters.[38]

The fact that the government offered money does not mean that officials were oblivious to the pitfalls of doing so. As Isaac Newton, who prosecuted coiners in his role as the master of the Mint, complained, "The new reward of forty pounds per head [for the apprehension of coiners] has now made Courts of Justice and Juries so averse from believing witnesses . . . that my agents and witnesses are discouraged and tired out by the want of success and by the reproach of prosecuting and swearing for money." But whether the payment of money invalidated the information was a complex issue and seemed to call for shades of gray. The acceptance of a reward did not necessarily delegitimate service.[39]

Richard Kingston displayed a mix of attitudes about informers and money when in 1695 he wrote a long report to Trumbull about his journey to the southeast coast to visit and expand a network of informers. He distinguished between those he held in esteem and those he thought were motivated solely by money. At Hythe, he told Trumbull, "[I] have often caused men and goods to be seized, by my intimacy with Mr. Monger an innkeeper there, who receives them and for a reward has discovered them; but since he is only true to them that bid most, I dare not confide in him." But he also matter-of-factly reported, "I have fee'd the drawer in the tavern at Greenwich from whom I shall have continual notice of what company frequents that ill place." Moreover, he condemned "the remissness of the late Secretary [John Trenchard] in rewarding such services" as the policing of smugglers. Later on he told Trumbull with no negative judgment that "the countrymen [were] well pleased with your gift of two guineas." Obviously, if the government trusted only those who gave information for free, it would get no information at all.[40]

Matthew Smith's model of truth as a commodity that could be legitimately sold also fails to capture the nature of most transactions between government officials and informers. The word "truth" poorly captures what it was that caused an official to offer something to an informer. Whether an informer was telling the truth, whether his information was helpful, and how much he should be given were separate questions. The market might be a good metaphor for what happened between informers and government officials, but only if the market being discussed looks more like Wall Street in 2007 than a stall in the early modern village square.

The price of information was neither "just" nor transparent. What was being "paid" was often hidden in lump sums or recast as "expenses." It might also be intangible, like a promise of future good will perhaps leading to a government job. Insofar as we can discern payment for services, the value assigned to information was not pegged to its "truth" in any straightforward way. That was in part because, of course, the buyers in this market, the government officials, did not know for certain what was true (if they already knew what was true, they would have no need to pay for information). It was also because officials making decisions about what to pay thought less about the truth or usefulness of the information and more about their current and future relationship with the informer.

Analyzing the nature of the exchange between government officials and informers is daunting because it is hard to assess what informers were paid. What the law mandated as a reward for the conviction of an offender does not begin to represent what the government actually paid for information. Unfortunately, that figure is impossible to define precisely. The secret service accounts and Treasury books only occasionally record specific sums given to specific individuals. More commonly, lump sums were handed to secretaries of state or other officials who rewarded informers at their discretion.

Some documents do provide a sense of the range of payments that might have changed hands. When the informer William Chaloner (about whom more below) submitted a petition for reimbursement, he claimed to have paid between a half crown and a crown per day over many months to several assistants. In 1694 James Johnston, secretary of state for Scotland, submitted to the Earl of Portland a statement of "Money laid out by me since the beginning of the year 1692 to people employed in Secret service." On each line he recorded the general nature of an undertaking and its total cost (for example, "for the discovery of several French officers that came to London with the French King's commission in their pockets, £5–10–0"). Unfortunately, Johnston's accounting method makes it hard to tell how among many individuals a payment was divided, what precise services were performed, or whether the money was understood to be a reimbursement of expenses or a reward exceeding expenses. Nonetheless, it is clear that Johnston made numerous small payments and occasional large ones. At the high end Johnston recorded a payment of £160 to "one man now in town" for "the discovery of the intended invasion from La Hogue," who "told as much of the business a month before the time as is yet known." Less spectacular but still large sums recorded in Johnston's accounts included £80 paid by the Earl of Nottingham to the chief discoverer of a secret printing press and £29 to the persons (he does not say how many) who discovered Colonel Parker's lodging (Johnston helpfully noted here that he was ordered to "spare no money" on this matter).[41]

Most of the payments were much smaller. A total of £6–15–0 was divided among three people who gave information about a design to betray Jersey and Guernsey to the French; £11 was split among "several" persons "employed to discover the name and lodgings of the Scotch officers lurking here in town"; £5–10–0 was given (to an unknown number of persons) for the "discovery of several French officers that came to London with the French King's commission." At the very end of his account, as an afterthought, Johnston noted he had "given at one time or other within these two years to above 30 men and more women whom I have employed partly to engage them, and partly in small pensions, and often because of their necessities (many of them being indigent officers) and for services that I have forgot to mark the particular charges of, about as near as I can compute it, £193."[42]

Johnston's account is especially useful in establishing a lower end of the scale of payment. It suggests most people received around £5, maybe less (depending on how one interprets the maddeningly ambiguous phrase "more women"). At the other end of the spectrum were the large sums paid to William Fuller. Many others fell in the middle. Matthew Smith got at least £20 from Shrewsbury (though he asked for more). The Lancashire Plot witnesses received for "expenses" between the time Lunt "revealed" the plot and the trial itself between £18 and £24 apiece. Because almost all of these payments were described as reimbursements for expenses, it is hard to know how much the informer profited. Clearly, expenses could be variously defined. Matthew Smith, after all, included the purchase of alcohol, equipage, and a horse in his account of "expenses."[43]

It would be a mistake, however, for would-be informers or historians to see informing as an easy path to wealth. The experiences of Edward Aneley and John Blackburne are a cautionary tale. The two men undertook the prosecution of the Yorkshire attorney Thomas Darby for speaking "horrible, treasonable and heinous words." The men had gone to exceptional trouble, traveling more than two hundred miles to London to give an information and then, encouraged by government officials, returning to Yorkshire to pursue the case at the assizes, managing and maintaining other witnesses through the course of a long trial. Their request was supported by Treasury solicitor Aaron Smith, who described the petitioners as "poor men and having families to maintain" and who deemed it "an act of justice and compassion" to compensate them with the £80 that Darby had paid as a fine. They were eventually paid out of the Exchequer, although it is not clear if all their expenses were covered.[44]

The informer Henry Oulding may also have spent more than he was paid. In March 1696, shortly after the discovery of the Assassination Plot, Oulding overheard Patrick Cunningham say to another man in an Exeter churchyard that they would "take of[f] the King's life in the winter if we cannot before for though the King hath escaped with his life now he shall shortly die before nine months be at an end." Oulding was the sole witness against Cunningham at the Exeter Assizes, where the defendant was convicted of the misdemeanor of speaking seditious words and fined 500 marks. Oulding spent £20 to attend the assizes as a witness, but that proved to be only a fraction of the price he paid to be an informer. According to a petition to the Treasury, Oulding endured attacks on his reputation and threats to his life, which caused him to quit his trade and flee to London for refuge, "by which means he hath expended and lost almost £300 and is now reduced to poverty having a wife and child to provide for." In 1699 he was finally given £50, along with the possibility of receiving more if Cunningham's fine was ever paid (there is, however, no indication as to whether it was).[45]

Aneley, Blackburne, and Oulding probably got paid because there was something outstanding about the defendants against whom they witnessed. Thomas Darby, against whom Aneley and Blackburne testified, was clearly someone whom Treasury solicitor Aaron Smith wanted to prosecute. It may be relevant that his name turned up elsewhere in the Northern Assize Papers in connection with a coining case. Patrick Cunningham, against whom Oulding testified, was important because his words might indicate an actual plot. Our judgment of the adequacy of the payments to these three informers would depend on answers to unanswerable questions: Did Oulding really need to flee Exeter? What were Aneley's and Blackburne's expenses, exactly? But whether the compensation was fair or not, the examples of Aneley, Blackburne, and Oulding show that even when the value of an informer's contribution was endorsed by government officials, payment came late and was uncertain.[46]

Government officials, moreover, might not always fully support informers. Owen Banahan, according to Aaron Smith, had been allowed a subsistence ranging from 30 shillings to 2 guineas per week by the orders of Secretaries Trenchard and Trumbull while he made trips as a spy to the court of St. Germain, but despite Banahan's "great zeal and faithfulness," the payments fell off so that Banahan's "condition and that of his family hath been very miserable and himself enforced for bread to list himself a common sentinel." Robert Alcock, according to his own petition, had done good service discovering "several notorious clubs and unlawful meetings of the Jacobites in the City, some of which have been convicted." The Treasury solicitor, Nicholas Baker, helpfully endorsed Alcock's petition with a certificate that Alcock had indeed been "very serviceable to his Majesty" and that he in the past had received subsistence from the government but was now for want of it "under great necessity." Alcock asked for eight months' arrears or a government job. The Treasury Lords left it to Nicholas Baker's discretion how Alcock should be compensated. A month later, though, Alcock complained that Baker had told him that he had no money in his hands particularly appropriated to such use and therefore "could do nothing in it." The Treasury Lords resolved to "speak with Mr. Baker." Alcock's third (and last) petition, in September, complained that after four months Mr. Baker had not been spoken to and that he could "not subsist longer without relief." It is impossible to tell at this distance why Alcock was so poorly treated. Perhaps two bureaucracies were trying to make one another bear the burden of payment.[47]

Sometimes the logic behind the refusal to reward informers is obvious. Government officials might withhold payment because they wished to deny the fact that they had solicited information. Thus James Vernon counseled Shrewsbury not to pay William Read and Mrs. Scott, who had given some helpful tips about the doings of the annoying Matthew Smith. "One time or another your Grace may think fit to give them some small thing," he warned, "but at present I can't believe it is advisable. I don't know what they may be able to discover, and what use one may make of it; in which case it will be fit they be able to make oath, that they have no reward given or promised them."[48]

An instructive saga revealing the vagaries of payment for informers is that of the spy Henry Crymes, who embedded himself in London Jacobite networks in 1695 (though it is possible he had been a spy since 1692). Crymes's particular friends among the Jacobites were Father Edwards and Mr. Spenceley, both of whom purportedly had regular contact with the court at St. Germain. Crymes reported what Edwards and Spenceley told him to Trumbull. Most of the information he obtained could be classified as hopeful Jacobite gossip about an imminent invasion. Crymes may have been a valuable asset to Trumbull, however, because of what he was willing to endure. After he was arrested, he assured Trumbull, "I am very well satisfied with my present confinement," and asked only to be "kept private" (that is, not be used as a witness) so as "to be still capable of doing the government good service." With the permission of authorities, Crymes received visits from his Jacobite friends while in prison and provided Mr. Spenceley with money that he himself received from Trumbull. If that was a strategy for enhancing his reputation in the eyes of the Jacobites, it worked. In February 1696 Crymes, now out of prison, was recruited by the Jacobite Major Bartram into the circle of conspirators who were to ambush King William as he went out hunting at Richmond, a scheme that came to be known as the Assassination Plot.[49]

Crymes did not become famous as the first discoverer of the Assassination Plot. As was noted above, the king and Portland first learned of the plot from Thomas Prendergrass and Francis De La Rue, two of the conspirators who had a change of heart. Crymes's independent and almost simultaneous revelation to Trumbull was neither publicized nor celebrated. Crymes never received anything like the reward bestowed on Prendergrass: a pardon, £3,000, land in Ireland, and a baronetcy.[50]

The lack of recognition meant that Crymes had further opportunity for serving the Williamite regime, albeit at the price of his freedom. Arrested as a conspirator, he was placed in what he described as an "easy" confinement in the house of the John Gellibrand, a royal messenger who had previously acted as a conduit between Crymes and Trumbull. Although he tried to persuade Trumbull to let him stage an escape with a fellow prisoner in order to boost his credit with the Jacobites, he remained in custody until at least June 1696, during which time he was paid and legally protected by the state.[51]

By November Crymes was at liberty again, this time offering his services to discover networks of Jacobite correspondence and transportation in Kent.

He claimed that he was owed favors by the notorious owler Stephen Lansfield of Romney Marsh, as well as by one Monger, a lodging house keeper of that town. The two men would be able to tell him about Jacobites landing in or escaping from England. Trumbull still ordered payments to Crymes, but Crymes complained of delays in payment and of seeing his "endeavors slighted." He had spent £25 by Trumbull's order to equip himself with a horse and was now in danger of being seized for debt.[52]

Like Matthew Smith, Crymes blamed financial constraints for his inability to do more glorious service. "I must beg leave to remind you," he scolded Trumbull, "that I gave you an account of the breaking out of this last plot ye same day Mr. Prendergrass gave it to the King, and if I had not then been straightened in the pocket, but been enabled to have gone into the best of companies, the government should not have missed Sir George Barclay, Harrison or any others they had a mind to take in England." Trumbull seems to have become disillusioned too. Crymes's letters became more boastful, his claims more extravagant. Crymes said that he was "promised a considerable post in the French land," that "not a man in England can serve you like myself," and that "no man in England's reputation is more clear with the [Jacobite] party than myself, and that can secure you such intelligence, which I think at this time of the day is very valuable, and not easily otherwise to be purchased by any secretary since this revolution." But Trumbull was not impressed, sardonically remarking of Crymes, "All his discoveries ended about saddles in the West." Nonetheless, Crymes remained connected to Trumbull and to Gellibrand, on whom Trumbull relied to "take care" of him. In 1698 he was paid a £50 reward for "discovering and seizing several libels."[53]

Although Crymes was compensated, the dramatic contrast between the rewards given to Crymes and those given to Prendergrass shows that informers were not paid in accordance with how hard they worked or with the truth or use-value of their information. It is likely that some informers with truly helpful information received relatively little because of social class: they were deferential, they accepted less, their expenses were low. Effective spies who remained under cover by definition could not be paid well, lest the payment draw attention. Those informers who were willing to be witnesses, too, had to wait for a reward, lest they seem to be testifying for profit. And as with Ormiston, an informer might be paid for fear that he would make trouble.

Chaloner and Price

How to put a value on information was a particularly vexed question in the Williamite regime's encounter with William Chaloner and Aubrey Price. James Vernon tellingly compared Price's information to a counterfeit coin, possessing "some varnish and gilding, but it is so thin, the base metal will soon appear through it." Chaloner's metaphorical language, too, connoted uncertain value. He was reported to have said he "would bubble the government who were the easiest to be cheated of any men in the world." As a noun, "bubble" was soon to mean an inflation of the value of stocks fueled by the ill-informed fantasies of the public (as in "South Sea Bubble," the great stock market crash of 1720). Chaloner's words, too, connoted value inflated by desire and fantasy: he implied that government's desire for a plot made plots worth selling and so called them into being.[54]

The story of Chaloner and Price draws together a number of themes already introduced in this chapter. Their accusation of the Duke of Shrewsbury neatly rounds off a trend previously identified. Moreover, like William Fuller and Matthew Smith, Chaloner found allies in Parliament and promoted himself through the press. Chaloner and Price also stand as a revealingly extreme case of the problem normally facing the government officials who dealt with informers. Paradoxically, in pursuing information that would help to sustain its credit (by thwarting counterfeiters and protecting Shrewsbury's reputation), the government risked undermining that credit by using state power to support men known to be coiners and con artists.

Such collusion with criminals had become a disturbingly common practice not only for secretaries of state but for local magistrates. Tim Wales and John Beattie have documented the proliferation or at least increased visibility of thief-takers in the late seventeenth century. Thief-takers straddled the border between crime and law enforcement. They helped victims to make a "composition" with a thief (that is, to buy their stolen goods back at a price that was less than their value but high enough to make the effort of stealing them worthwhile for the thief). The thief-takers were able to negotiate such settlements, of course, because they had connections among criminals, often heading up the gangs of thieves that committed the robbery in the first place. Yet they were tolerated and sometimes protected by magistrates. Such tolerance was justifiable as the least of all possible evils: thief-takers "helped" the victim, and because they were sometimes willing to act as informants and witnesses they helped to control crime. But it made the magistrate into the thief's accomplice, subjecting him (fairly or unfairly) to charges of corruption. Salathiel Lovell, recorder of London, incurred especially hot controversy over his close relations with thief-takers and thieves. Thief-taking was structurally analogous to informing: like the informer, the thief-taker was involved in the crime he tattled about. As James Vernon put it with his usual delicious honesty,

> witnesses may be pitiful fellows and such as have assisted in the same crimes, but may they not therefore be better able to discover them . . . do you think proceedings at law must stop till Cataline comes to accuse Cethegus? The generality of informers are scoundrels, and yet their oaths must pass till they are disproved.[55]

William Chaloner's career was related both structurally and practically to the world of the thief-takers. Like them, he simultaneously committed crimes and made himself valuable as an informant. Vernon described Chaloner to the Earl of Portland as one who "hath been long suspected for false coining, he was actually concerned in counterfeiting bank notes and found a way to get his pardon by discovering others, so that forgeries and coining may be said to be his profession, and he hath dealt in discoveries from time to time as they were necessary for his protection." According to Chaloner's sometime accomplice Price, Chaloner had said as much himself, declaring that "he would not pretend to serve them [the government] unless it were for some other purposes and to secure himself a protection" against prosecution for the coining of guineas, which was "Chaloner's way of livelihood."[56]

Chaloner, like the thief-takers, maintained connections to both sides of the law; not surprisingly, he consorted with thief-takers as well. When he presented an "abstract of services" to the government in 1695, the list he provided of persons able to vouch for him ran the gamut from government officials to quasi-criminals. On it were William Bridgman, clerk to the late Secretary of State Trenchard, and Treasury solicitor Aaron Smith. Chaloner also named John Gibbons, the Whitehall porter known to be a thief-taker who alternately protected and witnessed against coiners.[57]

Chaloner himself "compounded" in the manner of thief-taker with the Bank of England when having been apprehended for forging notes, he won his release by turning in his associates. He was said to be an associate of Matthew Coppinger, who robbed and extorted money from people under pretense of exposing them as coiners. Like Coppinger and Gibbons, Chaloner "discovered" crimes that he had encouraged. As Isaac Newton put it, he could not find that Chaloner "did ever make it his business to find out any treasons or conspiracies against the King and Kingdom but what were of his own contriving, as in the case of the printers."[58]

The printers mentioned by Newton were William Newbolt and Edward Butler, whom Chaloner had witnessed against in 1693 for printing King James's *Declaration*. At their trial the two protested that they were "but servants, and hired to work for their livelihood, the press was not theirs." Claiming to be mere employees did not save them from a death sentence, but they won reprieves by turning witness against others. According to Chaloner's "abstract of services," they made oaths against Henry Griffith, Dr. Brett, Henry Singleton, George Burden, and Edward Price for publishing libels or handing them to the press. Newton was later convinced that Chaloner had set them up:

> Chaloner to secure himself as a person serviceable to ye Government, persuaded Butler and Newbolt (at ye expense of several treats and some money) to print him 40 of those [King James's] Declarations pretending that they were not to be dispersed but sent to a private gentleman in the country and as soon as he had got ye papers he went to Secretary Trenchard and informed him that he had discovered and taken the Printer of King James's Declarations with their Press and receiving (as he gives out) a reward of £1000 has since bragged . . . that he fun'd [that is, tricked] the King of a £1000.[59]

The trepanning of Newbolt and Butler also featured prominently in a mock-heroic biography published after Chaloner's death, *Guzman Redivivus* (1699). The author might have taken his title from a serial, *The English Guzman*, published in 1683 to ridicule and discredit the Hilton gang, informers who targeted illegal meetings of dissenters. In any case, it presented Chaloner as being (like Hilton) a scoundrel masquerading as a patriot, who "whilst he was acting villainy in private, pretended himself to be still busied for the good of the public."[60]

Chaloner was able to find supporters within Parliament and the Privy Council for many years. In 1695 he presented an abstract of services to the government, accompanied by a petition asking compensation for £400 laid out in expenses as well as the sufferings he incurred when "confined as a close prisoner above five weeks amongst these traitorous persons the better to enable him to make a further discovery." In his list of services he listed the convictions not only of Newbolt and Butler but of many other printers and dispersers of seditious pamphlets, some of whom Newbolt and Butler also helped convict. Chaloner further claimed to have discovered the forgers of Nottingham's seals and tracked down the merchant John Commins, a key figure in Jacobite financial networks. Chaloner's claims were recognized as legitimate by some members of the Privy Council. Lord Monmouth advocated for Chaloner, pushing John Somers in May 1695 to see that Chaloner be paid "above £200," and Somers in turn confirmed to Portland that (the late) "Mr. Secretary Trenchard gave me a very long list of his services," which were further "verified by Mr. Aaron Smith's report." In November 1695 the king ordered a payment of £100 p.a. to Chaloner and directed that he should have employment.[61]

In the following months, Chaloner added to his record of government service. Appearing before a committee at Whitehall on 3 February 1696, he described a ring of counterfeiters who made guineas with dyes that had been stamped in the Tower (where the Mint was located) and implicated Roettier, the chief engraver of the Mint widely suspected to be a Jacobite. He further claimed (in what appears to have been a second examination) that the Mint coined counterfeit money and also coined money below standard weight.[62]

At the same time as he "served" the government, however, Chaloner was being pursued as a coiner by the recorder of London, Salathiel Lovell. He complained in a petition that Lovell had recruited as witnesses against Chaloner the very same coiners whom Chaloner had named to the Privy Council as part of the counterfeiting ring deploying Roettier's stamps. His complaint was certainly consistent with Recorder Lovell's known associations with thief-takers: Chaloner pointed out that "Abbott [the coiner] whom he [Chaloner] hath sworn against, hath had such favors from the recorder, as have been injurious to the government." Chaloner's and Lovell's mutual charges were aired before the Lords Justices in May, when it was resolved that informations from Chaloner and informations against him should be examined.[63]

How far Chaloner succeeded in persuading government officials that his information was valuable is unclear. Lord Chief Justice John Holt expressed some ambivalence to Trumbull, characterizing Chaloner as "a very cunning fellow, from whom I cannot procure any evidence against any particular person, though it appears there hath been a great mystery of villainy at the Tower." Chaloner's expertise on coining, though, gave him some leverage.

An Abstract of the Services done by William Chaloner Gent for his Ma:ties & Government.

That by Order of Mr Secretary Trenchard, he hath made it his whole business for a considerable time past to discover the Persons that counterfeited Passes in the name of the Earle of Nottingham, and were otherwise traiterously Acting against his Ma:ties and Government.

That he informed Mr Secretary that foure Persons in Peter Street Westm: were Printing the late K: James's Declarations, Passes in the name of the Earle of Nottingham & other traiterous Lybells, and who were the Authors, Handers, Printers, Publishers, and Disposers of the said Seditious and Treasonable Lybells, and where were severall other great quantities of Seditious Lybells, Letters, false Passes, Printing Presses &c. All w:ch Declarations, false Passes, Lybells, Presses, &c. have been taken with the Persons to whom they did belong; who have thereupon been Convicted some of High Treason and others of Misdemeano:rs and have been Sentenced to dy, Stand in the Pillory, fined, Imprisoned, Outlawed &c. for the same; Also where were kept two Printing Presses contrary to Law (viz:t).

W:m Newbolt taken in y:e Haymarket for printing & publishing 150 Seditious Lybells Entitled	King James's Declaration Great Britains just Complaint The Answer to D:r King The Jacobits Principles Vindicated The Common people of Engl:ds Peticon to the Parliam:t of England A Letter to D:r Tillotson The State of the Seven Provinces The Earle of Pembrookes Speech The French Conquest neither desirable nor Practicable The Originall Contract Song of an Orange Actus Quintus	This was Verified by the Oath of Mr Price, Chaloner, Hayward, Gillibrand at the Sessions, and by the Lybells taken upon him.
Ellinor Ross taken in Queen Street with 2 cart Load of Seditious Lybells Entitled	An Answer to D:r King A Letter to D:r Tillotson &c	This was Verified by Mr Gillibrand and Hayward who took them in her house.
John Gowen taken in Tyburn Road with severall Seditious Lybells, & for publishing the same Entitled	King James's Declaration A Book of Paradoxes Actus Quintus The Jacobits Principles Vindicated The Scotch Whim The Fr: Conquest neither desirable nor Practicable Great Britains just Complaint The Answer to D:r King The Common people of Engl:ds Peticon to the Parl:t of Engl:d A Letter to D:r Tillotson The State of the Seven Provinces The Earle of Pembrookes Speech The Originall Contract The Song of an Orange	This was Verified by the Oath of Mr Price, Hayward & Gillibrand at the Sessions and by the Lybells taken upon him.
Epiphanius Nytham taken near Piccadilly w:th many Seditious Lybells	of three severall Sorts	This was Verified by Mr Gillibrand & Mr Hayward who took them upon him
Mary Elliot taken in St James's w:th many Seditious Lybells	of three severall Sorts	This was Verified by Mrs Maris son and Mr Maris Servt who took them upon her
Car Taylor taken in Queen Street with Seditious Lybells Entitled	A Song Printed by Robin Hogg The Originall Contract Great Britains just Complaint The Answer to D:r King The late Kings Declarations The French Conquest	This was Verified by the Oath of Mr Price, Hayward, and Gillibrand at the Sessions, and by the Lybells taken upon him

The first page of William Chaloner's abstract of services. The left column lists publishers or distributors of seditious libels whom Chaloner helped to convict, the middle column lists titles of the libels, and the right-hand column gives the names of supporting witnesses. "An Abstract of the Services Done by William Chaloner" © The British Library Board, British Library Add. MS 72568, f. 48r.

He had already "compounded" with the Bank of England in discovering forgers, and in turn the Bank's director recommended he be included in a general pardon. In 1697 he gave a helpful demonstration of coining techniques to a parliamentary committee investigating alleged abuses at the Mint and published recommendations based on his own experience for making coins less vulnerable to counterfeit.[64]

One of Chaloner's supporters in these enterprises was the Whig MP Jack Arnold, who headed the committee on abuses at the Mint. Arnold already had a long history as a promoter of informers: in 1691 he had insisted on Crone's and Preston's confessions being brought before Parliament and had supported William Fuller. It was probably Chaloner's credit with Arnold that gave him access to another Whig MP, Arnold's cousin Harry Colt, who soon became the sponsor of Chaloner's next foray into "the service of the government." In 1697 Colt embarked on an independent intelligence gathering project. One of his informants was Catherine Bernard, a Dutch woman who had entered into an uneasy business partnership with Mrs. Scott, the niece of the Jacobite Neville Paine, whose house was said to be the resort of many disaffected persons. The lawyer John Robins of Lincoln's Inn, who had helped Chaloner negotiate his composition with the Bank of England, was also drawn into Colt's network, as was Chaloner himself.

Chaloner and/or Robins in turn introduced Colt to a young man, Aubrey Price, as a person well able to do him service. Price was a coiner and forger of Exchequer bills. Like Chaloner, he had made a composition with the Bank and named his accomplices. He apparently got his start as a spy when, with the help of Mrs. Bernard (Colt's informant), he insinuated himself into the confidence of the hot Jacobite Mrs. Scott. It is possible that Price's initial goal was not to spy on Jacobites but to obtain material for coining; a trunk of plate had been entrusted to Mrs. Scott's care by a Jacobite who had fled to the Continent, and it is likely Price made Mrs. Scott's acquaintance in order to get his hands on it.[65]

Whatever his motive, Aubrey Price did win Mrs. Scott's trust. He was introduced to her many Jacobite friends, who were under the impression that he would be able to carry messages from them to the court of St. Germain. According to the version of the story Price told to Vernon, Price then proposed to Chaloner and Robins that he use his access to Mrs. Scott's Jacobite network "for the service of the government," and they in turn chose Harry Colt as their conduit to the authorities.[66]

Harry Colt's Jacobite hunting project sprang from and became further entangled in the antagonism between the two secretaries of state, Shrewsbury and Trumbull. As noted above, Colt and Arnold both promoted informers like William Fuller. By 1697 their zealous pursuit of Jacobitism in high places had alienated powerful Whig politicians, including Shrewsbury and James Vernon. It was for this reason that, despite being Whigs, Colt and Arnold sought the patronage of William Trumbull and in doing so inserted themselves into the conflict between Trumbull and Shrewsbury. The solicitor, John Robins, too, sought Trumbull's favor, apparently with success.[67]

There is no evidence that Trumbull was directly involved in Colt's Jacobite-hunting activities. He was only informed after the fact by Robins of the allegedly important discoveries Colt and his spies were to make. Nonetheless, Colt was well aware of Trumbull's enmity with Shrewsbury. He was in fact part of the reason for that enmity. In April 1697, feeling that he had been marginalized, Trumbull had threatened to resign. He made it a condition of his remaining in office that Colt and Arnold would come into places. Lord Sunderland, newly appointed Lord Chamberlain, promised to help, but, as Trumbull recorded in his diary, Sunderland soon reported "that Arnold and Colt could not come into places without the Duke of Shrewsbury's consent, else an affront to him, they having been most violent against him." That fact that Trumbull did not "have credit enough to bring in a friend" intensified his alienation. Trumbull's enmity with Shrewsbury might well have shaped the direction that Colt's "discoveries" were to take, even if Trumbull did not dictate that direction.[68]

In June 1696 Colt brought Price's information to the Lords Justices, the councilors who met almost daily in the king's absence. The information met with a mixed reception. Some of what Price said was plausible and familiar. According to James Vernon (who acted as clerk to the Lords Justices and attended all meetings), several persons "whom nobody doubts to be Jacobites" were included in a list Price had obtained of potential Jacobite insurrectionists in Northamptonshire. Price also named as Jacobites the owler Stephen Lansfield, about whom William Trumbull had already obtained intelligence, and a Lieutenant Gargrave in Colonel Coote's regiment, whom the Lords Justices were inclined to believe guilty of at least making big Jacobite boasts. His accusation of the Earl of Yarmouth was greeted with more ambivalence. Yarmouth had initially refused oaths of allegiance to the Williamite regime and been imprisoned twice, but in 1696 he had taken the oaths and resumed his seat in the House of Lords. Vernon reported to Shrewsbury, "The Lords [Justices] give very little credit to what they have said of Lord Yarmouth, and don't like that the reputations of persons of quality should be tossed about."[69]

Price's biggest story, which was that Captain Roberts had proposed to him a plan to seize Dover Castle for King James II, was probably his least convincing. Captain Roberts was real enough: he was a known Jacobite, already under indictment for helping to convey some of the assassination conspirators to France. However, the local Dover justice of the peace, Michael Cole, had already arrested Price's servant Morris after he was heard speaking of this plot in an alehouse; the blatant indiscretion itself (to Vernon and apparently the Lords Justices) cast doubt on the seriousness or existence of the plot.[70] Even Harry Colt, Price's biggest supporter, had to admit that Price's youth and association with Chaloner lessened his credibility. Nonetheless, the Lords Justices agreed to pay Price at least £30 over the course of two months to defray his expenses in making discoveries.[71]

In late August, however, Price took a step that changed him from a slightly dubious informer into a dangerous one. He gave Colt secondhand information from Captain Roberts (the supposed organizer of the Dover Castle Plot) that implicated Secretary of State Shrewsbury yet again in Jacobite plotting. Price said Roberts told him that Shrewsbury had tried to help the notorious Jacobite conspirator John Fenwick escape to France.[72]

The ever-loyal James Vernon took on the job of defending Shrewsbury's reputation (for the third time in one year!). He assembled witnesses able to testify to Shrewsbury's zeal in pursuing and finally catching Fenwick, taking every opportunity to remind other government officials of this point. But this was not enough. Vernon wanted to discredit the accusers and to learn who had directed them to make the accusation. He considered consulting the thief-taker John Gibbons, whom he was sure knew something about Price, but feared Gibbons was a "tool with so devilish an edge" that it would be dangerous to make use of him.[73]

Vernon quickly decided to use Chaloner to testify against Price as a coiner or forger. He had leverage over Chaloner, he believed, because the Mint warden Isaac Newton had recently found a witness who could implicate Chaloner in a scheme to erase the denominations on Exchequer bills and replace them with higher ones (so that a £10 note might become a £100 note, for example). Unfortunately, Newton was reluctant to move against Chaloner immediately. As he explained to the Lords Justices, he did "not think the discovery yet ripe." Newton had only enough evidence to convict Chaloner of a misdemeanor and was waiting to have "fuller matters" against him. Nonetheless, the Lords Justices pressed Newton to get his proofs ready as fast as he could and take up Price and Chaloner. As Vernon explained it to Shrewsbury, "My wishes are that Price may first be taken up for coining, and that his blasting may begin from thence." For Vernon, pushing Newton to take up Chaloner was the first step in silencing Price.[74]

Vernon's decision to prosecute Price as a forger or coiner (rather than as a perjurer) was driven by his anxiety about public opinion. As Vernon explained to Shrewsbury, tampering with currency was universally loathed. Most people cared little about the plight of public officials wrongfully maligned, but "in what concerns property and the coin, and where every man may fear to be undone if the counterfeiting designs prove successful, the prejudices and indignation of the people will run all one way." Implicit in the comment was Vernon's assumption that people would be less unanimously indignant (in fact, they might be gleeful) when they saw public officials slandered. As he struggled to control the damage to Shrewsbury's reputation, Vernon worried that Price and his sponsors had already "spread abroad" rumors that Shrewsbury was accused. He was later vastly relieved to find that "at present the people are kept in the dark as to all this examination, and since it must have been taken up at one time or another, I can't but be glad that it is before the meeting of parliament, while one may have time and liberty to make an impartial inquiry into the credits of our informers."[75]

Vernon's scheme to "blast" Price for coining by pressuring Chaloner to witness against him soon wavered and altered. One reason for his unsteadiness was that discrediting Price proved difficult and not entirely desirable. Vernon came to be impressed with Price as a "cunning dexterous rogue" who handled questions with "great quickness and subtlety." Not only did he deliver "cautious lies that should have some semblance of truth," but some of what he said actually was true. Of Captain Lewin, whom Price had accused of Jacobitism, Vernon wrote with alarm that Price "does him no wrong, and yet this man's wife is now rocker to the Duke of Gloucester [son of Princess Anne]." Vernon was especially excited by Price's information about Neville Paine's niece Mrs. Scott. "If she were seized and would speak the truth," he told Portland, "something considerable might be known, it being evident she was a great confident of that party [the Jacobites]."[76]

Price was, then, "a proficient in the arts of cozenage," but Vernon was still eager that "his informations too may have as much weight given them as they will bear." Exactly how to make use of the occasional truths without giving credit to the lies remained problematic, so that, as Vernon put it, "The Lords [Justices] find such a mixture in the man of truth and lies, that it is a perplexed matter to know what to resolve on."[77]

Vernon changed course. Instead of using Chaloner as a witness against Price, he tried to use Price against Chaloner. He may have wished to take advantage of public anger at coiners and forgers; Chaloner, the most visible and notorious coiner of his day, might have been a better target than Price. Vernon may also have pursued this new strategy because Chaloner had not bowed to pressure to implicate Price, as Vernon had hoped he would. Rather, claiming that he was being persecuted by Newton because he was able to reveal corrupt practices in the Mint, Chaloner mobilized his ally Harry Colt to accuse the Lords Justices of "stifling discoveries."[78]

By late September, some doors had closed and some windows had opened. The jurists who at the request of the Lords Justices examined Price's information warned that Price was useless as a witness, and so too was Chaloner, both being men of "prostitute reputations." Vernon, however, had come to find a new use for Price. Fearing that Chaloner might be the greater threat, he was now hoping that Price would be able to lure Chaloner into revealing more deeply laid plans. Temporarily smiling on Price, the Lords Justices facilitated his release on bail, presumably in return for his promise of help against Chaloner. In the end, there was not enough evidence to convict Chaloner of anything. Chaloner and Price both walked free (though each did hang a few years later). Mrs. Scott was never caught.[79]

James Vernon's inability to effectively exploit the information of either Chaloner or Price underscores two separate though related problems. First, there was the dilemma inherent in any engagement with an informer or thief-taker: informers were scoundrels. It was because they were scoundrels that they could inform on other scoundrels, but to use a scoundrel as a witness was to give him credit. Vernon was unable to figure out how to use Chaloner and Price against one another because one would have to be credited in order to successfully prosecute the other.

Second, the government's desire for information not only allowed scoundrels to commit crimes they would have committed anyway, but it provided them with an incentive to pretend to commit crimes in order to inform about them later. It is striking how often in the course of questioning suspects brought in by Price's information that Vernon found that "treason" had been conjured up for theatrical effect. Price did report on treasonous talk, but Price himself had encouraged that talk. On 7 September, for example, the Lords Justices examined two of Price's catches, Horsenail and Robinson. As Vernon told it:

> Horsenail is 70 years old, owns a lot of idle conversation with a young fellow, and assures their Excellencies there was not a true word spoken by either one of them. He had writ to them indeed from Norfolk of men that would be ready to serve K[ing] J[ames], but he knew not one of them, nor ever opened his mouth about it. Robins[on] was an exciseman turned out, ready to steal for want, and one may perceive the discourses with both of them have been mere trepans.[80]

Ironically, some of Price's targets tried to inform on Price at the same time as Price tried to inform on them! The Earl of Yarmouth, when given a chance to defend himself, "owned a young man had been with him, whose name he did not know, pretending he brought him messages from France. The reason he [Yarmouth] gave for admitting him [Price] was, that if [he] had anything of consequence to impart, he might make use of it for the government." In Vernon's view, then, Price's reports were not so much false as inflated, bubbly. The men Price informed on really did speak treason in his presence. But they were either just bragging foolishly or were deliberately trying to entrap Price, competing with him at his own game.[81]

Vernon eventually had to admit that the one piece of information he regarded as being truly valuable—that there was a scheme by Chaloner and Price to change the denominations on Exchequer bills—might be an illusion conjured up by the government's sheer desire for information. Recall that this scheme had been the centerpiece of the case that Vernon intended to build against Price. Chaloner did indeed give information against Price, accusing him of being the first proposer of changing denominations on Exchequer bills. To that Price had a ready answer: that the counterfeiting scheme had been proposed to him first by one Randall, and that he had proposed it to Chaloner only "for finding out how far he was concerned in it."[82]

Vernon not only found it hard to determine who originated the denomination-changing scheme, but he came to doubt that there was such a scheme at all. Perhaps Chaloner had not been interested in forgery per se but rather in celebrity and political leverage. Chaloner, Vernon reported, had told Isaac Newton that he was "preparing something to be printed against [before] the meeting of Parliament, to show how counterfeiting Exchequer bills could be prevented" so that (in Vernon's opinion) "the House of Commons were to be amused with his tricks of this kind this winter, as they were the last with his coining." Two days previous to that, Chaloner himself had colorfully expressed to Newton his glee in conning authorities, saying he had "funned the King formerly, he had since funned the Bank, and he would fun the Parliament before he had done with them." Chaloner also said, according to Vernon, that "they did not care to make any profit by it [the forged bills], but their chief aim was mischieving the government." The plan to change denominations on Exchequer bills might, then, have been a publicity stunt from the beginning, meant to direct attention at a serious crime which Chaloner could then get credit for helping to prevent. If Vernon thought that was the case, his suspicions would have been confirmed by Price's account, given a few days later, of what Chaloner had told him of his plans to "bubble the government." Chaloner, Price recalled, advised him "to make his discoveries strong it was no matter whether they were truths or not, the Government wanted a plot and he must make one for them."[83]

Conclusion

The idea that the government "wanted a plot" brings us back to the quotation from Robert Ferguson at the head of this chapter. The story told here in a sense confirms Ferguson's claim that the government's desire for plots encouraged informers to fabricate them. The process by which this occurred, however, was less top-down and intentional than Ferguson would have us imagine. It was the very openness of the government to scrutiny—and the availability of a rhetoric of patriotism rather than top-down subornation—that legitimated informing and ensured that authorities would at least pretend to take informers seriously. There was a complicated dynamic of power between the state and the informers. Informers were hardly passive tools in the hands of the government. They had a "devilish edge."

Of course, informers might make the same complaint about government officials. The next section of this book considers the informers' experience and perspective.

CHAPTER 4

Identity, Honor, and Gender in the Narratives of Informers

Some of the dangers faced by state officials in dealing with informers were discussed in the previous chapter. Here and in the next chapter I examine the state-informer relationship from the other side. This chapter examines the narratives of a wide range of informers, asking how the act defined the informer's sense of self and relations with others. I consider first those informers who seem to have informed only once and about whom information is fragmentary. I then consider two kinds of long-term "career" informers: those who maintained a consistent identity as zealous Williamites, and those (including Catholics, ex-Catholics, and prisoners) for whom informing was a means of transforming their identities. Chapter 5 is a case study of one individual, Richard Kingston, and the ways his service to the state impacted his own credibility and that of the government.

Most scholars who have studied informing in modern contexts have found it hard to say whether denunciation should be seen as an instance of the state manipulating the individual or vice versa. Sheila Fitzpatrick finds wide variation among denunciation in Stalinist Russia, from manipulative "apartment denunciations" to denunciations driven by apparently sincere if paranoid desire to protect the regime from its enemies. It is not always possible to tell the difference, though, and many denunciators occupy a middle ground between interestedness and disinterestedness: denunciations of disloyal officials who abuse their power over subordinates, for example, serve the needs of the denouncer and the state alike. Jan T. Gross emphasizes that even (or especially) manipulative, self-interested informing ultimately strengthens totalitarian regimes, the essence of which is the erasure of the boundary between public and private. "The principal mechanism which accounts for the penetration of the state into the private domain has been the practice of denunciation," he writes. "The real power of a totalitarian state results . . . from its being at the disposal of every inhabitant, available for hire at a moment's notice." Joanna Innes, writing about an informer in a nontotalitarian context, also sees informers as ambiguously being used by and using the state at once: the mid-eighteenth-century informing constable William Payne certainly saw himself as a patriot, enforcing order and protecting England from the Catholic menace. Yet, his informing was also a way for him to impose himself on the world around him, and his priorities were not necessarily those of England's ruling class; in fact, his social superiors often failed to welcome his contributions.[1]

All of the above-mentioned scholars emphasize that informers made active choices to inform, and that it somehow suited their needs, whether material, psychological, or political. Yet the very fact that informers met their own needs by performing service to the state would have affected the state as well. For informers, the state was the audience before whom they told their stories. We do not need to posit that the Williamite England was a totalitarian regime to recognize that informers became invested in and identified with the government, which in turn was the source of their own credibility and legitimacy. Of course, the reciprocal relationship between the state and the informer could also compromise the credibility of one or both parties.

One-Shot Informers

The arbitrary survival of records and the sheer variety of pathways by which an information given in the 1690s might make its way to the historian's desk prevents us from quantifying informers. Nonetheless, it seems safe to say that the act of giving information to the government about threats to its security was more common after 1688 than it was in the Restoration, and that the vast majority of those who did it were not professionals or repeaters. There were more monetary incentives to do so, advertised in proclamations. Even without the promise of gain, the persistent threat of invasion may have moved informers.

Malicious or manipulative denunciations, like those described by Jan T. Gross and Sheila Fitzpatrick, must also have occurred, but their frequency is hard to assess. One striking feature of the period is the paucity of references to malicious informations, though there were some. The soldier Cornelius Sodington, petitioning to be restored to his post, explained that his wife had sworn high treason against him but that the information had been found false and malicious. Mary Cook, alias Nugent, described as "an Irish popish woman," was committed to Newgate for having sworn treason against William Tuff and Benjamin Parker, who "justified themselves to be loyal subjects, and made it appear that her malice against them was for getting her committed to Bridewell for pilfering." Lieutenant James Weames, indicted for speaking scandalous and seditious words, persuaded the court that the prosecution was "malicious and base." The witness against him, he said, had been his former servant "who had behaved himself very ill" and to whom he had given "some small correction, after which the fellow was heard several times to threaten him, that he would be revenged on him."[2]

That there were few complaints of malicious accusation does not necessarily mean that malice itself was rare. It is likely that we hear of malicious accusation only when the accused was confident of being believed. What the complainants listed here have in common is that their accusers were of lesser credit than themselves: a disobedient wife, an Irish Catholic female thief, and a disobedient servant. Where a strong disparity in relative credit between accuser and accused did not exist, victims of malicious accusation might have kept silent.

Another reason for the rarity of complaints about malicious accusation is that so much of what informers reported was open, public behavior. Many informations concerned things seen or heard by more than one person. A sheet marked "extracts of letters out from Norwich relating to papists" in Undersecretary of State John Ellis's papers shows that the identity, meeting places, and even general mood of Jacobites was widely known in local communities and provoked enough anxiety to motivate a denunciation. One extract noted that Sir Robert Yallop maintained a chapel where nonjuring ministers preached, and on the Sunday before the discovery of the Assassination Plot the text had been the especially threatening passage from Jeremiah, "I will send sword and famine and pestilence etc." Another extract reported that the keeper of the Goat Tavern, a Quaker, regularly received "a most dangerous" Jacobite newsletter that he never opened until Yallop came and which he shared only with those who "by their cant assure him they are of the party." Other extracts concerned Mr. Tasborough, described as "a wry cunning man," who was less discreet than the tavern keeper. Tasborough was believed to have a correspondence with St. Germain and had been publicly showing letters received from London promising that there would soon be news; so many had seen the letter "that it was the talk of the whole town."³

Anne Hancock's letter to Postmaster John Wildman on the subject of the suspicious Mr. Whitfield also conveys a whiff of the atmosphere of gossip circulating around known or reputed Jacobites. Hancock possessed both a sense of history and knowledge of social networks. She identified papists and disaffected persons with confidence. "The gentleman [Whitfield] converses with most," she told Wildman, "is one Adam Banks, in Watling Street, a woollen draper, a most famous Papist, and a rich merchant in Bow Lane, Mr. Wroth, and Mr. Lacy, who was hie shreeve [high sherriff] of Herfordshire in King James's time, and all most bigoted papists." Her animus against Whitfield was based on personal experience and predated the Glorious Revolution. She promised Wildman she could herself swear that "in King James's time" she had heard Whitfield "converting of all the company, and this was his words, that it was nonsense to think that there was any salvation, outside of the Roman Catholic Church." She had made inquiries as to Whitfield's habits and whereabouts, learning from a Captain Dellanel that "not one servant that belonged to my Lord could ever tell where Mr. Whitfield lodged nor how to speak with him except in the coffee house at Charing Cross." Some of the gossip she collected was just salacious: "I have heard today his whore [was?] out of a little bawdy house her name is Juxon but goes for his wife and by his name, at Mr. Cooper's house a Silver Smith at ye Golden Ball in Foster Lane." Hancock's letter further suggested that the talk in her community about Whitfield was driven by some frustration that a high-ranking person, referred to in the letter only as "My Lord," had bestowed favor on Whitfield but was ignorant of his true character. Sir Charles Harrow, she fumed, "was made acquainted with what a villainous character [Whitfield] had by a man of quality but it is supposed he did not make my Lord acquainted with it." The letter expressed confidence that her opinion was shared. There were (she reported), "a great many worthy gentlemen" who wished that someone would make Whitfield known "to my Lord, as he has been to all his acquaintance for a great villain."⁴

The fact that Hancock's convictions about Whitfield and his friends festered over time raises an important question: Why did people choose to report at the moments they did? Timing can tell us something about motivations, degree of enthusiasm, and countervailing pressures.

In some cases an informer moved quickly because he or she thought that there was immediate danger. The anonymous informations from Norwich discussed above were given in late February and early March 1696, in the immediate aftermath of the Assassination Plot, and so they emphasized things that looked to the writer or writers like evidence that Jacobites everywhere had been "big with expectation of some great thing to be done to their advantage." Another informer who acted quickly under a sense of threat was Dorothy Damram of Portsmouth. She went to the magistrate to report an alarming series of conversations with an acquaintance, Mrs. Smith, who lived at the Golden Patten in Southwark, after the latter had visited several ships in Portsmouth harbor and, coming ashore, reported that "'twas thought King James would be here again." Damram's suspicions were further aggravated when she heard Mrs. Smith say she was returning to London with a pack of forty letters, that "the morning she left London she had spoken with Mr. Pepys" and "that in some little time some of her friends would be in favor again, and then she should be better respected." Damram's evidence seems inconclusive. Nonetheless, the prospect of disloyalty in the fleet was frightening enough not only for Damram to report it but for officials to act quickly. The day after Richard Haddock, who received Damram's information, reported it to Secretary of State Nottingham, a warrant was issued to apprehend Mrs. Smith on suspicion of high treason.[5]

In other cases potential informers were reluctant to come forward. Middlesex justices in 1691 provided a "kind of balloting box" to receive anonymous informations about refusers of the oath of allegiance, which suggests that reluctance was expected. Information might come to the attention of authorities through a string of intermediaries, suggesting that the initial witness was prodded by someone else.[6]

One such reluctant witness was a barber, Mr. Marks. As he later told the Lords Justices, he had seen a person whom he "strongly fancied" looked like the late King James through a window in the apartment of James Roettier, the notoriously disaffected ex-engraver of the Mint still residing at the Tower. A few days later, Marks mentioned what he saw to his landlord Mr. Billers, a London Common councilman, after he had come to trim him and seen a note in his window directing a search for suspicious persons. Billers mentioned it to a third man, the broker Mr. Whiston, who (as Vernon put it) "carried it round the town," bringing Marks to a magistrate to make oath and insisting that Lord Lucas, the governor of the Tower, make a search. The Lords Justices, after hearing all the witnesses, were to decide the whole thing was "a foolish imagination." Whiston appears to have been the instigator of the proceedings: he expostulated to the Lords Justices about the "easiness of seizing the Tower" and described having seen a "very rich bed" in Roettier's home (whereas Lord Lucas found the bed "ordinary enough"). Marks, by contrast, had sat on the information for days, explaining that he had "only a strong suspicion of it, otherwise he should have taken other measures."[7]

A set of documents in the papers of William Brockman, a Kentish justice of the peace and sometime member of Parliament, offers a rare glimpse of the dynamic between those who knew of suspicious words and actions and those who actively organized that knowledge into information given to government officials. On 10 January 1695, Robert Robinson, having brought his four-year-old son with him to the Saracen's Head Inn at Milton (next to Gravesend), was moved to declare publicly that he "wished King William might not piss waking" until he had made Robinson's son Prince of Wales. The point of the remark (which was variously reported by other witnesses as being that William might not "piss walking" or "not have the power to piss") was elusive to Robinson's hearers as well as to historians. Robinson was perhaps thinking of gonorrhea and its connection to William's failure to produce an heir with Queen Mary, whose recent death (in December) had once again stirred up questions of legitimate succession. The remark could be glossed as a comment on the line of succession established by the new regime: according to one account, Robinson went on to explain that William had as much right to put Robinson junior in line for the throne as he did to put in Princess Anne's son, the Duke of Gloucester.[8]

Elizabeth Webb, the proprietress of the Saracen's Head, participated in the conversation; she pressed Robinson to clarify whether "the King" upon whom he wished the urinary disability was William or James. She found the story interesting enough to repeat to others, like William Thurloe of Gravesend, a baker, and Edward Milles of Milton, a carpenter. It seems that it was from Milles that the mayor of Gravesend, Walter Nynn, heard the story. Nynn, however, sympathized with Robinson. He summoned Elizabeth Webb to his house, berating her as a "busy gossiping slut and not fit to keep a public house for no persons were safe to come there."[9]

The story also reached Robert Paterson, a former excise man turned schoolteacher in Gravesend who was a zealous supporter of the new regime. For Paterson, Robinson's remark in the pub was the tip of an iceberg of Jacobite sympathies. Robinson, as Paterson was later to explain, was one of two "notoriously ill affected" men who "have much gloried in ridiculing the government." Robinson, a brazier by trade, had already "almost ruined" himself by "selling all his goods and appointing King James's return for his pay day." His companion in disaffectedness, John Seres, kept a coffeehouse that received Jacobite newsletters and had already stood in the pillory. Much to Paterson's annoyance, these two had lately been allowed to stand bail for a third Jacobite sympathizer, a Mr. Barnes, the new proprietor of the Five Bells in Northfleet, who was under indictment for assisting another suspect, Joseph Bradshaw, to escape from authorities. Robinson's history explains why Robert Paterson saw fit to make an issue of his words in a pub. It is not clear exactly what role Paterson played, but Nynn clearly blamed him (as well as Webb) for the fact that the story got around. He accosted Paterson at the Swan, another Milton establishment, reviling him for making "a great deal of trouble of a tale in a tub."[10]

At the end of January the General Court (comprising Nynn and the corporation of Gravesend) considered the charges against Robinson. Elizabeth Webb gave testimony but (according to Paterson) was "snubbed." John Seres by this time had disappeared. Mayor Nynn procrastinated in calling two other witnesses against Robinson, and in the ensuing delay Robinson also absconded. Mayor Nynn subsequently took steps to retaliate against Paterson and against other people in Gravesend whom he considered to be Paterson's allies. One target was William Thurloe, against whom Nynn put out a warrant as a "disaffected person." Nynn reportedly wished to have a similar warrant against Paterson but was dissuaded by the attorney George Morton, who pointed out that the charge would not be credible.[11]

Paterson at this point appealed to William Brockman. Outside intervention was needed and justified, he explained. The farce at the General Court had left many of its members so frustrated with Nynn's mismanagement that "they wished of Parliament that the mayor may be made sensible of his disloyalty which indeed being taken notice of to some purpose may be a terror to the disaffected." According to Patterson, there were "fifteen or sixteen witnesses to confirm all that I have given you [Brockman] account of" but they were reluctant to speak on their own accord, fearing that Nynn "would study to be revenged on them and their relations."[12]

Over the next months Nynn, having obtained a copy of Paterson's list of potential witnesses against him, did indeed retaliate against at least two of these people: the farrier James Hindmarsh and the carpenter Edward Milles. According to testimony Brockman collected, Nynn "hath forbidden his bailiff to employ Mr. Hindmarsh one of the witnesses so that he hath lost a customer and hath plainly told Mr. Milles another of the witnesses that he shall not build the booths for the fair which he hath been accustomed to do for many years." A few of the men Paterson had named as potential witnesses stood by him and expressed admiration even when their names leaked out. John Skarr, who described himself as a "waterman," was "reflected on" by the mayor as one of Paterson's "crew," to which (according to Paterson) Skarr responded that he was not "ashamed to be called one of my crew because he knew me to be an honest man [and] he loved me because I dared to be true to the government." But some of Nynn's targets turned on Paterson for having exposed them. Paterson ruefully reported that Hindmarsh had accosted him in the street and "began to reflect upon me at a strange rate saying that like an ill man I had forged his hand in setting it in a petition against Mr. Mayor for which Mr. Mayor had set his chamberlain to abuse him and he would arrest me for so doing."[13]

As Paterson put it to Brockman, "Those who are willing to attest to all things relating to ye affair request that some means may be used to seem to constrain them to testify the truth because they expect to be damnified in their respective occupations if they appear voluntary." There was clearly discontent in Gravesend with Mayor Nynn and his protection of Robert Robinson and John Seres, but few of the discontented wanted to be exposed as informers. Nynn could retaliate against them. Moreover, it is likely that there was a pro-Nynn party in Gravesend as well. One powerful Nynn supporter was the next mayor of Gravesend, who (Paterson complained) "told me plainly that I must prepare to resign [as schoolmaster] for he was resolved I should not continue for what I did to ye late Mayor he was resolved to make me suffer for."[14]

The presence of authorities hostile to would-be informers might also play a role in an intriguing story from the Leicester borough archives. The case at first appears to be about seditious words spoken by the town vicar, Mr. Newton, but was in fact much more about William Pollard, a barber-surgeon, whose gossip about Newton's words made him vulnerable to legal action. When Pollard told Newton (erroneously) that the French had landed, Newton had answered, "God speed them." Pollard had not gone to the mayor with this information; rather, he spread the story around, at least to his customers. Elizabeth Bent, a hosier's wife, was in the shop when Pollard told her what Newton had said, adding (as Elizabeth put it), "Mr. Newton was a hollowhearted and deceitful man, and several other railing words." The entire Newton family soon learned what Pollard was saying. Elizabeth Bent herself told or confirmed the story to Mary Newton, the vicar's "spinster" daughter. Mary was also sent by her mother (Mr. Newton being absent) to confront Pollard directly. William Pollard was predictably hostile. He called Mary a "damned bitch and said her father might kiss his arse."

Pollard's wife, however, tried valiantly to make peace. Intervening in the confrontation between William Pollard and Mary Newton, Mrs. Pollard told Mary that although she heard vicar Newton speak those words about the French, she "believed that Mr. Newton spoke the same words in jest." Mrs. Pollard also seems to have tried to intervene with Elizabeth Bent. About four days after Pollard had railed against Newton in Elizabeth's presence, Mrs. Pollard called to Elizabeth as she was passing by and inquired "whether Mr. Newton had spoken to her about going to Mr. Mayor." When Elizabeth confirmed that Newton had indeed asked, Mrs. Pollard tried to convince her that it was she herself and not William "that had spoke the said words" [that is, the words against Newton]. Clearly, Mrs. Pollard was afraid that Newton would press charges against her husband.[15]

The records do not reveal how this story ended. The fact that depositions were taken suggests that Mrs. Pollard's fear that her husband's words against the vicar would be viewed more harshly by authorities than the vicar's alleged well wishes to the French had some basis in reality. That the Newtons were far more powerful than the Pollards is underscored in Mary Newton's statement that her mother "hearing of [Pollard's words] sent this information to the said William Pollard to know the reason why he had so abused her husband in such a manner in his absence." There is more than a hint of imperiousness on the elder Mrs. Newton's part. Surely she would send her unmarried daughter to confront a male householder only if she thought Mary's superiority in status was seen to compensate for her inferiority in gender and marital status.

What was really going on? Perhaps the vicar was known to be a good Williamite and Pollard was spewing venom for some other reason. Or perhaps the vicar was a powerful crypto-Jacobite who could count on the protection of authorities. We cannot tell. The case is most useful for the questions it raises and possibilities it suggests. First, knowledge about seditious words could circulate around communities and come only indirectly to the attention of magistrates. Potential informers might make a choice not to go to the authorities, especially if the person about whom they wished to give evidence was powerful. The very indirectness by which the historian learns about Newton's apparently seditious words leads the historian to suspect that many seditious words were never recorded because most people (including Mrs. Pollard) did not want to incur the risk William Pollard ran by making a fuss.

The one-shot informers who surface in the archives, then, may represent the tip of the iceberg of people who had information that could be deemed valuable to the security of the state. Many men and women in Williamite England may have felt strongly enough about the new regime to take action to protect it, but we cannot assume they were a majority.

Still, it was possible to inform with passion rather than reluctance. Joshua Bowes, who in a letter to Trumbull wrote that he wished his body were transparent so that his "love and duty" for the king were readily apparent (see introduction), would stand as a shining example of a passionate informer. Bowes identified himself with loyalty to the state; informing was for him an arena in which he could articulate an ideal version of himself and ask state authorities to witness and confirm it. There are other informers who can be seen in the same light, for whom informing seems to have been a means of confirming or transforming identity. In the first group were those who informed repeatedly and consistently in order to establish themselves as a particularly zealous kind of Williamite supporter, often in the hopes of obtaining government favor. For the second group, the act of informing was both a result of and a means to changing their identity, especially their religious identity. I call them, respectively, patriots and chameleons.

Patriots

There was certainly no conflict between patriotic informing and self-interest. Joshua Bowes was eager to present himself as a zealous lover of the new regime, but the second part of his letter to Trumbull strongly suggests he was looking for a job:

> Sir I must confess it has been some trouble to me to see the King's enemies flourish with the King's preferments; whilst honest loyal men, men of understanding and integrity, and some that have been sufferers for a Protestant cause in the late King's reign have been discountenanced after unwearied applications: I am confident neither the King nor his Secretaries know it.[16]

The presence of crass material motives was entirely typical of the informers considered in this section. But the stakes went beyond material self-interest. For the informers discussed here, the credit of the Williamite regime became inextricably connected to their own personal credit. They conflated threats to the government with threats to themselves (and vice versa).

The papers of William Brockman, a Whig Member of the Parliament and justice of the peace in Kent, are a rich source for material on patriotic informers. Brockman was perhaps particularly receptive to pleas from public servants or would-be public servants who felt that their patriotism deserved greater reward or that they were disadvantaged by their loyalty to the government because of his personal experience. In 1691 Brockman had been instrumental in the prosecution of Godfrey Crosse of Canterbury, who was convicted and hanged for conveying intelligence to the French fleet. The case had been locally controversial, and Brockman was alarmed to hear that Alderman Jeffreys of Canterbury had made remarks to the effect that Brockman "murdered" Crosse. Jeffreys hastened to apologize, explaining that he meant only that Brockman had been a witness at the trial and had therefore "hanged" Crosse. The ensuing round of correspondence among Brockman's friends, Brockman, and Jeffreys about whether the apology was sufficient shows that the insult was seen as a serious political problem: it was, as Brockman's friend William Watson put it, "a plain demonstration of how persons of public spirit are used by the Jacobite party." Brockman himself admonished Jeffreys to take "due care, no reflection of aspersion be thrown out upon any one whatever . . . for ought said or done upon this occasion on behalf of the government."[17]

Given the seriousness with which Brockman and his circle took aspersions cast on patriots, it is natural that self-defined patriots would turn to Brockman for support. Two who did, the postmaster John Woodgate and the excise man/schoolmaster/customs officer Robert Paterson, left enough evidence of themselves in Brockman's papers so that we can trace their careers.

When John Woodgate assumed the position of postmaster at Canterbury in 1689, the office was already unprofitable. Throughout the late seventeenth century, Canterbury postmasters complained that the profits to be made by lodging travelers and letting out horses were undercut by the postmasters of Dover and Deal, who directed travelers to rival establishments. Moreover, as Woodgate was later to explain, the war with France had drastically curtailed traffic on the Dover Road. The allowance of £80 per annum that he received from the General Post Office could not cover the expenses of keeping the twelve horses and six boys needed to carry the mail.[18]

Woodgate's zeal for the government apparently garnered the sympathy of John Wildman, the first postmaster of the new regime. In 1691, Woodgate wrote to Wildman about Captain Crofts, the master of the Charles Galley, who "telling his mind when drunk" had announced his designs to fight against the Dutch rather than the French. It is not clear if Woodgate or Wildman was able to make the charge stick. Woodgate did promise to send witnesses to verify his story, and the Admiralty was shortly thereafter told to inquire into allegations against Crofts. After this the case drops from sight.[19]

Nonetheless, the information about Crofts allowed Woodgate to draw Wildman's attention to his longstanding problem with the Deal postmistress, Mrs. Elizabeth Watts, who directed people traveling from the coast to London to a rival establishment. To blacken Watts further, Woodgate obtained a copy of a court record indicating that she had been previously charged with perjury and sent it to Wildman. The postmaster general promised to "make Mrs. Watts comply and send all guides to the posthouse or she shall be no postmistress." Woodgate's political loyalty translated into protection from the postmaster general. "I have such a sense of your honesty and zeal for the government," Wildman wrote, "that I shall be glad to give you all the encouragement that shall be in my power."[20]

Woodgate undertook a second service in 1692, uncovering a ring of wool smugglers who carried correspondence between Dover, France, and Flanders. He later claimed to have used the profits of his office to finance the investigation. By this time, however, Wildman had been replaced as postmaster general by the Whig-Tory duo of Robert Cotton and Thomas Frankland. By late 1694 the new postmasters were demanding arrears that Woodgate owed them.[21]

Woodgate mounted a successful campaign to delay the payment of his debt. His petition to the Post Office was subscribed by several Whig members of Parliament, who attested that Woodgate was "active and zealous in their Majesties service." Woodgate had, they said, already tried to give up his job but had been prevailed upon by "the most loyal and eminent gent[lemen] and citizens to continue in that trust till this time to prevent their letters being ransacked and broke open as formerly by ill affected persons." Woodgate's indispensability to the government was further emphasized in a letter written on his behalf by the Kent Whig Basil Dixwell to Lord Portland. Dixwell deemed Woodgate the only "well-affected" person of his profession in Canterbury; it would be far better to remit his debts and increase his salary than to let him be ruined and suffer "the ill consequences of ill affected persons in his room besides the discouragement that the King's friends will receive by his being unkindly used."[22]

In the short run, the campaign worked: although Cotton and Frankland opined that Woodgate had channeled the profits of the Post Office to pay his personal debts, they submitted to an order by the Treasury Lords to give Woodgate an extra six months to pay. Nonetheless, tensions between Woodgate and his superiors continued to mount. The postmasters general soon accused Woodgate of deliberately misrepresenting what time of day letters arrived from Dover and Deal in order to cover up the fact that he held the mail for several hours before sending it on. They further pressured Woodgate by requiring his personal appearance in London.[23]

Although there is no record of what precisely transpired in London, it is clear that Woodgate had begun to link his troubles to the machinations of Jacobites. John Watts, who had succeeded his mother Elizabeth as postmaster of Deal, was heard to complain loudly that Woodgate "appeach[ed] him to be a Jacobite but he scorns that name." Brockman's friend Jacob Janeway of Canterbury reported, "I fear the Jacobites will still work his [Woodgate's] destruction for they have set all the engines the Devil can assist them with to work his undoing." Woodgate's campaign against Watts intensified in August when he informed William Brockman that Watts's father "was whipped at Sandwich for stealing of sheep" and that "his mother stands on record in court for perjury."[24]

Making such accusations, however, did not save Woodgate's job. When his arrears again became due in the middle of 1695, the postmasters general agreed to forgive part of his debt, but they put the business of collecting postage fees into the hands of a Mr. Fenner, while Woodgate was retained as a salaried employee for "riding work." Woodgate continued, though, to seek reinstatement. By June 1696, he somehow amassed money to pay what he owed the king, but the postmasters, understandably, wanted to keep Fenner in his new post. In response, according to Frankland and Cotton, Woodgate in September 1696 "did seize the letters, and receive the money due for the same"; further, he launched a formal complaint against the postmasters general and, while waiting for the complaint to be heard, continued to "receive money for letters due all that time," becoming once again "indebted to the [Post] Office £661."[25]

Although the nature of Woodgate's complaint is not revealed in the record, it might have been connected to charges of crypto-Jacobitism brought by another disgruntled postal employee, Ralph Blackhall. Blackhall was certainly aware of Woodgate and apparently adopted his cause. In November 1696, right after Woodgate had forcibly taken over the collection of letters from Fenner, John Robins reported to Trumbull that Blackhall "who brought before the Late Lords Justices the charge against the Post Office" now threatened to address the House of Commons with his complaints, one of which was that Frankland and Cotton intended to place John Wilson, a Canterbury innkeeper with alleged Jacobite sympathies, "in the room of Mr. Woodgate." Once again, then, Woodgate directly or indirectly promoted a narrative in which the security of the regime would be threatened were he removed from his post. This time, however, the narrative was less persuasive. In April 1697 Woodgate's complaint against the postmasters was heard. Woodgate later claimed that he had "proved all the matter and had thanks given him by my Lord Keeper, who owned he had done the King and Kingdom great service therein." Nonetheless, he was soon dismissed from employment.[26]

Frustrated by repeated failures to settle his accounts with Fenner and the Post Office, Woodgate took the bold step of printing an address to the House of Commons. In it he traced the roots of his difficulties to his "being so active in discovering the intrigues of those smugglers under which was carried on that pernicious correspondence with France" in 1692. The discovery, he contended, had "rather displeased than pleased the Postmasters General," who "refused to reimburse him" the £300 he claimed to have spent in the endeavor and "were picking quarrels with him, to turn him out of his place in 1697."[27]

This time, however, he was not able to save himself by politicizing his professional troubles. His failure might be attributed to the fact that Whigs no longer controlled the House of Commons. Moreover, the threat to the credit of the government that was carried by his charge of Jacobitism in high places probably outweighed any services he could perform for the regime. In any case, the printed paper backfired: Frankland and Cotton turned to the House of Commons for redress, complaining that Woodgate's libel violated their privileges as MPs, and after hearing parties on all sides the Commons voted that the printed paper was "false, scandalous, and malicious."[28]

Woodgate's political connections enabled him to survive in his post much longer than he could have otherwise. Robert Paterson's career had a rather different trajectory: until the very end of his career not even his friendship with Brockman could protect him. Nonetheless, Paterson and Woodgate shared a way of speaking about their troubles. Each appealed for Brockman's help on the grounds that his fate would affect the future of the new regime.

Robert Paterson's efforts to mobilize potential witnesses against the mayor of Gravesend were described earlier in this chapter. Brockman's papers allow us to reconstruct his career in more detail. Paterson trained as a gauger for the Excise and was assigned to his first post in Gravesend either just before or during the reign of James II. He quickly found it a sink of corruption. Local brewers were long accustomed to bribing excise officers to underestimate the amount of taxable beer they produced. They tempted Paterson with the promise of making three times his salary, and failing that, they "told him how it lay in the power of brewers to injure officers that were unkind sometimes by the interest they had with superiors." Paterson's predecessor, a Mr. Blincoe, was squarely in the brewers' camp. Having been ordered to show Paterson "his business" before departing, Blincoe orchestrated an evening of splendid hospitality to acquaint Paterson with the local brewers; finding Paterson stubbornly intended to honor his "sacred oath," Blincoe "did all he could to hoodwink [Paterson] by making the business as intricate as he could" and threatened to inform the Excise board that Paterson was not prepared for the demands of his job. When Paterson complained to Major Bird, the collector of the Excise, he was transferred to Romansgate in the Isle of Thanet, where, once again, the local brewers tried to corrupt him. Paterson was finally dismissed by his superior, Mr. Hornby, allegedly for "a false survey" but really, Paterson was later to insist, for having resisted "signing to take off the penal laws and test." He was replaced by John Young, a secular priest from St. Omers.[29]

The Revolution of 1688 brought a temporary reversal in Paterson's fortunes. Thanks to Brockman and two other prominent Kentish Whigs, Philip Boteler and William Honywood, Paterson was restored to a post in the Excise. At around the same time, Paterson came to Brockman with information about treason. As Paterson told it, he was approached by Daniel Deery, an Irishman who had formerly collected hearth taxes in Kent. Under the influence of drink, Deery confided to Paterson that he intended to join William's army in Ireland and then betray it by giving intelligence to the Jacobite enemy. Deery further confided to Paterson that he had embezzled £370 in taxes he had collected, with the assistance of the Quaker financier Thomas Calvert, to whom he customarily remitted his money. Calvert had agreed to withhold funds from the government but had demanded of Deery a share of the profits in return for his silence. Paterson duly informed Brockman, who in turn brought him to Secretary of State Nottingham. Calvert "was summoned to appear before the Exchequer bar to answer for the non-payment." Deery, thanks to Brockman's "indefatigable trouble," was taken up by messengers but later inexplicably released by Nottingham. He later tried to murder Paterson in London, and when that failed he swore "that he had such friends at the helm that I [Paterson] should never be easy in a public employment."[30]

Deery's words proved prophetic. Sir Henry Ashurst, the Whig MP who presided over the Excise office and was seen by Paterson as a sympathetic protector, resigned in 1691. Paterson's old nemesis, Mr. Hornby, was restored. Paterson was again marginalized, "set up for a mark for every knave to shoot at." The last straw for Paterson was that Hornby removed him from Kent, where there were "several honest gentlemen . . . [who] would support [my] integrity," and placed him in Middlesex, under "a supervisor who was well known to have alleged most false things against me. I resigned my employment to preserve my reputation a large sheet would not contain half the injustices done." Paterson then changed careers, opening a school in Gravesend, which he described to Brockman as a "petty subsistence."[31]

In 1695 Paterson, now a schoolmaster, turned again to Brockman in the role of a patriot beleaguered by corrupt men in power. His antagonist this time was the mayor of Gravesend, Walter Nynn. Throughout this episode (discussed above), Paterson (like Woodgate) was able to find protectors who saw high stakes in his struggle. Should Nynn go unpunished, as Tilbury's deputy governor St. Clare put it, "the Jacobites would increase and domineer over all the honest men in the county." Paterson was understandably eager to emphasize in his correspondence that other people saw him as both a man of integrity and a zealous supporter of the regime. He told Brockman that when Walter Nynn called in the attorney George Morton to take an affidavit from Robinson's wife alleging that Paterson was a secret Jacobite, Morton "dissuaded him from saying it was of dangerous consequence for I was known to be quite another person." Likewise, the town's minister repelled an overture from the mayor "to assist him in turning me out," but, said Paterson, "the minister hath instead of taking his part much blamed him for his malice and mismanagement."[32]

Still, the good public opinion of himself that Paterson was so careful to emphasize to Brockman must have had limits and did not protect him. His position was precarious. As noted above, some of the people whom Paterson had hoped to mobilize as witnesses against Mayor Nynn turned against him when they thought he was forging their names to a petition, and speculation ran rife that Paterson himself would soon be arrested and pilloried. Paterson's livelihood now began to suffer: twenty-two scholars were removed from his school. The threatened ruin of his school caused Paterson once again to seek government employment.[33]

Given the picture of self-sacrifice and indefatigable effort that he and his supporters had drawn, it is surprising how long it took for Paterson to find employment. In April he obtained recommendations from Tilbury's deputy governor St. Clare, the excise officer John Baron, and the Earl of Romney, all urging that the present gauger for the Excise in Gravesend, Captain Boad, be removed to make room for Paterson, which "will be in many respects for His Majesty's service and will be [en]couragement to Mr. Paterson and others to perform well their duty to the public." As if to demonstrate his usefulness to the king in Gravesend, Paterson's own letter to Brockman pleading for an excise job included a postscript reporting on the seditious words "reflecting against the Parliament" spoken at the Swan Tavern by the notorious Dover Jacobite Paul Pepper. Nonetheless, in November Paterson was complaining that he had been tricked out of employment.[34]

Finally, a year later, Paterson had left Gravesend for Folkstone (also in Kent) and had found employment in the Customs as a riding officer. We know this in part because Paterson continued to dutifully inform Brockman of seditious words spoken in his presence. In November 1696, he along with three other customs officers made affidavits about the disloyal grumblings of Henry Gerard, minister of Lydd. After that Paterson disappears from view, until April 1700 when he surfaces to provide Brockman with further details about his encounter with Daniel Deery.[35]

Woodgate and Paterson illustrate the difficulties of establishing personal credibility in the public eye faced by informers of consistently Williamite political principle. To some extent the Williamite state came to their aid in that struggle, though not always as fast or as well as they might have hoped. Informers with a more checkered history faced even greater challenges. They too turned to the state not only for reward or mercy but also as a validator of identity or credibility.

Chameleons

"Chameleons" (or "turncoats") had no longstanding record of Whig or Williamite politics, but at some point they remade themselves as supporters of the government (though sometimes also maintaining Jacobite or Catholic identities, ostensibly for the purpose of spying). Chameleons can further be divided into the involuntary and the voluntary. The most obvious and frequent way that a person in Williamite England changed sides to become an informer was under pressure. Such people faced different problems in establishing credibility with authorities and described themselves in different ways than did the turncoat who stepped forward voluntarily to inform on former companions. Granted, the voluntary/involuntary distinction is sometimes muddy: some prisoners, having been forced to turn informer, claimed that they had genuinely changed sides and hoped to make a longer-term career of spying on their former friends.

Voluntary Chameleons and Converts

Trying to figure out the real allegiances and origins of voluntary turncoats was tricky for secretaries of state, and equally so for modern historians. Some would-be spies approached government officials with narratives about receiving apparently spontaneous, unsolicited confidences from Jacobites. John Robinson of Liverpool reported that a papist who mistook him for a co-religionist had confided that King James would return soon and they had one thousand horses ready. Robinson subsequently made a bid to become an informer, telling John Morgan, the governor of Chester Castle, that he was confident he could make great discoveries. James Ormiston similarly said he was mistaken for a Catholic by one Captain Clifford. Sir Ralph Dutton, of Sherbourne, told Trenchard he had been pressed by an unnamed acquaintance to accept a military commission from King James and that he had done so in order to serve the government. Whether these men were really the innocent bystanders they pretended to be, or whether they had already done something to encourage the confidences of Jacobites, is unclear.[36]

The motives of those who admitted to having once been Jacobites are equally unclear. Their change might have been voluntary, forced by Jacobites, or an attempt to avert impending discovery. Edmund Everard presented his conversion as voluntary: he told Nottingham he went overseas to find out

Jacobite machinations "under a sense of having been deluded by 'em." Other turncoats/infiltrators may have already been rejected or at least suspected by their own party before becoming informers. Richard Kingston, the experienced government agent, suggested to Trumbull that Jacobites who had displeased their fellows might be ripe for recruitment by the government. "Mr. Platt at the Jacob's Well in Barbican," Kingston wrote, "has been a very stiff man for the Jacobites, but by taking the oaths [of allegiance] is become their aversion, and under his present discontent might be worked upon if the deputy of the ward would undertake the service."[37]

One turncoat who presented himself as motivated more by rejection from Jacobites than by a positive choice of allegiance to William was Owen Banahan. Before the revolution Banahan had been a quartermaster to King James. In 1689, apparently en route to Ireland to join James's forces, he was detained and imprisoned in Bristol. According to Banahan's later account, it was in Bristol that he first tried to rejoin Williamite society, marrying into an "honest family." But when his wife's relations learned of his Jacobite past, they booted him out. Again casting his lot with James II, Banahan traveled to the court of St. Germain, where he provided King James with a helpful list of Bristol officeholders sympathetic to the Jacobite cause, and then returned to England to deliver messages to James's supporters. But now Banahan's marriage became a problem for his Jacobite friends; James's advisors learned of his "fanatic family" and threatened him. In revenge, Banahan provided Williamite officials with information about Jacobite ciphers and couriers as well as his list of Jacobite-sympathizing Bristol politicians. Petitioning for reward in 1697, he recounted how he had helped to obtain outlawries against several prominent exiles at St. Germain and gave evidence leading to the indictment of the Jacobite courier Captain Williamson and the conviction and execution of Thomas Pike, alias John Latham, for coming from France without a license.[38]

Like Banahan, William Tyrwhit described himself as being motivated by revenge for his "ill usage" by Jacobites, but it took further pressure to make him an informer. As Shrewsbury tells the story,

> Some time since a young gentleman came to me [Shrewsbury] from France, who was bred a papist, served as lieutenant in the fleet till the late King went away, followed his fortunes into Ireland and afterwards went on board the French fleet, where, upon some suspicion, he was seized and

thrown into prison for above two years, and being released came straight away and surrendered himself to me, professing to turn protestant and to be very desirous to revenge himself upon the ill usage he received in France.³⁹

Both Banahan and Tyrwhit, then, were Jacobites who had fallen afoul of their fellows. Their choice to inform gave them new identities. But the choice was not entirely free. Banahan gave his information when he was caught traveling without a pass. Tyrwhit, who had desired to join the fleet as a volunteer, was pushed by Shrewsbury to turn informer, which (Shrewsbury reported) Tyrwhit "undertook very unwillingly, thinking it an employment not very becoming a gentleman." Only after Tyrwhit "did discover some things in which I [Shrewsbury] found him true" did Shrewsbury recommend him for naval service, and he became a midshipman aboard the *Stirling Castle*. For both Banahan and Tyrwhit, then, informing became a way to change allegiance.⁴⁰

Catholics: Taaffe and His Circle

Neither Banahan nor Tyrwhit reflected much on his religious identity. For some Catholic and ex-Catholic informers, however, religious identity was central to their stories about themselves. Not surprisingly, some converts used informing to solidify their change of religious allegiance: betraying former co-religionists would certainly confirm their new identities. Other Catholic or ex-Catholic informers seem to have maintained ambiguous or double identities with respect to both religion and politics. Yet another group of Catholic informers used informing to define an identity as Williamite Catholics, or "honest" Catholics.

One group of borderliners, both converts and "honest Catholics," were linked through their connection to John Taaffe, aka Father Vincent Taaffe, a Capuchin priest who renounced Catholicism in 1688. Taaffe may be best remembered for his role in the Lancashire Plot (see chapter 6), but here I will focus on his religious identity, his informing, and his relations with the "bondenliners" with whom he consorted: Madame Anne-Claude Archer, who was probably recruited by Taaffe to give evidence that the birth of the Prince of Wales in 1688 was a fraud and who stands as a rare example of a genteel Catholic female informant; John Lunt, also a Catholic, the star witness of the Lancashire Plot, and brother-in-law to Taaffe; and Agnes Barker, a Lancashire convert to Protestantism, who with her husband, William, assisted Taaffe as a witness for the Superstitious Lands Commission operating in Lancashire. Because Taaffe's life is documented relatively fully (albeit with maddening gaps), his story can organize the others.

Religious conversion and the ambiguity of religious identity were key elements in Taaffe's story. Taaffe renounced the Catholic religion in the presence of Thomas Tenison, the rector of St. Martin in the Fields, and three witnesses on 15 June 1688. The timing deserves some comment: 15 June was five days after the birth of the Prince of Wales and during the trial of the Seven Bishops. Taaffe was later to say that he chose a moment when the future of English Protestantism looked dim in order to prove his sincerity. This claim, though, might be taken with some grains of salt. By 15 June 1688, the loud outcry against the "warming pan fraud" and swelling of support for the Seven Bishops might have convinced Taaffe that it was a good idea to convert to Protestantism, suggesting the timing of his conversion was driven by pragmatism rather than sincerity. More important, there is no indication that his conversion was public. In March 1689, as the new regime was taking shape, Taaffe asked Tenison to help convince potential patrons and employers of his conversion by giving him "a certificate [of] how I changed before those [sic] times," which suggests his conversion during James's reign had been secret and perhaps that he was suspected of coming late at a convenient time to Protestantism. The lack of publicity is surprising, given that Tenison had staked his reputation on his ability to convert Catholics and would have seen Taaffe's soul as a feather in his cap. The most likely scenario, then, is that Taaffe did renounce Catholicism in June 1688 but kept his conversion quiet.[41]

Not surprisingly, Taaffe was dogged by questions about the sincerity of his conversion. Perhaps rightly so: in August 1688 he was seen serving Mass as "Father Vincent" to a (possibly francophone) congregation at the house of Simon and Mary Conjett in Dover, continuing what seems to have been a longstanding practice. He went to great efforts, though, to combat rumors that he was a Catholic. To demonstrate that the Catholic Church considered his defection notorious, he showed Tenison an excoriating letter sent to him by a Capuchin designed "to make me tremble" and hinted that his life might be in danger. Yet there are signs that Taaffe's newfound Protestantism was not widely known. On 29 March 1689, just a week after showing Tenison how angry and scandalized the Capuchins were at his defection, Taaffe told Secretary of State Nottingham about intelligence he received from an escaped Jacobite prisoner, Captain St. Ange. It is hard to see why St. Ange would have confided in Taaffe if he were aware of his conversion.[42]

What Tenison thought of Taaffe's efforts to prove his sincerity is unknowable as his side of the correspondence is absent. For whatever reason, he disappointed Taaffe as a patron. In June 1689 Taaffe, threatened with arrest by creditors and facing homelessness, lamented "the extremity I am put to for changing my religion." There is no record of contact between Taaffe and Tenison for another five years.[43]

Taaffe found new patrons and new ways to demonstrate zeal in prosecuting Catholics and Jacobites. He testified in the treason trial of Patrick Harding, a laborer residing in his neighborhood of St. Martin in the Fields, declaring that Harding had tried to recruit his help raising an army for King James. That might, again, suggest that as late as November 1689, when Harding made his overtures, Taaffe was still passing as Catholic.[44]

In 1690 Taaffe began what was to be a long and fruitful career as a star witness for the Superstitious Lands Commissions (discussed in chapter 2), using his familiarity with the affairs of Catholic landowners gained while a priest to lend credibility to his testimony. It was from Taaffe that the commissioners "learned" of a great synod for Catholics convened by the papal nuncio D'Adda in London, at which dozens of lay Catholic landowners arranged to convey their estates to the church. His contribution went beyond mere testimony, extending to the use of violence. He threatened the clerk of the commission, a Mr. Lutwych, to prevent him from revealing evidence of corruption. Along with William Barker, he also intimidated the tenants of the Catholic landowner Bartholemew Walmesley in a premature effort to transfer ownership. Barker and John Taaffe, it was alleged, had "struck a thousand terrors into the poor ignorant" tenants of Walmesley's Saintsbury estate by telling them (erroneously) that the estate had been forfeited "and notoriously forced a great number of the more affrighted tenants to enter themselves tenants to the crown and pay monies by way of atturnment" by threatening "that unless they complied the sheriffs of the county should turn them out of possession."[45]

Taaffe also made himself useful to the Earl of Bellomont, who was at the time conducting an inquiry intended to confirm that, as had been rumored, the baby born to James II and Mary of Modena in 1688 had been a fraud, smuggled into the queen's bed chamber in a warming pan. Working with Bellomont introduced Taaffe to what should by now be a familiar practice of casting suspicion on great men in high places. As Bellomont was an ardent Whig, his target was not surprisingly a Tory, Secretary of State Nottingham. In 1690 Bellomont wrote a memorandum accusing Nottingham of undermining his inquiry into the warming pan affair. The smoking gun in the case was thought to be letters written by Thomas Skinner to his daughter Madame de Labadie, the nurse to the Prince of Wales, which had been found in Mr. Skinner's trunk. A messenger had been sent to bring Mr. Skinner from Ireland for questioning. According to Bellomont, Nottingham, in whose keeping the letters had been placed, had ridiculed the discovery, stalled the messenger sent to apprehend Skinner, and leaked the discovery to newsmongers, presumably in order to discredit it or perhaps to give advance warning to those implicated. Taaffe provided Bellomont with information that implicated Nottingham as the leaker. Thomas Skinner's son, Taaffe said, had confided to Taaffe that he had been warned of his father's impending arrest by "a good friend he had in the Secretaries' office."[46]

The fact that Skinner junior so easily confided in Taaffe raises questions about Taaffe's religious identity and public reputation, suggesting again that he may have been passing in some quarters as Catholic. Bellomont's memorandum strengthens the impression that there was some secrecy or confusion about Taaffe's history. To show that Nottingham was responsible for the leaks to newsmongers, Bellomont cited the fact that newsletters written in September 1690 had identified "Father Vincent Taaffe" as having "brought two French priests" to the Earl of Bellomont to help discover papers relating to the birth. Nottingham, Bellomont explained, was the only person among the government officials aware of Taaffe's part in Bellomont's investigation who *also* knew that Taaffe had gone by the name of "Father Vincent." Such a statement suggests Taaffe concealed his past and perhaps that he identified as John and Father Vincent as occasion required. Somehow, however, Taaffe was notorious enough so that in 1691 Bellomont could complain that "endeavors have been used to asperse our witnesses on purpose to discredit their testimony, and particularly Mr. Taaffe is attacked."[47]

Up to this point we have treated Taaffe's Catholic persona as something that fooled Catholic Jacobites like St. Ange or Skinner junior into making confidences in the belief he was one of them. But Taaffe also acted as an intermediary with Catholics who, for whatever reason, *wanted* to share information.

There is fragmentary but compelling evidence that he was especially important as an intermediary between Bellomont and French-speaking Catholics. Tenison's papers contain letters to and from Taaffe in the French language. It is notable that Mary Conjett, at whose house "Father Vincent" served Mass in August of 1688, was known to authorities (who suspected her of abetting illegal travel to Calais) as "French Mary." As noted above, the piece of news that Bellomont complained had been leaked to newsmongers was that Taaffe had brought "two French priests" to give him information about the birth of the Prince of Wales.[48]

It is therefore tempting to think that Taaffe in his work for Bellomont established a connection with another French-speaking informer, Anne Claude Archer, who had made a deposition before John Holt in July 1691 regarding the warming pan baby. She described how her (former) friend the Dame de Longueil, newly arrived from France, had been strangely elated at the prospect of being the means to "chaser l'heresie d'Angleterre" and how she had found her friend "accouchée" in the company of Madame de Labadie and a deputy of the queen's midwife but with no baby in sight. The point, clearly, was that Madame Longueil was the true mother of the warming pan baby. Bellomont described Archer as a "gentlewoman of Lorraine and said to be of good quality" and "a Roman Catholic but no lover of the French King." He further added that she had been "prevailed on" after two months to disclose her knowledge by a person Bellomont employed to speak to her, and that this person had been instructed not to promise her any rewards but to "overcome her with arguments of the honesty and usefulness of discovering a gross falsity and cheat." There is no direct evidence that the person was John Taaffe. Nonetheless, the fact that Taaffe was mentioned by Bellomont in the cover letter as a witness in whose honesty Bellomont had confidence, and the fact that as both a priest and a convert Taaffe was adept at talking about morality, combined with Taaffe's fluency in French, makes it likely that Taaffe was the man who ministered so effectively to Madame Archer's conscience.[49]

Madame Archer can be identified almost certainly as the widow of the engineer Captain James Archer. Her history helps explain why her conscience was available for ministration. Significantly, she was a person comfortable with movement, change of allegiance, and change of nationality. Captain Archer was himself a multiple migrant. After his family had suffered the loss of lands in Ireland at the hands of "the late usurped power" (that is, the Commonwealth), James Archer had been "for twenty four years a captain in the French king's service during fifteen of which he was governor of a place." It was presumably in France that he met Anne, who describes herself as having lived in Lorraine.[50]

In 1669, having also fought against the Dutch, James was invited by Charles II to accept employment as "second engineer of England" in the Tower. His ties to England, however, were fragile. Discontented, he suggested in an angry petition to the Earl of Arlington that he be "given leave to go abroad with a letter of recommendation from the King and begin the world anew." Although James never did leave, his relations with the English government were soured by unfulfilled promises and financial stress. He complained that he was paid less than other foreign engineers who worked with him at the Tower, that a promised grant of £150 per annum promised by the Ordinance Office had never materialized, that all his remaining lands in Ireland had been sold, and that he was "indigent" and his family in a starving condition. After James's death his widow Anne continued to fight for compensation, with mixed success.[51]

Anne Archer's search for royal patronage continued into the reign of James II. Her deposition given before Holt details how she was encouraged by her friend the Dame de Longueil to apply for the position of "berceuse" (rocker) to the future Prince of Wales even before the prince's birth. Despite Longueil's assurances to Archer that she could do her great favors, however, the job never materialized. Perhaps bitterness over a broken promise led Archer to inform. But Archer might also have been motivated by factional struggles among the Catholic priests at court. Archer's director of conscience, Father Mansuet, had been confessor to King James, but he had been replaced because (as he later told Archer) he had refused to give his consent "a la supposition d'un enfant pour estre fait Prince de Galles." He was, moreover, denigrated by his colleagues. When Archer asked another priest, Father Le Blanc, "la raison de la disgrace du dit Pere Mansuet," she was told "brusquement" that Father Mansuet was "un vieux fou" who loved neither his religion nor his prince.[52]

Archer's account shows that the Catholic community even around the court of James II was not monolithic. Her association with priests opposed to the warming pan fraud did not prevent her from being detained by authorities in the winter of 1690–91, for reasons she said she did not know but perhaps simply because she was a French Catholic. However, at least in Bellomont's eyes she carved out an identity as a special kind of Catholic, one who was "no lover of the French King," who could be persuaded of her "duty" to discover the warming pan cheat.[53]

Madame Archer's self-definition as an honest, anti-Louis XIV French Catholic was also on display a year later when she gave an information to one M. Girard, who in turn passed it on to someone who gave it to Secretary of State Nottingham. Her access to information came from her Catholic identity, which let her know what was "confidently reported among papists" and prayed for "in all popish meetings and Mass houses." Madame Archer told Girard, among other things, that King James was to arrive shortly in London, that an army was organized to rise up in his support, that someone named "Cokeley" was a colonel in one of these regiments, and that "there were abundance of Frenchmen in this town that went to the Prot[estant] churches that were papists to her knowledge, and among the rest she named a Frenchman that lives with Sir Theophilus Oglethorpe."[54]

Madame Archer's information to M. Girard in 1692 provides strong evidence of her connection to John Taaffe: on almost the same day, John Taaffe approached the same unknown intermediary who had taken M. Girard's information. Although his story was more elaborate than Archer's and Girard's, and developed over the course of a week, it coincided with Madame Archer's in some key points: James would be in London in days, there was a Jacobite army ready to rise, one Cokeley was a colonel in that army. Taaffe also made the same point as Archer that thousands of French who pass for Protestants and go duly to the French Protestant churches were really Catholics, and 150 Jacobite officers had lately landed in ports "under the notion of refugiés who had escaped from France."[55]

Taaffe's 1692 information is worth considering in depth. It sheds further light on Taaffe's place at the borders of Roman Catholicism, and it provides a first glimpse of John Lunt, the third member of our group of converts. At the time Taaffe gave it, he was married to a Lancashire woman, Mary Woodward, and letting lodgings in his house on Berry Street. Taaffe in his information claimed that he and his wife were visited in April 1692 by his wife's sister, a papist. She came accompanied by a male companion. Taaffe was later, in his testimony at the Manchester trial in 1694, to identify that companion as John Lunt. At the time, however, and within Taaffe's statement, Mary's sister's companion was first identified as "Captain Blount," but he soon confessed to his hosts that his name was "Widdrington," thereby connecting himself to a well-known Northumberland Catholic and Jacobite family. Widdrington (alias Blount, alias Lunt) told Mary Taaffe on 21 April 1692 that King James would be in England in a few days, that there were 20,000 men in London ready to take arms for him, that most of these were Frenchmen who passed for Protestants but would reveal themselves as Catholics upon King James's landing, which would be near London. Widdrington also hinted to Mrs. Taaffe that several members of the Privy Council secretly supported King James, though he refused to tell her which ones, averring that "it was a resolved thing among them not to trust their secrets to any woman, for . . . all our designs have hitherto been betrayed by women." He further named officers in the forces that were to rise in arms for James (including Cokeley, who had also been mentioned by Madame Archer). He explained that the Jacobites were collecting horses, most of which were "sheltered" by Protestants to evade the laws prohibiting papists from owning horses. He asked Mrs. Taaffe to persuade her husband to pretend to own as his horse a gelding that he, Widdrington, had recently purchased.[56]

The request for a favor was accompanied by an implicit threat: Widdrington told Mrs. Taaffe that the forces that were to rise for King James "would kill man, woman and child that would not be quiet and befriend their designs, but that their orders were not to break so much as a glass window of those that would be quiet and give them no opposition." The Taaffes provided Widdrington lodging, a place to store his weapons and saddles, and eventually a shelter for his horse. But at the same time, John Taaffe communicated what he had learned to an anonymous government agent (who passed it to M. Girard, who passed it on to Nottingham).[57]

Taaffe's information presents challenges of interpretation. What did Taaffe think he was doing when he gave his information to a government agent? Was he passing on what Lunt told him, unedited? Did he believe it himself? It is possible that Lunt gave so convincing a performance as an officer in the secret Jacobite army and that he duped Taaffe into thinking that a Jacobite uprising was at hand. However, the strong probability of a prior connection between Taaffe and Madame Archer, coupled with the overlap in the substance of their informations, suggests Taaffe helped Lunt to construct the story.

Around Christmas 1693, more than a year after Taaffe gave his April 1692 information about "Widdrington," Lunt reappeared in Taaffe's life. This time Lunt presented himself not as a Jacobite but as a turncoat informer. According to a deposition that he gave some time thereafter to Secretary of State Trenchard, Lunt had had a conversion experience of a sort. Lunt said that after the failure of the naval invasion put an end to the plans for an uprising in 1692, he had gone to the court of St. Germain. There he had been recruited to travel back to Dover to take part in a plot to "cut off the Prince of Orange." But en route to England, Lunt became "somewhat troubled in his thoughts with what he had undertaken" and so conferred with "several priests" about the morality of the plan. Some of these, Lunt recounted, "were positively against it, as damnable, and others for it, as meritorious, which difference amongst themselves gave him, this informant, more disturbance," leading him eventually to change his allegiance. Like Madame Archer, then, Lunt stressed the existence of serious ethical divisions among Catholic priests. Also like Madame Archer, Lunt represented himself as a Catholic friendly to the Williamite regime, explaining to Parliament in 1695 that "the King does not desire any man to change his religion." But despite his avowed adherence to Catholicism, Lunt soon joined Taaffe as a witness for the Superstitious Lands Commission operating in Lancashire.[58]

It is likely through their work for the Superstitious Lands Commission that Taaffe and Lunt came to know William and Agnes Barker. This couple's motive and opportunity for informing might well have arisen from the liminal position they occupied between Catholic and Protestant communities in Lancashire. William seems to have been always Protestant. In 1693, after a stint as page to the (Tory Anglican) Earl of Darby, he had moved into the business of trading horses. Agnes was kinswoman to a prominent Lancashire Catholic family, the Dicconsons. She was raised a Catholic and, according to herself, converted to Protestantism in 1693 at around age twenty-seven.[59]

Both Barkers testified in the prosecutions on behalf of the Superstitious Lands Commission in Lancashire that Taaffe had organized, giving evidence to the effect that many of the witnesses whose testimony favored the Catholic defendants in the suit were in fact relatives, tenants, and/or co-religionists of the defendants. Agnes must have been struggling with a major transition in social and religious identity. She testified against people with whom she had recently attended Mass and against the interests of her own Dicconson kin. It was her very membership in the Catholic community that allowed her to describe the ties of kinship, friendship, and dependence that, in her view, had caused witnesses to lie on behalf of the Catholic landholders. At the same time, she was able to demonstrate how thoroughly she made the break by inserting anti-Catholic stereotypes into her testimony. The defendants' witnesses were lying, she asserted, because their priests told them it was not a sin.

Agnes Barker's newfound anti-Catholicism came to the fore when she described her outrage at the behavior of Thurston Stott, a Catholic tenant of the Catholic landowner Sir Thomas Gerrard. According to Agnes, Stott had fallen into conversation one day with herself and her husband. Stott openly admitted that although Thomas Gerrard was reputed to be owner of the Southworth estate in Winwick, he paid the rent to Jesuit priests. Stott also intimated to the Barkers that he might use his knowledge to blackmail his landlords into accepting a reduced rent, declaring that "unless the said priests or Jesuits would be content to receive their rent, out of the money raised by the sale of two cheese [sic] he would do them a displeasure or make a discovery or words to the like effect." The Barkers eagerly reported the conversation with Stott to John Taaffe, who warned them that Stott, when formally questioned by the inquisition investigating lands given to superstitious uses, would deny everything. Much to Agnes's indignation, Taaffe was right: Agnes was "very much astonished" to see Stott deny everything, including having had the conversation with herself and her husband. As a result, Agnes said she was "very much inclined to believe that he [Stott] had or depended upon an absolution from the popish priests or Jesuits." In support of her theory, she added that "he is now in much greater esteem and repute amongst them than he was before." William Barker echoed his wife's story and her view of Catholics in his own testimony, telling how he had heard a priest endorse the bearing of false witness.[60]

The Barkers' testimony shows the complexity of their relationship to the Catholic community. On the surface, Agnes had made a clean break, which the giving of testimony both reflected and perhaps reinforced. Yet under the surface, the Barkers' relationships with Catholics were more intimate, albeit exploitative. As a horse dealer, William was the person with whom Catholics needed to negotiate if they were to have horses at all. According to Agnes, the Catholic gentleman (and Lancashire Plot defendant) Sir Rowland Stanley not only purchased horses from her husband but also tried to get William to hold the horses for him to prevent their being seized. It was also said (granted, by hostile observers) that, being appointed by authorities to seize the horses of Catholics and recusants worth more than £5, he would seize horses under as well as over that value and then sell them back to the owners or to their friends at a profit. The story that William and Agnes told about their conversation with Thurston Stott is striking simply in that it shows they had the conversation with Stott after Agnes's conversion. Perhaps it was Agnes's liminal position that attracted Stott's confidence: if he was contemplating the blackmail of his Jesuit landlords, he might have seen Agnes as a natural ally. Even if the Barkers were lying about their conversation with Stott, their testimony nonetheless tells us that they assumed it would be believable that they conversed with known Catholics.[61]

Further evidence that Agnes had not entirely broken her ties to the Catholic community comes from her testimony before the House of Lords in the aftermath of the Lancashire Plot trial. The question facing Parliament was whether Taaffe, who had initially helped to "discover" the plot but had later sabotaged the prosecution in the case by testifying at the trial that the discovery was a fraud, had been suborned by the defendants, one of whom was Agnes's kinsman William Dicconson. Agnes, now Taaffe's bitter enemy, told the Lords of a conversation she had had with one of her Dicconson relations shortly before the trial. "I was at Captain Dicconson's," she testified, "I said I hear Mr. Taaffe was come in" (that is, changed sides). To which her cousin replied, "Yes, but he cost us dear." Agnes must have expected that the picture of herself casually conversing in the home of her Catholic cousin about how Taaffe had been bribed to change sides would be believable to her audience.[62]

If the Barkers had until 1694 retained a connection with Lancashire Catholics, it is likely that the connection was shattered by the trial and ensuing enquiries. One effect of the trial was to intensify their local reputation as informers. On the eve of the Lancashire Plot trial William Barker was identified as a man who had offered one Mr. Cheshire, a mercer at Warrington, £100 per annum if he would become a witness for the prosecution "and swear what he would dictate to him." Whether it was true or not, the report is evidence of William's reputation.[63]

In the wake of the Lancashire Plot trial, the Barkers seem to have moved into a closer alliance with the Williamite regime and into a more hostile relationship with their neighbors. By September 1695 William had been appointed postmaster in Warrington. In addition, he was an active but perhaps lonely scourge of Jacobites. He undertook the prosecutions of both Matthew Mainwaring, whom he described as "but a mean fellow in the world yet he is very great with the Jacobites," and of Matthew Page, who had come into the marketplace at Warrington to announce (one presumes jubilantly) that King William had been killed.[64]

William and Agnes had by now developed a close relationship with the pamphleteer and government agent Richard Kingston. Kingston was later to incorporate the Barkers' testimony into his *True History of the Several Plots and Conspiracies* (1698) to help prove that the Lancashire Plot had been real. But Kingston and the Barkers had been friendly since at least September 1695, as is shown by a small run of surviving letters. William Barker appealed to Kingston for help financing the prosecutions he undertook and in obtaining an increase in his salary. Kingston in return received information about Lancashire Jacobites, flattery, and even a promise from Agnes of the gift of a "pot of woodcocks."[65]

The letters between the Barkers and Kingston testify not only to the couple's gratitude to the Williamite regime but also to their isolation from their neighbors. When he undertook to prosecute Matthew Page for announcing King William's death, Barker told Kingston that the prosecution "has made me worse hated than before, but while I do my duty I do not value their bad looks." When on 31 August news came to Warrington that the king, far from being dead, had captured Namur, the only celebratory bonfire in the town was lit by William Barker, and (he grumbled to Kingston) "all the companions I had was one mercer and two butcher." In the course of asking Kingston to help him obtain a raise in his post office salary, he further revealed that his unpopularity in Warrington was forcing him to give up his side business as an alehouse keeper. He had, he complained to Kingston, "so disgusted the Jacobites (which is generally all the country) that none of them will come near me and as formerly I vented ale in my house of six bushels a week I now vent not above so much in a month and no one in the town will rent me a house but of an extravagant rate so truly I resolve it may be to give over keeping a public house."[66]

The Barkers, then, became increasingly dependent upon the government as their local ties weakened as a result of their role in the prosecution of the Lancashire gentlemen. The trajectory of their former friend Taaffe, who had changed sides and given testimony on behalf of the defendants, was quite different. Not surprisingly, in trying to establish his credibility during and after the trial he also had to change sides in political terms. Taaffe had up to 1694 cultivated Whig patronage: he had helped Bellomont to attack Nottingham and had used Bellomont's connections to give Lunt access to the Whig Secretary of State John Trenchard. Whigs and dissenters like Aaron Smith, Harry Baker, and the Earl of Warrington had been the major players in the Superstitious Lands Commissions. But as the Lancashire Sham Plot affair became the takeoff point for a Tory attack on Whigs, Taaffe naturally found himself on the Tory side. It became necessary for him, then, to present his past in a way that fit comfortably with his bid for Tory patronage. Taaffe told his story in at least three contexts: at the trial itself, at the later parliamentary inquiry, and in what appears to be a widely circulated manuscript narrative.[67]

Taken together, Taaffe's several accounts of himself reveal what Taaffe wanted authorities and the public to know about him in 1694, when he needed to explain why, after having promoted John Lunt's allegations against the accused Lancashire plotters, he was now alleging that Lunt had made up his stories. He tried to establish his credibility by aligning himself with morality and the Church of England, both of which were under attack by Lunt and his crew. Taaffe opposed his own moral decency to Lunt's lack thereof on several fronts. He explained in the trial at Manchester that in 1692 he had banished Lunt from his house after learning of Lunt's association with two notorious housebreakers. In his manuscript narrative, he emphasized Lunt's bigamy. The Whig Treasury solicitor Aaron Smith, along with Harry Baker (Taaffe's erstwhile colleague on the Superstitious Lands Commissions), loomed large in the narrative as exemplars of the threat to the Church of England. Traveling with Taaffe to Lancashire to investigate the alleged Jacobite conspiracy, both men manifested their hatred of the Church of England with all manner of "atheism, blasphemy and all other sorts of profaneness." Smith "wished for old Oliver again, saying, the times were never so happy as under him, and that he had not so much animosity against the Papists of the Church of Rome, as those of the Church of England, for they were for monarchy and hierarchy." Smith had also colluded to cover up Lunt's bigamy: when Lunt had been arrested upon a complaint by one of his wives, Smith had come to Lunt's defense, bailing him out, hectoring, and "threatening what he would do" to the woman "for taking up the King's evidence." Baker gleefully anticipated that the discovery of the Lancashire Plot "would make a thorough Reformation, and down Bishops and Cathedral laws," for (said Baker) "we can never be happy whilst there is a bishop or minister of the Church of England left."[68]

Playing to Anglican and Tory prejudices required Taaffe to rewrite aspects of his past, in particular his work with Bellomont. Although Taaffe in his trial testimony and manuscript narrative acknowledged a longstanding relationship with Bellomont, he mentioned nothing of his role in Bellomont's inquiry into the birth of the Prince of Wales, explaining only that Bellomont had procured him a pension because his father had been killed in the king's service. He further suppressed his earlier history as an informer. When he described his 1692 encounter with Lunt/Widdrington, he did not mention that he had pretended to cooperate with "Widdrington" with the intention of informing on him to a government agent. Instead, he said he had vehemently refused to help Widdrington get a recommendation from Mr. Dicconson to take to France, declaring that he "would not meddle with anybody that was friend to King James" and that he had offered to help Widdrington find a job under the Williamite regime only if he would take the requisite oath of allegiance.[69]

Also missing from Taaffe's story in 1694 was any hint that he had ever, himself, accepted the premise that great men in government like Nottingham could conspire against it. Instead, he said in his narrative that he had believed Lunt's story about the Lancashire Plot until Lunt began to name "such honorable persons" as (among others) the Marquis of Carmarthen, the Duke of Devonshire, the Marquis of Halifax, and the Earl of Nottingham! It was then, Taaffe explained, that "I thought their [Lunt's] plot a fiction, for I could not imagine those men should plot against the life of the King, that had hazarded their own to bring him to the throne."[70]

Taaffe thus completely reversed his earlier attitude toward the government. Instead of accusing great men in power of suppressing plots or being themselves plotters, he maintained that unscrupulous informers routinely charged innocent persons with treason for political ends. The picture of state officials, especially Trenchard, as being too credulous about plots fit well with arguments that had already been made before the trial and which were to become part of the subsequent Tory narrative about it.

We get only short glimpses of Taaffe after 1695. He was briefly arrested after the Assassination Plot, perhaps because his betrayal of Lunt at the trial of the accused Lancashire plotters made it seem like he was now part of a Jacobite conspiracy himself. He was considered a person of interest by Secretary of State John Ellis, who asked the customs officer Captain Barron to search for him. It is possible that the combination of his testimony in the Lancashire trial and his troubles with the government earned him the trust of Lancashire Catholics, who gave him an annuity in gratitude. But as always with Taaffe, there was more than one side to his identity: he seems to have also been working against Catholics as a government spy. In 1697, Solomon Smith of Liverpool and his friend Thomas Davis masqueraded as Catholics in order to obtain intelligence about Lancashire Catholics. Keeping Secretary of State Ellis informed of his progress, Smith noted that he and Davis routinely met with Taaffe at night "in a wood near Standish, where he gives us all the intelligence he can learn."[71]

The Catholics and ex-Catholics discussed in this section all used informing to redefine religious identity or to negotiate an unstable position. Informing could excuse ambiguity or hypocrisy: it was possible to justify being two things at once if it was in service to the state (most spectacularly in Taaffe's case, perhaps also in Agnes Barker's). For the two consistent Catholics, Lunt and Madame Archer, informing was the means to forge an identity as the good rather than bad kind of Catholic. These informers sought out the Williamite state as an audience to aid them in the process of self-definition and self-transformation.

Prisoners: Involuntary Turncoats

Not all "conversions" were voluntary. The largest category of side-changers were those who were forced to change sides. Much of what the Williamite government learned about their enemies came from people who gave information or testimony under some kind of pressure. After Mrs. La Fore of Dover was detained by authorities, Shrewsbury directed the mayor to discharge her but to caution her that to avoid future trouble she would be required to give notice of suspected persons coming to her house. Similarly, in 1692 Nottingham directed the mayor of Rochester to prosecute one Mrs. Nash (for an unspecified offense), "unless she makes a discovery." At the extreme end of the spectrum was the threat of death. The printers William Newbolt and Edward Butler, convicted of treason for publishing copies of King James's *Declaration*, saved their lives by becoming witnesses against Henry Griffith, who (according to witnesses at their own trial) had been seen at their printing house asking for copies of James's *Declaration* to be made. Many coiners and some highwaymen obtained reprieves, or tried to, by giving information. Even prisoners who were executed, like Anderson the printer, were at least rumored to be giving information.[72]

The coerced informants and prisoners discussed here had much in common with the chameleons and turncoats discussed above. Their "real" commitments are often obscure (to contemporaries as well as historians). They often tried to maintain contradictory allegiances and to establish credibility in the eyes of the Williamite state without losing a reputation for honor among Jacobites. This section examines how some prisoners responded to that challenge. It is necessary first, however, to describe the conditions under which negotiations between prisoners and the state took place.

Negotiations between authorities and Jacobite prisoners were watched intently. Jacobite visitors to prison tried to assess and prop up the resolution of their detained companions. After John Crofts was put into the custody of messengers, the Jacobite "Mrs. Brown" reported to her husband abroad that Croft "has been examined before the secretary and they design to make an evidence of him," although Crofts himself seems to have been saying otherwise: "He cries that he knows nothing and that he's an honest man and truly will not tell lies for all the world." Her letter offers clues as to why she and her fellow Jacobites might be skeptical of Crofts's loyalty. In addition to demanding money he said he was owed, Crofts "desired me to give him money for a suit of clothes," but she declined to pay him while he was in prison, fearing "he would but drink it out."[73]

Matthew Crone put on a more impressive show. His exchanges with his Jacobite visitor, Mrs. Alithea Clifford, were anxiously recorded by the Earl of Clarendon, one of the people against whom Crone (Jacobites feared) might be induced to provide evidence. When Mrs. Clifford went to see Crone after he was convicted of treason, "he said he was too young to be a martyr, and she believed that rather than die he would tell all he knew." But the next day, Clarendon noted with relief, Mrs. Clifford said, "Crone was in a better humor and talked courageously." That Crone confessed, though not the actual contents of that confession, became publicly known. Narcissus Luttrell, wondering whose information had led the government to take up several men for conspiracy on 22 June 1690, noted that "some think [it was] Crone, others think Gadbury."[74]

The public (and not just the Jacobite public) was conscious of the negotiations between prisoners and authorities. Lord Preston's waffling was an open secret. As Luttrell put it in his diary, Preston "is very busy in writing in the morning (some think a discovery of the plot) and in the afternoon burns it and drinks with his Jacobite friends." Anne Merriweather's progress was eagerly followed by Williamites and Jacobites alike. While awaiting trial, she had let it be known to her friends that she intended to "die a martyr" rather than name her accomplices. Speculation ran rife following her conviction as to whether the prospect of death by burning would shake her resolution. Opinions varied: one newsletter reported that "she continues obstinate and will not be wrought into compliance," but Luttrell heard the same day that she "has declared this afternoon she will discover her accomplices and those that set her on work, provided she may have her pardon."[75]

Public awareness of negotiations between the state and potential prisoner-informers made credibility a complex problem for both parties. Government officials worried that criminals, already problematic as witnesses, would be more problematic if the public knew they had traded information for clemency. The agent Richard Kingston showed some sensitivity on this point when, informing Trumbull that three owlers now in the messenger's custody were available to be interrogated, he assured him that "if it be objected they are prisoners and hope to save themselves by this recrimination, I will help your honor to twenty more witnesses." When one Mr. Bateman and his wife were sentenced to death in Flanders for desecrating and robbing a church, they offered to reveal a plot against William; although they managed to save their lives, Shrewsbury thought them useless as witnesses as "they appear to be both people of such a character, and some things they say seem so improbable, that though they have had the good luck by these means perhaps to save their own lives, I think they ought not to take away the life of anybody." The mercy shown to the Batemans may have damaged the government's credit. Robert Ferguson, the Jacobite pamphleteer, held them up as examples of the questionable informers upon whom the government (he claimed) routinely depended.[76]

If credit was central to the survival of the regime, it was even more central to the survival of prisoners. Their lives depended on being believed by government officials, yet their circumstances made their credibility hard to establish. The very fact that they were known to have informed under pressure might cast doubt on what they said. Moreover, a prisoner who had given information in exchange for a reprieve might be threatened again with execution by officials who believed that he or she had withheld something. For this reason, prisoners who would turn informer to save themselves had not only to give information but to demonstrate repeatedly that it was true, valuable, and complete. Their survival might also hinge on whether they were willing to testify in court. But again, their value as legal witnesses could be compromised by the fact that they had been prisoners. The negotiations between prisoners and government officials were for these reasons lacking in clear ground rules or guarantees.

Establishing credibility was especially vexing for prisoner informers because they were concerned with more than one audience. They wished to be believed by government officials, but they did not want Jacobites to see them as disloyal or dishonorable. Some prisoners wanted to retain the confidence of Jacobites because they intended to remake themselves as spies for the government. Others, less calculating, simply needed to maintain a sense of personal honor. It is not always possible to tell the difference between the two groups. In either case, however, the Williamite state became the audience for and validator of the informer's honor-preserving narratives. In that sense, whether they were sincere about changing allegiance or not, these prisoners found themselves dependent upon the state.

Lord Preston, whose waffling Luttrell so amusingly commented upon, exemplifies some of the strategies coerced informers used to preserve their honor by constructing a new relationship with the state. Preston repeatedly insisted that he entirely depended on and was assured of the king's mercy, thus downplaying the uncomfortable fact that he had won a series of reprieves by turning informer. When pressured by officials who thought he was still holding back information, Preston became indignant at their lack of trust in him, asserting his own confidence in the king's mercy to argue that his information had not been given in any hope of a pardon. "I did never pretend to make any terms in favor of my life before my confession," he insisted, but had rather "truly and sincerely" confessed all he knew, "relying upon his Majesty's clemency, and the hopes that had all along been given me of life, and indeed in my own construction, did almost amount to an assurance." Preston's adaptation of religious language here is fascinating: just as the elect were assured of God's mercy although they have done nothing to deserve it, so Preston has lived with assurance of William's mercy given so freely that he would have spared Preston without requiring a confession from him. Thus Preston's confession was given voluntarily and must be sincere. Perhaps Preston thought the king would be flattered by the structural alignment of himself to God. But whether that flattery would have won the authorities over is a moot point. Preston did give further information and was finally pardoned. His efforts not to be seen as someone who would trade information for clemency are especially poignant, as he failed to convince his fellow Jacobites of his integrity. His political life at an end, he devoted himself to a translation of Boethius, with whose suffering he identified.[77]

Matthew Crone faced even more complex challenges in preserving a sense of honor. He simultaneously tried to convince authorities that he had changed sides to become a loyal Williamite and that the faith of Jacobites in him was still so firm that he would be able to spy on his former companions. Crone's imprisonment in 1690 had provoked anxiety in the Jacobite community. Having acted as a courier between St. Germain and English Jacobites, he was in a position to name contacts and accomplices. After his conviction in June, Crone told authorities enough to obtain a series of reprieves, but not enough to be released or pardoned. Lord Preston's confession in May 1691 renewed the government's interest in Crone, whom Preston had mentioned. If Crone could be brought to corroborate Preston's testimony, it would greatly strengthen the case against persons Preston had named (the Earl of Clarendon, James Graham, William Penn, Lady Dorchester). Government officials arranged for a confrontation, in which Preston (whom Crone had denied knowing) recognized Crone, which in turn led Crone to offer the government new material. In return, Crone was immediately released from close confinement and allowed to return to the press yard, to "eat, drink, and converse as formerly." He was also given another reprieve and a promise from his interrogators of "interceding for his pardon."[78]

Having turned informer, Crone now enthusiastically changed sides, affirming, "I have but lately engaged to serve the government, but no private gentleman now employed will serve more faithfully than I." In addition to informing, Crone offered to keep authorities apprised of what he learned from Jacobites who came to visit him in prison. But performing this service in turn depended upon the continuing trust of the Jacobites in Crone himself. Strangely, Nottingham became Crone's confidante as Crone became increasingly enraged by the fact that his erstwhile companions suspected him of having informed. When his Jacobite visitors asked him what he had told authorities, Crone told Nottingham, "All that I said in answer . . . is that I wondered what grounds people could have to suspect a man that had been so faithful to them; that I thought it very impertinent of any one to give their opinions of me in that manner upon a sinister imagination." He underscored the point a month later with an ostentatious refusal to take money that his Jacobite friends sent him, saying, "I would receive no person's moneys that held me under such apprehensions as they had been please[d] to do."[79]

Crone's refusal to take money from his Jacobite friends was in part a ploy to get money out of Nottingham, to whom he had previously expressed a fear of "falling under the disgrace of wanting bread." But he seems to have been just as concerned with maintaining an internal sense of honor even in the act of betrayal. In describing his refusal of money, his thinking took another twist: he was not just putting on a show of indignation for the Jacobites but living by his own moral code, for "to receive money from people I act against is contrary to my principles."[80]

Nottingham became the primary audience before whom Crone affirmed that he had been and deserved to be trusted, even by Jacobites. His written narratives given to Nottingham emphasized the trust and even intimacy that Crone had enjoyed in Jacobite circles. For example, Crone described a consultation at the house of James Graham (Lord Preston's brother). Going into an upstairs parlor, Crone and a companion found the Lady Dorchester, commonly known to have been the mistress of James II, asleep in a chair by the fireside. The group commenced debating about whether King James should stay in Ireland or attempt an invasion. Dorchester firmly expressed herself to be of the opinion that James should try to come back to England.

> My Lady drawed her chair close to me, and speaking softly to me, begged that I would not give the King any other advice than to come away [from Ireland] speedily. Some of the company apprehending what her Ladyship said to me, occasioned a laughter among them, saying something to this purpose, that the Lady Dorchester was clearly for having the King's person as near her as might be.[81]

The sharing of a wistful laugh with the king's mistress and her male friends over her longing for her absent lover is one of several charming, intimate vignettes in Crone's written informations. The secretaries of state would also have read about the dislike between Lady Oglethorpe and Mrs. Alithea Clifford and about how Crone and Mrs. Clifford obtained wet balls of laundry powder from a shop at the old Exchange and hid documents inside of them. None of these stories were essential to the security of the Williamite regime. Taken together, they were essential to Crone's ability to present himself as someone intimate with and completely trusted by Jacobites; comfortable informality with Jacobite women in particular seems to have been an important indication of Crone's status as an insider. His narratives did not simply ask the secretaries of state to trust his information but to trust that he was trusted by Jacobites. Perhaps, one might speculate, he was trying not only to convince the secretaries of state but also to convince himself.[82]

Gender and the Informer

Crone's stories about the sexual jesting with Lady Dorchester and buying wet washballs with Mrs. Clifford invite some discussion of the sometimes striking invocation of gendered stories and imagery in discourse by and about informers. The defense of sexual "honesty" could reinforce or stand in for the defense of other kinds of honesty that were rendered vulnerable by the act of informing. Moreover, gender distinctions have been a primary means by which societies define and enforce boundaries; in turn, discomfort about the clarity of boundaries can be expressed metaphorically as anxiety-inducing ambiguity of gender. That may explain why Titus Oates's sexual interest in other men became a focal point for his critics: his "sodomy," as Paul Hammond has brilliantly argued, disrupted sexual and social boundaries and therefore both expressed and contained the fear of the more significant destruction of order and identity that his informing unleashed.[83]

Some female informers were also attacked in terms of sexual transgression. Elizabeth Cellier, for example, was relentlessly painted as a whore. So too was Mrs. Hansard, who came to James Vernon with an offer to help capture the Irish Jacobite McDonnell. Vernon eagerly passed on the information that Mrs. Hansard had come to England in men's apparel and had a "very cracked reputation in Dublin," that "Colonel Cunningham and Palmer . . . can give an account how chaste she was," and that "I find she has a passion for Mrs. Dixey, her kinswoman." When informing Shrewsbury that Mrs. Hansard planned to lure McDonnell to a meeting with her at Covent Garden Piazza, where soldiers would arrest him, Vernon remarked, "I know not what sort of jilt she will prove at last." Vernon's language left it unclear whether he expected Mrs. Hansard to "jilt" McDonnell by betraying him or to "jilt" Vernon himself by not following through, but since "jilt" meant "prostitute," it sexualized her actions either way. Because female informers straddled the boundary of private and public, or because the trade in knowledge was associated with the trade in sex, informing by women could carry a sexualized stigma.[84]

Vulnerability to sexualized attack, however, did not prevent women from giving information to the government. Many did, and did so in ways that indicate gumption. The illiterate servant Anne Brown signed with her mark a deposition concerning suspicious remarks made by Christopher Clapham, Esquire, apparently undeterred by the gap in status between them.

Bob Ferguson or the Raree Show of Mamamouchee Mufty. Satirical portrait with the recognizable face of Titus Oates, highlighting the ambiguity of the informer's religious, national, sexual, and class identities. Although Oates appears to be the subject, the title implicates Robert Ferguson, another Whig associated with Shaftsbury whose true allegiance was, like Oates's, hard to pin down. "Mamamouchee" connotes both Turkishness and false gentility: it is the fake honorific title that Molière's pretentious "Bourgeois Gentilhomme" claims to have been given by the sultan. Reproduced by permission of The Huntington Library, San Marino, California.

At the other end of the educational spectrum, Alice Barton, the wife of a clerk, signed with her own name a long account of a political debate between herself and the Jacobite-sympathizing clergyman William Cade occurring in her own house, in which she articulately defended the legitimacy of the new regime. No one seemed to have found that remarkable.[85]

Nonetheless, in some cases a female informer's information was discounted on grounds of gender. As noted above, Elizabeth Webb, the proprietress of the Saracen's Head, was reviled by Mayor Nynn as such a "busy gossiping slut that she ought to have her license taken from her for coming to declare what her guest had said." The widow Elizabeth Wattell of Maidstone was a person of sufficient status that the incumbent MP Thomas Bliss came to her "for her interest for Parliament men." She answered to the effect that King William must not like the current Parliament, or he would not have sent them home. Bliss shot back that the king was a "usurper" and "arbitrary as the K. of France was." Wattell gave a deposition to the mayor about Bliss's words, which ultimately attracted the attention of Secretary of State James Vernon, and Bliss was prosecuted. However, Wattell's gender, as Attorney General Edward Northey warned Vernon, did present some difficulties in mounting an effective case. In a letter to Vernon, Northey noted that "there is but one witness, and that a woman," and "it may be a question whether she will have so much credit with a jury as on her single testimony to convict Bliss."[86]

The twenty-six trials for speaking seditious words held at the Old Bailey during William's reign reveal both a surprising gender equality and some important ways in which female witnesses were treated differently. In eighteen of these cases, the gender of the witnesses was not indicated. Of the remaining eight trials, there were five in which the prosecution witnesses were male and three in which they were female. The gender ratio seems surprisingly even. Yet there were striking differences in the way the reputations of male and female witnesses were discussed. In two of the five male-witnessed cases, the reputation of the witness(es) was not discussed at all. In another two, it was mentioned that the witnesses were drinking; in one of these the defendant was also drunk, and the point seems to have been made more as an explanation than as an attack on credibility. The reputation of only one male witness, a former servant who had been dismissed by the defendant for "ill behavior," was seriously attacked.

By contrast, in the three trials where the prosecution witness(es) can be identified as female, the reputation of each one was attacked in court. Ann

Knot allegedly said in the presence of Mary Skinner, "God Damn King William I would clip his ears for a groat if I could come near him," but Skinner's testimony was disregarded when Knot brought a witness to prove there was "a grudge betwixt them ... for that Skinner was jealous of the prisoner." Sarah Ghoste, a defendant, was also able to convince the court that the women who heard her say "King William was the son of an Whore" had a "spite against her, because they had been at law together" and like Ann Knot was acquitted. The only female witness in a case that ended in conviction was the exception that might prove the rule. Defendant Jacob Duchfeild claimed that the unnamed woman "swore against him out of malice, because he would not yield to her unlawful desires." The witness's husband, however, "stood by her in court" and asserted that "she was no such person." In this case, alone of the three, the defendant was convicted.[87]

Such cases underscore the absence of a level playing field for female informers. All women were disadvantaged, although some women were disadvantaged more than others. Married women (Alice Barton and the witness against Duchfeild) who had husbands to back them up fared better as witnesses.

The cases also call attention to the complexity of the definition of female reputation. Sexual transgressions were implied in many of the slurs, but a woman's reputation could not necessarily be reduced to sexuality. Two of the women described above who suffered attacks on their reputations were not attacked for sexual transgressions per se: in Ghoste's case the issue was a previous law suit between women, and Mary Skinner was accused of holding an unspecified "grudge" involving "jealousy" against Ann Knot (which might be sexual jealousy, but might not). Walter Nynn's epithet "busy gossiping slut" directed against Elizabeth Webb was also, like the charge of "jealousy" against Ann Knot, open to more than one reading. "Slut" had connotations of both whoredom and dirty housewifery; given that Webb was an innkeeper, the latter could be just as devastating as the former. Still, the fact that even the slurs that were not necessarily sexual carried a possible sexual meaning or edge to them reinforces the initial point: female informers, already vulnerable to the charge of political transgression in the sense that they at least took part in a conversation where seditious words were spoken, were further open to charges of sexual transgression as well.

Their own vulnerability to charges of sexual transgression might explain why so many female informers made a point of commenting on the sexual misdeeds of others, as if to implicitly establish their own virtue. Thus, an anonymous female correspondent from Kent made clear to the Earl of Dorset that Madame Lupin was a "slut" who "went up out of this country great with bastard not many years ago" and "has some correspondence with ill men for no good ones will have anything to do with her." Anne Hancock's information to Wildman about Mr. Whitfield included the salacious tidbit, "His whore [was?] out of a little bawdy house her name is Juxon but goes for his wife and by his name."[88]

Male informers could be associated with sexual transgression as well. Oates has already been mentioned. Colorful slanders, too, were directed against Richard Kingston. He was accused by Robert Ferguson of polygamy in 1694; in 1700 Matthew Smith repeated the charge in his *Reply to an Unjust and Scandalous Libel* and added in rape and sodomy. The male informer Aubrey Price was described as having initially a feminine appearance, such that (according to James Vernon) he was taken "for a woman in disguise."[89]

Such images of gender ambiguity were put forward by commentators in conjunction with doubts about the informer's credibility. What about images put forward by male informers themselves? Male informers might well have been eager to establish themselves in the eyes of others as proper men playing conventional masculine roles, as husbands and fathers who could govern and provide for a family. However, what male informers said about themselves suggests that the act of informing itself was in tension with that role; insofar as male informers tried to claim masculinity, they also destabilized its meaning.

"Patriotic" male informers inevitably confronted a contradiction between the ideal masculine role of patriarch/householder and the role they embraced as zealous supporter of the new government. The contradiction is evident in many petitions submitted to the government by informers for compensation, wherein the imminent starvation of a family was a common trope. Although this strategy emphasized their position as husband and father, it also required them to admit to *failure* as husbands and fathers.[90]

Some men who fell into the "patriotic informer" category saw that failure as a virtue and displayed the suffering of their family to demonstrate their allegiance to the government. Joshua Bowes declared himself willing to part with his beloved wife and children for the king's sake. Robert Paterson also implicitly placed loyalty to the state above loyalty to the family when he described to Brockman how, after he had resisted bribes from the brewers, the brewers had turned to his wife.

> [When] the other brewers could not prevail with me they ploughed with my heifer for my predecessor's wife brought her acquainted with the brewers' wives who told her what had been done by others and what advantages I might make of my employment and made my wife like Job's passionately charge me with my folly that I did not take the like care of my family as others of theirs which made me tell her if she was not satisfied with what I was honestly able to do she must go look for better maintenance, an answer as unpleasant to her as to her clients.[91]

This unusually frank narrative of marital discord was meant to restore Paterson's standing as a responsible husband even as he conspicuously failed to do what would have been considered the most essential husbandly task of keeping his wife in line. Intriguingly, it echoes a pattern that Ann Hughes has identified in the printed narratives of the mid-century Leveler John Lilburne, in which a man's sense of political duty trumps his obligation to ensure his family's comfort, leading to conflict with his wife. In fact, Paterson's plight seems more extreme than Lilburne's, in that he admitted that he failed to reform his wife with his reproaches and hinted that he was ready to cast her off. Loyalty to the government legitimated what must have been controversial behavior.[92]

A comparison of Paterson's narrative with Lilburne's may lead us to posit a shift in what constituted acceptable behavior for men. Some zealous supporters of the regime embraced alternative ideals of masculine behavior in which uxoriousness was suspect and family seen as a hindrance. When John Macky the riding surveyor (discussed in chapter 2) became a widower, he told Secretary of State John Ellis, "I am sorry for the loss of the woman who was as good as women generally are, but not so much for the loss of the wife, seeing there is certainly no happiness comparable to the tranquil liberty a man enjoys single." To some extent, the king's own behavior might have made it possible for his supporters to imagine freedom from family obligations as an ideal. Although the conjugal love between William and Mary was made much of for propaganda purposes at the time of the 1689 settlement and again at Mary's death, William was away from home during much of the marriage, and by the late 1690s (when Macky wrote) he was indeed enjoying the "tranquil liberty" of a single man. It is possible, then, that the patriot male informers discussed here did not see themselves as "failing" in a patriarchal role but rather as embracing one possible ideal of masculinity in a context where ideals of masculinity were shifting and contested.[93]

Male informers used gendered representations in a variety of different ways to solve the problems inherent in trying to establish credibility while being an informer, and hence inherently untrustworthy. Matthew Crone, for example, can almost be said to have feminized himself, as in his story about buying washballs with Mrs. Clifford. However exceptional and weird the representation, his example can stand as the exception that proves the rule: he invoked feminine, domestic images not to establish himself as a loyal Williamite but rather to underscore his intimate access to Jacobite inner circles.

John Taaffe made use of gendered representations in yet a different way. His wife Mary played a conspicuous part in his 1692 deposition describing his first encounter with John Lunt alias Widdrington. In part, Mary was prominent because her Catholic connections helped Taaffe to maintain a relationship with the Catholic community. But she was also of obvious rhetorical value. Her presence in the narrative helped Taaffe establish a new kind of masculine identity, as a head of household rather than a priest, in a way that enhanced his credibility and licensed his informing. Using Mary as a foil, Taaffe showed himself to be conscious of his position and authority. When Lunt/Widdrington came to Taaffe's house in 1692, he confided initially in Mary but refused to tell her which members of the king's Privy Council were secret Jacobites, averring that "it was a resolved thing among them not to trust their secrets to any woman, for . . . all our designs have hitherto been betrayed by women." Taaffe, by contrast, was able to learn the secret: Widdrington "having first conjured him as he was a gentleman," told Taaffe that one of the traitors in the government is "Lord G." The glimpses Taaffe gives us of his marriage show his mastery both of his wife and of masculine knowledge. When Widdrington told Mary the name of a French general currently hiding in London, Taaffe tells us, Mary forgot the name, but "her husband bidding her recollect the name if she could" listed all the French generals he could think of, until Mary was able to recall that the general was Catinat.

Taaffe also used his wife rhetorically to solve the problem of how to acknowledge apparently fearful actions without being discredited by them. Taaffe described how Mary, hearing Widdrington's threat that "they would kill man, woman and child," was "startle[d]" and "said she hoped there would be no danger for her husband and her." Mary's fear in turn legitimated Taaffe's own: it allowed the reader to believe that Taaffe's cooperation with the Jacobite Widdrington was undertaken for the honorable purpose of protecting his family. Taaffe depicted himself as managing to extract yet more information from

Widdrington by playing the role of nervous householder. To learn where the Jacobite forces were aiming their attack, "Mr. Taaffe pretending fear asked the captain's advice whether to get out of harm's way it were not best for him to remove into the City" and thereby learned from Widdrington that the City was the main target. Mary's presence seems essential to Taaffe's ability to manipulate fearfulness as a strategy to spy on Widdrington, or to recount that spying, without losing face. Had Taaffe expressed fear for himself rather than his family, he would have appeared weak.[94]

In many cases, informers often found themselves in a tenuous relationship to established ideals of behavior: informing itself almost by definition carried distasteful connotations of treachery to former friends, put an individual's credibility under scrutiny, left women and men alike open to sexualized insults, and embroiled men in an uncomfortable choice between responsibilities to the family and responsibilities to the state. That recognition in turn helps us to underscore the importance of the state in the lives of informers.

Although (as suggested above) the Williamite state might have helped to generate some alternative models for male behavior, it obviously did not create the notions of proper roles for men and women that operated in the narratives of informers, nor did it invent the idea that people should appear upright and trustworthy. Its role in the lives of informers was not to dictate ideals of behavior. But by being present as an audience and conferring a stamp of legitimacy on informers' narratives, it did enable informers who might otherwise be anxious about their lack of conformity to those ideals to understand themselves in a more flattering light. Sometimes representatives of the Williamite state were the informer's only sympathetic audience. Richard Kingston helped Agnes and William Barker to deal with alienation from Catholic neighbors and kin, and William Brockman helped Robert Paterson to account for his marital difficulties in a way that did not undermine his sense of masculinity.

Thus if we wish to explain why people informed, we might look beyond motives of money and self-preservation and consider the ways in which the Williamite state was a resource and audience for people in the process of constructing or transforming identities. In some cases, the very need to reconstruct identity was caused by the act of informing itself. In others, a person may have been engaged in a troubling change prior to becoming an informer. It is often hard to decide which of these two scenarios best describes a given case. What matters most for our purposes is that the credit of the informer came to be closely connected to the credit of the state. That point in turn has important implications for how we assess the "modernity" of the Revolution of 1688. If one mark of a modern revolution is that it transforms "subjects" who merely submit to rule by the state into citizens who identify themselves with the state and construct their sense of self through service to the state, then the informers discussed in this chapter seem to have experienced 1688 as a modern revolution.

CHAPTER 5

Credit and Credibility in the Worlds of Richard Kingston

Richard Kingston was a paid intelligence agent, a pamphleteer, and a figure of enough notoriety to symbolize the ambiguities of the government's credit in his own person. His life and writings provide a rare opportunity to look at how knowledge of conspiracy was made and presented to the public as well as a glimpse of the struggle with personal credibility that a person who made and presented that knowledge faced.

As a pamphleteer, Kingston devoted himself to proving the truth of plot revelations and the trustworthiness of government officials. His *True History of the Several Designs and Conspiracies against His Majesties Sacred Person and Government* (1698), published in the wake of the Assassination Plot, used the undisputed veracity of that plot, as demonstrated by confessions and conviction, to "prove" that the far more dubious Lancashire Plot was equally real and to link that in turn to all other known and alleged Jacobite conspiracies. Kingston further upheld the credit of the government by responding to Matthew Smith's charges that the Duke of Shrewsbury had ignored early warnings of the Assassination Plot (discussed in chapter 3). He was probably the author of a hostile picaresque biography of the informer William Fuller, who had insinuated the existence of treason in high places and accused the Earl of Nottingham of covering up the truth about the birth of the Prince of Wales. In attacking Fuller, then, Kingston was defending the integrity of a former secretary of state (his own employer), and by extension affirming the government's credit. Kingston further defended the government when he attacked the Earl of Peterborough, who had been recalled from his command of forces after alienating England's Spanish allies but whose hyped-up heroism had become a rallying cry for the Marlborough-Godolphin ministry's opponents.[1]

But Kingston was a spy, and spies are by definition liars. If Kingston's reports to the secretaries of state can be believed, Kingston managed to convince Jacobites that he was one of their number in order to attend their meetings and read their correspondence; he even wrote pro-Jacobite pamphlets to learn the identity of their printers. By the middle of the 1690s, Kingston's name was a signifier of duplicity. The Jacobite pamphleteer Robert Ferguson attacked him in two separate pamphlets in 1694. Kingston's history, Ferguson said, began with "forging his own priestly orders," moved on to "polygamy, as well as the most prodigious and criminal offenses," and ended with the defrauding of one Sir Samual Astry of several hundred pounds. He alleged that Kingston went about the country in disguise, "sometimes in the habit of a parson, and assuming his characters at another time in lay garb, and personating in one place a physician, and in another a discarded Jacobite officer," all in order to trepan people into speaking favorably of conspiracy to him and so give the government's claim that it was besieged by Jacobites a false patina of plausibility. Not surprisingly, Kingston's employers in the government were not entirely confident of his credibility. Kingston was part of the government's solution to the problem of its own credibility, but he was also part of the problem.[2]

The study of a "life and writings" brings home, in an especially acute way, the epistemological problems associated with the subject and period covered in this book. The prevalence of identity fraud (literary and commercial), the irregularity in the keeping and survival of records, and the deception inherent in informing have all been discussed in previous chapters; these impact negatively the historian's ability to provide a reliable narrative of an individual career in ways to which this chapter calls attention. The tentativeness of the conclusions herein is inevitable, but I hope instructive.

The Good Spy? Styles of Informing

Kingston is remembered by historians as a valuable and trusted government spy, indeed, in the words of Paul Hopkins, "the best agent the government ever had." It is worth asking how Kingston attained that status, if the reputation was earned, and what, if anything, made Kingston different from the unscrupulous plot-discoverers like Matthew Smith and William Fuller whom he attacked. From the papers of some of the secretaries of state whom he served, as well as clues in his published writings and in writings about him,

I have pieced together what I can of Kingston's career. It appears from this evidence that Kingston was indeed *sometimes* trusted and *sometimes* valued, but to different degrees at different times. The nature of his work changed with time and political circumstance, and his credibility with his employers was not always secure. This section looks at Kingston's career, with an eye to what it taught him about establishing credibility.[3]

Kingston began his working life as a clergyman and writer. His publishing career seems to have begun with a sermon preached at St. Paul's Church in 1665, exhorting repentance as a response to the plague then ravaging London. He published more sermons in the 1680s, including a virulently Tory assault on the Rye House plotters, the Whig Exclusionists, and dissenters in general in 1683. How Kingston (or "Dr. Kingston," as he was sometimes known) became a government agent is not clear. It is possible that he used his connection to Lord Lucas, the Governor of the Tower, to bring himself to Nottingham's attention. Alternatively (or simultaneously), it seems he obtained the confidence of King William's favorite, the Earl of Portland; this is suggested by the fact that Nottingham, in correspondence with Portland, referred to Kingston as "your doctor" or "your friend." Nottingham's trust, however, did not come easily. The secretary of state expressed some skepticism in a letter to Portland: "I don't know what to make of your doctor," Nottingham wrote in June 1692, "for Mr. Attorney can get nothing from him upon oath." By August Nottingham was more enthusiastic, telling Portland that Kingston "is very active and zealous and would do great service if there could be found another person to corroborate his testimony." A month or so later, Kingston had obtained financial compensation and perhaps a regular salary, or so he implied in his jaunty promise to Nottingham, "As I eat the King's bread so I am ready if opportunity offers to make a dutiful return."[4]

In the first year or so of his government service Kingston tried out different styles of informing and learned how to make himself a valued agent. Some of these experiments look like dead ends. For example, in 1692 Kingston engaged in making spectacular accusations against men and women in power. After this one incident, he never did it again. Looking at the episode is useful because it puts into relief Kingston's more characteristic and long-term approach to intelligence. It also clarifies what he did or did not have in common with Matthew Smith and William Fuller, the two agents (or self-described agents) against whom he directed such fierce attacks.

Presumed portrait of Richard Kingston, on the frontispiece of his *Pillulæ Pestilentiales; or, A Spiritual Receipt for Cure of the Plague* (London: Edward Brewster, 1665). Reproduced by permission of The Huntington Library, San Marino, California.

Kingston's experiment with spectacular informing began when, in a written affidavit, he accused the Earl of Marlborough and Princess Anne of treason. Such charges were unoriginal and so had the virtue of plausibility. Marlborough had already been suspected and sent to the Tower; Princess Anne's antipathy to her sister Mary, as well as her close friendship with Marlborough's wife, Sarah, were well known. Kingston apparently hoped to make himself especially valuable to Nottingham by offering to testify. At the same time, he pleaded to be allowed to delay giving evidence publicly, lest it compromise his ability to learn more secrets: "This is a critical minute, and if the enemies of the government persevere in their heights, a greater and more ample discovery (I hope) will quickly be made; and therefore for the service of the government I could wish to be a little longer concealed till I can strengthen my testimony."[5]

Kingston's informing here was dramatic, self-dramatizing, and a little dubious. He wrote as if he had unrestricted access to Jacobite inner circles and as if he was so trusted by men and women of great rank that they did not hesitate to spew treason in his presence. From Bath he reported to Nottingham that he had "the honor of kissing the Princess's hand, at which time her Highness was pleased to say she had notice of my coming." He went on to record the princess's rant against William and Mary, her hopes for a French invasion, and even her laughable comparison of herself to Queen Elizabeth I. Kingston swore that the Earl of Marlborough, too, spoke treason freely in his presence, saying that William's government "could not last long; for it was not to be endured any longer, but every good man ought to lay his helping hand to put an end to it." Kingston compounded the drama with a tone of patriotic martyrdom. "Though men under my present circumstances seldom meet with a favorable opinion," he complained to Nottingham, "your lordship hath to do with an honest man, and one that prefers the service of their Majesties and the protestant religion beyond my own safety."[6]

Ironically, when Kingston later penned pamphlets against Fuller and Smith, he ridiculed behaviors that closely resembled his own in this episode: their protestations of patriotism, their propensity to record long orations by Jacobites, their presentations of themselves as being at the center of conspiracy and confidantes of important traitors. Perhaps Kingston's animus against them was related to his own experience with a spectacular style of informing.

As it turned out, Kingston was not called upon to testify against Marlborough, and he never did anything like that again. It is possible that his gambit was so successful that it won for him Nottingham's confidence and a steady salary, at which point it was not necessary to take the risks associated with making spectacular accusations. Or it is possible that the risk of having to testify publicly, thus lessening his potential usefulness as a spy, was too great. Whatever the reason, the rest of Kingston's intelligence was about a different sort of subject and written in a different tone. Instead of presenting himself as a confidante of royal traitors, Kingston learned to talk as if he knew that he was on the margins of Jacobite circles. He made no pretense that his information was comprehensive or that he had caught the chief culprit in the act of plotting. Rather, he seemed to recognize that his reports provided only part of a larger whole. His reports were not about earls and princesses, but about innkeepers, customs officers, postmasters, and printers. They concerned the nitty-gritty details of how Jacobites communicated with one another.

Kingston and the Press

One of Kingston's greatest assets as a spy was his experience as a writer and his familiarity with the world of publishing, including Jacobite publishing. It is hard, in a society where the government at least pays lip service to the idea of free speech, to imagine the degree of distress that the appearance of Jacobite pamphlets provoked in government circles. Thomas Comber, the dean of Durham, described such pamphlets as an "infection, which creeps secretly into the bowels of the nation and may make a sudden and dangerous eruption if not suppressed by a little more severity then hath yet been showed against those who so manifestly attempt to involve us all in blood and ruin."[7]

The appearance of Jacobite pamphlets caused such consternation in part because their very availability suggested the government was too weak to suppress them. Moreover, their publication helped to create a sense that James's return might be imminent. William's invasion of England in 1688 had been accompanied by a well-run public relations campaign, with justificatory pamphlets and declarations distributed at the moment of his landing, and so it would be reasonable to expect that the Jacobites would likewise time the appearance of their pamphlets to go hand in hand with an attempt to recapture the throne. Richard Kingston linked pamphlets with invasion plans when he reported to Nottingham that the Jacobite Robert Ferguson's "history of King William's descent is ready for the press but he says he will not print it until King James is ready to land." One can imagine that the appearance of cartloads of King James's *Declaration* (in which the deposed king exhorted his subjects to return to their allegiance) must have seemed to many people to herald an invasion. For that reason, the printers and distributors of it were savagely persecuted. By keeping alive the hopes that the king would return, the hard core of Jacobite supporters was able to keep the much larger group of soft supporters interested in and attached to the cause.[8]

Kingston was a walking encyclopedia of Jacobite texts and authors. He informed Nottingham, for example, that the writer of *The Humble Petition of the Commons of England to Their Representatives in Parliament* was "Mr. Pitts, a non-jurant clergyman." He went on to keep Nottingham apprised of Jacobite works-in-progress. In August 1692, for example, he reported that "Dr. (George) Hickes is answering Dr. King's book and Mr. Dodsworth is writing the history of the Revolution." In September he identified Mr. [Charles] Leslie as "author of many dangerous pamphlets" and reported that Leslie, too, had "under hand an answer to Dr. King," and a few months later he followed up by naming the printers of that book. In November, Kingston reported, "The libel called *the Substance of King William's Speech*, the mock speech to parliament, and a paper as bad as the worst called *The specimen, or State of the Nation*, were all printed by Capt. Philips, who lives somewhere in Piccadilly, and goes by the name of Major Fox."[9]

Like many other government agents and informers, Kingston was obsessed with the prolific Jacobite pamphleteer Robert Ferguson. He triumphantly wrote Nottingham that he had made Ferguson's acquaintance and planned to bring a witness to their next meeting, where he would encourage Ferguson in talking treason for the sake of collecting evidence against him. Although he failed in this task, Kingston did keep Nottingham apprised of Ferguson's schemes: these included a plan to write pamphlets to be sent into Holland that would sow discord between the Dutch and their English allies, and another scheme to spread an "ingenious lie" that the Prince of Wales (James II's son) had converted to Protestantism.[10]

By using his talents as a writer, moreover, Kingston gained access to Jacobite printers and publishers. As he told Nottingham in August 1692, he wrote a Jacobite pamphlet in order to learn more about the Jacobite press.

> By pretending a paper to print, I was not without hopes of discovering the press, and yesterday was earnestly solicited for it because another was delayed till mine could accompany it. I have finished it, such as it is, . . . I will read it among them tomorrow night for their approbation and then

deliver it to my confident, who, under the pretext of correcting it at the press, shall discover where they are at work before the composer shall be able to set it.[11]

That stratagem ultimately led Kingston to one of his greatest triumphs, the capture and conviction of Anne Merriweather. Mrs. Merriweather had assisted in the distribution of King James's *Declaration* in 1692, and the government hoped that she could be induced to name her accomplices. She resisted pressure throughout her detention and trial, and only when she was convicted of petty treason and sentenced to death by burning did she finally break down and turn informer.

Kingston was deeply involved in all stages of the case. He described in detail how Mrs. Merriweather received wet copies of the *Declaration* from the printer and hung them up to dry in her garret, then delivered them to others to be dispersed throughout the country. He knew her family connections and the hiding places in her house. He provided Nottingham with the name of a friend who might be induced to "peach" her and lists of interrogatories "from which she cannot extricate herself." Kingston also helped coerce Henry South into being a witness for the prosecution. South, Kingston reported, was very uneasy to be made an evidence and "shaked hard to writhe his neck out of the collar; but finding that myself and Mr. Keate, were resolved to accuse him, if he refused to do the government justice, he grew more tame and pliable." Finally, Kingston himself drafted letters to Merriweather, as if from a friend, warning her not to run the hazard of a trial because she could not hope for clemency. His zeal, even sadism, in pursuit of a confession, suggest his deep investment in the project of dismantling the Jacobite press.[12]

Jacobite Communications

Alongside reporting on the way that Jacobites communicated with the public, Kingston explored the many ways they communicated with one another. In order to learn what Jacobites in England thought their military prospects would be, he attended Jacobite meetings, where he met emissaries from the Jacobite court at St. Germain, read correspondence from Jacobites abroad, and helped draft the replies.[13]

Kingston might in this manner have learned of French plans for the abortive invasion, which really did occur in the spring of 1692. He reported to Nottingham that he was introduced to "Mr. Marsh a Benedictine monk" who had arrived from the court of St. Germain and "confirm[ed] the design of invading England this summer, but makes it depend upon a sea fight, in which they [the French] promise themselves a victory." After the French invasion was thwarted at the battle of La Hogue, Jacobites (erroneously, as it turned out) expected another attempt, and Kingston dutifully reported on all of them. Thus, in September 1692 one Mr. Cary had come with a letter from King James promising a descent in winter. Within a month, Kingston found that "the Jacobites do now very warmly discourse their hope of K[ing] J[ames]'s descent in the spring."[14]

Jacobite expectations seemed to be constantly disappointed, and constantly postponed, to the point where Jacobites themselves were confused. Of King James's anticipated descent in the spring, for example, Kingston noted that the report "has not yet gained credit enough with the officers as to encourage them to talk of [en]listing men." Likewise, Kingston wrote in January 1693 that one Colonel Fountaine received a letter describing impressively large numbers of men and ships poised for a French-Jacobite invasion. But Kingston also said that he had been among some of the "most eminent" of the Jacobites, and "though they all say a descent is intended, they deny it will be so early as is generally discoursed, because none of the officers have had notice and they have had no particular commands from King James. They have no other notice to occasion these rumours, except what comes from private persons in correspondence to England." In March Kingston noted that the hope of Scots-led reinforcements from Denmark landing in Scotland and converging with James's invasion from Dunkirk, which he had first reported in January, was now "lost in a fog."[15]

Kingston's reports on what Jacobites thought would happen, then, were not very valuable as military intelligence. But perhaps the accuracy of Jacobite rumors of an imminent landing was not the point, to Kingston nor to the secretaries of state. Nottingham maintained a network of spies in France who provided him with more accurate information than Kingston ever could about the size of the French fleet, the attitudes of the French court to helping James, and where troops might be massing for an invasion. Nonetheless, Kingston's reports mattered because Jacobite rumors and expectations affected the strength of Jacobitism. The continually disappointed and continually revived hopes of a French-Jacobite invasion sustained a community of potential Jacobite supporters, and for that reason they were a threat to the Williamite regime.[16]

That Kingston understood this dynamic, and that he tried to intervene in it, is strongly suggested by a puzzling document in Nottingham's papers, a "copy of a letter" in Kingston's handwriting, apparently written by a Jacobite at the court of St. Germain to a Jacobite in England. Although at first glance the document might appear to be a letter that Kingston intercepted, it is more likely a letter that Kingston himself wrote, with the intent of either printing it or circulating it in manuscript through English Jacobite networks. The "author" of the letter laments the failure of understanding between English and French Jacobites. The French, he explains, have been waiting for the English to organize an uprising before they invade, whereas the English Jacobites are waiting for the French to invade before organizing an uprising. Given that no domestic Jacobite uprising seems at hand, he cautions his English friend not to expect a French invasion in the foreseeable future. It is likely that Kingston composed this letter as a piece of what is today called "disinformation," meant to pour cold water on Jacobite enthusiasm in the hopes that the softer supporters would just give up.[17]

One important lesson that Kingston learned from his surveillance of the Jacobite press and Jacobite communications, then, was that information had a life of its own. It did not have to be accurate to be powerful.

Reform and Policing

Kingston's familiarity with Jacobite networks of communication taught him much about England's leaky borders and poor security. He saw that Jacobite emissaries traveled and corresponded with relative ease to and from the Continent and within England and Scotland. This could in turn be blamed on negligence and corruption in the Customs office, the navy, the Post Office, and among the king's messengers, officers who arrested and detained suspects. Kingston became an active, enthusiastic participant in the project of reforming all these institutions and creating better systems of policing and surveillance.

Both Nottingham and Trumbull were receptive to such projects.[18] Kingston certainly tried his hand at a proposal at least once. Thus, Trumbull wrote to Portland on 25 June 1695 with the details of "Dr. Kingston's project for preventing correspondence with France." It is possible, too, that Kingston was the author of the document in Nottingham's papers entitled "suggestions for an intelligence service" (discussed in chapter 2), which contained the

Kingston-like suggestion that "a good pen be employed (in a concise manner) relating to the affairs of government, to obviate malignant objections and to maintain truth in its own colors; and those prints be sent, gratis, to the several great towns." Another attempt at system building was the up-to-date, corrected list of code names used in Jacobite correspondence that Kingston presented to Trumbull. Noting the addition of two hundred items, he bragged of the usefulness and accuracy of his book and called attention to its novelty, "since no other Minister has had one but you."[19]

Kingston also delivered a systematic analysis of the morals and loyalty of the king's messengers. A long list of messengers and their addresses in Trumbull's papers has annotations by Kingston commenting on the virtues, or more often lack thereof, of each man. Some of the entries alleged simply general incompetence or dishonesty. Gellibrand of Southwark was dubbed "a rattlehead," and Richard Hayward was described as a "careless drunken sot." Peter Tom, according to Kingston, "neither minds nor understands his business," while "I have nothing against [Charles Coachman] but his invincible ignorance and unfitness for office." Kingston also identified a number of scams for robbing both the government and innocent persons in which messengers were involved. Henry Allen, for example, arrested people without warrant and "discharged them again for money without acquainting the Secretary." John King charged prisoners per diem fees for their diet and lodging and then presented a bill to the government for the same expense. In some cases, Kingston suggested messengers were actually Jacobites, such as Frances Clerke, who "keeps company with Jacobites and is much commended by all that party for a very honest man." Because messengers were the first to receive arrest warrants, they were well positioned to warn the targets of those warrants that it was time to escape. Kingston alleged that Ralph Gibbs "hath been often accused by his fellows for betraying them, and for taking money of Mr. Newbury for giving him notice what warrants were issued." Likewise, William Jones was "the common intelligencer to the Jacobites what is done in the Secretaries office," and Robert Knoller "took money thrice of Mr. Stafford for giving him notice there was a warrant against him." Benjamin Morris's "wife is a papist, and communicates all she knows to that faction." Some messengers let prisoners have unauthorized visitors. Charles Morris, for example, "took money of William Canning, Mr. Brett, and Mr. Wilcox to suffer their friends to come to them." Others, like Henry Allen and Richard Hayward, let prisoners escape.[20]

The full range of Kingston's concerns is best seen in his town-by-town account of his trip to the coasts of Kent and Sussex to assess the state of security there. He drew a devastating picture of incompetence, corruption, and treason at all levels. At Dover, he found that a corrupt jailer had allowed four French prisoners to escape. At Margate, a trustworthy officer was unable to stop smuggling because he lacked the power to inspect ships. At Deale, the lieutenant of the castle routinely slandered the government, and "thus are the King's garrisons made sanctuaries for his enemies." Indeed, Kingston elaborated, "I have visited all the castles and forts in these coasts hither, and find everything so much perverted that they are wholly insignificant to the end they are designed to serve." The navy was also unreliable. Kingston heard a story that the king's ships had remained at anchor "and there rode all the time as idle spectators" when the Marquis of Carmarthen's barge was attacked. They "never assisted and said they must not unless they had orders. The like has been done one time or another in all the harbours, merchant men taken out of the harbors by privateers and our own men of war look on the whilst."[21]

Meanwhile, at Foulston (Folkestone), smugglers who carried both contraband goods and Jacobites into England were aided by an inverted incentive structure that rewarded customs officers for looking the other way:

> The owlers [smugglers] do almost what they please, and transport who they please, having always a greater force to accomplish their ends than the king can raise to oppose them; and though the officers know some of the persons, yet dare not prosecute them because the commissioners for the customs will not bear them out, and they are not of ability to follow the law themselves.

The soldiers assigned to patrol the marshes where Jacobites were known to take shelter were just as bad. Kingston reported from Romney and Lydd:

> In this marsh is part of a troop of dragoons, but seldom any officer: and if they are called to assist the King's officers refuse it unless they had command from their officer, who is either not to be found or at too far distance to fetch when he is wanted; some care I think should be taken that the soldiers should assist the officers when called.[22]

Kingston and Politics

Despite its systematic approach, Kingston's report on his journey to the coast had a strong partisan element. It was peppered with jibes at the negligence of John Trenchard, the Whig secretary of state who had succeeded Nottingham and preceded Trumbull (both of whom were Tories). With respect to the impudence of owlers, Kingston observed that what "has lately hindered the seizure of several persons was the remissness of the late Secretary in rewarding such services, but I hope this malady will be cured for the future." Kingston's account of the escape of the Jacobite Edmund Gee also trashed Trenchard, more generally pointing to the existence of corruption at the highest levels of (Whig) government:

> This Gee, a busy bold clockmaker in Rye, was sent over to reside at Bullen [Boulogne] to receive from and transmit intelligence to the party for which he has an allowance from the party in England: and I can prove £6 paid him since he has been in France by Mr. Gribble, a merchant in Rye. . . . Sir John Trenchard was acquainted [of this matter] about five or six months since, and what has made it sleep so long I cannot imagine since I am sure this correspondence does continue. I am told by that party, that colonel Austin in the Admiralty is Gribble's friend. Thus the government is at great charge, and some men at great peril in discovering this commerce, and when they have the offenders and good proof of the crimes they let them go unpunished.[23]

Kingston's careful analysis of cracks in the nation's security thus also worked as a scathing indictment of the Whigs. He played on and inflamed partisan divisions within the government.

The question of how politics affected Kingston's career and writing must be handled with attention to chronology. His party preferences were not consistent. Despite his early expression of Toryism (in his 1683 *Vivat Rex*), Kingston came to support the Revolution of 1688. Indeed, his rather late and admittedly unoriginal *Tyranny Detected; and the Late Revolution Justify'd* (1699) put forward Whiggish-sounding arguments about the right of resistance and the contractual nature of the English monarchy. In an interesting about-face, he lambasted the Tory clergy who (like himself!) had in Charles II's reign urged the divine right of kings and indefeasible hereditary right.[24]

Kingston may also have reversed his allegiance in his choice of patrons amongst the secretaries of state, moving from Tories to Whigs. His first strong relationships were with the Earl of Nottingham and William Trumbull, both Tories; but he later defended the Whig Shrewsbury from Matthew Smith's accusations, even at a time when Trumbull was supporting Smith. Whether Kingston's ideological commitments changed, or whether he just supported whichever powerful men would accept his service, is unclear.

The revving up of party antagonisms was another inconsistent feature of Kingston's career. It was conspicuous in one phase of it; but, like the spectacular style of informing with which he experimented in 1692, it seems to have been something he tried and later dropped. Some of the change can be attributed to the impact of the discovery of the Assassination Plot in 1696. It might also be attributed to a broader shift in Kingston's career, from spying to writing. In Kingston's published work, all traces of party animosity seem to have vanished.

Kingston's tendency to politicize his intelligence was especially pronounced in his correspondence with Trumbull in 1695 and 1696, including his account of his journey to the coast. As shown above, he blamed Whigs and especially Trenchard for letting Jacobites operate with impunity. It is possible that Kingston's animus against Trenchard sprang from his loyalty to his first employer, the Earl of Nottingham, who had lost his job at around the same time that Trenchard was appointed to the secretaryship of state. Widely blamed for the miscarriage of the Smyrna fleet, and further embroiled in a scandal involving the appearance of his signature on forged passes, Nottingham was forced to resign in November 1693, leaving Trenchard in charge. It is unclear whether Kingston continued to work as a spy during Trenchard's term as secretary of state. Very little of Trenchard's correspondence survives. Robert Ferguson, in his 1694 pamphlets attacking the government for the Lancashire Plot prosecutions, anticipated (wrongly) that Kingston would be a witness against the defendants and accused him of luring people deliberately into conspiracy with talk of plots, but Ferguson is hardly a trustworthy source.[25]

Whatever the state of relations between Kingston and Trenchard, the appointment after Trenchard's death in April 1695 of another Tory, William Trumbull, was greeted by Kingston with warm enthusiasm. He aggressively courted the new secretary, whom he praised as "another Nottingham." Meanwhile, he offered Trumbull a paranoia-inducing education in the partisan politics of the secretary's office, drawn from Nottingham's unfortunate experiences. His letters relentlessly conveyed the message that as a Tory,

Trumbull was already under suspicion, as Nottingham had been before him. In May, Kingston wrote Trumbull that his appointment of Francis Winnington, a suspected Jacobite, as recorder of Tewksbury, had led to talk of Trumbull being an instrument of "popery and slavery." In July, he warned Trumbull about William Brockman, the Whig MP and justice of the peace, whom he described as

> an over busy man of the 48 size and cut, that in conjunction with Sir Bazill Dixwell has a great hand in placing and displacing officers of all sorts; he has treated your honor [Trumbull] very untowardly in this country, and made very sad prognistications of ill things that are to happen upon the management of so great a tory.

In November, he again warned Trumbull that Whigs complained "that you caress the Jacobites and slight those in the King's interest."[26]

Kingston also played to partisan prejudices in his advice to Trumbull to pay off the dubious freelance informer James Ormiston (discussed in chapter 3). Ormiston had worked for the Whig Treasury solicitor Aaron Smith. That was, for Kingston, the tip of an iceberg of Whig connections. Kingston further told Trumbull that Ormiston had been "recommended to Sir John Trenchard by [the Scottish] Secretary Johnston's brother, [that is, Alexander Johnston]" and was "one of Mr. Johnston's tools to cheat the government."[27]

Kingston's strategy of exploiting party antagonism may have made him an object of attack. Shortly after Kingston made his trip to the coast and scathing indictment of Trenchard, Trumbull received denunciations of Kingston's character. In Trumbull's papers there is a copy of a letter from the Reverend John Knighton to Thomas Tenison, the archbishop of Canterbury, which alluded to the existence of an abandoned wife and a new mistress and averred that Kingston was "suspected of highway robbery." Moreover, whereas Kingston routinely described himself as "Master of Arts of both universities," Knighton asserted he had "been to neither" and that "I have always doubted his being in orders." Around the same time that Knighton's letter was written, moreover, Trumbull was told by the Earl of Portland, William III's closest advisor, that "something happened at Gravesend last year, known to Mr. Vernon, which throws doubts upon his [Kingston's] honesty."[28]

Although Portland's letter does not specify what happened in Gravesend, it is possible that he was referring to Kingston's part in the battle between

Mayor Walter Nynn and the patriotic schoolmaster Robert Paterson (see chapter 4). Nynn had come into the possession of a list of potential witnesses whom Paterson had mobilized against him. It was said that Nynn had obtained that list from a mysterious gentleman who had come from London bragging of his high-ranking political contacts and promising (in return for a substantial fee) to help the mayor to recover a debt owed by the Commissioners for Sick and Wounded Seamen. There is some evidence that Richard Kingston was that mysterious gentleman or was at least suspected to be so. Kingston is mentioned (as "Dr. R—— K——") in a note in the papers of Justice of the Peace William Brockman, who had investigated the affair. Although the note is difficult to interpret, it suggests that Kingston claimed to have been sent to Gravesend by a privy councilor, whom he refused to identify.[29]

If Kingston was indeed the mysterious gentleman who slipped Mayor Nynn a list of enemies, his motive in doing so is obscure: perhaps it was greed, or the joy of putting obstacles in the path of zealous Whigs like Paterson, or the power that came with making people think he had access to the powerful. Of course, at this distance it is impossible to be sure that the mysterious gentleman really was Kingston. Nonetheless, the fact that Kingston's name surfaced in the investigation of the mysterious gentleman's identity is itself significant. Portland's cryptic remarks about events in Gravesend, coming shortly after Robert Ferguson portrayed Kingston in his *Letter to Trenchard* as a master of disguise, underscore the extent to which Kingston was (justly or not) associated with duplicity.

It is hard to know how seriously Trumbull took the warnings from Knighton or Portland about Kingston, but his relationship with Kingston cooled over time. The correspondence between them, which had at one point been several letters a week, trailed off. Although Trumbull remained in office until December 1697, the last datable letter from Kingston in Trumbull's private papers is 21 February 1696.[30]

It is unclear whether Kingston worked for the government as a spy again. Some evidence that he remained in the employ of the government comes from his literary war with William Fuller. In his *Life of Wm. Fuller, alias Fullee*, Kingston recounts how Fuller tried to persuade local officials in Newcastle that he had been appointed by Lord Portland to manage the affairs of the town, and how James Vernon (now secretary of state) had exposed Fuller as a fraud. Several letters to and from James Vernon in the summer and autumn of 1698 do in fact document such an attempted fraud, which suggests that Kingston might have had inside information from the secretary of state's office when he wrote his book.[31] That Kingston retained his ties to government officials is also suggested by the passages in *Life of Wm. Fuller, alias Fullee*, wherein, as will be discussed below, Kingston describes what were probably his own adventures accompanying William Fuller on a wild goose chase in Sussex in pursuit of the elusive Jacobite Colonel Parker and leads the reader to think that he was trusted by the secretary of state. To my knowledge, however, there is no direct evidence that Kingston had the same relationship (or volume of correspondence) with either Vernon or Ellis that he did with their predecessors, Trumbull and Nottingham. The nature of his continuing service as a spy remains a mystery.[32]

In any event, Kingston in the late 1690s turned his energies to writing. In 1698 he produced his lengthy *A True History of the Several Designs and Conspiracies against His Majesties Sacred Person and Government*. The picture of the government that Kingston drew in his *True History* was radically different from what he had presented in his correspondence with Trumbull, or even Nottingham. There was no mention of partisan divisions within the government; Kingston simply wrote of "the government." Also conspicuously absent from Kingston's published writing was any trace of an allegation that anyone inside the government was complicitous, willfully or negligently, with Jacobites. Kingston made no mention of the cracks and vulnerabilities in the nation's security that he had exposed in his surveys of the coast and account of the king's messengers. Local magistrates and officials were described as competent. Indeed, on one occasion where Kingston had to explain how a glitch in evidence gathering allowed a conspirator to escape trial, he chalked it up to a small act of forgetfulness on the part of customs officers rather than (as we might imagine from his previous writings) deep corruption or crypto-Jacobitism.[33]

The gap between Kingston the spy and Kingston the pamphleteer was especially clear when Kingston printed in his *True History*, as examples of Jacobite wishful thinking, copies of letters in which Jacobites gleefully remarked upon the disloyalty of England's fleet, the vulnerability of her defenses, and the numbers of local magistrates and gentlemen secretly loyal to James II. Ironically, the claims made in these (fictitious?) Jacobite letters were similar to what Kingston himself had reported to Trumbull. In his *True History*, by contrast, he was quick to assure the reader that defenses *were* strong and people *were* loyal. He seems to have changed his mind.[34]

Kingston also changed direction by offering his services to Trumbull's rival, the Whig Earl of Shrewsbury, when Shrewsbury was accused by Matthew Smith of ignoring his information about the Assassination Plot (see chapter 3). Trumbull embraced Smith and his accusations and spent many years trying to expose Shrewsbury as either an incompetent or a closet Jacobite. Trumbull's relations with Smith seem to have begun around the time his relations with Kingston dropped off, in May of 1696. Meanwhile, in a stunning about-face, Kingston offered his services to Shrewsbury, whom he defended by publishing two pamphlets attacking Matthew Smith: *A Modest Answer to Captain Smith's Immodest Memoirs of Secret Service* (1700) and *Impudence, Lying, and Forgery Detected* (1700).[35]

This change of sides might never have been complete or comfortable. Although Shrewsbury and his undersecretary, James Vernon, were in contact with Kingston by 1698, they were less than enthused at having him as a defender in 1700.[36] Vernon, who handled most of Shrewsbury's business (including his defense against Smith), showed a marked distaste for Kingston, numbering him among the "scribbling fools, who imagine others will be as pleased with what they write, as they themselves are." He regretted not having been able to dissuade Kingston from publishing, for if "I had been consulted I would not have advised his [Kingston's] coming into a print . . . thinking it much the best way not to thrust oneself between plot-makers, who generally make more mischief than they mend." He was resigned, in the end, to let Smith and Kingston "bespatter" one another but urged Shrewsbury to disassociate himself from Kingston. Vernon recommended that Kingston be instructed to disavow all knowledge of Shrewsbury and "make it understood that he does it [writes] of his own head" lest "your Grace [Shrewsbury] should be charged with having solicited him to write on that subject, or that it was done by your means and procurement." Sure enough, Kingston presented himself in his book as "so perfect a stranger to the D[uke] of S[hrewsbury] that he never had the honor of speaking to him but once in his life."[37]

It is clear from Vernon's reaction to the prospect of being defended by Kingston that Kingston was not able to establish himself persuasively as a loyal servant of the government. If anything, Vernon saw Kingston as a chameleon, a bit like the duplicitous creatures that (as will be seen below) populated Kingston's own books. For example, Vernon repeated to Shrewsbury the story (which was also told by Matthew Smith) that in order to enhance his status as a pamphleteer Kingston would publish pamphlets on both sides of an issue: he had written a pamphlet "reflecting on the House of Commons" and then made "an answer to it himself with a reply upon that answer."[38] Vernon also found, in a similar vein, that Kingston showed off his skill in deciphering secret codes by decoding letters that he had in fact written himself: "Dr. Kingston either sent or brought your Grace a letter in Characters of his own writing and introduced himself by pretending he had the skill to decipher it."[39]

Kingston's reputation became more exposed in public after he engaged himself against Smith. In his *Reply to an Unjust and Scandalous Libel* (1700) Smith picked up on charges that had been earlier made by Ferguson and also circulated among government insiders. He ended his book by presenting Kingston with a set of "interrogatories," which "I know he can truly answer, though I question whether he will or no." The questions (to which the obvious answer was "Richard Kingston") echoed and amplified Ferguson's themes of disguise, fraud, false clerical credentials, and sexual deviance. To give just a few examples:

> Question 1. Whether he knows the man that forged letters of orders, and stopped a woman's mouth in a Hay-Loft with the sleeve of his gown, while he committed adultery, if not a rape upon her, and was ignominiously chased by the Bishop of Ex—— (then of Bristol) out of his dioceses? . . .
>
> Question 4 Whether the same man did not personate the late Bishop of Peterborough (Doctor White) and borrow four guineas of his landlord . . . and whether having given that landlord the slip, he ever had the honesty to return his money? . . .
>
> Question 8: Whether he knows a sham clergyman, that stands indicted for sodomy and bigamy.[40]

Smith's attacks did not, of course, put an end to Kingston's career. He went on to publish a further reply to Smith, an attack on William Fuller, and a later attack on the Earl of Peterborough. He continued to publish religious works into the first decade of the eighteenth century, including a *Discourse on Divine Providence* (1702) and a two-volume exposé of the French Camisard prophets, the title of which (*Enthusiastick Impostors, no Divinely Inspir'd Prophets*) gives the gist of the argument. For all this output, and for all his service to the government, he is said to have died in poverty.[41]

Proof and Persuasion in Print

Given that Kingston was so often depicted as the human embodiment of falsehood itself, it is striking to find him presenting himself consistently as a tireless investigator and teller of truth. In his *True History of the Several Designs and Conspiracies* (1698), he avowed that neither political allegiance nor hope of preferment "hath influenced me in the least to deviate from what I ever accounted the soul and life of history, TRUTH," and in a later pamphlet he dubbed himself a "friend to *Truth and Justice*." Conversely, his works were deeply concerned with falsehood, full of memorable charlatans and shapeshifters. These included "Mr. Bromfield, a pretended Quaker, and so dextrous and bold a counterfeit that he was able to personate the disciple of any sect, member of any faction, or person of any quality"; the Camisard disciple Miss Betty Grey, who pretended sudden blindness and chokings that were miraculously cured in the presence of the faithful; and of course, the colorful con artists Matthew Smith and William Fuller.[42]

Kingston's work brought together issues of credit in the multiple spheres of commerce, religion, politics, and printing. He often made use of the association of (financial) credit and credibility to cast doubt on the claims of the government's critics. The satirical *Life of Wm. Fuller, alias Fullee*, for example, was essentially a long primer in how to cheat one's creditors. Fuller, in this narrative, gets lodgings, meals, an education for his sister, nice clothes, and loans of money all by pretending to be a rich man who just happens not to have ready cash on hand. He puts off his creditors repeatedly with elaborate excuses, promises them government jobs that it is not in his power to offer, and pays his debts with notes drawn on well-known merchants or aristocrats who of course turn out (when presented with the notes by the unwitting victim) to have never heard of him.

Credit in the world of books, too, was an issue with which Kingston grappled. One of his reports to Nottingham detailed the uncertainty among Jacobites themselves as to whether printed documents could be trusted. The appearance of James II's *Declaration*, he wrote, "was such a surprise to all the designing party among the Jacobites, who knew nothing of it nor believed it [to] be King James's, that it has caused a great deal of trouble in finding out the truth of it." It was only after conversations with the printers and distributors that Kingston was able to ascertain "that it really was King James's *Declaration*."[43]

In practice, it is impossible to separate these different arenas in which credit was required and contested. To discredit Matthew Smith's charges against government officials, for example, Kingston set out to prove that Smith had not written the books in which his charges were made but that the book had been written by the Grub Street hack Tom Brown; this claim was then backed by the word of booksellers of Kingston's acquaintance, whose credibility in turn was contested in the ensuing pamphlet war. Credit troubles in the realms of books, politics, and money were tied together by Kingston in one story about William Fuller, wherein Fuller cons a bookseller into giving him money by "pretending to furnish him with Secrets of State, which he had been let into, and promises of preferment at court." In Kingston's writing, problematic credit of one sort impinged on credit in other realms. The goal is not to decide if Kingston was really telling the truth but to understand his methods of persuasion, and the obstacles to it, in the context of the crises of credibility discussed above.[44]

Ironically, the very difficulties of trusting printed works that plagued seventeenth-century readers impinge on the twenty-first-century historian trying to analyze Kingston's methods of persuasion. It is not always easy to establish Kingston's authorship. For example, Kingston is credited in bibliographies and catalogues with having written the first and second parts of *The Life of Wm. Fuller, alias Fullee, alias Fowler, alias Ellison, &c* ("Printed to prevent his further imposing upon the public," 1701), as well as with the 1692 *The Life of William Fuller, the Late Pretended Evidence*, from which the 1701 work is partly plagiarized. These texts, however, are anonymous. Moreover, after Fuller complained in his *Fuller's Non-Recantation to the Jacobites* that Kingston had written anonymously against him, the preface to the second part of the *Life of Wm. Fuller, alias Fullee* offered a denial (of sorts) that Kingston had authored the first part, excoriating Fuller for "scandalously abusing Mr. K—— a person who is otherwise taken up than in writing against a Fellow whose very actions are sufficient to expose him."[45]

There is some reason to think that in this one instance Fuller is more believable than Kingston, and that Kingston really did write at least the first part of *The Life of Wm. Fuller, alias Fullee*. The book has some stylistic similarities to works more reliably attributed to Kingston (such as the use of Latin tags and the printing of original letters). A further reason to suspect Kingston was the author of *The Life of Wm. Fuller, alias Fullee* is that the book contains a very flattering picture of a person who, although unnamed in the text, is almost certainly Kingston himself. Given Kingston's penchant for self-promotion, inserting a glowing and thinly disguised self-portrait into his own book seems entirely in character. The story, as told in *The Life of Wm. Fuller, alias Fullee*, is that Fuller had boasted to the Lords of the Council that he could locate the notorious and elusive Jacobite Colonel Parker. Not quite trusting Fuller, but unwilling to pass up the opportunity, the Lords appointed "a gentleman, well known to the government, to accompany him into Sussex." The "gentleman" is not named in the text, but his travails are described with admiration and striking sympathy. *The Life of Wm. Fuller, alias Fullee* recounts Fuller's many cheats on this expedition and his shabby treatment of his companion, who was, however, a "longheaded man" who "knew well enough that a fellow who had put such a trick upon the government could never more obtain to be countenanced by it."[46]

Since Fuller in his own autobiography identified the gentleman sent to accompany him into Sussex as Richard Kingston, it seems clear that the "longheaded man" described by Kingston is Kingston himself, and that Kingston was writing a glowing account of himself in the third person. It is, after all, hard to imagine that an author who wasn't Kingston himself would admire the gentleman so much, recount his travails in such detail, and yet neglect to name him. In any case, for purposes of this discussion I will treat *The Life of Wm. Fuller, alias Fullee* as Kingston's work. Even if I am wrong, the problems of establishing credibility in print discussed in relation to this text are relevant to Kingston's career and to the themes of the present book.

How, then, did Kingston (or whoever wrote the works attributed to him) think that his own truth-claims would be believed? Beyond simply proclaiming his devotion to TRUTH, Kingston used a number of techniques to establish credibility. Many of these are reminiscent of tactics that were deployed by members of the Royal Society, such as the use of "plain style," the printing of documentation, and the invocation of gentlemanly social status to confer credibility.

Just as Robert Boyle deployed a "plain style" in his lab reports to enhance the impression of truthfulness, so too Kingston asked his readers to equate unornamented prose with credibility. "As the Author lay under no necessity to disguise or perplex the TRUTH," he wrote in the preface to his *True History*, "so he has all along taken care to express himself in such a plain, familiar style, as is the language of business, and lies within the reach of the meanest capacity." This he contrasted to the harmonious periods and beautiful turns of language employed by recent French writers to "prevail upon his [the reader's] passions," under whose "rhetorical flowers" was concealed a snake, "for as it was not their design ... to confine themselves to the severity of TRUTH, which does not require such artifices to recommend it, so they fondly thought to conceal and supply the defect of it by the elegance of their expressions."[47]

Further guaranteeing the truth of his book, Kingston pointed out, was his use of citations and printed documentation:

> I have, after the example of some of the most celebrated historians of this and the last age, cited my Authorities all along in the margin, which are printed at large in the appendix, and those the reader may consult at leisure for his farther satisfaction.[48]

Kingston thus grounded the authority of the book not on himself but on the transparent evidence. He was merely an editor, arranging it in chronological order, "so that all the business I had to do, was but to digest these materials into a proper method, according to the series of time, when the most remarkable incidents happened, and to collect out of them what I thought most convenient to be inserted into the narration."[49]

Kingston's *True History* contained numerous references in the margin. Some led to documents printed in the appendix of the book, others to documents existing (or alleged to exist) outside the text. His attacks on Smith, Fuller, and the Camisards also frequently mentioned sources and reproduced documents (like Fuller's fraudulent instruments of credit). Kingston also printed letters from eyewitnesses (who, for example, heard Camisard preachers or saw them perform miraculous cures) and on occasion told readers whom they could ask for confirmation of a given statement.

As Steven Shapin has argued, social status and financial credit played a large role in the credit-establishing techniques of natural philosophers, who regarded objectivity as the monopoly of gentlemen. It is not surprising, then, that Kingston also invoked social status and financial solvency to tell readers whom to believe. William Fuller's fraudulent financial credit was for Kingston closely connected to his lack of credibility in the political sphere, and Kingston harped relentlessly upon Fuller's low origins and blamed Fuller's problems on his attempt to climb out of his proper sphere:

The world had never heard of such a person as Fuller, had Fuller been content to have been known for nothing else but what his birth and education entitled him to. But since he has justled [*sic*] out of his sphere . . . it is but necessary, for the sake of truth, to bring him back to the remembrance of his parentage, and recall him from his high posts, to give a visit to the joints of mutton in his father's stall, and cast an eye upon the day labourer's house where his mother . . . first drew breath.[50]

Kingston was eager to establish the opposite point about himself. When attacked by Matthew Smith, he made an appeal "to all the tradesmen I have dealt with, who I am sure will all give the best words they have." He made a point of his consistent employment, having "served his Majesty above Eight Years." Education was a theme in battle as well. Kingston made a point of using Latin tags; by contrast, he called attention to Matthew Smith's ignorance of Latin and to William Fuller's "false spelling" to undermine their credibility.[51]

Kingston's methods of establishing credibility were inconsistent and problematic, however. If anything, his example might lead us to question how persuasive the familiar model of gentlemanly credibility really was when invoked not in the limited confines of the Royal Society and its journals but in the open arena of printed political polemic.

Plain style, for example, was used in much of *True History*, but not consistently, and in other writings by Kingston it barely featured at all. Moreover, Kingston's use of plain style for the simplest reader was already undermined by the Latin tags he used to establish his own educational attainments. Kingston further departed from "plain style" when he delivered bawdy accounts of the hetero- and homosexual adventures of William Fuller or of the Camisard Betty Grey's ecstatic, near-literal impersonation of the "Great whore of Antichrist."[52]

Social status, too, failed to settle questions of credibility in Kingston's representations of himself and others. The members of the Royal Society described by Shapin were indeed all gentlemen. If the hostile reports on Kingston can be believed, Kingston himself was not. He was described by John Knighton in a letter to the archbishop of Canterbury as the "son of a farmer" who had been "apprentice to a tailor." By contrast, Matthew Smith really was the nephew of William Parkyns, the wealthy Jacobite gentleman convicted of participation in the Assassination Plot. Even William Fuller might have had stronger claims to gentlemanly status than did Kingston. Though his mother's husband was a mere butcher (and not, as Fuller claimed, an eminent grazier who victualed the king's navy), Kingston also hinted loudly that Fuller's mother had cuckolded her husband and had been impregnated by Cornelius Harfleet, Esquire, making William Fuller "a gentleman's graft upon a Butcher's Crabstock." Reference to social status also failed to resolve questions of credibility in Kingston's writing on the Camisards, as some of their English adherents, like John Lacy and Richard Bulkeley, were indeed gentlemen. Above all, the problem with linking credibility to gentle status was that gentle status could be faked. William Fuller, in Kingston's account, was able to make tradesmen, rich merchants, innkeepers, and clerics *think* he was a man of wealth, breeding, and education by his appearance and conversation.[53]

Kingston's efforts to establish credibility by providing citations and reproducing documents in his texts were also problematic. His marginal notes did not do what a modern reader would expect a footnote to do, that is, to direct her to a place (a book, an archive) where she would find the document to which the footnote refers and thus be able to see for herself if the evidence given supported the author's claim. Some of Kingston's references did indeed direct the reader to an appendix where letters and affidavits were printed. Nonetheless, for these printed documents to function as "proof," the reader would have to trust that what was printed in the appendix really did exist outside of Kingston's printed page. Moreover, contrary to the claim made in the preface, not all the sources cited in the margin appeared in the appendix.

Kingston referred readers to documents in the possession of the government, such as "Goodman's depositions in the secretaries office."[54] The "virulent paper," a draft of James II's *Declaration* to his supporters to be published on his landing, that was "found in Mr. Standish's closet at the search made at Standish Hall July 16 1694" (and was therefore a crucial proof of Standish's involvement in the alleged Lancashire conspiracy) was not reproduced by Kingston, on grounds that it was "so stuffed with scandal, malice and bitterness of the [Jacobite] party against the King and government that I think it not worth the charge and trouble of procuring a copy, much less to recite it unless I designed to affright the modest, or poison the unwary reader." Rather than reproduce the document in the appendix, Kingston simply assures the reader that it was "found by Captain Baker, the original delivered by him into the House of Commons." Perhaps the oddest of Kingston's footnotes was the one that leads the reader not to an object but to a person: "Mr. Clark is now in England, and I appeal to him for the Truth of it."[55]

The inadequacy of the printed page to stand as irrefutable proof became an explosive issue in Kingston's pamphlet war with Matthew Smith. Kingston's argument in his *Modest Answer to Captain Smith's Immodest Memoirs* was that Smith's *Memoirs of Secret Service*, which printed letters between Smith and the Duke of Shrewsbury, failed to accurately reproduce these letters, which Kingston had been able to see in the original. The relationship of original letters to printed reproductions became even more vexed when Kingston tried to handle an apparent betrayal by one of his original informants. Kingston had asserted that Smith had said in the presence of himself, William Read, and Francis Jermy that he had reason to believe Shrewsbury was complicit in the Assassination Plot. Smith, in his reply to Kingston's book, countered by printing a certificate from William Read saying that Kingston's statement was "utterly false" and that "I never did hear Captain Smyth speak immodestly, unhandsomely, or disrespectfully about the Duke of Shrewsbury." Not surprisingly, Kingston responded in turn by claiming that the certificate from Read that Smith printed was a forgery.[56]

Kingston's *Life of Wm. Fuller, alias Fullee* (both the first and second parts) also elaborately confronted the problems involved in proving things with books. He showed more awareness in this text than in others that a printed document may not substitute for the original. Thus, Kingston printed notes written by Fuller to be drawn on eminences like the Earl of Portland and promised the reader that the originals could be seen "at the Cock-Ale House without Temple Bar." Likewise, Kingston avowed himself "ready to appear before any person in Authority and produce the originals [of Fuller's letters] with a sufficient proof they are all his." Thus, Kingston dealt with the inadequacy of the printed text to provide proof by directing the reader to something outside the text.[57]

Kingston also wrestled in his books about Fuller with the problem of using anonymous information. As Kingston described it, Fuller's victims were reluctant to have their names printed, and Kingston showed himself respectful of their wishes. He withheld, for example, the names of the "persons of honor and quality," including "no less than twenty eight Lords, Spiritual and Temporal" whom Fuller accused before Parliament in 1692. Kingston also concealed the names of two innkeepers whom Fuller had humiliated "at their request, not to be exposed, unless there be farther occasion for it." Not surprisingly, Fuller (in a response to the first volume) complained of Kingston's failure to name sources, and (in Kingston's words) "intimate[d] that if the Author had his accounts from unquestioned Authority, he would not withhold the names of the persons who gave 'em him, from the knowledge of the public." To Fuller's criticism, Kingston responded that it was the "urgent desires" of Fuller's victims that caused him to withhold names, but that "the several relations [that is, narratives] come from unquestioned hands and men of integrity." Paradoxically, this concealment was meant to enhance the credibility of the story Kingston told: being conned by Fuller would be so humiliating that it was believable that his victims would want to remain hidden. It also, again, gave Kingston an opportunity to gesture at the existence of testimony and documentation that lay outside the book, without actually giving the reader that testimony or documentation (so the reader was led to believe it existed without actually seeing it). Kingston might have concealed the names of the innkeepers Fuller cheated, but "if the reader inquires about Namptwich he may hear the story more at large."[58]

It is easy to scoff at Kingston's "evidence." A modern historian who wants to assess its value as proof of Jacobite plots will no doubt judge that Kingston's printed affidavits, printed signatures, and references to inaccessible documents did not actually prove much. Nonetheless, even the very obvious flaws in Kingston's method should lead us to ask why he thought it would be persuasive.

The state itself seems to have been important for Kingston as a guarantor of his credibility. It is striking that he cited votes of Parliament to establish truth. The long list of William Fuller's aliases and occupations that comprised the full title of his *Life of Wm. Fuller, alias Fullee* included the designation "by vote of Parliament an imposter." Likewise, Kingston affirmed that his own credibility was demonstrated by his eight years of service to the government and referred the reader to "the Right Honorable the several Secretaries of State with whom I have had the honor to be concerned." Moreover, many of the documents that Kingston cited in his *True History* were said to be in the possession of the secretaries of state, the Parliament, or privy councilors or safely locked in the Tower of London. One message here was that truth was, literally, in the possession of the state.[59]

Kingston also put faith, or asked the reader to put faith, in the possibility of the face-to-face questioning of human sources. As noted above, many of

Kingston's texts featured stories of Kingston himself tracking down relevant witnesses; implicitly, the reader was invited to follow in his footsteps. It was as if Kingston's solution to the limited capacity of print to carry "proof" was to send the reader out into the world. His truth-claims seemed to depend on the existence of an extensive but finite community of which the reader and he were both members. The brilliance of Kingston's writing was precisely its capacity to create the illusion that such a community existed outside the text, that one could access it if one wanted to, and that even if one did not bother trying one could have the virtual experience of having been there.

There was of course a circularity to both of these ways of establishing credit. The state established Kingston's credit, but Kingston's writing itself was necessary to establish the credit of the state. Likewise, the community of real witnesses outside the text backed up the claims of the text, but it was the text itself that created the strong impression that such a community existed.

Conclusion

Richard Kingston has plunged us into a world of spin, which spins so fast that a historian cannot always be sure which end is up. But let me try.

Kingston's career alerts us to the ways that government intelligence and government propaganda—the finding of "truth" and the telling of "truth"— were closely intertwined in this period. What Kingston learned as a spy about the importance of rumor and information certainly influenced his work as a writer. Conversely, the Williamite regime clearly saw the creation of its own image as part and parcel of what we would call "national security."

Kingston's struggles with credibility bring home just how important credibility was, the extent to which it rested on fictions, and how hard it was to maintain. His tactics for creating an impression of veracity illustrated this point: he was able to create entities through print (like the state, or like a closed community of truth-seekers and accessible truth-tellers) that sustained his own credibility as a writer, including the credibility of his claim that these entities existed in the first place! But of course, fictions are never incontestable. For all the brilliance of his technique, Kingston was dogged by suspicion.

Kingston's sad situation in turn should be put in the larger context of the Williamite regime's particularly acute need for credit in its early years. It needed not only to survive the Jacobite challenge but also to persuade its subjects that it was capable of doing so. Ironically, then, establishing credit of this sort required psychological warfare, spying, the control of information, and campaigns of misinformation; in short, it required people who lied. And it further required that those people who lied be held at arm's length. The regime's quest for credit, then, created Richard Kingston and at the same time made Kingston's own credit an unattainable dream.

CHAPTER 6

Loyalty and Credibility in the Lancashire "Sham Plot"

Nothing of public concernment has been so variously discoursed of at home and abroad, as the Lancashire Plot.
—[RICHARD KINGSTON], *A True History of the Several Designs and Conspiracies against His Majesties Sacred Person and Government as They Were Continually Carried on from 1688 to 1697* (1698)

Two plot "discoveries" of the 1690s, the Lancashire Plot of 1694 and the Assassination Plot of 1696, had very different consequences for the credit of the government. Looking at how they were handled by authorities and how they were represented to the public brings together threads followed throughout the book. Plots can be seen as occasions that destabilize and redraw boundaries of loyalty, provide opportunities for informers and witnesses to construct their own credibility in the eyes of community and the state, and spotlight tensions between liberty and security. The Lancashire Plot is the subject of this chapter; the Assassination Plot is discussed in chapter 7.

In October 1694 thirteen wealthy men from the counties of Lancashire and Cheshire (henceforth referred to as the "Lancashire gentlemen") were brought to trial on charges of treason before special commissions of Oyer and Terminer held in Manchester and Chester. Most of the defendants were Catholic. They included Caryll Viscount Molineux, the former lord lieutenant of Lancashire under James II, and representatives from some of the most prominent local families, for example, the Blundells, the Gerrards, and the Dicconsons. A few defendants were Protestant non-jurors, like Peter Legh of Lyme the elder. The chief prosecution witness was John Lunt, who testified that he had been sent from Ireland by James II in 1689 to deliver commissions to the Lancashire gentlemen and others to be officers in a secret Jacobite army.

Lunt's story was backed up by George Wilson and John Womball. Wilson, once a failed innkeeper in Flintshire and more recently chamberlain of the Ragged Bear and Staff in Smithfield, testified that he saw Lunt deliver the commissions to the prisoners, and also that he received money from defendant Rowland Stanley to enlist soldiers for King James. John Womball, universally described as a "broken carrier," said he had transported arms for the accused.

Lancashire, with its large Catholic population and easy access to Ireland, had long been an object of anxiety for the Williamite regime. Plots had been revealed, and Catholics and suspected Jacobites had been rounded up in 1689 and in 1690. It was natural to expect that the trial of the Lancashire gentlemen would prove what officials thought they already knew. But in that Manchester courtroom the case soon fell apart. Lunt's performance as a witness was almost comically unconvincing. Asked to identify one of the accused men, he pointed to the wrong defendant. A string of witnesses testified to Lunt's career as a highway robber and bigamist.

The decisive blow to Lunt's credibility came from John Taaffe, his brother-in-law and erstwhile accomplice. Taaffe had initially helped Lunt obtain a hearing for his plot discovery from Secretary of State John Trenchard. But Taaffe had changed sides: on the witness stand he recalled how Lunt had gleefully drawn up lists of wealthy men whom he intended to accuse of treason in order to acquire a share of their forfeited estates. To stop Lunt's murderous perjuries, Taaffe had recruited friends and kinsmen of the defendants to volunteer as collaborators to Lunt and in this way extract from him a detailed explanation of his plans to "run through all the gentlemen in England." Two of these men, Leigh Bankes and Roger Dicconson, appeared in court to back up Taaffe's testimony. The first batch of defendants was promptly acquitted by the jury, to rejoicing in the streets of Manchester. The second batch was brought to the bar the next day, but no witnesses appeared against them. The trial at Chester was similarly aborted. All defendants were dismissed, though not before the presiding judge, Sir Giles Eyre, delivered a helpful lecture on comparative law. "Gentlemen," he explained, "most of you . . . have been brought up in France, where the complexion of government is much different to this of ours, here the King rules by law, there his will and pleasure is law; and therefore let me advise you to study to be quiet . . . go and sin no more, lest a worse thing befall you."[1]

"Go and sin no more" was hardly the apology that men who had been detained three months might have expected. What is more striking, however, is that Eyre was almost the only person who thought the trial of the Lancashire gentlemen actually vindicated English justice. Controversy about the Lancashire "sham plot" raged on after the trial. The whole affair revealed disturbing things about the government, whichever side one took. Either the regime persecuted the innocent, or it was unable, through ineptitude or worse, to protect itself from a real plot.

The Lancashire Plot allows a glimpse of post-1688 England at a moment of intense uncertainty. The trial and subsequent doubts about it played into a wide crisis of credit and credibility for the government, occurring at a time when the "credit of the government" was quite literally at stake, in a financial sense. The problematic credibility of witnesses in the plot was associated with the problematic value of England's coin by the Jacobite pamphleteer Robert Ferguson. Accusing several Whig Treasury officials and secretaries of state of fabricating charges against the Lancashire gentlemen, Ferguson wrote that the entire sham plot was like a false coin, "minted by Harry Baker, Alexander Johnstone, and Hugh Speke, and afterwards made current through the kingdom, by the credit which the two secretaries, Johnstone and Trenchard have stamped upon it."[2]

The Lancashire Plot affair furthermore shone a spotlight on the profound tension between the government's promise to secure liberty, which itself justified the Revolution of 1688, and the need to protect Williamite England from its enemies, raising painful questions about whether the new regime really differed from its predecessor. It allowed Tories to present themselves, rather than Whigs, as defenders of the subject's liberties, and as such was an important part of the context in which elements of the Tory party became a "country party," claiming to represent the "true whig" principles of the revolution.[3]

The Story (to the Best of My Knowledge)

In June 1694 John Taaffe brought his brother-in-law John Lunt to Secretary of State Trenchard to give a deposition about the secret Jacobite army being raised in the north of England. For several months Lunt had been providing testimony for the Superstitious Lands Commission operating in Lancashire, as had John Taaffe and another Lancashire Plot witness, John Womball. As Paul Hopkins has persuasively argued, the connection between the Superstitious Lands Commission's inquiries in Lancashire and the "discovery" of the

Lancashire Plot was hardly accidental. The same Catholic gentlemen were targeted. John Taaffe, for example, had testified for the Superstitious Lands Commission that Lord Molineux, Sir William Gerrard, and Bartholemew Walmsley had donated large sums to the Jesuits at a convocation held at the papal nuncio's house in 1686; these men were all later accused by Lunt. Moreover, when Lunt and Taaffe traveled to Lancashire in June 1694 to make searches and arrest suspects, they were accompanied by Harry Baker and financed by Treasury Secretary Aaron Smith, both of whom were deeply involved in the Superstitious Lands Commission. It is likely, as Paul Hopkins has argued, that Lunt and Taaffe were motivated to "discover" the Lancashire Plot to make the superstitious lands allegations more convincing and to forestall a prosecution for perjury, which Lancashire Catholic landowners (including the men they accused) had been pursuing against them.[4]

The connection between the Superstitious Lands Commission and the Lancashire Plot "discovery" was of ideological as well as causal significance. Harry Baker and Aaron Smith (and the Superstitious Lands Commissions more generally) were associated with Whiggery and dissent. That was in turn to shape the politics of responses to the trials and the way Taaffe told the story. Taaffe attributed his decision to change sides at Manchester to Baker's and Smith's obvious hostility to the Church of England.

As Taaffe later told the story, he had brought Lunt and his revelations to Secretary of State Trenchard because he initially believed in the existence of the Lancashire Plot but had been disillusioned by the anti-Anglican irreverence of Smith and Baker. He also became "sensible that the whole was a roguery." Having recognized Lunt's dishonesty, however, Taaffe did not know what to do, until the internal quarrels of Lunt, Womball, and Wilson give him an opportunity. Lunt complained to Taaffe that Wilson and Womball were "ungrateful rogues" and said he wanted to get some "gentlemen" to replace them on his roster of witnesses. Lunt's thirst for gentlemen to act as witnesses inspired Taaffe to resolve upon a daring design. He would find "gentlemen of reputation" and introduce them to Lunt. Lunt would then "open himself freely" to these men, giving them instructions as to what they were to swear against the victims. At that point, Taaffe and the gentlemen would all expose Lunt to the secretary of state.[5]

To recruit these men, Taaffe turned to Mrs. Dicconson, wife of the prisoner William Dicconson, who it seems was acquainted with Taaffe's wife. Through Mrs. Dicconson, Taaffe enlisted three Protestant gentlemen:

Edward Beresford of Grey's Inn, Leigh Bankes (kinsman to defendant Peter Legh), and a Mr. Bagshaw, also of Grey's Inn. Mrs. Dicconson also introduced Taaffe to Roger Dicconson, defendant William Dicconson's brother, who seems to have acted independently of the other three. Eventually, Roger Dicconson and Leigh Bankes were to back up Taaffe as witnesses for the defense in Manchester, leading to the spectacular acquittal.[6]

To tell the story from Taaffe's point of view, however, imposes a false neatness on it. The defense of the Lancashire gentlemen was a multipronged affair, in which friends and relatives of the defendants acted independently of Taaffe or of one another. The family of defendant William Blundell compiled a set of "notes to discredit" prosecution witnesses, while Roger Kenyon, the Tory MP, deployed a network of gentlemen and ladies who reached deep into local society for information. Lady Standish, for example, reported to George Kenyon (Roger's son), "I have made some inquiry of the man called Lunt, but cannot yet hear that he had a wife in our neighborhood, nor that [his?] family does not own that they know him; but will enquire farther after him." No further information is forthcoming about who was interviewed. But there were clearly far more people gathering evidence and volunteering information than ever testified at the trial. The standard version of the story in which Taaffe's clever heroism saved the gentlemen is based on Taaffe's narrative and obscures much important activity.[7]

One aspect of Taaffe's narrative that is worth taking seriously, though, was his acknowledgment that defending the Lancashire gentlemen was dangerous. As Taaffe told it, many of the people whom he tried to recruit to his cause were wary of him. When Taaffe first changed sides, for example, he had approached Mr. Allenson, who was minister at the defendant Peter Legh's chapel at Newton. But Allenson "being fearful of him or not crediting him, gave no heed to him." Even Beresford, Bagshaw, and Bankes, the friends of Peter Legh who joined in Taaffe's scheme to entrap Lunt, were nervous. Despite his solicitude for Peter Legh, Mr. Beresford had "no inclination to meet or converse with [Taaffe]." Bagshaw at first agreed to meet Lunt at the Ship Alehouse by Temple Bar but "upon further thought and reflection, was unwilling to go, till he had further consulted what was advisable and safe." In the end Leigh Bankes was the only one of the three to give testimony at the trial about his encounter with Lunt. And even Bankes, who did meet Lunt once, backed out of a second meeting with him on the advice of a lawyer. Bankes told the House of Commons that he distrusted both Taaffe and Lunt.[8]

It is at first glance surprising Bankes, Bagshaw, and Beresford, all of whom were Anglicans, did not bond more closely with Taaffe, who defined his motives purely in terms of saving the Church of England from the Presbyterian threat. Perhaps Taaffe's history of conversion made him seem untrustworthy. The fear of how authorities would respond to their entrapment of Lunt may also have contributed to the reluctance of Taaffe's potential recruits. Not only would these men have to persuade Lunt that they were willing witnesses, they would then have to convince authorities that they were acting a part when consorting with Lunt but were now telling the truth!

Taaffe's recruits did in fact experience hostility. When Leigh Bankes approached Lord Chief Justice Holt offering to make a sworn statement about that encounter, Holt refused to take his affidavit because it was improper for him as the judge in the case to see evidence in advance. The immediate effect of approaching authorities was to make prosecutors aware that efforts were being made to discredit the witnesses. Leigh Bankes told the House of Commons that Aaron Smith had threatened Peter Legh's sister, saying "she had given then more trouble than all the rest, and Smith said Mr. Beresford and himself [Leigh Bankes] were ill fellows and ought not to be let loose."[9]

The most damning claim about government resistance to the truth came from the pamphleteer Thomas Wagstaffe, who asserted in his pamphlet *A Letter out of Lancashire* that the government issued warrants before the trial to seize anyone attempting to suborn or discredit the king's witnesses. There had been, he claimed,

> A mighty hunt . . . made about the Town by Officers and Messengers after men who said anything tending to the reproach of the King's Witnesses, together with warrants of a strange and illegal nature, to seize and take up men and their papers for conspiring and endeavoring to suborn (as the warrants word it) witnesses against the lives and credit of several witnesses for their Majesties, against persons charged with High treason; Upon which some very worthy and considerable men were taken up, and kept close-Prisoners for some time, and are yet under bail, contrary to all law and justice.[10]

A set of notes made by the Tory former Secretary of State Nottingham echoed this charge with more specificity. A paper entitled "Observations of Some Practices before the Trial" alleged:

> Unprecedented warrants were issued out and by virtue thereof divers persons were taken into custody who not only by a fair and honest enquiry to

serve their friends had detected the dishonesty of Brereton, who was one of the evidences; and these persons were kept in custody till that day the judges were gotten as far as Coventry in order to the trial of the gentlemen. Kitson and Coachman two messengers had the warrants; and Mr. Deputy Newberry was one that was taken into custody and I think Mrs. Cotton and Mrs. Anvill.[11]

    It is hard to confirm or disprove the charge that the government deliberately suppressed evidence against prosecution witnesses prior to the trial. The State Papers contain a tantalizing warrant, dated shortly before the trial at Manchester began, against the persons named in Nottingham's "Observations" paper (Newberry, Cotton, and "Mrs. Ward alias Anvill") for "conspiring to suborn witnesses against the lives of credit of several witnesses for their Majesties against persons charged with High Treason." Exactly what they were alleged to have done, unfortunately, is not clear: they (naturally) never appeared at the trial in Manchester, and so what they had to say against the prosecution witnesses, if anything, remains mysterious.[12]

    Nonetheless, some government officials might have been aware that the case against the Lancashire gentlemen was not solid; if so, it might explain the apparent indecision that beset the proceedings. It is otherwise puzzling, for example, that three months elapsed between the arrests of the Lancashire gentlemen and their trials. Most of the defendants were taken up in July, held in Chester Castle, then brought to London at the beginning of September. By that time, Lunt had been arrested for bigamy but bailed out by Aaron Smith. Meanwhile, the arrival of the accused in London raised expectations that a trial would happen shortly. But there were delays and also negative publicity. Dyer's newsletter, according to Luttrell's diary for 4 September, "ridiculed the said plot by saying there was only some few rusty swords, fowling pieces and hunting saddles found with the conspirators." Then on 10 September Edward Harley noted the appearance of "a very smart libel . . . entituled *A Letter to Lord Chief Justice Holt concerning the plot*, indicating the scheme, and Hugh Speke and Baker the managers. It is very likely to come from Ferguson." Another anonymous pamphlet attributed to Ferguson appeared, the *Letter to Trenchard*, bearing the date 9 October, and was reportedly circulated in Manchester to stir up a hostile mob. This pamphlet in effect printed the case for the defense before the trial began, telling the story of how Taaffe arranged for Leigh Bankes to pretend to be a potential witness in order to get Lunt to reveal the nefarious scheme.[13]

One revealing sign of government uncertainty was a change in the venue for and the judges chosen to preside over the trial. As noted above, when Leigh Bankes approached Lord Chief Justice Holt offering to make a sworn statement about that encounter, Holt refused to accept Bankes's affidavit because it was improper for him as the judge in the case to see evidence in advance. Sometime in September, however, the government decided to return the defendants to the north for their trials, under Giles Eyre and the commission of Oyer and Terminer. The fact that Holt subsequently either removed himself or was removed from the case might suggest that some government officials were losing confidence in the case. Holding the trial outside of London may have been a way to avoid public scrutiny.

Whatever the case, government officials certainly had strong hints before the trial that Lunt and his fellow witnesses were unreliable: as noted above, the case for the defense was already in print! Why, then, did they proceed with the trial? There were, in fact, good reasons to take Lunt seriously. Shrewsbury might well have remembered that Lunt had been jailed at Coventry as a potential conspirator in 1689. Authorities had in the past received intimations of a secret army being raised in Lancashire. As early as October 1689, Manchester justices of the peace had informed Secretary of State Shrewsbury that many local Roman Catholic gentlemen had gone into hiding in the country, preparing for an invasion or insurrection. In February 1690 the Irish ex-soldier John Kelly had made what Shrewsbury described as a "large discovery" of a conspiracy of papists in Lancashire, which had caused Shrewsbury to issue warrants for the seizure of several Catholic gentlemen. Then again in May 1690 Robert Dodsworth attended the House of Commons to give an account of a planned insurrection in Lancashire, leading to more arrests.[14]

Paul Hopkins, the foremost historian of early Lancashire Jacobitism, maintains that Jacobites were indeed raising an army in Lancashire, although not all the informants who alleged it existed had first-hand information. Hopkins describes Lunt as an "accomplished fantasist" who was not actually privy to the plot but managed by some lucky guesses to name some real conspirators. For our purposes, whether there was or was not plotting is not important; the key point is that there was already a history of allegations about a secret Jacobite army at the time Lunt appeared on the scene.[15]

Even if government officials heard stories that the witnesses were suborned perjurers, moreover, they might not have been dissuaded from holding a trial; they knew that such accusations might be countered simply by turning the accusation back on the accuser. It is easy to counter a conspiracy theory with an even bigger conspiracy theory. During the Popish Plot scare in the 1680s, the "popish midwife" Elizabeth Cellier "discovered" that the allegations against Catholics to kill the king and destroy London were really part of a plot by Presbyterians to kill the king, destroy London, and blame it on the Catholics. She had found proof of this Presbyterian plot, she claimed, in papers buried in a meal tub. Not surprisingly, she soon found herself accused of fabricating the so-called Meal Tub Plot. That is, according to her detractors, Cellier, a Catholic, had a plot to falsely accuse Presbyterians of falsely accusing Catholics of doing what Catholics were in fact doing! The subtitle of Robert Ferguson's 1681 pamphlet *No Protestant Plot*, written in defense of the Earl of Shaftsbury (discussed below), expressed the opposite but structurally identical theory: that is, that "the present pretended conspiracy of Protestants against the King and Government, [was] Discovered to be a conspiracy of the Papists against the King."[16]

Similarly, Taaffe's charges that Lunt had lied and suborned others to do so were turned against Taaffe. Immediately after hearing of the acquittals at Manchester, Shrewsbury, while admitting he was still mostly in the dark and "cannot yet be very clear in relating the contrivance," was already speculating that there was some sort of elaborate deception: "There appears to have been a great villainy [amongst? against?] the King's witnesses, and some who put them upon swearing this plot, in order afterwards to discover their perjury," he told Blaithwayt. Within weeks after the trials, those who believed that the Lancashire gentlemen really were guilty had constructed a satisfying narrative, according to which the wealthy defendants had suborned Taaffe, and Taaffe in turn had suborned Leigh Bankes and the other witnesses who testified against Lunt.[17]

There was thus no reliable, agreed-upon way to decide on the reality of the alleged plot: all stories about its truth or falsehood hinged upon the credibility of witnesses, which in turn was supported or undermined by other witnesses whose credibility was subject to debate. If government officials pressed forward with the trial of the Lancashire gentlemen, it might have been because they had no good reason to believe Taaffe over Lunt.

The government's failure to respond to warnings that the case against the Lancashire gentlemen was deeply flawed might also have been due to sheer lack of coordination or communication. The job of managing the prosecution and paying out almost £800 to cover the expenses of witnesses and legal officials was left to Aaron Smith. By contrast, although Trenchard and Shrewsbury took Lunt's deposition in June, it is hard to find evidence that either closely followed the trial preparations. Shrewsbury, as we saw above, was genuinely confused by the dénouement of the trial, unable to "be very clear in relating the contrivance."[18]

The idea that Trenchard or other courtiers deliberately framed the Lancashire gentlemen, however, gained traction after the trial. Tories launched a campaign in Parliament, the press, and the courts to discredit the Whig government officials deemed responsible for the prosecution. A central theme of the pamphlet literature was that the enemies of the subject's liberties were hidden but high ranking. As the anonymous author of *The Lancashire Sham-Plot* put it,

> Yet it won't be amiss to give you a hint
> Of this cursed sham plot and what by it was meant,
> And of those of great note that had a hand in't
> Which nobody can deny
>
> This sepentine monster was first hatch'd in hell
> And nourished by some that I know very well:
> But I dare not speak out, nor all the Truth tell
> Which nobody etc.
>
> But this I'll affirm, and if need I can swear
> We've had a sham-plot at least once a year
> And till one does take, they'll go on still I fear
> Which nobody etc.
>
> Yet no man can say but the last was well laid,
> And Breerton, Wilson and Lunt were well paid,
> And encouraged with Gold to set up their Trade
> Which nobody etc.[19]

For the pamphleteer Thomas Wagstaffe, the false oaths of the witnesses pointed to "a great deal more behind the curtain, some secret and invisible springs which moved the machine, some who contrived the business, prompted these ungodly instruments, and taught them their lesson, and abetted them in the prosecution and management." Wagstaffe declined to name names but inserted a heavy hint that the ministerial Whigs had deliberately fabricated a plot in order to intimidate members of parliament to "give or be hanged," that is, to vote in favor of a controversial money bill which they otherwise would have rejected out of fear of being accused of being traitors themselves. Thus, Wagstaffe concluded, "perjured villains were set up and maintained to overawe the parliament" and "scare people out of their liberties."[20]

Tories spearheaded inquiries in both the Commons and the Lords, hoping to use the "sham plot" scandal to discredit Whigs in the ministry. These efforts failed: both Houses voted (albeit with significant division) that the officials who initiated and oversaw the trials had acted appropriately, and the Commons voted that there was indeed a dangerous plot.[21]

The arena of battle then shifted to the courts. The three major witnesses (Lunt, Wilson, and Womball) were held for trial at the King's Bench, on charges of conspiracy, but the trials never took place. They were then convicted of perjury at the Lancashire Assizes in August 1695. That conviction was rescinded, however, when the three men persuaded the court that they had received no notice of the trial.[22]

There are no detailed records of the court proceedings, but the political stakes were high enough that Tory politicians, like the Earl of Nottingham and the MP Roger Kenyon, became deeply involved in pursuing the perjury case against the Lancashire Plot witnesses. Not surprisingly, the fact that Lunt, Wilson, and Womball escaped punishment only confirmed in these critics their belief that high government officials had connived with the perjurers and were now protecting them to protect themselves.[23]

The truth of these charges is hard to assess, but a cryptic letter from Chancellor John Somers to the Earl of Portland, indicating that Portland and the king thought the trials of the Lancashire witnesses should be "taken care of" but that neither Somers himself nor anyone in public employment should "meddle in that matter," could be glossed as confirmation of Tory suspicions. There was certainly continuing solicitude for the Lancashire witnesses on the part of government officials. In 1696 John Womball was put into line for a vacancy in the customs service, and the Lords Justices agreed to give Lunt and Womball allowances. In November 1696 the three prosecution witnesses were granted a *nolle prosequi* to prevent further prosecution. It is easy to see why friends and allies of the Lancashire gentlemen would think they had been robbed of justice.[24]

Supporters of the government, however, were equally bitter about the affair. They were convinced that the Lancashire gentlemen really were guilty but had escaped justice by suborning Taaffe and the other witnesses who testified against Lunt. Some accused the king's counsel, Sir William Williams, of deliberately losing the trial. The pain that the episode occasioned for Whigs can be glimpsed in Burnet's *History of His Own Time*, which presents the government's humiliation in the Lancashire Plot trials as the background to the also humiliating passage of the Treason Trials Act. It was only with the discovery of the apparently more real Assassination Plot in 1696 that the government had a chance to vindicate itself.[25]

Religion, Party Politics, and Loyalty

The Lancashire Plot affair raised questions about how to distinguish between the loyal and the disloyal. The traditional default category for identifying disloyalty was Catholicism: Catholics had been suspected of disloyalty since the sixteenth century and after 1688 were assumed to sympathize with their co-religionist James II. Nonetheless, Anglican Tories and dissenting Whigs used the Lancashire Plot affair to cast suspicion on one another and portray themselves as the most reliable support for the regime. In the process, Catholics found themselves, ironically, in a position to make a case for their own loyalty to William and Mary.

"Papists" in Lancashire and elsewhere certainly constituted a ready-made set of "usual suspects" to be rounded up at moments of crisis. As early as 22 December 1688, just as James II was escaping to France, the House of Lords (at that time the only legitimate institution of government left standing) issued orders that all papists, with the important exception of householders who had resided there three years, depart London and Westminster and the surrounding area ten miles adjacent. London and Westminster justices of the peace accordingly issued warrants to constables to search out popish recusants and ask them to depart and to report lists of names. In Lancashire, numerous Catholic gentlemen were rounded up by Lord Lieutenant Charles Brandon and detained until the following June.[26]

It is significant, however, that even when "papists" were targeted for searches or round-ups, officials in practice felt little obligation to limit themselves to "legal papists" (persons who had had refused to take the Declaration against Transubstantiation). The assertion that a papist or reputed papist was

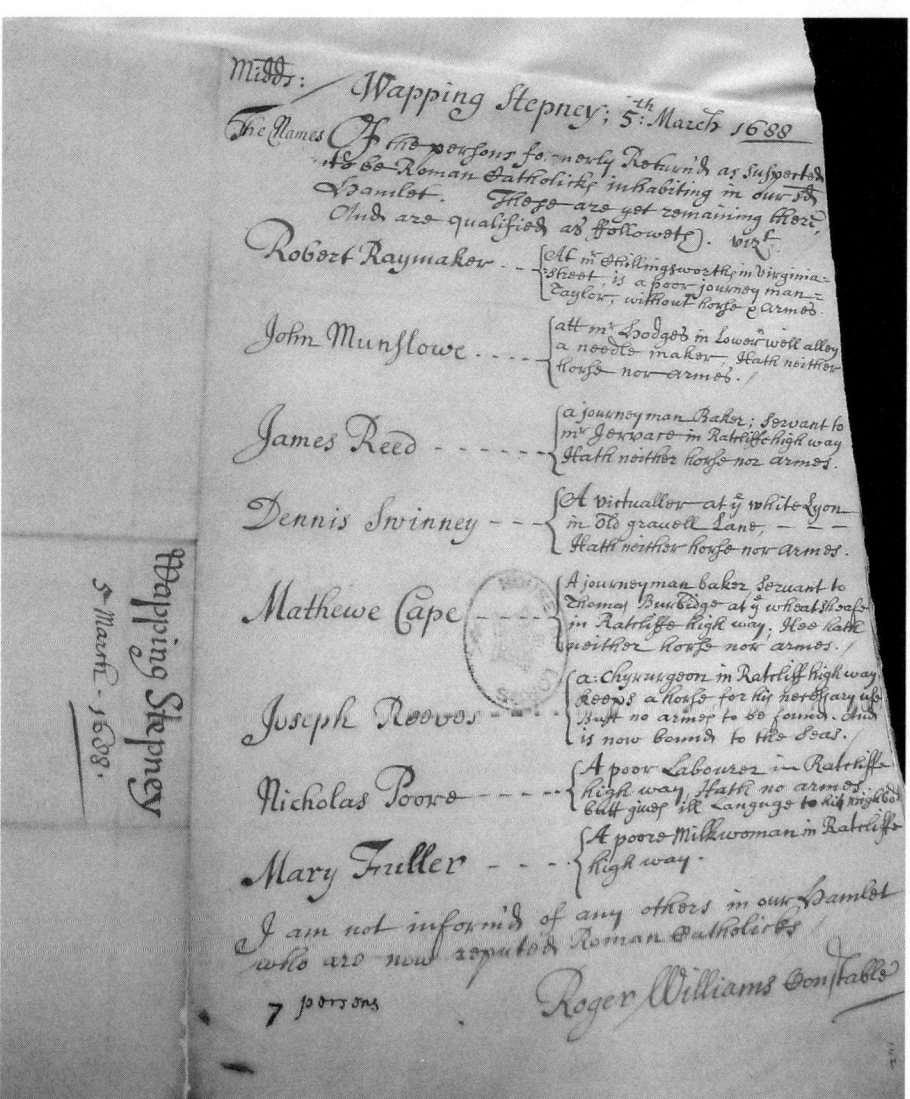

Example of a constable's "return of papists," as required by the House of Lords in 1688. Constable Roger Williams of Wapping found seven Roman Catholics and noted their addresses, occupations, and whether they possessed horses and arms. Return of Papists by Constable Roger Williams for Wapping, 1688. HL/PO/JO/10/1/402/6—Main Papers, Parliamentary Archives, London.

present in a group, or was the owner of a house where a group met, was enough to license a search that would include disaffected persons regardless of religion. Thus, a warrant might be given to "apprehend several dangerous and disaffected persons who meet and cabal at the houses of several persons in Westminster who are papists or reputed papists." Colonel Edward Matthews was ordered to "search for concealed arms belonging to papists, and to apprehend all Irish papists together with other traitors and conspirators." Lord Lumley received instructions give orders for disarming papists and their adherents. A similar slippage from defining Catholics as the objects of an action to targeting a wider group can be seen in the orders given by Lancashire justices of the peace to the bailiffs of Wigan, in Lancashire, to search for "absconded papists," Irish and popish soldiers, and "any thievish, roguish, or other felonious or suspected persons to be robbers of houses." The promiscuous accretion of terms—papist and reputed papists and adherents of papists and disaffected persons—suggests that authorities knew perfectly well that Catholicism in and of itself was not the equivalent of disloyalty and that not all the people they wished to target were Catholic.[27]

In Lancashire in particular, it would be a mistake to assume that Catholics were marked as a distinct and distinctly disloyal group. A long history of friendship and cooperation between Catholics and some Tory Anglicans, at least among elites, dated back to the shared experience of being Cavaliers in the civil war. Powerful Anglican Tories like Roger Bradshaigh in Wigan were known to protect Catholics and were associated with crypto-Catholic Jacobitism. Such an association seems to have lain behind the notorious remark of the judge Giles Eyre that among the trial defendants "Protestants of the Church of England, as they call themselves, were mingled with Papists as the Iron and the Clay in Nebuchadnezzar's image."[28]

The well-known Anglican-Catholic friendships had given Lancashire Tories (as well as Catholics) a bad name. In the early 1690s, Whigs successfully exploited the Williamite regime's perception of Lancashire as a dangerous place, campaigning to replace local Tory justices with Whigs and persuading William to choose as lord lieutenant the ardently Whig Charles Gerard, Lord Brandon (later Second Earl of Macclesfield), rather than the Tory Earl of Derby. As Lionel Glassey points out, petty issues of patronage in Lancashire became tangled with national party conflict. The story of the Preston House of Correction is revealing. In 1689 the new Whig sheriff, John Birch of Ordsall, had dismissed William Tomlinson, the keeper of the Preston House of Correction, on grounds of suspected Jacobitism. Birch received support for this move from Lord Brandon and the Whig secretary of state Shrewsbury. The majority of local justices, however, voted to restore Tomlinson to his post, finding the charges of Jacobitism unfounded. Local

Tories enlisted the Earl of Nottingham, the Tory secretary of state, in the cause of restoring Tomlinson to his post. So high did passions run that when the Lancashire justices ordered Tomlinson's replacement, William Higgonson, to step down, Higgonson barricaded himself in the House of Correction and refused to come out.[29]

The House of Correction affair clearly rankled with Tories, so much so that Taaffe tried to invoke the memory of it during his testimony at the Manchester trial. Testifying to John Womball's motives for perjury, Taaffe recalled that Womball had told him he intended to ask his "very good friend" Lord Macclesfield (that is, Brandon) "for his interest to assist him to be made governor of the House of Correction at Preston in Lancashire." As Taaffe must have known, an audience of local jurors would readily assimilate this information to a narrative about false accusations of Jacobitism being used to gain appointments to political office.[30]

Whigs welcomed Lunt's revelations. The discovery of the plot would demonstrate the laxity of the Tory JPs who had allowed conspiracy to flourish, and the alleged involvement in it of Protestant non-jurors like Peter Legh would prove Anglicans were untrustworthy, in turn paving the way for Whig electoral victories. For the Whig MP Thomas Norris of Speke, the Lancashire Plot affair drew attention to Tory perfidy and also brightened Whig political prospects. Norris complained that arrests of suspects had been difficult because "the Popish gentlemen have such private retreats and so many friends" and because of the "irregular and undutiful" behavior of local justices of the peace. He then opined, "If some of the men now apprehended be not brought to their trials, it will turn to our prejudice; I am fully satisfied that if you fairly convict a number, especially of the protestants, it will be in our power to choose (even in this county) much better members of parliament in case of a dissolution."[31]

The immediate aftermath of Lunt's revelations only confirmed the image of Lancashire as a place where so-called Protestants of the Church of England consorted with papists and Jacobites. The difficulty of making arrests caused the Whig JP Thomas Lee in Croxton to tell Secretary of State Trenchard that his neighborhood was swarming with Jacobites ready to rebel: "My abode," he wrote, "is in the crowd of enemies to the government; it is certain they are in great consternation, and riding about continually, as I now am informed they have done in the night for some time past." Lee was dismayed in particular by the recalcitrance of the locals. At Chester, where the prisoners were to be held, he found the head military officer, an ensign Robinson, uncooperative; in general, he found men "timorous in their evidence concerning their neighbors." The negative image of Lancashire as a place of lawlessness was further promoted by Richard Kingston in his *True History*, which described how "the Popish mob at Manchester, animated by reading Ferguson's libel (which was in almost every hand in that Country)[,] had resolved to prevent the trials of the prisoners, by stoning the King's evidences to death, as they came into the town." For Whigs, the trials promised to be convenient political theater which would establish that Lancashire needed yet firmer Whig control.[32]

Whig efforts to associate Tory officeholders with Jacobitism, however, were undercut by the memory of how, in the 1680s, some Lancashire Whigs had collaborated with the regime of James II in the hopes of achieving toleration. The most important and successful of these "Whig collaborators" was Charles Gerrard, Lord Brandon, who became the Earl of Macclesfield in 1694. Immediately after the Revolution of 1688, Brandon remade himself as a Williamite Whig and became lord lieutenant of the county, replacing the Tory Lord Derby. Brandon's history, then, was the Achilles' heel in any representation of the Whigs as friends and the Tories as enemies of the Williamite regime.[33]

The memory of Whig collaboration with James II helps to explain why Tories, in particular Roger Kenyon, defended the Lancashire gentlemen and criticized the government's conduct of the trial. Kenyon's support for the mostly Catholic defendants was not based on any preexisting sympathy for Catholicism. Kenyon before the Revolution of 1688 had profited greatly as a collector of recusant fines. He was rumored to have "got as much by managing the convictions of the Roman Catholics that he redeemed a mortgage of 15 hundred pounds upon the Estate." His callous insistence on distraining a Catholic widow's property, in fact, provoked a notorious riot at Wigan in 1681.[34]

Kenyon's defense of his Catholic neighbors was therefore surprising. It is best understood as an attempt to construct an alternative narrative about loyalty, party, and religion in Lancashire in which Tories were the best supports of the regime and Whigs were the greatest threat.

While Whigs tried to paint Tories as Jacobites and crypto-Catholics, Kenyon wanted to draw attention to Brandon's history as a collaborator and cast doubt on his loyalty to the Williamite regime. Kenyon's actions in 1694 continued a long-running campaign to call Brandon's loyalty into question. Two manuscripts in Kenyon's papers, probably produced shortly after the revolution as part of an attempt to block Brandon's appointment as lord lieutenant, detailed Brandon's Jacobite and pro-Catholic inclinations. Brandon had been "a violent assertor of [James II's] dispensing power," had pressed the people "to choose men for the parliament that would take away our penal laws and tests," consorted with Catholic priests and "all the popish gentry," and had taken up arms for James II at the time of the revolution. According to Kenyon, Brandon was still courting popish supporters. As Kenyon recalled, although Brandon had put the "chief papists" in prison, he had given them extraordinary freedom, so that

> each had so much liberty as to choose his lodging, to remove at pleasure upon any dislike to any other lodging, to meet and dine together, where they pleased, to converse without any restraint with any that came to them, together or apart, and some of them were frequently permitted to go to their own homes and to return upon parole without any keeper. . . . [A] little before the election of this parliament, to sweeten them for their interest, they were all discharged upon bail. . . . [W]hen the Lord Brandon came down and set up his friend Sir Samuel Gerard to be chose at Lancaster, several papists, which before absconded, came to give votes for his friend, Sir Samuel, his Lordship personally appearing to manage that election."

How, then, was Brandon (now Earl of Macclesfield) concerned in the Lancashire Plot trials? Ironically, he had been far away at the time of the arrests and so had little direct involvement. But that makes it all the more striking that Kenyon insisted on associating the prosecution of the Lancashire defendants with dissent in general and as much as possible with Lord Macclesfield. Richard Kingston reported that special efforts had been made by the Lancashire gentlemen and their allies at the time of the parliamentary hearings to "vilely abuse" Macclesfield. Macclesfield, in response, reviled Roger Kenyon and his son George, describing the latter (who was seeking a job as recorder of Wigan) as the "son of old Kenyon who not only follows his father's steps but was chosen by a party who profess themselves for King James, ridiculed the Lancashire Plot, and by the contrivance of old Kenyon prosecuted the king's witnesses for perjury." Both Kenyon and Macclesfield, then, insisted on making the Lancashire Plot affair about one another.[36]

Kenyon attacked other Whig dissenters too, like the "furious fanatic" Aaron Smith. He took Giles Eyre's remarks about Nebuchadnezzar's image quoted above to be "a side-blow at the Church of England." The indictment of dissent directly, and of Macclesfield implicitly, provided a springboard for rewriting narratives of loyalty and disloyalty in Lancashire in such a way that suspicion would fall onto dissenters rather than Anglicans.[37]

Although his hatred of Macclesfield and dissent remained a constant for Kenyon between 1688 and 1694, his position on Catholics did a 180-degree turn. Perhaps his views were softened by the trial itself, where he might have heard Catholics described as loyal to the new regime. One defense witness, a former deputy lieutenant of Lancashire, reported that the Catholic defendant Thomas Clifton "several times expressed . . . much zeal and affection for the present government, saying how much the persons of his religion ought to be satisfied with their usage under it." For whatever reason, Kenyon moved from a story, based on his memory of James's reign, in which Catholics and dissenters colluded against Tories, church, and King William to one in which dissenters posed the real danger and Anglicans and Catholics might ally against them. The granddaughter of Catholic defendant Lord Molineux remarked upon Kenyon's dramatic change of heart, saying that she never expected Kenyon to have shown himself "so much a friend to the Roman Catholics as she heard [he] had done." It may have been the beginning of a beautiful new relationship between Kenyon and Lancashire Catholics: in 1696 he was apparently giving legal advice to those wishing to avoid recusancy charges.[38]

The shifting of religious and political alignments in Lancashire was one important result of the sham plot scandal. Of course, the very terms of the transformation were unstable. The narrative about Presbyterians courting the papists that backed up Kenyon's antipathy to Whig dissenters depended on the assumption that it was a bad thing to court papists. It is unclear how long Kenyon would remain friendly to Catholics in Lancashire. But for a moment, Catholics benefited from his about-face.

For Kenyon, in sum, the Lancashire Plot controversy became a stage on which to combat Jacobite-baiting by Whigs directed against Tory churchmen and to show that the Tories rather than the Whigs might be the best friends of the Williamite regime. He was not entirely successful. The aftermath of the parliamentary hearings and the failure of attempts to try Lunt, Wilson, and Womball might suggest the opposite. But the fact that Kenyon could and did try to challenge the easy assumption that Whigs were more loyal than Tories showed that the lines separating the loyal from the disloyal had become muddied and confusing. Robert Ferguson, in an entirely different way, saw opportunity in that confusion as well.

Robert Ferguson, the Rule of Law, and the Specter of Williamite Tyranny

Robert Ferguson wrote two pamphlets in 1694, *A Letter to the Right Honourable Sir John Holt, Kt. Lord Chief Justice of the Kings Bench; Occasioned by the Noise of a Plot* and *A Letter to Mr. Secretary Trenchard, Discovering a Conspiracy against the Laws and Ancient Constitution of England: With Reflections on the Present Pretended Plot* (hereafter referred to respectively as the *Letter to Holt* and *Letter to Trenchard*). Both texts charged William with continuing the tyranny of his predecessors. Much of their rhetorical force was derived from Ferguson's personal history, which was widely known. In the Restoration, Ferguson had been a committed Whig allied with Shaftsbury and other opponents of Charles II. When Shaftsbury in 1681 had been jailed on charges of plotting insurrection, Ferguson had defended him in a successful pamphlet, *No Protestant Plot*. The appearance of that pamphlet prior to Shaftsbury's trial probably influenced the grand jury to return a verdict of *ignoramus* on the indictment and free the accused. By repeating his past performance, and again publishing pamphlets prior to a trial, Ferguson brought home the point that nothing had changed since the time of Charles II.

There were strong echoes of *No Protestant Plot* in both *Letter to Holt* and *Letter to Trenchard*. All these pamphlets argued that the king's evil ministers had trumped up charges against political enemies and suborned witnesses to swear against them. In 1681 and in 1694 Ferguson used the same tactic of naming the anticipated witnesses and then discrediting each one. He also cited the same passage from Tacitus, describing how, in the reign of Tiberius, "trepans and false informers, who had been always found a public mischief, and whom no penalties or punishments could sufficiently restrain, were then encouraged and emboldened by rewards." *No Protestant Plot* and *Letter to Trenchard* both alleged further that people who could prove prosecution witnesses had been bribed to perjure themselves had been taken into custody and silenced prior to trial. Ferguson seemingly brought the memory of 1681 to bear on his understanding of 1694, in order to emphasize the tyranny of the Williamite regime.[39]

Another important point of continuity between Ferguson's earlier and later writings was the clever tactic of denying the existence of a conspiracy, on the one hand, and justifying it, on the other: if you falsely accuse people of plotting, Ferguson suggested, you cannot blame them if they then plot.

Ferguson believed that the attempted judicial murder of Shaftsbury by the state had driven the earl to organize a real insurrection (though not assassination) in 1682. As he put it in *Letter to Holt*, "The interposition and influence which some of King Charles's ministers had, both in forging and forming that pretended plot (in [16]81) and in suborning miscreants to support the belief of it by falsehood and perjury, was that which gave provocation and encouragement to the designed insurrection in 1682. For when men can't find safety in their innocency, they will seek to obtain it by their swords." This move served Ferguson well precisely because his agenda was not simply to defend Shaftsbury and the Lancashire gentlemen, respectively, but also (and here was a contradiction) to subtly justify the insurrections that these "innocents" were accused of fomenting.[40]

Ferguson did not simply repeat himself, however. There were subtle but important differences between his writings of 1681 and 1694 that underscore the changed context of the 1690s. One conspicuous change was that in 1694 he adopted a confessionally neutral approach to sham plots. In the early 1680s, Ferguson had believed Titus Oates about the Popish Plot, or at least said he believed him. *No Protestant Plot*, moreover, maintained that the fabrication of sham plots was something that papists do to cover their own designs against the government. Ferguson recalled, for example, that Mary Queen of Scots encouraged her Catholic followers to pretend that their stockpile of arms and horses was for the purpose of defending Queen Elizabeth from the Puritans. By contrast, the 1694 *Letter to Holt* was confessionally evenhanded. Ferguson admitted that Oates was a perjurer. He described informers as ideologically and religiously indifferent, driven only by money, "trained up to swear men out of their lives ... if they might be plentifully paid and rewarded for it." "Having breakfasted on those of one party," Ferguson continued, informers "were willing to sup on them of another, for being habituated to blood, it was indifferent to them whom they murderously destroyed; and all that obtained a room in their thoughts, was the being assured beforehand in whose slaughter they should make the better meal."[41]

The encouragement of informers was now, in 1694, redefined as a matter of tyranny rather than popery, and specifically of tyranny exercised by money. Ferguson was therefore able to tie a critique of informers to a country critique of the court's control of Parliament through bribery and placemen. "And it is beyond all contradiction," he wrote, "that whosoever will hire and bribe Members of Parliament to subvert and destroy the constitution and murder the Kingdom ... such persons will never scruple the ruining individual persons by the worst and most infamous arts."[42]

The metaphor of informers as members of Parliament, and government ministers as the hirers of both informers and placemen, resonated with an emerging "country ideology" expressed elsewhere in the pamphlet literature, criticizing high taxes, the war, the presence of Dutch soldiers, and the expansion of executive power. For example, Wagstaffe's *Letter out of Lancashire*, published right after the trial, was kinder to MPs, but it made essentially the same point as Ferguson, that the trials were connected to the aggrandizement of power by the court over Parliament. The trial had been timed, the author argued, just before the next session, to intimidate members into voting for a money bill:

> The timing of this highly deserves consideration, it was just before the present session of Parliament, and in all probability, the money bill will not pass so easily, at least in such proportions, as some men may require, such prodigious sums having been given already, and the kingdom exhausted to the very bones; But here was a method to ram it down their throats, the destroying evidences hang over their heads, and there was no medium, either give or be hanged.[43]

Ferguson's 1694 pamphlets also differed from *No Protestant Plot* in taking up questions of civil liberty that were not on the agenda in the 1680s. In that sense, the radicalism of his critique was made possible by the revolution itself. The most striking feature of his Lancashire Plot writings is his far-reaching critique of practices of detaining suspects. Although the suspension of habeas corpus had been condemned in other Jacobite and Tory literature, Ferguson's *Letter to Trenchard* outlined problems that the Habeas Corpus Act, even when not suspended, did not address. Ferguson pointed out that even when people were eventually able to make use of habeas corpus, they could be destroyed by the expenses of being in custody, the absence of any limits on the bail that could be set, and the long vacations between law terms. That was especially the case because secretaries of state had been able to issue blank warrants or warrants in which no particular crime was specified, and were able to issue warrants against persons on suspicion even if there was no witness to make an oath against that person. Ferguson thus set a high standard of proof to be met before anyone could be detained: no one should be arrested at all unless the warrant specified not only the crime and the person but also the witnesses that had sworn to it. Ferguson also drew attention to the powers of the royal "messengers," who were now making arrests and detaining suspects privately, on warrants from the Privy Council or secretaries of state rather than judges. Messengers who confined prisoners to their houses, Ferguson complained, did not have to obey the same rules as actual jailers, who at least had to keep records. Ferguson also decried the absence of procedures for handling papers seized from suspects. Messengers were allowed to carry away jumbles of uncatalogued paper; consequently, incriminating evidence might be slipped in, or (almost as bad) prisoners might lose valuable business records and be ruined.[44]

In comparison to other writings critical of the Lancashire Plot trials, Ferguson's *Letter to Trenchard* clearly stood out from the pack. In contrast, Wagstaffe in his *Letter out of Lancashire* simply made a conventional demand for the passage of a bill to regulate treason trials. Roger Kenyon and the Earl of Nottingham, for their parts, both attacked the proceedings against the defendants, but on much narrower grounds and within the framework of existing law and decency as they understood it, decrying, for example, irregularities in the selection of the jury panel and the lack of assistance given to the deaf and senile defendant Lord Molineux.[45]

Even when he joined Tories and Jacobites in defending the Lancashire gentlemen, then, Ferguson retained a distinctly Whig ideological stamp. Some recent historians have found the term "Whig-Jacobite" useful to capture Ferguson's complexity. Mark Goldie, Clare Jackson, and Melinda Zook all see consistency in Ferguson's critique of Restoration tyranny and his critique of the Williamite regime: his radical about-face, the turn from Whiggery to Jacobitism, was not really an about-face at all. The observation that Ferguson was (certainly in his own eyes) consistent needs, however, to be complicated by an acknowledgment that in almost every respect Ferguson's rhetorical strategies hinged upon creating uncertainty about his own allegiance, and about the allegiance of others.[46]

Underneath the forthright critique of the regime as violating the subject's rights there was a complicated, subversive game: Ferguson gestured at layers upon layers of secret agendas, casting doubt upon prevailing categories of loyalty and disloyalty and making his own position hard to decode. The most consistent thing about Ferguson was his conviction that nothing was what it seemed. The protagonists of Ferguson's writings on the Rye House Plot, for example, were men who joined the conspiracy for the sake of stopping it but covered their true intentions by being louder than anyone else in promoting it. In Ferguson's 1694 Lancashire Plot pamphlets, James II's ministers were alleged to have conspired with the Prince of Orange. The government spy Richard Kingston was described in *Letter to Holt* as traveling in disguise, "sometimes in the habit of a parson, and assuming his character; at another time in a lay garb, and personating in one place a physician, in another a discarded Jacobite officer; and all to try whether he can decoy any into a compacential [*sic*] hearing of a conspiracy against the government."[47]

The most chameleon-like figure in Ferguson's narrative was his former associate from Shaftsbury's circle, the current secretary of state John Trenchard. In 1682, Ferguson reminded readers, Trenchard had reneged on a promise to bring troops from the west to assist Shaftsbury's (real and justifiable) planned insurrection against Charles II, allegedly pleading that he was ill from a venereal infection. And so Trenchard, described by Ferguson as a chronic hater of monarchy, was now pursuing the overthrow of a government by means more suitable to his cowardly nature: running the government so badly that William's subjects would inevitably rebel. To encourage suspicion of Trenchard, Ferguson let drop that he had been caught with a picture of the Prince of Wales. Yet even Trenchard's method of fomenting revolution by encouraging tyranny, as Ferguson presented it, was not what it appeared: Ferguson intimated the bad policies that provoked anti-government plotting were actually helpful to the government, as they made the government's allegation of conspiracies more believable! Trenchard's motives were thus presented as ultimately unknowable; the byzantine, Machiavellian calculations lying behind his actions could always, in Ferguson's mind, be given another twist.[48]

Ferguson's tactic of confusing or reversing political categories enabled him to discredit the government not simply on grounds that it was tyrannical but also on grounds that its own apparent supporters wished to undermine it. His obsession with the difficulty of knowing what side a person was really on allowed him to intervene in the debate about oaths of allegiance. He suggested in *Letter to Trenchard* that very few people actually believed in William's lawful right to the throne and that most who did take oaths of allegiance did so on defactoist grounds.

> Most of those who serve this government, as well as those who refuse allegiance to it, believe him [William] on the throne to be only King de facto, but not de jure: Nor is this merely the opinion of your non-swearers and those

> called Jacobites, but it is the firm belief of two in three of your swearers, who are vulgarly stiled Williamites: for the utmost that either law or religion will allow them to acknowledge, is, that he is king by exercise but not by right.[49]

Such a claim effectively erased the distinction between a non-juror and a defactoist juror. That erasure in turn worked on several levels. On the surface, Ferguson called for compassion for those who posed no danger to the government, "who cannot nicely distinguish themselves from under the obligations that they owe to King James, that are nevertheless willing to remain quiet under the power that is over them, and to sleep in whole skins." At the same time, he justified whatever it was that non-jurors might have done in reaction to their bad treatment.

> I am inclinable to believe, that had not those styled Jacobites been made all of them uneasy in their fortunes, and many of them impoverished, by double taxes . . . they would sit as silent and quiet under this administration as any others whatsoever, though they cannot equally approve and commend it.

Even more subversively, Ferguson suggested to those who had sworn allegiance to the government that there wasn't anything separating them from so-called Jacobites. That could be taken as an invitation to join an insurrection.[50]

Ferguson's insistence on seeing disguise everywhere he looked, along with his insistence that nothing really separated jurors and non-jurors, wrought havoc with the boundaries of allegiance. Even if his intentions were Jacobite, the significance of the pamphlets was less in winning adherents to Jacobitism than in putting front and center the difficulty of assessing the loyalty or the credibility of anyone. In this respect, Ferguson's project of confusing his readers as to who was really on what side oddly converged with Kenyon's. Kenyon also wrought havoc with the boundary between loyalty and disloyalty, if with perhaps a less disruptive intention. He helped to open up a space where Catholics could present themselves as loyal while casting doubt on the Lord Brandon, one of the regime's loudest supporters.

Together, Ferguson and Kenyon exacerbated the sense of uncertainty about how to distinguish between the loyal and the disloyal, which in turn fueled bitter fights over the wording and enforcement of oaths of allegiance that continued throughout the 1690s and beyond. Their weird alliance demonstrates the convergence of several strands of anxiety and discontent. An Anglican discourse about the rise of fanatics converged with a country discourse about corruption and tyranny, converging in turn with a Jacobite effort to delegitimate the revolution. These in turn, as will be seen below, played into worries about social hierarchy and commercial credit. Such issues were not the same, but they could feed one another; someone drawn into one discourse might more readily respond to the others. It was the combination that made them persuasive, creating a crisis of credibility for the Williamite regime.

Credit and Credibility

The deceptiveness of appearance and the difficulty of knowing what or whom to believe was a central issue in the Lancashire Plot affair. The defense of the Lancashire gentlemen hinged on masquerade: Taaffe and his allies had playacted to lure Lunt into revealing his deliberate perjury. The credibility or lack thereof of the prosecution witnesses was also the object of intense research by families and friends of the defendants prior to the trial, and after the trial the credibility of defense witnesses was attacked by those who thought the gentlemen guilty after all. Questions of credibility were not confined to defendants and prosecution witnesses. Many people were drawn at some stage of the proceedings into vouching for or discrediting others.

Many of the people who argued about the plot took social status to be an indicator of credibility. Perhaps the most spectacular example of social class being used to establish credit and discredit came in the performance of Roger Dicconson, one of the men Taaffe recruited to pretend to be a willing false witness in order to lure Lunt into revealing his scheme. Dicconson gleefully described how, posing as a Mr. Howard, he tested Lunt's hubris and ignorance by asking him if he knew Roger Dicconson (to which Lunt confidently replied he knew him well). The most delicious moment in Dicconson's testimony came when he described the obviously lower-class Lunt dismissing the only slightly more plebian Wilson and Womball as "a couple of blockheads," while fawning over his new gentleman friend "Mr. Howard." At the end of the meeting, according to Dicconson, Lunt offered to embrace Howard/Dicconson, which, Dicconson told his audience, he avoided. The repudiation of Lunt's physical embrace, and Dicconson sharing his revulsion with his hearers, worked to establish bonds of class solidarity between Dicconson and his gentlemanly audience, underscoring his status as a gentleman despite being a Catholic and despite his disguise.[51]

Notions of social hierarchy were also important for Roger Kenyon and his circle, but in a slightly different way. Lunt and his fellow prosecution witnesses were certainly shown *not* to be gentlemen. Beyond that, however, they were disorderly: they were discredited not simply because they stood at the bottom of the social hierarchy but because they disrespected their superiors and flouted morality. Roger Kenyon penned a biographical narrative about Lunt in which he portrayed him as a disloyal, pilfering, and sexually invasive servant. Thus, Lunt was discharged from the service of his first master, Mr. Smith of Quineyborrow, for "having grown so saucy as to pretend to love his master's daughter." Likewise, Kenyon claimed that when Lunt was postillion and undergroom to Lord Oswaldston in 1682 he cut out and sold the rich lining of his lady's coach and as a consequence was sent to Bridewell. Kenyon's circle of correspondents contributed to this picture. Richard Townley wrote that Lunt (prior to 1689) had a reputation as an "idle and ill man" who had once "pretended to be contracted to a cook-maid of mine, and . . . had made a great bustle about her, even though she was married." Further inquiry undertaken by Townley's servants had revealed that Lunt already lived with a woman who "was esteemed, and owned herself, his wife." Thomas Fleetwood reported to Kenyon that an old woman (possibly the wife of Lunt's father)

> told me many of his rogueries, too long to writ[e], when he was young. His first master was one Mr. Hastings, with whom he stayed not long; then went to the Mr. Smith you mention, and he, beginning to bear up to his daughter, he turned him off. Hence, he went to London, and one of Smith's servants, that was in love with him, followed him to London, and put him prentice, to a shoemaker, where he stayed 2 or 3 years, and then fell out with his master and listed himself a soldier.

Prosecution witness George Wilson was another disruptive plebian, and Kenyon collected a number of complaints that he had dumped his children on the care of the parish.[52]

Robert Ferguson's pamphlets also linked the credibility of witnesses to financial solvency, although in a way that was perhaps more meaningful to tradesmen than to rural gentlemen. Whereas Kenyon and Roger Dicconson focused on violations of traditional social hierarchies to discredit prosecution witnesses, Ferguson focused on credit fraud, perhaps to appeal to a potential audience in the trading town of Manchester where his pamphlet was distributed prior to the trial. Thus, he described Harry Baker as a person of "infamous character . . . against whom there are so many actions for debt." About Alexander Johnstone (the brother of Scotch Secretary James Johnstone),

Ferguson wrote, "The Court hath been a sanctuary to him . . . to cover him from paying his creditors." Ferguson alleged that another witness, Captain Brewerton, stole from his landlady and cleverly avoided paying rent to another landlord in France by leaving him, as a valuable "security," a chest that turned out to be filled with stones. And Lunt "being asked by a poor man for a debt which he owed him . . . he instead of that caused him to be apprehended as a traitor" and likewise requited Mr. Noel of Dover for his kindness in lending him money by accusing him of high treason. Mr. Slingsby, a witness against Crosby, "fastened on a gentleman a sham bill of fifty pounds."[53]

The prosecution witnesses were not the only people whose credit was at stake in the Lancashire Plot affair. As friends and family of the defendants conducted their research into the backgrounds of witnesses, they had occasion to take the testimony of a wide range of people, whose credibility then came up for judgment. The document entitled "notes to discredit witnesses" preserved in the Blundell family's papers lets us trace these trains of accreditation. In the document we find a list of particular allegations against prosecution witnesses, and for each allegation, names of people able to support it. For example, one Mr. Ashton, who said that Womball tried to suborn him to swear against Peter Legh, is listed under the heading "To discredit Womball." On a separate list, John Pownall and Thomas Bumford are named as witnesses "to Ashton's credit." Likewise, Richard Shaw, his wife, and six other people were listed as able to testify that another prosecution witness, Breerton, had sworn revenge upon the defendant Sir Rowland Stanley; a further witness, "Alder Mannering" (Alderman Mainwaring?) was entered on the list as a witness "to the credit of Shaw and other witnesses."[54]

The investigations by friends of the Lancashire gentlemen thus called forth a large number of local "informers" who gave direct and indirect evidence about the reliability of potential witnesses, opening up a much wider dialogue about who was and was not credible in local society. The motives of these local informers are often obscure. Did they know or care how their information would be used? Were they bribed by the friends of the Lancashire gentlemen, as was later alleged? Were they coerced? Did they manipulate the gentlemen and gentlewomen who came to make inquiries, grabbing a chance to spread gossip for their own purposes? Did the informants have political views or party identifications?[55]

In most cases these questions are not answerable. Even when information is available, it can be ambiguous. Consider, for example, the servant of

Richard Brooke who testified against his own son at the behest of his master. Brooke's letter to Kenyon introducing the unnamed servant portrays the man as "willing" but also implicitly invokes the all-important power of masters to give or withhold character references, thus making the historian wonder how voluntary the testimony would have been:

> This bearer (an old servant to this family and therefore I presume no stranger to you) is willing to do his country right by giving evidence against his own son (one of their majesty's witnesses). And his testimony (if material) may be the more significant on the account of his relation, however if he can any other way be useful to [the defendant] Mr. L[egh] you may command his utmost either at Manchester or Chester and I think you may trust him otherwise he should not have this character under my hand of your faithful servant.[56]

It is certainly likely that social elites used their power to bring subordinates to testify. Kenyon's correspondent Henry Prescott reported some frustration in Wales, where "I met with many gentlemen who could say they believed [prosecution witness George Wilson] to be a rogue, a villain, a violent papist . . . but none were willing to be subscribers even to their own words." Prescott relied on the assistance of Sir John Conway to persuade the local vicar, John Edwards, to make a sworn statement. Conway likewise prevailed upon Mr. Thomas Carter to promise that his own servant, John Bryan, would testify. Prescott's letter gives the unmistakable impression that people made formal statements only when pressured to do so.[57]

Other informers seem to have come forward voluntarily because they were already angry with one of the witnesses. Anthony Heathcote of Buxton in Derby, described as a "gent," had a personal grievance against George Wilson, to whom he had lent £60 to open an inn, only to find that Wilson's circumstances were much worse than had been supposed, that Wilson was already greatly in debt and besides "lived a lewd life."[58]

Sometimes the motives of informers are maddeningly elusive. Consider, for example, a letter from Bridget Molineux to her cousin, Thomas Legh (uncle of defendant Peter Legh). She had found someone (a Mr. Cheshire) to say that one of the likely witnesses at the trial had been suborned:

> Just now we have an account from Mr. Hawarden of Weedens who was lately sent to, by one Mr. Cheshire a mercer of Warrington to come to him, and after some discourse told him that not long ago a gentleman came to

him to change a penny, and after some discourse told him that he had been very conversant and always in the company of the [prosecution] witnesses when they were in Lancashire, and after several kind offers they proposed to assure him a £100 per annum, if he would become a witness amongst them, and swear to what he would dictate to him. This Mr. Cheshire is much concerned that innocent men should be so much abused, and is willing to take his oath of this before any magistrate, which if you think to ye purpose you may communicate it with what speed possible to Mr. Kenyon which if you please you may do by my servant Birch tomorrow morning who is to meet him at Cheekerbent on Saturday, . . .

PS he will discover the party when upon oath which by circumstances I find to be Mr. Barker.[59]

Bridget Molineux's letter opens up a fascinating and frustrating array of questions: who was Mr. Hawarden, and why was he the intermediary between Mr. Cheshire and Bridget? Cheshire's motives were also opaque: it is strange, after all, that a suborned witness would publicize his subornation. It is possible that Mr. Cheshire was concerned, as he said, "that innocent men should be so much abused," but it is also possible that he mentioned the sum he would be paid for lying in order to encourage the defenders of the Lancashire gentlemen, like Mr. Hawarden, to enter a bidding war. Although it cannot answer these questions, the document does reveal that the trial was talked about in advance, that it was known that the subornation of witnesses would be an issue, and that someone wanting to share such information would seek channels by which it would come to someone who could make use of it. It points to a dynamic in which the knowledge that gossip was desired actually created the gossip.

Insofar as it is possible to find recurring themes in the lives of people who participated in all this talk, those themes are trade and travel. People who had something to say of relevance tended to be in some form of trade, like Mr. Cheshire the grocer or William Barker, the Superstitious Lands Commission's witness, who was a dealer in horses and later tried to keep an alehouse (see chapter 4). Robert Ferguson's researches on the plot also benefited from the willingness of tradespeople to complain about those who ripped them off. People who traveled also appeared frequently as witnesses or commentators on the credibility of witnesses. Kenyon learned much from informers who had stayed at one of the inns where Taaffe, Lunt, Wilson, or Baker had lodged, such as the Wheat Sheaf in Manchester. Travelers were especially helpful in cutting through aliases. Simon Arrowsmith had been underjailer at Lancaster and had known Lunt when a prisoner there. He had met Lunt again in Manchester and recognized him, but Lunt insisted his name was "Smith." When Arrowsmith saw Lunt again at Wigan, Lunt explained, "He durst not own his name at Manchester because it might hinder the design they were then there upon."[60]

Travel across religious boundaries was also common among witnesses. Agnes Barker and John Taaffe were both converts from Catholicism. Womball was said to be married to a papist. Even more intriguing is John Brown, whose information about Womball's violent anti-Catholicism is contained in the "notes to discredit witnesses" in the Blundell manuscripts. Brown was present when Womball "upon discourse about papists said tis no more sin to hang a papist than a dog." Given that Brown was privy to Womball's speech, one can assume that he was not himself Catholic. Yet the fact that his statement is in the Blundell papers shows he was willing to talk to and help Catholics.[61]

Perhaps the best generalization that can be made (out of what are already generalizations) is that people who contributed information in the cause were in some way engaged in negotiating credit and identity: they did not experience their place in society as being fixed in a stable hierarchy but rather had experienced situations in which they had needed to establish their own credibility or assess that of others. They lived in a world where judgments of people were constantly necessary. Giving information about other people involved in the case was both a way of sharing judgments made and perhaps of establishing their own credibility as well. We cannot know exactly what motivated each informant to say what he did about whom he did. But taken together, informers' statements suggest that the micropolitics of establishing the credit of the humble interacted with the macropolitics of establishing the credit of the government. The trials were a site on which many different kinds of political battles were fought out.

Conclusion

The Lancashire Plot was a critical but as yet underexamined moment in the political history of the Williamite regime. It was, first, a test of the new regime's credibility: it raised questions about whether William had lived up to promises to protect the subjects' liberty as well as about the effectiveness and loyalty of those charged with protecting the government's security. Most observers would have found the government's credibility shaky on one or the other of these points. The immediate result of the Lancashire Plot was distrust.

Ironically, it would be possible to emerge from this chapter with a sunnier picture. The trial was (as Sir Giles Eyre saw it) in one sense a vindication of English justice. Although it is important not to downplay the sufferings of innocent defendants held for three months, the Manchester trial did end in an acquittal. But the fact that so few people saw this as a good thing is also sobering.

The Lancashire Plot affair can be seen paradoxically as a moment of political opening and a moment in which lines were hardened. It provided opportunities for many people to make claims for loyalty and to have a voice, however small, in matters of political importance. A wide range of people gave evidence formally or informally. Tories and Catholics made unusual claims to be reliable supporters of the regime. At the same time, there is no evidence that anyone persuaded anyone to change their minds. It is easy to see why the affair exacerbated party conflict. Whether one believed the "Whig" or "Tory" versions of the story depended on whether one believed Whigs or Tories to be credible people. Moreover, a belief in one version tended to confirm the heinousness of anyone who embraced the other version. There seemed to be no possibility of mediation between the "mutually exclusive conspiracy theories" that Whigs and Tories put forward about the Lancashire Plot. "Truth" seemed to be a matter of party allegiance. The divisions exacerbated by the Lancashire Plot were only partly healed by the discovery two years later of the Assassination Plot, which created (at least temporarily) more consensus.[62]

CHAPTER 7

Representation, Politics, and Law in the Assassination Plot

The credit of the Whig-dominated government was at risk in February 1696. The Bank of England had been established, but its success depended upon the recoinage of the currency, a complicated and potentially disruptive project that had only just gotten under way. Queen Mary's death in 1695 had diminished the government's claim to legitimacy by hereditary right. The Lancashire Plot fiasco, combined with general war weariness, had enabled some Tories in Parliament to transform themselves into a more ideologically appealing "country" opposition purporting to defend society from an overweening central government. The parliamentary session of 1695 saw resistance to new taxes, inquiries into corruption, and challenges to the Bank of England. It also, finally, produced a Treason Trials Act, much to the dismay of the government. The Whig memoirist Gilbert Burnet opined that "the design of [the act] seemed to be, to make men as safe in all treasonable conspiracies and practices as was possible."[1]

In this context, the timely discovery of a plot to assassinate William was a lucky break for the government. The response to the plot, however, called attention to the conflict between liberty and security, which again posed significant challenges for a regime's capacity to earn its subjects' trust. It was not taken for granted that the credit of the regime would emerge stronger from the Assassination Plot discovery.

The Assassination Plot can be defined narrowly or broadly. Narrowly, it was a plan to ambush King William in a narrow lane between Richmond and Brentford as he returned from hunting. The organizer of the plan (which is sometimes dubbed the "Turnham Green Plot") was Sir George Barclay, a Jacobite officer who had come over from France for the purpose. Barclay worked closely with some other high-level organizers—Robert Charnock,

George Porter, Ambrose Rookwood, Robert Lowick—each of whom separately recruited assassins. Altogether about forty men were said to have been recruited for this attack, which was planned for 15 February but postponed to 22 February after the king failed to go hunting on the fifteenth.[2]

Broadly defined, the Assassination Plot was a plot to encourage a French invasion and raise a rebellion at home to restore James II. One key moment in this more broadly defined Assassination Plot was a meeting held at the King's Head Tavern in Leadenhall Street sometime in May or June 1695, at which a group of plotters resolved to send Robert Charnock to France to invite King James to invade. In the eyes of the government, the participants in the King's Head Tavern meeting were just as guilty of "assassination" as the men who planned to attack King William, and considerable efforts were made to bring them to justice.

Those efforts only partly succeeded. Some conspirators, like George Barclay, escaped. The greatest problem prosecutors faced was the scarcity of credible witnesses. The two best, Thomas Prendergrass and Francis De La Rue, were plotters who had changed sides and came forward to warn King William. Unfortunately, neither of these men had been at the King's Head Tavern meeting, and each could identify only a fraction of the larger group of plotters. The witness with the most valuable information to offer was George Porter, who had been (with Charnock) among the leaders recruited by Barclay and had turned witness to save his own life. His credibility was therefore problematic. Other conspirators who later confessed or were convicted—William Bois, Thomas Bartram, Brice Blair, George Harris, Cardell Goodman, Alexander Knightly, and Peter Cook—posed the same problem.

The government's choice of whom to try, and when, was determined by the witnesses they had available. In the end, the list was small. The first defendants convicted were three men directly involved in the planned attack on William: one of the chief organizers—Robert Charnock—along with Edward King and Thomas Keyes. The last of these, a trumpeter, had a very small role in the plot. He had been servant to George Porter and had, he said, just done what his master told him. He seems to have been included in the trial simply because he was so easy to convict: his own master testified against him! The next two conspirators tried, John Friend and William Parkyns, were not assassins themselves but had helped to organize and finance the assassination or the rebellion. Several more trials and one notorious attainder secured convictions for some actual would-be assassins (Ambrose Rookwood, Charles Cranburne, Robert Lowick, and Alexander Knightley) and men who had been present at the King's Head Tavern meeting (Peter Cook and John Fenwick).

Perhaps the most important achievement in the trials for the government lay not in the number of convictions it obtained but in having persuaded the courts (and, through the press, the public) that the broad and narrow versions of the Assassination Plot were an organic whole, that the purpose of killing the king was to enable the invasion and rebellion to succeed. This was an ideological victory. The assassination of a king was something so horrifying that not even Jacobites could bring themselves to say it: they preferred to speak of "levying war upon the person of the Prince of Orange" or "attacking the Prince of Orange at the head of his guards." As one pamphleteer commented, kings and princes "always abhorred assassination," so much so that the martyred King Charles I "would not agree to permit Oliver Cromwell to be assassinated, though he was a usurper." Gathering arms and horses for the day when King James returned, carrying letters to France, facilitating the transfer of money, or distributing commissions to officers in a secret Jacobite army, in contrast, did not evoke the same outrage. Persons who prepared for war, even for a civil war, could be considered soldiers, and for that reason honorable. By insisting that the assassination was inseparable from the uprising and invasion that would follow on its heels, the government tried to infuse the latter with the horror evoked by the former.[3]

Representing the Revolution

Defining the Assassination Plot broadly made it possible to rewrite recent history. In hindsight, the Assassination Plot discovery lent credence to the Lancashire Plot. Clues to the connection were eagerly awaited and reported. Luttrell, for example, noted in his diary in June, "Mr. Knightly, prisoner in Newgate, has given some light into the conspiracy as also the Lancaster Plot." *A True History of the Horrid Conspiracy*, published sometime in June, eagerly reported that "one of the evidences . . . made such a discovery as did in a great measure confirm the Lancashire Plot; which the disaffected party had so much labored to ridicule." Two longer and more reflective histories of the plot, James Abbadie's *History of the Late Conspiracy* (1696) and Richard Kingston's *True History of the Several Designs and Conspiracies* (1698), wove the Lancashire Plot (as Lunt had described it) into a seamless narrative culminating in the Assassination Plot.[4]

England's currency woes were another one of the government's embarrassments that could be reinterpreted in light of the plot discovery. Abbadie reminded readers of his *History of the Late Conspiracy* that Titus Oates's revelations of 1678 had been reckoned a fable because they contained "some things which were looked upon as incredible, by reason of the enormity of the crimes." Among these allegations was one that conspirators had adulterated money and exported currency. Now, said Abbadie, "later experience has convinced us that they were really true; especially what relates to trade, exportation of species, and the debasement of money."[5]

Defining the Assassination Plot broadly also helped to enhance the affective appeal of the regime. Paul Monod's work has rightly called attention to the openly sentimental side of Jacobitism. Jacobites were certainly thought by their contemporaries to play shamelessly with emotions, inflaming passionate attachments to the Stuarts at the expense of the rational logic of self-preservation (it was for this reason, of course, that women were considered especially susceptible to their siren song). Moreover, Jacobites may have had advantages in the contest for the hearts as opposed to minds of the English people. They could make use of patriarchalist idioms, using familial attachments to fuel political allegiances. They also benefited from a tradition, established in the wake of the civil war, of elevating "loyalty" to the top of the hierarchy of laudable feelings.[6]

But Williamites should not be stereotyped as "rational." Despite, or perhaps because of, the obvious emotional appeals of Jacobitism, William's supporters strove to imbue the English people with a passionate attachment to both the person of the king and his government. At the same time, the affective culture of the Williamites could not simply repeat older, conventional forms of royalism. Personal loyalty to William had to be distinguished from personal loyalty to James, and loyalty as a value had to be reconciled with revolution. When James Abbadie wrote triumphantly that "loyalty is become *at last* the distinguishing mark of honest men" (italics mine), he implied that it was uniquely in William's reign that loyalty was an admirable trait. The challenge for Williamites, then, was to harness older royalist tropes and impulses, take them away from the Jacobites, and combine them, however improbably, with contractarian defenses of 1688.[7]

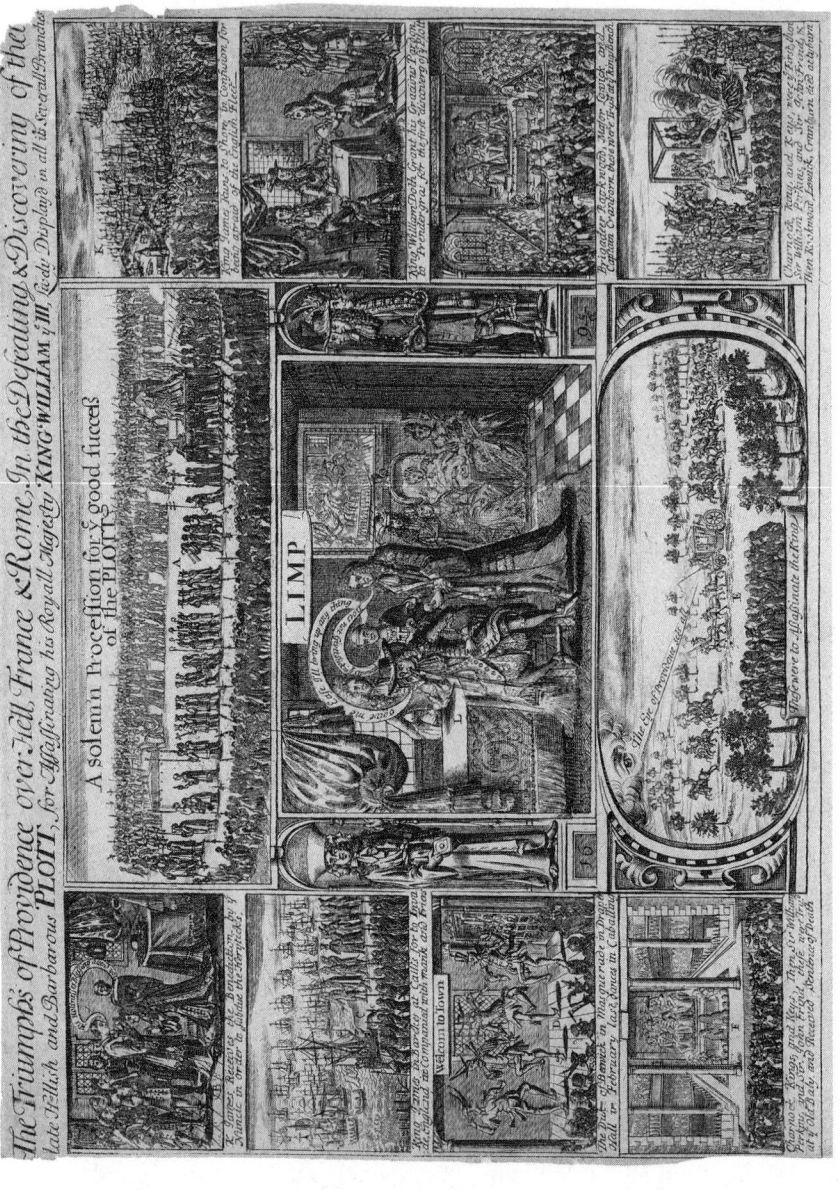

The Triumphs of Providence over Hell, France, and Rome, in Defeating and Discovering of the Late Hellish and Barbarous Plott (1696). This beautifully engraved broadside celebrates God's miraculous intervention, the thwarting of a French invasion, William's mercy to the virtuous informer Prendergrass, and the rule of law. The banner LIMP reminds viewers of the close tie between the exiled royal family (James, Mary of Modena, and the Prince of Wales) and Louis XIV. By permission of the Folger Shakespeare Library.

Abbadie's *History* serves as an excellent example of how Williamite writers harnessed traditional royalism to their cause. The king was portrayed in the narrative as having a special, God-given status as the only person who could protect England and Europe from the French. William's survival, Abbadie insisted, could hardly be a chance event; rather, there were "conspicuous marks of the finger of God" in it, and "it would be impious and absurd, to ascribe our deliverance to a lucky concourse of fortuitous acts." According to Abbadie, "God saw, and blasted their dark contrivances, and delivered Him whom he had made the deliverer of so many nations."[8]

This providential and even Christological language, however, sat alongside the language of consent, natural right, and the ancient constitution, to which Abbadie was also committed. "Tis impossible," Abbadie wrote, to dispute William's right to rule "without denying us the common and most essential privileges of a nation." Indeed, "the safety and consent of the people were the primitive and most sacred foundations of sovereign authority." And "by the fundamental constitution of our government, the people are originally free, and royal authority limited."[9]

Abbadie thus combined what have been often regarded as incompatible accounts of monarchy. He achieved this powerful synthesis by insisting that the defense of the king and the defense of the nation were literally the same. His *History* harped incessantly on the unity between king and people. "Never was the interest and happiness of a Prince so inseparably united to that of his people," Abbadie gushed. The conspiracy itself "served only to strengthen the union betwixt the king and his people, by the interest of their mutual preservation." Perhaps the most striking image in the entire pamphlet was that of William as a mother.

> Those who fancy it unreasonable to suppose that one may be King of England, or even heir to the crown, without endeavoring to destroy the nation, will never be able to comprehend the motives that should oblige his majesty to expose his person for the preservation of his people: they know not . . . that a true king may be distinguished by the same marks by which Solomon distinguished the true mother.

The "true mother" of the story, of course, was recognized by her care for her child's life, while the false (Jacobite) one was willing to let the baby be divided in two and hence destroyed. Just as the discord of the Jacobites was further linked to an agenda of destruction, the unity of William and the nation was founded upon the principle of preservation.[10]

To defend William was therefore to defend the one person who could protect the nation. To kill William, conversely, was to kill the nation. Abbadie reminded readers that as the nation had made William king, it was itself the real object of the assassination attempt. Thus, "those who are possessed with so Brutish a fury, as to imagine that he [William] may be assassinated without a crime, because he suffered our representatives to place him upon the throne, do at the same time pronounce a bloody sentence against the Parliament, and condemn the whole kingdom to havoc and desolation." At a more pragmatic level, Abbadie treated the assassination as part of the invasion attempt. Killing William would disorganize and make vulnerable the nation: "They [the Jacobites] knew that His Majesty was the life and soul of his subjects, that his wisdom secured 'em from the devices, as his valor protected 'em from the attempts of their enemies: and therefore resolv'd upon the compendious way of destroying England in the person of its great defender." There was thus no conflict between an older ethic of obedience to and sacrifice for the king and a newer one of self-preservation. We have now been shown "that his Majesty's life is necessary for the preservation of his people; and that his subjects are inseparably united to him, both by duty, interest and inclination."[11]

The identification of king and nation allowed Abbadie to appropriate the rhetoric of "loyalty" which had so powerfully served Jacobites and, before them, the regimes of Charles and James II. He challenged the stereotype of the English as a rebellious, discontented people that was promulgated in Jacobite works, such as Orleans's *History of the Revolutions* (as well as famously by Dryden's *Absalom and Achitophel*). In a conscious attempt to reverse the use of labels, he turned the charge of rebellion upon the Jacobites: "They are perpetually talking of fidelity and obedience, and seem to make loyalty their idol; though they are usually the principal promoters of rebellion, and seldom or never well-affected to the government under which they live." True loyalty lay with supporters of the Williamite regime. At the same time, Abbadie implied that loyalty to King William was different from, and more right than, loyalty to the late King James: "Loyalty is become at last the distinguishing mark of honest men, and traitors to their country are looked upon as traitors to the government."[12]

What, then, of disloyalty? Abbadie's account of the plot and plotters was constructed to meet the regime's political needs. He carefully refrained from identifying a particular political or religious group as "Jacobite." That strategy would have backfired. First, it would have been unconvincing in light of the diverse profile of the plotters. Second, it would have played into the hands of critics like Robert Ferguson, who had already used the Lancashire Plot example to argue that the government used plot accusations to attack political enemies.

Still, while avoiding the equation of the Assassination Plot with any political party or religious group, Abbadie nonetheless portrayed it in a way that preempted criticism of government policies. He represented Jacobitism as a specific manifestation of an older, more destructive entity known as the "faction," which was "a secret cabal that has long been contriving our ruin." Significantly, the faction predated the Revolution of 1688: Abbadie held it responsible for the Gunpowder Plot, for the English Civil War, and for tempting Charles II to rule without Parliament. Jacobitism was only its current form. The faction thus had no particular ideological content beyond the destruction of the nation. Moreover, it had a chameleon-like ability to switch ideological location, taking on the colorings of absolutism or republicanism as needed:

> It has been, upon all occasions, the constant practice of the faction, to accommodate their notions to the various humors and inclinations of those whom they endeavor to draw into their party. For as they entertain some of their proselytes with projects to destroy the liberty and privileges of the nation, they insinuate themselves into the good opinion of others by exclaiming against the prerogatives of the Crown. . . . For 'tis their usual custom to tamper with the most violent persons of all parties, that, by animating 'em one against another, they may divide the nation into opposite and irreconcilable factions.[13]

The faction, according to Abbadie, intended to destroy the nation by fomenting divisions within it. That view provided Abbadie with both an explanation for recent discontents and a strong argument for ending them. If, as Abbadie insisted, the faction were "a set of men who seem to be in love with disorder," then they could be blamed for all existing conflicts between Anglicans and dissenters, king and Parliament, ministers and backbenchers: "It has been the constant practice of the faction, to fasten their own crimes upon us and to ascribe the disorders and divisions, which they kindle and foment among us, to the genius of the nation, and the humor of the people." Moreover, disorder played into their hand: "They love confusion and expect to live by it." Abbadie thus sternly warned his readers that anyone who criticized the government was an unwitting tool of the faction. The "country" opposition to the court, those who criticized military expenditure, favored the buildup of the navy at the expense of the army, or "seemed dissatisfied with the court" came in for a particular pounding from Abbadie as unwitting "tools for the carrying on of a design of which they were wholly ignorant."[14]

Though the number of actual Jacobites was, for Abbadie, reassuringly small, the number of those who might be manipulated by them was alarmingly large. And for these, ignorance would no longer (once they read his book!) be an excuse. Abbadie sternly admonished,

> There are a considerable number of deluded and unthinking persons, who suffer themselves to be led by those who are superior to them both in wit and malice. But though the simplicity of such undesigning tools may in some measure extenuate their guilt; their obstinacy makes 'em as dangerous as the fiercest and most desperate traitors.

Dissent in the polity was thus acknowledged, dismissed, and squashed all in one blow.[15]

Redefining Enemies: The Politics of Loyalty Oaths

As the foregoing discussion of Abbadie suggests, the "unity" that the Assassination Plot created was entirely compatible with (or a precondition for) an aggressive campaign by Whigs to marginalize a country opposition and to expel Tories from positions of influence. The potential use of the plot to intimidate Parliament into passing a money bill was suggested by the Whig MP Roland Gwynne shortly after the conviction of William Parkyns and John Friend. Parkyns and Friend had been convicted primarily for having financed and organized the projected Jacobite uprising. Parkyns was said to have met with a number of gentlemen in the north of England, but the names of these gentlemen had not surfaced. Roland Gwynne thus reasoned that the "disaffected party" contained men who hoped Parkyns and Friend would die quickly lest they be named. For that reason, Gwynne argued, the two should be kept alive:

> You saw how the disaffected party were dejected this day upon the report made of the examination of Mr. William Parkyns and Sir John Friend, and their owning that a great many were concerned in the Plot. When they are executed these men will know themselves safe from being accused by them, and may perhaps recover their spirit and oppose the good Bill [that is, the money bill] ordered this day to be brought in.

If the convicted plotters were reprieved, however, "It will be believed that they make a further discovery, and that party will be kept under fresh apprehensions that they will not dare to oppose us in any thing, for certainly they [Friend and Parkyns] can accuse a great many if they please."[16]

Despite Gwynne's recommendation, Parkyns and Friend were executed. But the plot discovery did allow Whigs to finally achieve what they wanted since 1689: a new loyalty oath that demanded a tougher standard. In 1689, the oath of allegiance required from officeholders was relatively undemanding. Takers had to promise to obey William and Mary but were not asked to declare them to be "rightful and lawful" monarchs. After 1696, the "Act for Securing His Majesty's Royal Person and Government" required officeholders to subscribe to the "Instrument of Association." This "Association Oath" not only described William as "rightful and lawful king" but also committed all subscribers to

> engage to stand by and assist each other, to the utmost of our power in the support and defence of his Majesty's most sacred person and government against the late King James and all his adherents, and in case his Majesty come to any violent or untimely death (which God forbid), we do hereby further freely and unanimously oblige ourselves to unite, associate and stand by each other in revenging the same upon his enemies, and their adherents.[17]

Meanwhile, and confusingly, the 1689 oath of allegiance (requiring merely obedience to William) continued to be used as a litmus test to identify the disaffected, but the penalties for refusing it were increased. The penalties set in 1689 for refusing the oath had been relatively mild. Now, in 1696, any person refusing to take the 1689 oath of allegiance when tendered to him would be liable to suffer all the "penalties forfeitures sums of money disabilities and incapacities which . . . are inflicted upon Popish recusants duly convicted of recusancy." This new use of the oath of allegiance marked a significant change in how enemies were defined and the relative positions of Catholics, non-jurors, and Tories.[18]

If Protestant non-jurors were now to be treated as if they were recusants, loyal Catholics might have finally in 1696 been given an opportunity to distinguish themselves from disloyal Protestants. Some of them did take the Association. Moreover, Middlesex justices of the peace took time to record the names of six persons who "did appear and declared themselves Roman

Catholics and only took the oath of fidelity." Maddeningly, no text of this "oath of fidelity" was supplied, but it was clearly intended to allow self-confessed Catholics to establish their loyalty to the new regime.[19]

In practical terms, this change did little to improve the situation of Catholics, but it was of symbolic importance. The acknowledgment that Protestant non-jurors were as disloyal as disloyal Catholics, whereas Catholics might be loyal, meant that the divide between loyal and disloyal no longer mapped directly onto the confessional divide between Protestants and Catholics. The possibility of Catholic loyalty was acknowledged several times from the bench during the Assassination Plot trials, especially that of John Friend. Friend tried to discredit the testimony of the conspirator turned witness Brice Blair, whom Friend had allegedly recruited to form a regiment; he argued Blair should be ignored because "a papist is not a good witness to prove a protestant a traitor within the st[atute] of 25 Edward III," thereby prompting the solicitor general to remind the court that "there was no such thing as a protestant in the time of Ed[ward] III." In his summation of the case, Lord Chief Justice Holt argued that the longstanding objection to believing Catholics, viz. that priests gave Catholics a dispensation to lie in order to injure Protestants, could not apply to those Catholics whose testimony helped to "defeat the designs of the Popish Party." Despite the continuing penal laws, he asserted,

> Papists are legal witnesses, and though there are severe laws to punish them for their non-conformity to the Church of England, and for other [sic] their Popish practices; yet I know of no law that renders them infamous, or incapable of being witnesses.[20]

The trial of Alexander Knightley, a Catholic, provided another occasion for Holt to affirm that Catholics might and should be loyal to the new regime. The lord chief justice lectured Knightley that his Catholicism was no excuse for treason. To think so was "folly and ingratitude,"

> For there is no English Papist that is master of any property, but he is interested in the preservation of this government, to which the whole party of them hath been, and still are continually obliged for its moderation and justice; for instead of being exposed to the severity of those laws to which they are obnoxious, they have had the same indulgence in the enjoyment of their religion, and the same protection, and as much benefit in the distribution of the common justice of the realm, as any other of the king's subjects;

therefore none could ever expect to mend their condition under a French domination . . . the English Papist, as well as Protestant, would have been reduced to a most dismal state, if you had obtained your end.[21]

The aftermath of the Assassination Plot seems, then, to have been when the equation of Protestantism and loyalty, Catholicism and disloyalty, was dismantled: for the first time, Protestant disloyalty was recognized as existing, and Catholics were given a chance (at least in Middlesex) to prove themselves loyal. However, the goal of changes in legislation was not so much to benefit Catholics as to put the spotlight on Tories. As the Association Oath's promulgators must have known, a number of Tories who had been willing to sign the 1689 oath of allegiance balked at signing the Association: most prominent among these was the Earl of Nottingham. The Association encouraged Whigs to undertake the purges of the militia and judicial bench that they had long desired.[22]

Powers of the State

One advantage to the broad definition of the Assassination Plot is that it legitimated rigorous measures taken against a wide group of suspected persons, most of whom had no direct connection to the Turnham Green Plot. Port officials were strictly enjoined to prevent anyone leaving England without a pass. The provisions of the 1689 "Act for Amoving Papists and Reputed Papists from London" were ordered to be enforced. Luttrell reported the seizure of about 300 horses in London belonging to suspicious persons. In the counties, justices and lords lieutenants were ordered to tender oaths systematically to papists and non-jurors and to report anyone who did not comply directly to the secretaries of state.[23]

Although quantification is tricky, published lists of persons detained in custody allow a few rough estimates. A list printed at the back of *A True Relation of the Horrid Conspiracy against the Life of the King*, published sometime between 3 April and 23 April 1696, contained the names of 107 prisoners (including 5 executed) held in the Tower, Newgate, the Gatehouse, and the Fleet, mentioning as well that there were "a great number of gentlemen and others in the custody of messengers; and there is hardly a gaol in England, but what has more or less in them." A sequel to that pamphlet, *A Continuation of the History of the Plot*, published shortly after 29 April, gave a longer list, this time including (in addition to those held in the four above-mentioned prisons) the names of prisoners held in the Marshalsea and King's Bench Prison as well as those in the custody of messengers or confined to their own houses. The compiler this time counted 323 names (including 8 executed) and again alluded to the further existence of an "abundance of those held in the county gaols." A slightly longer list, with 330 names, was published in a single-sheet broadside sometime after 9 May. Of these 330, 168 persons were listed as being held in the custody of a messenger.[24]

Some of the persons seized in the wake of the Assassination Plot had previously attracted the attention of authorities. The owlers James Hunt and Stephen Lansfield, for example, were taken into custody when habeas corpus was suspended, as was Paul Pepper, a Dover attorney who had been mentioned as a plotter by John Lunt in his 1693 information given to Trenchard. Thomas Noel, a customs officer known to be involved with smuggling, was also detained. Shirley Prettyman, a would-be informer who had plied Trumbull's with empty promises that Catholic priests would confide their plots to him, landed in the custody of messengers. So did the infamous John Taaffe. The vast majority of names appearing in various lists of the detained, however, are not recognizable (to me) either as people mentioned directly in the examination of participants in the Assassination Plot or as persons already under suspicion.

A handful of surviving petitions from prisoners suggests something of the circumstances and much about the human cost of detention. Nicholas Nolan, suffering in "poor and deplorable condition" on the Common side of Newgate, complained that there was "nothing alleged against him but being a Roman Catholic and a native of the Kingdom of Ireland." Thomas Cappock, a periwig maker by trade, spent seven months in Newgate, having been brought down by the messenger Thomas Davis from Montgomeryshire upon suspicion of the late conspiracy, though there was "no oath made against him." He described himself as the victim of an "unjust and malicious persecution." Thomas Hawley, formerly chief porter of the Tower of London, was in custody eleven weeks after "some one had maliciously whispered something against him" to the effect that he intended to betray the Tower. Gilbert Jones of Barking in Essex did have witnesses swear against him before JPs Nathaniel Finch and Carey Mildmay, "that your petitioner had said some words which might give occasion to suspect that your petition was not well affected to his Majesty and government," but he claimed that "he hath always been well affected" and "hath demeaned himself accordingly." He had been confined about two months, from which he asked to be released as "he has to take care of his poor mother and her family as well as his own . . . both families by reason of your petitioners confinement being reduced to great straits."[25]

Even the restoration of habeas corpus later in the year did not help those who were too poor to make use of it. An especially sad case was Thomas Segar, described as "a very poor man" more than sixty years old with a wife and small children. He admitted that he might have spoken the words alleged against him but said it was the "effect of the distraction he sometimes is under and no otherwise." His petition was subscribed by the constables, parish overseers, and a justice of the peace in the parish of St. Andrews, Holborn, confirming that Segar had lived "peaceably and inoffensively" and had taken the oaths. It is not clear how long Segar was detained, but he appears as "Thomas Segar starving in the Gatehouse" on a list of "persons in custody of the king's messengers who were committed a good while since, upon suspicion only, and against whom no information is yet brought, and who are so poor they are not able to get their liberty by habeas corpus." Barnet Davison's poverty likewise prolonged what might have been imprisonment due to mistaken identity. As he explained it

> Barnet Davison, arriving in Leicester last March was apprehended suspected to be that Davis mentioned in the late proclamation. [He] was committed and brought to Newgate where he has lain since to his great loss and damage, and that since His Majesty's most honorable privy council being satisfied of his innocency therein, was graciously pleased to make an order that he should be cleared upon bail . . . but being a stranger had no friends in London to procure any bail and was forced for want of bail to continue a prisoner in the same destitute condition.[26]

Although the justification for suspending habeas corpus was to catch potential plotters, detentions extended to a much wider group of people. The vast majority of those detained, however, never came to trial. That suggests that the government was not able to try and convict as many people as it had intended. To understand that failure, and its political significance, it is necessary to turn to the trials and the challenges that the government faced in securing convictions while maintaining legitimacy.

The Theater of the Law

No historian has doubted the existence of the Assassination Plot, and I do not intend to be the first. My concern, however, is not with whether it was true, but with how it was shown to be "true." What follows is not an exhaustive account of plot or trials but a consideration of the challenges regarding evidence and law that faced the government in conducting them.

One large problem was the nature of the evidence. As noted above, most of the potential witnesses were themselves involved in the conspiracy and had turned witness to avoid prosecution. Two other plotters, Alexander Knightley and Peter Cook, gave information and escaped execution but were ultimately not used as witnesses because they had been convicted.

The two most important and problematic witnesses were George Porter and Cardell Goodman. Of the two, Porter was the first to make himself available. He was the most important witness in the first trial held, that of Charnock, King, and Keyes. Porter's value lay in the fact that he alone among the available witnesses had direct, frequent contact with Robert Charnock, the only other high-level planner who had fallen immediately into the government's hands. Moreover, Porter linked the narrow and broad iterations of the plot. He not only planned the ambush at Turnham Green but also attended the infamous meeting at the King's Head Tavern, at which Charnock and others agreed to invite James II to invade England. As Porter was at the time the only attendee that meeting who was willing to be a government witness, prosecutors needed to establish his credibility.

Making Porter seem credible was not easy. He was a conspirator himself, a Catholic, known to be in debt, and rumored to have a lewd life. His credibility was enhanced, however, by the sheer unthinkability of acquitting Charnock, who had a long record as an open Jacobite and whose role in the Catholic takeover of Magdalen College had made him hated by Tories as well as Whigs. Porter's credibility was also helped by the presence at the trial of two more apparently sincere and voluntary witnesses, De La Rue and Prendergrass, who were free from the taint of having bargained for their lives. From the government's perspective, the single most important outcome of the trial of Charnock, King, and Keyes was to establish Porter as a credible witness.

The capture of Cardell Goodman soon gave authorities an even more promising but more problematic witness. Goodman, an actor and former lover of the Duchess of Cleveland, was especially valuable because he claimed to have been at the King's Head Tavern meeting with Charnock, Porter, and the others. That meant that he could serve as the necessary second witness to back up Porter's testimony against others who allegedly attended the meeting but had yet to be convicted, such as Peter Cook, the Earl of Ailesbury, John Fenwick, and Lord Montgomery. Goodman's first and only appearance in court was in the trial of Peter Cook, where he supported Porter's story about the meeting in the King's Head Tavern.

Goodman's credibility seemed even more vulnerable than Porter's. The defense in Cook's trial reminded the court that Goodman had been convicted for attempting to poison the Duke of Grafton, though he was pardoned for it. Charles Edwards (alias Douglas), himself a prisoner, testified that while in prison Goodman had told him that he would swear against Cook because Cook had sworn against him, and "he or I must perish." Some staff members at the King's Head Tavern had no memory of seeing Goodman there. Such assaults on Goodman's credibility were especially dangerous because they weakened Porter's as well (since the two had concurred) and so might throw into doubt the conviction of the now-executed John Friend (whom Porter and Goodman had both placed at the same King's Head Tavern meeting). Ironically, the fact that Porter's credit depended on Goodman's was now given as a reason to believe Goodman: the solicitor general argued that the witnesses whom the defense had brought to show Goodman was not at the King's Head Tavern "do falsify not only Mr. Goodman, who swears that he was there; but they likewise falsify the evidence of Mr. Porter . . . and therefore these men's testimony tends to overthrow both witnesses as well as one; and I must tell you, that if Mr. Goodman be not a legal witness, because he has sworn a thing that is not true, then Mr. Porter is not a good witness, who has sworn the same thing."[27]

The dubiousness of key witnesses was one challenge facing the government. A second challenge was the law itself. The Assassination Plot trials occurred at a moment of anxiety and confusion surrounding the imminent implementation of the new Treason Trials Act, which was to take effect on 25 March. Whigs saw the act as a dangerous brake on the power of the government to protect itself. One telling vignette that emerged during the trial of conspirator Robert Lowick confirmed that the act might have been seen as a boon by would-be conspirators. According to witness Richard Fisher, Lowick had believed that he would be safe if he spoke of treasonable practices to only one person at a time, for "there was an act of parliament on foot, that under [that is, fewer than] two witnesses nothing should affect a man's life in treason."[28]

Not even Lowick's lawyer, Bartholomew Shower, endorsed Lowick's interpretation of the Treason Trials Act, which was indeed a misreading (see below). The story is important, however, because it demonstrates that there was much uncertainty, among potential traitors and lawyers alike, about how the act might affect prosecutions for treason. Even more important, the passage of the Treason Trials Act put the fairness of the government's proceedings under a spotlight even before the act went into effect and potentially struck at the heart of the new regime's legitimacy: that the conduct of treason trials needed to be reformed suggested that the courts after 1689 had proceeded unfairly. The prosecutors and judges in the trials taking place before 25 March were thus under pressure to show that even "unreformed" trials were fair. After 25 March, their task was to show that they could still obtain convictions. The trials thus became a site on which both the legitimacy and the security of the new regime were tested.

Robert Charnock, the most articulate of the first batch of defendants, consciously used his trial to question the regime's legitimacy. He aggressively claimed rights for himself, in part to enhance his chances of acquittal but more importantly to expose the hypocrisy of his prosecutors. In challenging both Porter's and De La Rue's credibility, he cheekily invoked the memory of the Whig martyr Lord William Russell. The three witnesses against Russell in 1683 (Sheppard, Rumsey, and Lord Howard of Escrick) had all admitted involvement in the so-called Rye House Plot, and at least one of them could further be described as a "trapanner." Robert Atkyns, in his 1689 *Defence of the Late Lord Russel's Innocency*, had written:

> Now were I a juryman, I should think no such witness a credible witness, as should appear either by his own testimony, or upon proofs made by others against him, to have been *particeps criminis*; for that proves him to be a bad, and consequently not so credible a man; especially if it can appear the witness has trapanned the prisoner into the committing of the crime: Then the witness will appear to be guilty of a far higher crime than the prisoner, and therefore ought not to be believed as a credible witness against the prisoner; for he is a credible witness that has the credit of being a good and honest man, which a trapanner cannot have, and this trappaning proves withal, that the trapanner did bear a spite and malice against the person trepanned.

In the bottom right panels of *The Triumphs of Providence*, the rule of law brings about the just punishment of the conspirators. Detail of *The Triumphs of Providence over Hell, France, and Rome, in Defeating and Discovering of the Late Hellish and Barbarous Plott* (1696). By permission of the Folger Shakespeare Library.

Charnock in 1696 quoted Atkyns almost verbatim to make a case against Porter and especially De La Rue, who had by "his coming to me after he resolved to discover, plainly declares that he set himself to be a trapanner." Charnock continued, "I have read in a book of Sir Robert Atkins that to be a *particeps criminis* proves a person to be a bad man, and consequently not so credible, especially if it can appear the witness has trepanned the prisoner into committing the crime."[29]

Charnock also made arguments that echoed those made by John Hawles in his 1689 *Remarks upon the Tryals of Edward Fitzharris, Stephen Colledge, Count Coningsmark, the Lord Russel, Collonel Sidney, Henry Cornish, and Charles Bateman*, a pamphlet that had been intended not to change the law but rather to show that "no law in England" had warranted the practices of courts in the two late reigns (see chapter 1). Hawles had contended that defendants needed to know the details of the acts alleged against them so that they could plan a defense. How, for example, could a person provide an alibi if he was not informed of the time and place of an alleged act? "It is almost impossible," Hawles wrote, "for an innocent to defend himself, unless he had notice of the fact intended to be insisted upon at the trial." Hawles had also criticized the tradition of denying treason defendants the right to counsel during trial. The rights he claimed for defendants in treason trials were already available in cases involving lesser or civil charges, and the rights were denied not because anything in English law justified the denial but because they had fallen into disuse or been improperly understood.[30]

Ironically, Charnock claimed the same rights that Hawles had insisted on for defendants in the two previous reigns during a trial where Hawles himself conducted the prosecution in his capacity as solicitor general! Charnock pointed to the vagueness of the date of the alleged crime: when the prosecution witness Captain Porter was asked to give an account of "your knowledge about the first beginning of this conspiracy the last year," Charnock immediately objected that his indictment had specified only one date, 10 February 1696, which could not be considered "last year." Lord Chief Justice Holt then explained that "a man may certainly be indicted for a treason committed this year, and upon his trial evidence may be given of the same treason committed the year before." To which Charnock replied with a complaint Hawles himself had made about the Rye House Plot trials: "But then how can a man prepare for his defense?" He continued, "If one year may be put in the indictment, and another year brought in in the evidence, how shall any man be able to apply himself to his defense, whose thoughts run only upon the time laid in the indictment?"[31]

Charnock's other complaint was designed to raise the question of whether the Treason Trials Act was relevant to his trial. He complained he had been given no copy of the indictment, and no counselor was present with him at the trial. These, everyone acknowledged, would be required if he were to be tried only a few days later, once the Treason Trials Act went into effect. Charnock argued that he should be allowed them now, because of the "equity" of the act: "the ground of that act, which is the reasonableness and equity that all prisoners should be made capable of fairly defending themselves, is now in force." His argument was virtually identical to Hawles's 1689 argument that the rights a defendant needed to adequately defend himself were already part of or in harmony with existing law, and that the denial of them, however common, was already illegal. William Parkyns followed Charnock's lead at his own trial. He described the Treason Trials Act as "a beneficial law made, which if my trial had been put off a few days, I should have had the benefit of." But he also (somewhat paradoxically) suggested that he should get the benefit of the act no matter when his trial occurred, by insisting that the court read the preamble to the Treason Trials Act, which began: "Whereas nothing is more just and reasonable than that persons prosecuted for High treason . . . should be justly and equally tried." These words, Parkyns argued, showed that the act was "declarative of common law, because it says it was always just and reasonable" and that "what is just and reasonable tomorrow, sure, is just and reasonable today."[32]

Charnock's and Parkyns's multipronged assaults on the fairness of the proceedings produced a strong and equally complex response from the court and the government. Answering Charnock's contention that Porter could not be a "legal witness" because "he owns himself a partner in a bloody design, and to convict me, swears to take away my life, to save his own," Holt rhetorically asked, "Who can tell better what was intended and done in such a conspiracy than he that was a party in it?" It was, Holt asserted, "certainly a hard matter to discover crimes of this nature, if the accomplice in those crimes shall not be allowed to be good witnesses against their fellow conspirators." Holt was careful to buttress the bald claim with some subtler distinctions meant to establish that the government's methods did not invite perjury. In response to Charnock's complaint that Porter was testifying to get a reward, Holt pointed out that Porter would receive no reward for Charnock's conviction: the proclamation issued at the outbreak of the plot had offered a £1,000 reward for the *apprehension* of the named suspects, regardless of whether they were convicted or not. Holt further emphasized that Porter had not actually been indicted for his part in the conspiracy; if he had been, Holt acknowledged, it would have been "quite another operation."[33]

The court also rejected the defendants' arguments about the meaning of the Treason Trials Act. The judges responded (to Charnock) that the Treason Trials Act was not "declaratory" of the law as it was but was rather a new law made by statute, and again (to Parkyns) that the Treason Trials Act "was not a law till the time comes that the parliament hath appointed for its being a law." Although the court's denial that the Treason Trials Act was declaratory ironically repudiated John Hawles's 1689 arguments, it also conveyed a positive ideological message that Parliament (not the courts or tradition) constituted the highest legal authority. In this sense, it reinforced a point that was, as we saw in chapter 1, especially important to Whigs.[34]

The court implicitly made a further point that it was possible to conduct a fair trial without the Treason Trials Act and that there was still a large distance between trials that had been conducted in the old regime and those conducted after 1689. The trials held before 25 March 1696 proceeded in many respects with conspicuous consideration for the defendants. All were allowed pen, ink, and paper, a courtesy not extended to many defendants in the 1680s. Moreover, at Charnock's request, the witness De La Rue was removed from the courtroom while Porter was testifying. When Charnock complained that he had been unable to consult with counsel before the trial, and when Friend complained he had been given a slightly erroneous copy of the jury panel, the judges acknowledged that the defendants were indeed entitled to counsel before trial and accurate jury lists, although in each case the court blamed the defendant or his counsel for the mistake.[35]

Showing consideration for the rights of defendants before the Treason Trials Act went into effect was one way to reduce the sense that the act would be a radical rupture. The other way was to blunt the impact of the act's onset by controlling and limiting the meaning of the provisions that regulated the number of witnesses required to convict. There was much confusion as to what the act would require as sufficient evidence. As noted above, Major Lowick believed that the Treason Trials Act would make it necessary to have two witnesses to prove every fact (and thus that he could protect himself by speaking to one person at a time). William Parkyns apparently thought the same thing, complaining that there were not two witnesses to any single species of his alleged treason. The assassination of the king and the organization of an insurrection were, for Parkyns, two separate species of treason, and each required two witnesses.

Parkyns's argument gave the three presiding justices (Holt, Treby, and Rokeby) a chance to explain the existing law of treason and to assure the court that the Treason Trials Act would not have changed the rules. With respect to the law as it would exist until 25 March, each justice explained at length that it was not necessary to have two witnesses to every overt act of treason, but that (as Holt put it) "if there be one witness to one overt act, and another witness to another overt act of the same species of treason, that is all that the law requires." How one interpreted that statement, of course, hinged on how one interpreted the phrase "same species of treason," and the judges were explicit in their answer. Invoking the treason statute of 25 Edward III, which famously defined treason as "compassing and imagining the death of the King," they argued that assassination and insurrection were *both* aspects of such compassing and imagining, for, as Treby put it, "It cannot be supposed but that he that would have an invasion and an insurrection against the king's person, does intend the destruction of the king."[36]

The judges further commented on the new Treason Trials Act, emphasizing that had it already gone into effect it would have made little difference in the evidence required to prove treason, for the act "declares it is sufficient, if there be one [witness] to one overt act, and another [witness] to another [overt act]; but it must be of the same head, or species of treason," and "deposing the king and assassinating of him, and preparing to raise an army against him, or to excite an invasion, are but one sort of treason." In response to Parkyns's assertion that the act would have benefited him, the judges answered that "it would have been the same thing as to this matter, for this act declares the very same thing, as to the two witnesses." Thus, even as they avoided implementing the Treason Trials Act early for Parkyns's benefit, the judges conveyed the impression that they were not frightened by the act, that it would not have really made a difference.[37]

The court thereby took an important step to control the ways in which the Treason Trials Act would be interpreted even before it went into effect. The trial of Ambrose Rookwood helped them to limit its meaning after 25 March. Rookwood's lawyer Bartholomew Shower objected to the introduction of evidence that Rookwood had provided conspirators with a list of men to take part in the ambush to George Harris, on grounds that the indictment had never mentioned Rookwood had given such a list. The Treason Trials Act, Shower pointed out, stated "that no evidence shall be admitted or given of any overt Act that is not expressly laid in the indictment." The court, however, argued that evidence about the list given by Rookwood to Harris was acceptable because the giving of the list was an act which was itself evidence of the "overt act" that *was* alleged in the indictment, which was that Rookwood did "meet and consult" about how to effect this treason. Were this not the case, the attorney general noted, "all the evidence must be put in the indictment," which would be impracticable. The court's rejection of Shower's argument signaled that the "overt acts" specified in indictments could be interpreted broadly, and thus that evidence about an array of related acts could all count as evidence of one "overt act." The conclusion contemporaries could draw was that the Treason Trials Act had been respected and granted new (not eternal) rights but had not let Jacobites operate with impunity, as had been feared.[38]

Frustrations and Failures

The trials of ten conspirators held in common law courts might have sent a positive message that the government was at once tough and lawful. Nonetheless, prosecutors' limited ability to win convictions against suspects against whom they had strong evidence (let alone against the ones who escaped) would also have been apparent to the public. The trials actually held represented only a fraction of the trials that government officials had planned. By the end of 1696 officials had experienced several significant frustrations, which are described below. These in turn shed light on the reasons for and significance of the new regime's most controversial legal move, the attainder of John Fenwick.

There were several lines of inquiry that government officials were eager to follow but which resulted in legal dead ends. First, the government hoped to identify the northern gentlemen who had met with William Parkyns, as was established at his trial, to plan an insurrection. A second high-value target for the government was William Berkenhead, who organized a network conveying Jacobite people and correspondence, and who was potentially a witness against many other Jacobites. He was not easy to crack. As Vernon told Portland, "It is certain he knows a great deal but continues very obstinate."

The government did make progress, however, in gathering witnesses for an impending trial meant to break Berkenhead's obstinacy. The longtime owler James Hunt had been questioned and was prepared to testify against him, as were Hunt's wife and the conspirator turned would-be witness Peter Cook.[39]

A third line of inquiry by the government officials was meant to produce convictions for more of the men directly involved in the planned attack on the king. They seemed almost within reach. The conspirator Alexander Knightley had given an early confession in the (false) hope of avoiding trial and had named (among others) John Counter (alias Rumsey) and John Bernardi. When Counter was apprehended at the end of May, he possessed papers that gave tantalizing evidence about the payment of subsistence money to the would-be assassins, including Counter himself and John Bernardi.[40]

None of the above-mentioned government plans came to fruition. Parkyns went to his death in April refusing to name any accomplices in his scheme for insurrection. In October, Berkenhead escaped shortly before his trial, and (more mysteriously) James Hunt was spirited away to France. As Luttrell reported it, "A French vessel landed about 20 armed men near Rumney Marsh, who broke into the house of one Hunt, a noted owler near that place, and carried him on ship board for France, he having lately made a discovery of several people that corresponded there; and Berkenhead, who lately broke out of Newgate, is said to be one that carried him away." The case against Counter and Bernardi could not be brought to trial. Knightley, who had named them in a confession, was a convicted felon who, because he was not pardoned, was not eligible as a witness. That meant, as James Vernon had to admit at the end of December, that the only legal witness against them was George Porter.[41]

Perhaps the greatest frustration for government officials was their failure to convict all of the persons present at the infamous meeting at the King's Head Tavern (and a subsequent meeting at Mrs. Mortimer's), where it had been decided to send Charnock to France to encourage King James to invade. Porter had willingly given details of those meetings, at which were present (he said) himself, Charnock, Fenwick, Cardell Goodman, Peter Cook, the Earl of Ailesbury, and Lord Montgomery. Porter on his own was, of course, insufficient as a witness, and Charnock went to his death refusing to testify. But once Goodman became a willing witness and Peter Cook was apprehended, the government had reason to hope that they could convict more of the participants in the King's Head Tavern meeting. Goodman, in a bid for clemency, gave a long statement confirming Porter's story. He was accordingly brought as a witness at Peter Cook's trial. Despite the many challenges to his credibility (discussed above), his testimony led to Cook's conviction in May.[42]

It would have been natural for government officials to expect that Goodman and Porter would together stand as witnesses against more participants in the King's Head Tavern meeting, for example, the Earl of Ailesbury (held in the Tower) and Sir John Fenwick (finally captured in June). But using Goodman as a witness soon became problematic. Peter Cook, in a bid for clemency, turned informer and confirmed that he had met Fenwick, Montgomery, and Ailesbury at the King's Head Tavern. Unfortunately, Cook's information contradicted Cardell Goodman on a crucial point: Cook said that the discussion of sending Charnock to France happened before dinner and that Goodman had come in after dinner. Moreover, Cook threatened that if he were executed he would contradict Goodman in his last dying speech.[43]

As James Vernon explained to Portland, Cook had put authorities in a dilemma. On the one hand, Cook was willing to be a witness against Ailesbury or Fenwick, and he promised Vernon not to contradict Goodman. But even so, Vernon simply could not trust him to perform as a witness. He was underwhelmed by Cook's intelligence, finding him "very defective in his judgment" and a "trifling man." Vernon worried that although Cook "would not willfully contradict Goodman . . . his parts are not much to be trusted upon cross interrogations." On the other hand, Vernon took Cook's threat to discredit Goodman in his scaffold speech seriously enough that he advised delaying the execution, at least until after Goodman had had the chance to testify in the upcoming trial against John Fenwick. In the end, Cook was neither allowed to testify nor executed; he was kept alive (and silent) for months with a string of short reprieves. Meanwhile Goodman, whose fragile credibility Vernon had been seeking to protect, absconded to France on the eve of Fenwick's scheduled trial.[44]

By December, the government confronted the limits of using normal trial procedure. Many conspirators remained at large. There were some persons in custody (Fenwick and Ailesbury) universally believed to be guilty who could not be convicted in a court of law because there were not two witnesses against them. As is well known, the regime turned to attainder to deal with the vexing case of John Fenwick. But Fenwick was not the only conspirator who invited the circumvention of normal legal procedures. At the end of the year Parliament's "Act to Attaint Such of the Persons Concerned in the Late

Horrid Conspiracy to Assassinate His Majesties Royal Person" provided that the conspirators who had not yet turned themselves in (George Barclay, Johnson alias Harrison, Durance, Major Holmes, and several others) were to be "convicted and attainted of High Treason and shall suffer the pains of death and incur all forfeitures, penalties and disabilities as traitors convicted and attainted of High Treason." The act further provided that several persons in custody against whom there was as yet insufficient evidence for conviction would continue in custody for another year without bail or mainprise unless discharged by the Privy Council. These included John Bernardi and John Counter, along with four others specifically named (Robert Cassells, Robert Meldrum, James Chambers, and Robert Blackbourne). Despite the restoration of habeas corpus, Parliament continued to pass special acts to retain these men in prison.[45]

Fenwick's attainder was controversial, so much so that it was the last in English history. Why, given that Fenwick was (in Paul Hopkins's words) "small fry," did the government bring the attainder and Parliament agree to it? The decision to attaint Fenwick can best be understood in the context of the struggle for credit, which Fenwick threatened in several different ways. He was conspicuous for daring theatrical gestures designed to shame the government. In 1691 he had insulted Queen Mary, refusing to doff his hat and reportedly making obscene gestures when he encountered her in St. James's Park. He had taken part in the infamous Dog Tavern riot, during which Jacobites forced passers-by to drink to the health of the Prince of Wales.[46]

After his capture, Fenwick tried to preserve himself in ways that continued his pattern of insulting the regime. An intercepted letter written by Fenwick to his wife at the time he was caught suggested bribing the jury. Then, in September, he wrote a confidential letter to William offering "a sincere and ingenious confession of all I know of men who correspond with France, employed by him [William] in places of trust in the government, fleet and army." These men included Admiral Russell, Sidney Godolphin, Lord Marlborough, and the Duke of Shrewsbury. If Fenwick thought his revelations would win William's clemency, he was wrong: the king complained that Fenwick "only accuses those in my service, and not one of his own party." But, as discussed in chapter 3, embarrassing rumors spread which drove Shrewsbury to the verge of resignation. From the government's point of view, Fenwick's revelation was the latest in a string of acts in which he had mocked the credit of the regime, in this case by implying that not even its own supporters really supported it.[47]

For the government, the point of dealing with Fenwick in Parliament was not simply to kill him but to discredit his accusations—and to expose the accusations themselves as part of a plot to discredit the government. How, exactly, to do that was the subject of several weeks of deliberations among Shrewsbury, Vernon, Somers, Sunderland, and other advisors. These men opted for a show of openness. They decided to have Russell himself, one of the accused, bring Fenwick's revelations about treason within the regime to Parliament. The ground was carefully prepared, with influential MPs apprised in advance that the king had rejected Fenwick's information. When Russell on 6 November presented the House of Commons with a copy of Fenwick's paper accusing himself and others of secret Jacobitism, the House resolved unanimously that Fenwick's information was "false and scandalous, and a contrivance to undermine the government."[48]

The vote that Fenwick's information was false was connected, ideologically and strategically, to the vote to attaint him. In practical terms, the threat of attainder was intended to pressure Fenwick to reveal who had put him up to making his accusations, to reveal the deeper plot. Ideologically, both votes affirmed the importance of the Parliament, as the arbiter of truth, the guardian of the regime, and the highest court in the land. The right of attainder symbolized Parliament's status as the superior judicial authority, so much so that an early version of the Treason Trials Act (1691) was rejected by the House of Commons in 1691 precisely because it bound Parliament in attainder proceedings to follow the same rules as common law courts. Arguments by supporters of Fenwick's attainder emphasized the exalted place of Parliament. As Lord Cutts put it, "No superior is to be circumscribed by an inferior: and I would ask, if the courts below are not inferior to the parliament? There is nothing to limit us, but the law of Nature, the Law of God, and the Law of Parliaments." The author of the manuscript pamphlet giving reasons to attaint Fenwick saw Parliament as the natural remedy for defect in common law: if Fenwick deserved to die, he asked, "and a formality at common law of two witnesses is wanting to his trial, may it not be done by the highest court of equity in the nation, with the safety of their conscience and their honor?"[49]

Fenwick's attainder could be seen, then, not as a failure of procedural justice but as a demonstration of Parliament's prestige as the guarantor of justice and security. That demonstration was especially important given the continuing anxiety about whether the Treason Trials Act would limit the government's ability to secure itself through the courts. These considerations, combined with Fenwick's obvious guilt, made the attainder less damaging to the government's legitimacy than one might have feared.

There was of course a cost to the attainder. Eloquent arguments were made against it on grounds that it made a mockery of the safeguards for defendants that the new regime had so proudly honored and enhanced. Attainting Fenwick in Parliament rather than trying him at common law allowed the government to change the rules of evidence: there was only one witness, Porter, to testify to Fenwick's involvement in the King's Head Tavern meeting, but the government introduced depositions that Goodman gave at Cook's trial and called in members of the petit jury from that trial to recall what Goodman had said. As one member of Parliament said in opposing the bill, "To say that a man's life may be taken away by two witnesses in one place and by one in another, is to say, that there is no certain rule to prove a man guilty of a crime that may forfeit his life, which is not admitted in any country whatever." The vote for the attainder was far from unanimous. It passed the Commons by only 189 to 156, and the Lords by an even narrower vote of 68 to 61.[50]

It is likely that the mixed reaction to Fenwick's attainder discouraged Parliament from trying the procedure again. It was not, for example, used against Counter, Bernardi, and the other men consigned to prison by a special act of Parliament because there was only one witness against them. Arguably, the restraint itself helped legitimate the proceedings: Fenwick was an isolated case, and he was obviously so very guilty.

Conclusion

By this means our liberty becomes a noble freedom. It carries an imposing and majestic aspect. It has a pedigree and illustrious ancestors. It has its bearings, and its ensigns armorial. It has its gallery of portraits; its monumental inscriptions; its records, evidences, and titles.
—EDMUND BURKE, *Reflections on the Revolution in France* (1790)

And all this is permitted or connived at, under a Government, the voice of whose people is almost perpetually boasting of Liberty and Property.
—*A Short History of the Life of Major John Bernardi* (1729)

When Edmund Burke endowed "our liberty" with its gallery of ancestral portraits, he probably did not mean to include John Bernardi's. To be fair,

Bernardi would not have wanted to include himself in the lineage of English liberty: the signs of nobility he displayed were meant to evoke a continental aristocratic heritage. Still, his image in the frontispiece to his book testifies to an urgent wish to be remembered, and we might honor that wish. Perhaps Bernardi is part of the story of English "liberty" after all, in more ways than one.

In the lineage of liberty-promoting ideas, Bernardi's text is a bridge between the Whig-Jacobitism of Robert Ferguson and later eighteenth-century movements targeting corruption. In his account of his life, Bernardi described how his erstwhile friend George Harris was tempted by huge rewards offered to informers in 1696 to falsely accuse him, and how he was kept in prison without trial for thirty-three years. He exposed the hollowness of the new regime's claims to protect liberty, much in the way that the "Whig-Jacobites" Ferguson, James Montgomery, and Bartholomew Shower had done. By 1729, however, Bernardi was no longer refighting the revolution. Jacobite sentiment was conspicuously absent from the narrative; Bernardi had kind words for William, Queen Anne, and King George, all of whom he believed intended to relieve him. He blamed his ordeal on a systemic corruption: the Treasury solicitor who would have helped him for a bribe, the councilors who blocked the merciful king from reading the petitions of subjects, the "windings, turnings and labyrinths of politicians" which cannot be "easily traced and found out by a simple and well-meaning honest man," the lawyers and jailers who bilked prisoners of their fortunes. His unfavorable comparison of Newgate to the Bastille found an echo in the Gordon Riots and in the writings of Thomas Paine.[51]

Even as Bernardi's text called for liberty, however, it had conspicuous problems of authenticity. He used several credit-establishing strategies at once: he should be believed because he was a gentleman *and* because he printed relevant documents. Yet neither of these really assures a reader. The picture on the frontispiece was a representation of a portrait already ensconced over a commemorative plaque in a hall of ancestors. But of course, it was really just cheap print. What the "true copy of the Diploma or Patent of Empire granted to the Author's Grandfather in the Year 1629" that was printed in the book actually proved was anyone's guess. Bernardi was less than forthcoming about the reasons why the government insisted on his guilt. He claimed that he was held only because of George Harris's false accusation, but records of examinations in the papers of the Earl of Portland show

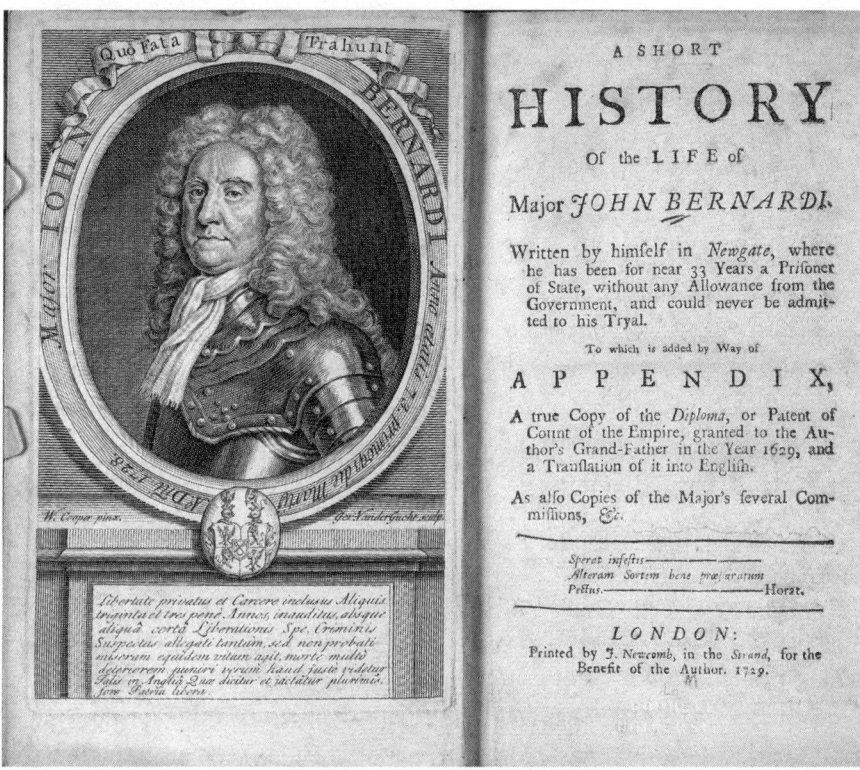

Frontispiece and title page of *A Short History of the Life of Major John Bernardi. Written by Himself in Newgate; Where He Has Been for Near 33 Years a Prisoner of State, without Any Allowance from the Government, and Could Never Be Admitted to His Trial* (London: J. Newcomb, 1729). Division of Rare and Manuscript Collections, Cornell University Library.

that Alexander Knightley had informed on Bernardi, and that Bernardi himself admitted to involvement in the plans for an insurrection.[52]

Even in the problematic character of its truth-claims, though, Bernardi's text might have a place in our sense of political lineage. The urgency and uncertainty of the truth about plots and about the people who discovered and prosecuted them gave rise to the debates within which Bernardi's critique of liberty resonates.

Insofar as he really (probably) was involved in trying to overthrow the Williamite regime, Bernardi too deserves some credit for shaping what modern "liberty" looks like. In a broad sense, it was the insecurity created by people like Bernardi that provided the context in which the new regime worked out vital questions about law and citizenship: how to define and treat categories of suspected persons, what kind of loyalty to demand of subjects, how to try criminals. The fear of plots also created new kinds of political power emanating from "below." The regime depended on ordinary men and women to preserve it, and they in turn found in informing a way to voice concerns to the state (not just concerns about plotters but about neighbors and about their own identity and reputation). The publicity surrounding plots meant that the government had to at least maintain the appearance of credibility in its handling of plots. We cannot, then, understand what the first liberal post-revolutionary regime came to look like without taking into account the impact of plots and the fear of plots.

More specifically, the Assassination Plot itself ironically made a great contribution to the regime's long-term survival (thus allowing it to become "Old Corruption"). In many ways, the government's response to the crisis in 1696 was exactly what Whigs had been advocating in 1689: more demanding loyalty oaths to effectively distinguish the well-affected from the disaffected and a purge of the Tory officeholders who could swear allegiance only weakly. The prestige of Parliament was affirmed. Whig theories of government by consent were given new emotional weight by being hooked to more sentimental and traditional forms of royalism. It is customary to add at this point that the success of the (Whig-promoted) Bank of England and the Great Recoinage also secured, literally, the government's credit. Very true. But without the rush of support for the regime created by the Assassination Plot, the recoinage (a high-risk, controversial undertaking perceived as burdensome to the poor) might have gone less smoothly.

None of this is to say that the Whig version of the revolution that crystallized in 1696 was permanent: Tories soon made a comeback, William's personal popularity faded, and policies regarding loyalty oaths or the treatment of Catholics took more twists and turns. By then, though, the Nine Years' War had ended, the recoinage was complete, and the survival of the new regime was less in doubt. One important sign of the difference in political climate before and after 1696 was the fate of high-ranking men upon whom suspicion was cast. When John Wildman was accused of plotting against the government, he was fired. When the Earl of Marlborough was accused, he was sent to the Tower. By contrast, when, after 1696, the Duke of Shrewsbury was implicated in treason (first by Fenwick, then by Smith, then by Aubrey Price!), his offers to resign were resisted and the government closed ranks against his accusers. It might have still been possible to insinuate the existence of treason deep within the government, but the government was confident in itself. For the temporary stability we can thank the Assassination plotters, including (probably) John Bernardi.

Most of all, though, John Bernardi's place in the lineage of English (or American) liberty is that he was treated in ways presumed incompatible with a regime dedicated to liberty and property and that this treatment was forgotten. The question he raised so painfully is still with us: What does a liberal regime do with persons who are almost certainly guilty and dangerous but cannot be successfully convicted in a court of law? However we answer that question, an acknowledgment of Bernardi's situation makes our story of the Revolution of 1688 and its relation to "liberty" less smooth and happy than Burke would have had us believe. For this reason, Bernardi is not just part of late eighteenth-century England's lineage but of our own.[53]

Notes

Note: All years begin on 1 January. Place of publication is London unless otherwise stated.

Abbreviations

BL Add.	British Library Additional Manuscripts
CJ	Journals of the House of Commons
CSPD	Calendar of State Papers Domestic
CTB	Calendar of Treasury Books
GD	Anchitell Grey, Debates of the House of Commons, from the Year 1667 to the Year 1694 (D. Henry, 1763)
HMC Downshire	Historical Manuscripts Commission, Report on the Manuscripts of the Marquess of Downshire (H.M. Stationery Office, 1924–40)
HMC Finch	Historical Manuscripts Commission, Report on the Manuscripts of the late Allan George Finch (H.M. Stationery Office, 1913–2004)
HMC Kenyon	Historical Manuscripts Commission, Manuscripts of Lord Kenyon (H.M. Stationery Office, 1894)
HMC Lords	Historical Manuscripts Commission, Report on the Manuscripts of the House of Lords (H.M. Stationery Office, 1889–1900)
KHLC	Kent History and Library Centre, Maidstone
LancsRO	Lancashire Record Office

LBHR	Narcissus Luttrell, *A Brief Historical Relation of State Affairs from September 1678 to April 1714* (Oxford: Oxford University Press, 1857)
LI	[James Vernon], *Letters Illustrative of the Reign of William III from 1696 to 1708. Addressed to the Duke of Shrewsbury by James Vernon, Esq.*, ed. G. P. R. James (Henry Colburn, 1841)
LJ	*Journals of the House of Lords*
LJ minutes	Lords Justices' minutes
LMA	London Metropolitan Archives
LPD	*Parliamentary Diary of Narcissus Luttrell*, ed. Henry Horwitz (Oxford: Clarendon, 1972)
LPL	Lambeth Palace Library MS
NUL	Nottingham University Library
OBO	*Proceedings of the Old Bailey Online*, http://www.oldbaileyonline.org/ (references by case number)
ODNB	*Oxford Dictionary of National Biography* (Oxford: Oxford University Press, 2004)
RO	Record Office
SR	*Statutes of the Realm*, ed. John Raithby (George Eyre and Andrew Strahan, 1810–22)
ST	T. B. Howell, *A Complete Collection of State Trials . . . from the Earliest Period to the Year 1783* (Longman, Hurst, Rees, Orme and Brown, 1816)
TNA	The National Archives

Introduction

1. Paul Hopkins, "Sham Plots and Real Plots in the 1690s," in *Ideology and Conspiracy: Aspects of Jacobitism, 1689–1759*, ed. Eveline Cruickshanks (Edinburgh: J. Donald, 1982).

2. Some inspiration for these questions about how to identify and punish collaborators with the previous regime is drawn from Tina Rosenberg's study of Eastern Europe, *The Haunted Land: Facing Europe's Ghosts after Communism* (New York: Random House, 1995).

3. For a recent celebration, see Michael Barone, *Our First Revolution: The Remarkable British Upheaval That Inspired America's Founding Fathers* (New York: Crown, 2007). For a critique of Burkeian influence on historiography, see Steve Pincus, *1688: The First Modern Revolution* (New Haven: Yale University Press, 2009), 22–25.

4. [John Somers], *Vindication of the Proceedings of the Late Parliament of England* (Dorman Newman, 1690), 9.

5. On the Popish Plot, which most historians regard as a sham, see John P. Kenyon, *The Popish Plot* (London: Heinemann, 1972). There is more controversy about the reality of the Rye House Plot and the guilt of particular individuals. Recent works that accept the veracity of the Rye House Plot are Melinda S. Zook, *Radical Whigs and Conspiratorial Politics in Late Stuart England* (University Park: Pennsylvania State University Press, 1999); and Richard Ashcraft, *Revolutionary Politics and Locke's Two Treatises of Government* (Princeton: Princeton University Press, 1986). For a more skeptical assessment, see K. D. H. Haley, *The First Earl of Shaftsbury* (Oxford: Clarendon, 1968), 707–28.

6. John Dunn, "Trust and Political Agency," in *Trust: Making and Breaking Cooperative Relations*, ed. Diego Gambetta (Oxford: Basil Blackwell, 1988), 83.

7. John Dunn, *Locke* (Oxford: Oxford University Press), chap. 2; Locke, *Second Treatise of Government*, paragraphs 209–10.

8. [John Locke], *Letter Concerning Toleration* (Awnsham Churchill, 1689), 7.

9. This point is made by Craig Muldrew, *The Economy of Obligation: The Culture of Credit and Social Relations in Early Modern England* (New York: St. Martin's, 1998), 124, 321–25. Hobbes explains the impossibility of trust in a state of nature succinctly in *Leviathan*, book 1, chap. 13, and elaborates through chaps. 14 and 15.

10. Thomas Hobbes, *Leviathan* [1651], ed. C. B. Macpherson (Penguin, 1968), 233 (book 2, chap. 18).

11. On the Royal Society, see Steven Shapin and Simon Schaffer, *Leviathan and the Air-Pump: Hobbes, Boyle, and the Experimental Life* (Princeton: Princeton University Press, 1985). Two important accounts of trust in an economic context before the late seventeenth century are Muldrew, *Economy of Obligation*; and Francesca Trivellato, *The Familiarity of Strangers: The Sephardic Diaspora, Livorno, and Cross-Cultural Trade in the Early Modern Period* (New Haven: Yale University Press, 2009). For currency issues, see Carl Wennerlind, *Casualties of Credit* (Cambridge, MA: Harvard University Press, 2011).

12. For the forging of Nottingham's seals, see *By the King and Queen, a Proclamation. Whereas in order to the holding a correspondence with Their Majesties Enemies* (Charles Bill, [9 March] 1693). For suspicions that Nottingham counterfeited it himself, see information from Richard Holland, 14 October 1693, *HMC Finch* 5:262. Discussed more generally by Sonia Anderson in ibid. 5:xxvii–xxviii (preface). For Sprat's case, see *A Relation of the Late Wicked Contrivance of Stephen Blackhead and Robert Young* (1692) and *A Second Part of the Relation* (1692).

13. Adrian Johns, *The Nature of the Book* (Chicago: University of Chicago Press, 1998).

14. Mark Knights, *Representation and Misrepresentation in Later Stuart Britain: Partisanship and Political Culture* (Oxford: Oxford University Press, 2005).

15. Shapin and Schaffer, *Leviathan and the Air-Pump*; Steven Shapin, *A Social History of Truth: Civility and Science in Seventeenth-Century England* (Chicago: University of Chicago Press, 1994); Peter Dear, "Totius in Verba: Rhetoric and Authority in the Early Royal Society," *Isis* 76:2 (June 1985): 144–61; Barbara J. Shapiro, *A Culture of Fact: England, 1550–1720* (Ithaca: Cornell University Press, 2000).

16. *LPD*, 24 (24 February 1692); *CJ* 11:579 (6 November 1696); *ST* 12:1403–5.

17. Diego Gambetta, "Can We Trust Trust?" in Gambetta, *Trust: Making and Breaking Cooperative Relations*, 217–18.

18. Wennerlind, *Casualties of Credit*. Letters to Undersecretary of State John Ellis document disruption caused by the recoinage. See, e.g., A. E. (from Yarmouth) to Ellis, 13 December 1695, BL Add. 28924, 103–4; and Thomas Power to Ellis, 7 January 1696, ibid., f. 105.

19. For interregnum defactoism, see John M. Wallace, *Destiny His Choice: The Loyalism of Andrew Marvell* (Cambridge: Cambridge University Press, 1968); and Quentin Skinner, "Conquest and Consent: Thomas Hobbes and the Engagement Controversy," in *The Interregnum: The Quest for Settlement, 1646–60*, ed. G. E. Aylmer (MacMillan, 1972). For defactoism in the Revolution of 1688, see Mark Goldie, "The Revolution of 1689 and the Structure of Political Argument: An Essay and an Annotated Bibliography of Pamphlets on the Allegiance Controversy," *Bulletin of Research in the Humanities* 83 (1980): 473–564. William Sherlock, *The Case of the Allegiance Due to the Sovereign Powers* (W. Rogers, 1691).

20. Exactly how many people believed the Williamite regime's legitimacy rested on their consent, and how many accepted it on other grounds (defactoist,

providentialist, or because of Queen Mary's hereditary claim) is still debated by historians. Representative statements of opposing positions are Mark Goldie, "The Revolution of 1689 and the Structure of Political Argument"; and Steve Pincus, *1688: The First Modern Revolution*, chap. 14. It nonetheless seems safe enough to say that propagandists and government officials in William's reign regarded a narrative of consent as one important resource for legitimating the regime in a way that their predecessors under James II and Charles II did not.

21. The suspension of habeas corpus has been importantly discussed in a recent article but not as part of an assessment of the revolution. See Paul Halliday and G. Edward White, "The Suspension Clause: English Text, Imperial Contexts, and American Implications," *Virginia Law Review* 94:3 (May 2008): 575–714.

22. Herbert Butterfield, *The Whig Interpretation of History* (New York: W. W. Norton, 1965), v; Edmund Burke, *Reflections on the Revolution in France* (J. Dodsley, 1790), 46. Thatcher is quoted in Edward Vallance, *The Glorious Revolution 1688: Britain's Fight for Liberty* (New York: Pegasus, 2008), 1. See also Pincus, *1688: The First Modern Revolution*, chap. 1, for the persistence of the image of 1688 as a nonrevolution. Michael Barone, *Our First Revolution: The Remarkable British Upheaval That Inspired America's Founding Fathers* (New York: Crown, 2007), 3, 231, 232, 23.

23. Vallance, *Glorious Revolution*, 17; Pincus, *1688: The First Modern Revolution*, 475.

24. Vallance, *Glorious Revolution*, 18; Tim Harris, *Revolution: The Great Crisis of the British Monarchy, 1685–1720* (London: Allen Lane, 2006), 515–16.

25. Pincus, *1688: The First Modern Revolution*, chap. 2.

26. Ibid., 7. For skepticism, see Edward Vallance's review, *New Statesman*, 22 October 2009.

27. Sheila Fitzpatrick, "Signals from Below: Soviet Letters of Denunciation of the 1930s," *Journal of Modern History* 68:4 (December 1996): 831–32; Colin Lucas, "The Theory and Practice of Denunciation in the French Revolution," *Journal of Modern History* 68:4 (December 1996): 768–85. On Muscovy, A. M. Kleimola, "The Duty to Denounce in Muscovite Russia," *Slavic Review* 31:4 (December 1972): 759–79. For an argument that modernity matters more than a particular revolutionary ideology, see Peter Holquist, *Making War, Forging Revolution: Russia's Continuum of Crisis, 1914–1921* (Cambridge, MA: Harvard University Press, 2002), esp. chap. 7.

28. Joshua Bowes to Trumbull, 29 June 1696, BL Add. 72535, ff. 226–27.

29. Lucas, "Theory and Practice of Denunciation," 770–71, 781–85.

30. M. W. Beresford, "The Common Informer, Penal Statutes, and Economic Regulation," *Economic History Review*, n.s., 10:2 (1957): 221–38; Mark Goldie, "The Hilton Gang and the Purge of London in the 1680s," in *Politics and the Political Imagination in Later Stuart Britain*, ed. Howard Nenner (Rochester, NY: University of Rochester Press, 1997). On Whig martyrs, see Lois G. Schwoerer, "Lord William Russell: The Making of a Martyr, 1683–1983," *Journal of British Studies* 24:1 (January 1985): 41–71.

31. [Edward Stephens], *Phinehas: or, The Common Duty of All Men* (Richard Baldwin, 1695), 10–11; Faramerz Dabhoiwala, "Prostitution and Police in London, c. 1660–c. 1760," (D.Phil. thesis, University of Oxford, 1995), 153, 167–68.

32. Lucas, "Theory and Practice of Denunciation," 775–76, 779.

33. *LBHR* 2:236 (29 May 1691); anonymous to Dorset, KHLC U269/C120/5.

34. Fitzpatrick, "Signals from Below," 866.

35. Joanna Innes, *Inferior Politics: Social Problems and Social Policies in Eighteenth-Century Britain* (Oxford: Oxford University Press, 2009), chap. 7.

36. Sheila Fitzpatrick and Robert Gellately, "Introduction to the Practices of Denunciation in Modern European History," *Journal of Modern History* 68:4 (December 1996): 748.

37. Alan Marshall, *Intelligence and Espionage in the Reign of Charles II* (Cambridge: Cambridge University Press, 1994).

38. For Ireland, see, e.g., S. J. Connolly, *Religion, Law, and Power: The Making of Protestant Ireland, 1660–1760* (Oxford: Oxford University Press, 1992); for Scotland, see Clare Jackson, "Judicial Torture, the Liberties of the Subject, and Anglo-Scottish Relations, 1660–90," *Proceedings of the British Academy* 127 (2005): 75–101. Tim Harris, *Revolution: The Great Crisis of the British Monarchy*, provides an excellent overview of the differences between Irish, Scots, and English experiences of 1688.

Chapter 1. Debates on National Security

1. For Armstrong's body, see 5 April 1689, *LBHR* 1:518; see also 19 May 1689, ibid., 1:537. Richard Greaves, "Thomas Armstrong," *ODNB*; John Hawles, *Remarks upon the Tryals of Edward Fitzharris et al.* (Jacob Tonson, 1689), 83–84.

2. *The Prince of Orange His Declaration. Shewing the Reasons of This Present Invasion* ("Given at our court at The Hague," 1 October 1688).

3. Lois G. Schwoerer, "Lord William Russell: The Making of a Martyr, 1683–1983," *Journal of British Studies* 24:1 (January 1985): 41–71. Debate on the Heads for a Bill of Indemnity, 16 May 1689, *GD* 9:252–76.

4. For legislation against Catholics, see "Act for the Amoving Papists and Reputed Papists from the Cities of London and Westminster and Ten Miles Distance from the Same," *SR* 6:60–61; and "Act for the Better Securing the Government by Disarming Papists and Reputed Papists," *SR* 6:71–73. For debate on expanded treason bill, see 10 December 1692, *LPD*, 309 (10 December 1692). The proposed "Bill for Preservation of their Majesties Persons and Government" provided that speaking words against the government would be punished the first time as a praemunire, the second time as high treason, and that to express the same in writing or printing is high treason.

5. [Robert Ferguson], *A Letter to Mr. Secretary Trenchard: Discovering a Conspiracy against the Laws and Ancient Constitution of England: with Reflections on the Present Pretended Plot* (1694), 33. For an important discussion of Ferguson, see Mark Goldie and Clare Jackson, "Williamite Tyranny and the Whig Jacobites," in *Redefining William III: The Impact of the King-Stadholder in International Context*, ed. Esther Mijers and David Onnekink (Aldershot: Ashgate, 2007), 177–99.

6. *LPD*, 316 (14 December 1692).

7. Grosvenor was reported to have said, "If you will do as I would have you, send away King William, and send back for King James." Grosvenor vehemently denied it. *GD* 10:78–79 (26 April 1690). Other quotations in the order that they appear here are *GD* 10:86, 82, 87, 77, 83 (26 April 1690).

8. Goodrick and Harcourt, *GD* 10:81, 77–78 (26 April 1690).

9. Clarges and Falkland, *GD* 10:83, 77 (26 April 1690).

10. *A Modest Enquiry into the Causes of the Present Disasters in England* (Richard Baldwin, 1690), 13–14.

11. For Baldwin's arrest, *LBHR* 2:78 (15 July 1690); warrant, 16 July 1690, *CSPD 1690–91*, 70; George Mackenzie to Earl of Nottingham, July or August 1690, *HMC Finch* 2:392–93.

12. On oaths and penalties, see Rachel Weil, "National Security and Secularization after the English Revolution of 1688," in *After Secular Law*, ed. Winnifred Sullivan, Robert Yelle, and Mateo Taussig-Rubbo (Stanford, CA: Stanford University Press, 2011). The "Act for the Abrogation of the Oaths of Supremacy and Allegiance and Appointing Other Oaths," *SR* 6:57–60, required that refusers of the oath of allegiance take the Declaration against Transubstantiation and, refusing that, be deemed popish recusants. The declaration was first used

only to determine the religious identity of members of Parliament under Charles II.

13. Draft of papist toleration bill, *HMC Lords 1689–90*, 385–88; cf. John Bossy, "English Catholics after 1688," in *From Persecution to Toleration: The Glorious Revolution and Religion in England*, ed. Ole Peter Grell, Jonathan Israel, and Nicholas Tyacke (Oxford: Clarendon, 1991), 371–72.

14. Robert Cotton, 14 May 1689, *GD* 9:246; similarly John Lowther, 15 March 1689, *GD* 9:168–69.

15. Hawles, Howe, Capel, and Tredenham, *GD* 9:322–23, 318, 326, 318–19 (15 June 1689).

16. Cotton and Howe, *GD* 9:320, 318 (15 June 1689).

17. On Act for Restoring Corporations, Henry Horwitz, *Parliament, Policy and Politics in the Reign of William III* (Manchester: Manchester University Press, 1977), 42; *CJ* 10:322–23 (2 January 1690). For the debate of 10 January 1690, *GD* 9:510–20. The bill passed but the proviso was rejected.

18. Cotton, 12 June 1689, *GD* 9:296 (12 June 1689). Cotton should not be confused with his Whig namesake, Robert Cotton of Cheshire. Ettrick, *GD* 9:382 (1 July 1689); Tredenham, *GD* 9:246 (14 May 1689).

19. Papillon, *GD* 9:319 (15 June 1689); Rich, *GD* 9:531 (20 January 1690); Austen, *GD* 9:378 (1 July 1689).

20. Rich and Howard, *GD* 9:325, 324 (15 June 1689). For similar sentiments: Jack Howe, 1 July 1689, *GD* 9:378–79; Hugh Boscowan, 15 June 1689, *GD* 9:320. *A Letter to a Friend, upon the Dissolution of the Late Parliament, and the Calling of a New One* (n.p., 1690), 1. The pamphlet was condemned by the new, Tory-dominated Parliament as a libel.

21. *GD* 9:244–52 (14 May 1689); *GD* 9:538–47 (21 January 1690); *GD* 10:2–3 (21 March 1690). For the king's speech offering list of persons, *CJ* 10:349 (22 March 1690). The final result, with its list of exceptions, is "An Act for the King and Queens Most Gracious Generall and Free Pardon," *SR* 6:174–79.

22. Hampden and Somers, *GD* 9:545–46, 541–42 (21 January 1690).

23. Temple and Cotton, *GD* 9:245, 246 (14 May 1689). Which Robert Cotton is not specified, but this was likely the Tory from Cambridgeshire. The Tories Joseph Tredenham, Christopher Musgrave, Gilbert Dolben, and William Ettrick also spoke in favor of starting with persons. See *GD* 9:240, 249, 538, 539.

24. Colonel Birch, *GD* 9:249 (14 May 1689).

25. Dolben, *GD* 9:539 (21 January 1690).

26. Paul Halliday and G. Edward White, "The Suspension Clause: English Text, Imperial Contexts, and American Implications," *Virginia Law Review* 94:3 (May 2008): 575–714.

27. Nottingham to William, 5, 7 June 1690, *HMC Finch* 2:288, 289; William to Nottingham, 10 June 1690, ibid. 2:293.

28. Shrewsbury to mayor of Bristol, 26 December 1689, *CSPD 1689–90*, 369–70.

29. On this point, see *Reasons for a New Bill of Rights: Humbly Submitted to the Consideration of the Ensuing Session of Parliament* (n.p., 1692), 21.

30. Luttrell reports that Edward Hales and Obadiah Walker were committed by the House of Commons for high treason in reconciling to the Church of Rome after they had made use of habeas to apply for bail, 26 October 1689, *LBHR* 1:596–97 (26 October 1689). For Lancashire, *LBHR* 2:45 (23 May 1690). For order to detain, Nottingham to Mr. Taylor, 12 July 1690, *CSPD 1690–91*, 63.

31. John Farmer to Nottingham, 8 November 1689, *HMC Finch* 2:259–60.

32. 15 August 1690, *LBHR* 2:90. See also Carmarthen to William, 12 August 1690, *CSPD 1690–91*, 95: "The French are gone from the coasts, the militia are dismissed, . . . and I believe it will be ordered tomorrow in council that all the prisoners shall be bailed except those against whom material evidence can be produced."

33. *Reasons for a New Bill of Rights*, 14; *A Short History of the Life of Major John Bernardi: Written by Himself in Newgate, Where He Has Been for Near 33 Years a Prisoner of State, without Any Allowance from the Government, and Could Never Be Admitted to His Trial* (J. Newcomb, 1729).

34. *GD* 9:52 (5 February 1689); *GD* 9:66–67 (6 February 1689).

35. *GD* 9:65–70 (6 February 1689).

36. 1 March 1689, *GD* 9:133, for vote of thanks. For first debate on suspension, *GD* 9:129–41.

37. "An Act for Impowering His Majestie to Apprehend and Detaine Such Persons as He Shall Finde Just Cause to Suspect Are Conspiring against the Government," *SR* 6:57. See Clarence C. Crawford, "The Suspension of Habeas Corpus and the Revolution of 1688–89," *English Historical Review* 30 (October 1915): 613–30. See also Halliday and White, "Suspension Clause."

38. For debate on committal by privy councilors, *GD* 10:87–95 (28 April 1690). For indemnity legislation, see "An Act for Preventing Vexatious Suits against Such as Acted in Order to the Bringing in Their Majesties or for Their Service," *SR* 6:153–54; and "An Act for Preventing Vexatious Suits against Such as Acted for Their Majesties Service in Defense of the Kingdom," *SR* 6:411–12.

39. Birch and Ettrick, *GD* 9:265, 266 (22 May 1689).

40. Alexander H. Shapiro, "Political Theory and the Growth of Defensive Safeguards in Criminal Procedure: The Origins of the Treason Trials Act of 1696," *Law and History Review* 11:2 (Autumn 1993): 220. According to Samuel Rezneck, one of the articles in the *draft* of the Declaration of Rights had called for "constructions upon the Statutes of Treason, and Trials and Proceedings . . . in cases of Treason, to be regulated." This article was, however, dropped and a weaker one put in its place. Samuel Rezneck, "The Statute of 1696: A Pioneer Measure in the Reform of Judicial Procedure in England," *Journal of Modern History* 2:1 (March 1930): 14, n. 32.

41. Rezneck, "Statute of 1696," esp. 16–21; Trevor and Harley, *GD* 10:286 (28 November 1692).

42. Rezneck, "Statute of 1696," 6.

43. *LPD*, 236 (18 November 1692).

44. John Hawles, *Remarks upon the Trials of Edward Fitzharris, Stephen Colledge, Count Coningsmark, the Lord Russell, Colonel Sidney, Henry Cornish, and Charles Bateman* (Jacob Tonson, 1689), esp. 64; cf. Rezneck, "Statute of 1696," 13–14. For Treby, *GD* 10:174 (18 November 1691).

45. On claims to legality by James II's regime, see Howard Nenner, *By Colour of Law: Legal Culture and Constitutional Politics in England, 1660–1689* (Chicago: University of Chicago Press, 1977). Bartholemew Shower, *An Antidote against Poison* (Charles Mearne, 1683). Shower's call for reform is *Reasons for a New Bill of Rights* (1692).

46. Finch and Clayton *GD* 9:133, 134 (1 March 1689). Mr. Finch could be Heneage Finch, MP for Oxford University, or his brother Edward, MP for Cambridge. Both were Tories as well as brothers to the Tory secretary of state, Daniel Finch, Earl of Nottingham.

47. For Abjuration Bill, *GD* 10:75–87 (26 April 1690). For debate on Bill for Securing the Government, *GD* 10:87–98 (28–29 April 1690). For Williamson, *GD* 10:86 (abjuration), 87–88 (securing the government); for Goodrick, *GD* 10:80 (abjuration), 89 (securing the government); for Thompson, *GD* 10:77 (abjuration, albeit cryptically), 88 (securing the government).

48. Howard, *GD* 9:269 (22 May 1689).

49. Draft speech by Roger Kenyon against a bill for indemnity [1689], LancsRO, DDKe 6/38, discussed in Horwitz, *Parliament, Policy, and Politics*, 98; Foley, 1 *LPD*, 455–56 (1 March 1693). Two indemnity bills passed: "Act for Preventing Vexatious Suits against Such as Acted in Order to the Bringing in Their Majesties or for Their Service," *SR* 6:153–54; and "An Act for Preventing

Vexatious Suits against Such as Acted for Their Majesties Service in Defense of the Kingdom," *SR* 6:411–12.

50. Clarges and Capel, *LPD*, 126–29 (13 January 1692); Treby, *LPD*, 98–100 (31 December 1691); Report of conference between managers for Commons and Lords, 13 January 1692, *GD* 10:233.

51. Montagu, *LPD*, 98–100 (31 December 1691); Dolben, *GD* 10:220 (31 December 1691); summary by managers for the House of Commons in their conference with the Lords, 13 January 1691/92, as reported in *GD* 10:229.

52. 11 December 1691, *GD* 10:210.

53. John Bellamy, *The Tudor Law of Treason* (London: Routledge, 1979), 11.

54. 21 March 1689, *GD* 9:180–83. See also Alan Marshall, "Fitzharris, Edward (d. 1681)," *ODNB*.

55. Philip Hamburger, "The Development of the Law of Seditious Libel and the Control of the Press," *Stanford Law Review* 37:3 (February 1985): 661–765. Williams and Garroway, *GD* 9:304, 303 (13 June 1689).

56. Oates's petition to the Commons, *CJ* 10:44–45 (23 May 1689). See also *To the Right Honourable the Lords Spiritual and Temporal, and to the Honourable the Knights, Citizens, and Burgesses in This Present Parliament Assembled; the Humble Petition of Titus Oates, D.D.* (Richard Janeway, 1689).

57. *HMC Lords 1689–90*, 76–77, 80–82, 80–81 (26 April 1689).

58. *HMC Lords 1689–90*, 78–80, 77. For Bracton, Withins cites book iii, chap. 6; for Peter Cary's case, *Croke's Reports I*, 405.

59. *HMC Lords 1689–90*, 78–80.

60. *LJ* 14:234 (6 June 1689); *HMC Lords 1689–90*, 80. Withins had prosecuted Fitzharris, helped in implementation of quo warranto, and condemned Algernon Sidney. Holloway was a little more moderate. For example, he supported the right of the Seven Bishops to petition. But he prosecuted Stephen College and was considered under the influence of Jeffreys. Stuart Handley, "Wythens, Sir Francis (c. 1635–1704)," *ODNB*; Stuart Handley, "Holloway, Sir Richard (bap. 1627, d. 1699)," *ODNB*.

61. For Commons resolution about stifling the plot, *CJ* 10:177 (11 June 1689). My account of the bill that passed the Commons is reconstructed from the Lords' attempts to amend that bill and Commons' response to those attempts. The Commons' bill described the judgments in King's Bench as "erroneous, illegal, cruel, and of evil example to future ages," according to *CJ* 10:263–64 (13 August 1689). The discussion of proposed amendments recorded in *LJ* 14:276 (12 July 1689) also shows that the Commons' bill contained a clause reversing

"the judgments of King's Bench, and the judgments given [i.e., by the Lords] on the said writs of error."

62. The first clause is reconstructed from the report of the committee to prepare reasons for a conference with the Lords, *CJ* 10:263–64 (13 August 1689). The second is from the discussion of amendments reported in *LJ* 14:276 (12 July 1689). The Lords' proviso against Oates witnessing is *LJ* 14:276 (12 July 1689). Oates was pardoned not just for the perjury but also for publishing his petition to Commons while his case was in the Lords, which breach of privilege had landed him in prison. Alan Marshall, "Oates, Titus (1649–1705)," *ODNB*.

63. Of the peers who signed their names to a dissent from the vote upholding the King's Bench ruling, a dissent from the amendments made by the Lords to the Commons' bill and/or a dissent from the Lords' vote to adhere to their amendments, the vast majority of those who can be classified were Whigs. A list of thirteen (out of twenty-three) dissenters to the 31 May vote to uphold the King's Bench conviction can be found in *LJ* 14:228 (31 May 1689). Two separate groups of dissenters signed statements objecting to the Lords' amendments to the Commons' bill, *LJ* 14:277–78 (12 July 1689). The names of twenty-three lords appear as dissenters to the 30 July vote by the Lords to adhere to their amendments, *LJ* 14:299–300 (30 July 1689). The identification of most of these as Whig is taken from Henry Horwitz, *Parliament, Policy and Politics*, app. B, 335–37.

64. The Lords' view, as described by Robert Howard, *GD* 9:288 (11 June 1689); Earl of Rochester's report for the committee to draw up Lords' reasons for insisting on their amendments, *LJ* 14:295 (26 July 1689).

65. Statement of dissent from Lords' amendments, *LJ* 14:277–78 (12 July 1689); statement of dissent by several peers from the adherence by House of Lords to their amendments, *LJ* 14:299–300 (30 July 1689). Similarly, the report of Littleton's committee, appointed to respond to Lords' amendments, states that Lords' amendments "weaken the declaration of law made in this bill," *CJ* 10:230–31 (22 July 1689). "Declaration of Rights," *CJ* 10:28–29 (12 February 1689).

66. Report of the committee to prepare reasons for a conference with the Lords, *CJ* 10:263–64 (13 August 1689).

67. Ibid.

68. *To the Right Honourable, the Lords Spiritual and Temporal, and to the Honourable the Knights, Citizens, and Burgesses in This Present Parliament Assembled; the Humble Petition of Titus Oates, D.D.* (Richard Janeway, 1689); H. C. Foxcroft, *Life and Letters of Sir George Saville, First Marquis of Halifax* (Longmans, 1898), 2:218, n. 4; printed paper discussed by the House, entitled

"The Case of Titus Oates D.D. Humbly Offered to the Tender Consideration of the Right Honourable the Lords Spiritual and Temporal, and Commons, in Parliament Assembled," *LJ* 14:219–20 (25 May 1689). For the attack on Carmarthen, see Andrew Browning, *Thomas Osborne, Earl of Danby and Duke of Leeds, 1632–1712* (Glasgow: Jackson, Son, 1951), 1:450–54.

69. Hawles and Howard, *GD* 9:290288–89 (11 June 1689); for pro-Oates Lords, *LJ* 14:277–78 (12 July 1689); Howe, *GD* 9:287 (4 June 1689).

70. Oates's petition to the Commons, *CJ* 10:44–45 (23 May 1689); Oates, *To the Right Honourable the Lords Spiritual and Temporal*; for Oates's supporters in Lords, *LJ* 14:299–300 (30 July 1689); *LJ* 14:277–78 (12 July 1689).

71. Report of Littleton's committee, *CJ* 10:230–31 (22 July 1689); Howard and Capel, *GD* 9:288, 292 (11 June 1689).

72. Mark Goldie and Clare Jackson, "Williamite Tyranny and the Whig Jacobites."

Chapter 2. A Trusted Government?

1. William Ashworth, *Customs and Excise: Trade, Production and Consumption in England, 1640–1845* (Oxford: Oxford University Press, 2003), chap. 7. Steve Pincus, *1688: The First Modern Revolution* (New Haven: Yale University Press, 2009), esp. chap. 6.

2. I focus here on local officeholders most concerned with the regime's security. For other important offices, and the importance more generally of local officials, see Mark Goldie, "The Unacknowledged Republic: Officeholding in Early Modern England," in *The Politics of the Excluded, c. 1500–1850*, ed. Tim Harris (Basingstoke: Palgrave, 2001), 153–94. For an important conceptualization of the English state, see Michael J. Braddick, *State Formation in Early Modern England, c. 1550–1700* (Cambridge: Cambridge University Press, 2000).

3. "Suggestions for an Intelligence Service," *HMC Finch* 4:160–61.

4. For the constable, see J. Southerne to Mr. Warre, 31 December 1691, *CSPD 1691–92*, 46–47. For some other references to escapes, see Nottingham to mayor of New Romney, 26 April 1692, *CSPD 1691–92*, 254; letter about Oliver d'Overy's escape, 2 June 1693, *CSPD 1693*, 168; *LBHR* 3:88 (2 May 1693) on escape from Thompson the messenger; *LBHR* 3:206 (17 October 1693) on Ipswich and Beccles jailers letting prisoners escape; Shrewsbury to attorney general, 13 August 1694, *CSPD 1694–95*, 262, reporting Colonel Parker's escape; *LBHR* 3:389 (27 October 1694) on escape of Earl of Clancarty from the Tower; Richard Kingston's paper "The abode of several messengers," BL Add. 72570,

ff. 63–64, accusing messengers Richard Hayward and Henry Allen of letting prisoners escape; and Proceedings concerning allegations that Christopher Warren of Plymouth let French officers escape, TNA T1/4/66. For complaints about Dungeness lighthouse keepers, see William Carter to Nottingham, 7 May 1691, *HMC Finch* 3:52; and Nottingham to Abraham Stock, 6 June 1691, *HMC Finch* 3:101.

5. *LBHR* 1:505 (23 February 1699); *GD* 9:164–65 (15 March 1689); John Morgan to Shrewsbury, 22 June 1689, *CSPD 1689–90*, 161. On Robert Minors, *LBHR* 1:586 (30 September 1689); *CSPD 1689–90*, 254, 256–58, 265 (13 September and following, 1689).

6. On Shales, *GD* 9:450 (26 November 1689) and passim. On rotten victuals, letters from Torrington and Russell, August 1689, *HMC Finch* 2:234–41; *GD* 9:441–46 (23 November 1689).

7. Separate letters from Shrewsbury, Somers, Trenchard, and Godolphin to William, 15 June 1694, *CSPD 1694–95*, 179–86.

8. John Drysdell to John Foche, 18 January 1696, TNA T1/43/16.

9. Elizabeth E. Hoon, *The Organization of the English Customs System, 1696–1786* (New York: Augustus Kelley, 1968), esp. chap. 1. For one account of difficulties preventing smuggling, see customs commissioners' report, 14 August 1690, TNA T1/9/32. For problems of policing lasting well into the eighteenth century, see Ashworth, *Customs and Excise*, esp. chaps. 8 and 9. For proposal to customs commissioners, dated 16 August 1689, TNA T1/4/57, ff. 202–5.

10. Shrewsbury to Jephson, 3 December 1689, 24 January 1690, *CSPD 1689–90*, 342, 427. For Trumbull, BL Add. 72569, ff. 16–19. See also Trumbull to Treasury Lords, 6 July 1695, TNA T1/34/10. On Noel, BL Add. 42596, ff. 117–18, 121; Trenchard to mayor of Dover, 11 February 1694, *CSPD 1694–95*, 25; warrant for Noel, 5 July 1694, ibid., 212; petition of Henry Allen, 18 August 1696, TNA T1/39/46.

11. Howard Robinson, *The British Post Office: A History* (Princeton: Princeton University Press, 1948).

12. [John Wildman], *An Advertisement from Their Majesties General Post-Office, London* [1689].

13. BL Add. 61690, f. 1.

14. Elias Burns and John Short to Wildman, 22 August 1689, BL Add. 61689, f. 12; Marshall's petition, ibid., f. 72; Woodward, BL Add. 61690, f. 34; Hermon, BL Add. 61689, f. 27; Elizabeth Gaylord to Wildman, BL Add. 61690, f. 26; see also ff. 86–87, depositions alleging loss of a package, and f. 96, letter of support for Gaylord signed by twenty Totnes residents.

15. Julius Deedes to Wildman, 4 August 1689, BL Add. 61689, f. 73; Paper endorsed "Mrs. Watts procures hands against the behavior of Mr. Hulke of Deale," BL Add. 61690, f. 24.

16. For examples of complaints about packet boat operators, see Ralph Bell to customs commissioners, 22 October, 7 December 1689, BL Add. 61689, ff. 104, 112. Wildman inaugurated an alternative packet route to the Continent via Corunna in order to control the problem: Maurice Ashley, *John Wildman: Plotter and Postmaster* (New Haven: Yale University Press, 1947), 284–85. On newsletters, Trumbull to Treasury Lords, 14 April 1696, enclosing paper signed by Ralph Blackhall, TNA T1/37/22; see also *Part of the Illegal and Evil Practices of His Majesty's General Post Office*, TNA T1/42/51; Murcott to Wildman, BL Add. 61690, ff. 22–23.

17. Sawtell to Mason, 19 August 1690, and Mason to Sawtell, 26 August 1690, BL Add. 61689, ff. 143–46; *Part of the Illegal and Evil Practices of His Majesty's General Post Office*, TNA T1/42/51; LJ minutes, 26 August 1696, *CSPD 1696*, 362.

18. Petition of Joseph Wartman, Wildman Papers, BL Add. 61690, f. 31. For examples of job applications asserting Williamite loyalty and/or applications endorsed by prominent Whigs, BL Add. 61689, ff. 13–14, 17, 21, 31, 43, 45, 47, 49, 70, 75; BL Add. 61690, ff. 1, 20, 34, 39.

19. BL Add. 61690, ff. 55, 39; *Part of the Illegal and Evil Practices of His Majesty's General Post Office*, TNA T1/42/51; LJ minutes, 19 August 1696, *CSPD 1696*, 353.

20. For Murcott's accusations against Castleton, Watkinson, Howell, Kempton, and others, BL Add. 61690, ff. 16–17. For Farmer's version, J. Farmer to Francis Golling, 22 August 1689, BL Add. 61689, ff. 82–83. See also Isaac Ward's accusation against Golling, BL Add. 61690, ff. 3–4; Lunn [to Wildman], 24 September 1689, BL Add. 61689, f. 90; Meredeth Bromhead and Robert Mason to Wildman, 5 November 1689, ibid., f. 106.

21. Lunn [to Wildman], 24 September 1689, BL Add. 61689, f. 90.

22. J. Farmer to Francis Golling, 22 August 1689, BL Add. 61689, ff. 82–83.

23. Paper by Murcott, BL Add. 61690, f. 23v.

24. Shrewsbury to Wildman, 12 December 1689, *CSPD 1689–90*, 354; papers relating to officers in Dover, KHLC U1015/O26 (items 2 and 3); "James Lingo Complaint about Mr. Bastinck," KHLC U1015/O27/3.

25. Nottingham to Bastinck, 19 September 1690, *CSPD 1690–91*, 26. Further evidence that Bastinck was still employed at this time comes from his petition to the Treasury for more funds (undated), to which Wildman responded critically on 31 July 1690: TNA T1/9/21, ff. 71–74.

26. Ralph Bell to customs commissioners, 22 October, 7 December 1689, BL Add. 61689, ff. 104, 112; Shrewsbury to Wildman, 28 January 1690, *CSPD 1689–90*, 432. See also ibid., 448. For Wildman's connection to Williamson and the Montgomery Plot, see Ashley, *John Wildman*, 284–85, 293.

27. Stock to Nottingham, 28 May 1693, *HMC Finch* 5:134; TNA T1/27/68; Richard Kingston, "A Journey into Kent and Sussex Begun July 9th and Ended July 27th," [1695], BL Add. 72570, ff. 50–51.

28. Thurloe is quoted in Ashley, *John Wildman*, 156–57. For Wildman's role, ibid., 155–58. On Restoration practices, see Alan Marshall, *Intelligence and Espionage in the Reign of Charles II, 1660–1685* (Cambridge: Cambridge University Press, 1994), chap. 2.

29. Queen Mary to Charles Viscount Lansdowne, 9 July 1690, *CSPD 1690–91*, 57; warrant for James Lawrence, 7 March 1693, *CSPD 1693*, 58; on Gadbury's packet, BL Add. 61689, ff. 135–36.

30. Samuel Morland [to Shrewsbury], 18 June 1689 (with enclosure and note in Shrewsbury's hand), Historical Manuscripts Commission, *Report on the Manuscripts of the Duke of Buccleuch* (His Majesty's Stationery Office, 1903), 2:48–51.

31. Complaint of Samuel Morland [1690?], *HMC Finch* 3:455–56; Robert Gorge to William Trumbull, 6 December 1695, *HMC Downshire* 1:594–95.

32. Carmarthen to William, 13 June 1690, in Andrew Browning, *Thomas Osborne Earl of Danby and Duke of Leeds, 1632–1712* (Glasgow: Jackson and Son, 1944), 2:163–64; Mary to William, 7/17 July 1690, in *Appendix to Sir John Dalrymple's Memoirs of Great Britain and Ireland, Part the Second* (W. Strahan, 1773), 133 (appendix to book 5). For letters intercepted by Monmouth, and Marlborough's views, see Ashley, *John Wildman*, 296–97. For Wildman's dismissal, ibid., 294–98.

33. For Hawkins, 13 April 1689, *CSPD 1689*, 61; 28 May 1689, ibid., 123; *LBHR* 1:540 (31 May 1689); for Saffin, Shrewsbury to mayor of Exeter, 24 April 1690, *CSPD 1689–90*, 564; 3 May 1690, *CSPD 1690–91*, 4; for Bristol mayoralty, William Jackson to Shrewsbury, 4 September 1689, *CSPD 1689–90*, 241; Shrewsbury to Jackson, 10 September 1689, ibid., 247–48; for Tomlinson, Lionel K. J. Glassey, "The Origins of Political Parties in Seventeenth-Century Lancashire," *Transactions of the Historic Society of Cheshire and Lancashire* 136 (1987).

34. Lionel K. J. Glassey, *Politics and the Appointment of Justices of the Peace* (Oxford: Oxford University Press, 1979), esp. chap. 4; on Sacheverell Clause: Henry Horwitz, *Parliament, Policy, and Politics in the Reign of William III* (Manchester: Manchester University Press, 1977), 42–43.

35. Nottingham to Lord Brandon, 12 July 1690, *CSPD 1690–91*, 64; BL Add. 42596, ff. 129–51; Torrington to Nottingham, 11 June 1690, *HMC Finch* 2:293; paper endorsed "Disaffection of the City and Corporation of Chichester," [c. 1697], KHLC U269/O56 (73); similarly, see Mr. Westmoreland to Ellis, 25 November 1697, BL Add. 28881, ff. 543–44, for reported disaffection of Reading's corporation.

36. Petition from mayor and aldermen of Canterbury, 15 March 1692, TNA T1/17/69; *The Complaint of the Inhabitants of the Island of Guernzey* (1690), ed. G. Stevens Cox (Mount Durand, St. Peter Port, Guernsey: Toucan, 1970).

37. Stokes to Shrewsbury, 25 April 1689, *CSPD 1689–90*, 75; Shrewsbury to Stokes, 13 February 1690, ibid., 461. Ironically, it was Francis Bastinck (see above) who had complained to Shrewsbury of the mayor's laxness.

38. [William Carter], *An Abstract of the Proceedings of W. Carter; Being a Plea to Some Objections Urged against Him* (printed for the author, 1694), 22–23. For raid on Deedes's barn, customs commissioners' report, 13 April 1692, TNA T1/18/14, ff. 54–60.

39. J. C. Appleby, "Neutrality, Trade and Privateering, 1500–1689"; J. S. Bromley, "A New Vocation: Privateering in the Wars of 1689–97 and 1702–13"; and A. G. Jamieson, "The Channel Islands and Smuggling, 1680–1850," all in *A People of the Sea: The Maritime History of the Channel Islands*, ed. A. G. Jamieson (London: Methuen, 1986); Shrewsbury to governor of Jersey, 19 March 1690, *CSPD 1689–90*, 515; information by Charles LeHardy [1691], *CSPD 1691–92*, 48; "Abstract of what passed in council concerning Jersey," 10/27 August 1691, *CSPD 1690–91*, 478–80; "Narration of things in as they now are in the Island of Jersey," *CSPD 1693*, 446–47.

40. Examinations about Pepper's escape, BL Add. 42596, ff. 117–18.

41. Nottingham to Harris, 21 August 1690, *HMC Finch* 2:421–22.

42. Petition of William Cotton, December 1693, TNA T1/25/8. For an intriguing albeit unsuccessful proposal to carry on illegal trade with France for purposes of spying, see "Mr. Roope's Proposal," BL Add. 72569, f. 43. On Gibson, Vernon to Mackye, 17 November 1698, BL Add. 40772, ff. 320–21.

43. For concerns about collusive capture, see Bromley, "New Vocation," 113.

44. For Letherhead's pass, see "Instructions for William Gatley" (with note of similar pass for John Letherhead), 27 April 1691, *HMC Finch* 3:41. For troubles with customs, see Russell to Nottingham, 3 June 1691, ibid. 3:94; William Carter to Nottingham, 11 July 1691, ibid. 3:153.

45. Letherhead to Nottingham, 25 July 1691, *HMC Finch* 3:177–78; Letherhead to John Lowther, 5 October 1691, TNA T1/15/41, ff. 157–58; William Carter to Nottingham, c. 25 July 1691, *HMC Finch* 3:375.

46. The suspicion that Watkins was supporting Letherhead is confirmed by the fact that he soon returned the goods he seized from Letherhead, understanding (as Letherhead put it) "that I was upon some service for their Majesties," Letherhead to Nottingham, 25 July 1691, *HMC Finch* 3:177–78; customs commissioners' report, 7 October 1691, TNA T1/15/46, ff. 184–85.

47. Letherhead to Lowther, 5 October 1691, TNA T1/15/41, ff. 157–59; customs commissioners' report, 7 October 1691, T1/15/46, ff. 184–85; memorial of Joseph Beverton, 30 October 1697, TNA T1/48/40.

48. P. A. Hopkins, "The Commission for Superstitious Lands in the 1690s," *Recusant History* 15 (1980): 265–82.

49. Deposition of Agnes, wife of William Barker of Warrington, 11 June 1694, TNA E134/6W&M/Trin9; examination of John Taaffe, BL Add. 36913, ff. 177–78; Hopkins, "Commission for Superstitious Lands."

50. Memorial of Joseph Beverton, 30 October 1697, TNA T1/48/40. Petition of Joseph Beverton (no date), Somers Papers, Surrey History Centre 371/14/M/4. Roland Gwynne to Vernon, 10 July 1698, BL Add. 28883, ff. 33–34; order to pay expenses, 22 May 1696, *CSPD 1696*, 199.

51. *Memoirs of the Secret Sevices of John Macky* (n.p., 1733), iii iv; Instructions from Trenchard to Macky, 10 May 1693, *CSPD 1693*, 131; J. D. Alsop, "Macky, John (d. 1726)," *ODNB*.

52. W. C., *England's Interest by Trade Asserted*, 2nd ed. (printed for author, 1671), preface.

53. William Carter, *An Abstract of the Proceedings to Prevent the Exportation of Wooll Un-Manufactured: From the Year 1667 to This Present Year 1689* (J. Streater, 1689), 6, 7, 3, 22–24, 18, 10; petition of William Carter, 14 May 1691, TNA T1/14/17, f. 53. For more on vexatious lawsuits, see "Case of William Carter," TNA T1/6/3, ff. 13–14. Note: *An Abstract of the Proceedings to Prevent the Exportation of Wooll* is found nested inside at least two other publications: *A Summary of Certain Papers about the Woollen-Manufacture* (J. Streater, 1689); and *An Abstract of the Proceedings of W. Carter; Being a Plea to Some Objections Urged against Him* (1694).

54. Carter, *Abstract of the Proceedings to Prevent the Exportation of Wooll*, 2–6. That customs officers sometimes compounded with smugglers to get immediate profits, rather than prosecuting the case in the Exchequer, was also alleged in a 1689 proposal to improve the customs, TNA T1/4/57.

55. Carter, *Abstract of the Proceedings to Prevent the Exportation of Wooll*, 21, 2. The Christ's Hospital story is also told in *England's Interest by Trade Asserted*, preface.

56. Customs commissioners to Treasury, 8 August 1689, TNA T/1/52, ff. 173–74; petition of William Carter, TNA T1/6/3, ff. 11–12; "Case of William Carter," TNA T1/6/3, ff. 13–14.

57. For Carter obtaining compensation: TNA T1/6/15, ff. 63–64; TNA T1/8/25, ff. 94–97; TNA T1/11/30, ff. 115–16. For threats by creditors and further complaints: Carter to Treasury, 9 December 1690, TNA T1/11/23, ff. 97–98; Carter to Treasury, 13 January 1690, TNA T1/11/30, ff. 125–26; and petition of William Carter, 14 May 1691, T1/14/17, ff. 53, 55.

58. *England's Interest by Trade Asserted*, 43; "Some Considerations Humbly Offered" [around or before May 1691], TNA T1/14/17, f. 55; *An Abstract of the Proceedings of W. Carter* (1694), preface; William Carter, *Usurpations of France upon the Trade of the Woollen Manufacture of England* (Richard Baldwin, 1695), 21.

59. *An Abstract of the Proceedings of W. Carter*, preface. The description comes from a hostile broadside quoted by Carter, but Carter conceded the fact.

60. Carter, *Abstract of the Proceedings to Prevent the Exportation of Wooll*, 8–9.

61. *An Account of Some Proceedings Lately Made for an Effectual Prohibition of the Exportation of Wooll, &c. Recommended to the Woolen Manufacturers of This Kingdome* [1685], 2, 6–7.

62. Pincus, *1688: The First Modern Revolution*, chap. 12; *England's Interest in Securing the Woollen-Manufacture of This Realm* (Joseph Streater, 1689), preface; *An Abstract of the Proceedings of W. Carter* (1694); "To the Merchants, Clothiers and Drapers &c."

63. Petition of William Carter, TNA T1/11/30, ff. 121–22.

64. "Instructions for Gatley" [27 April 1691] and passes for Gatley and Letherhead, *HMC Finch* 3:41; Carter to Nottingham, 29 April, 4, 7, 14 May 1691, ibid. 3:41, 46, 52, 61; Russell to Nottingham, 3 June 1691, ibid. 3:94; Carter to Nottingham, 25 July 1691, ibid. 3:375.

65. Carter to Nottingham, 11 July 1691, *HMC Finch* 3:153; Nottingham to Carter, 17 July 1691, ibid. 3:161; Russell to Nottingham, 3 June 1691, ibid. 3:94.

66. Memorial of Joseph Beverton, 30 October 1697, TNA T1/48/40.

67. For second voyage, Carter to Nottingham, 4 July 1691, *HMC Finch* 3:140. For proposed third voyage, Carter to Nottingham, 18 August 1691, ibid. 3:218–19. On Watkins: Letherhead to Nottingham, 25 July 1691, ibid. 3:177–78;

treasury commissioners' letter about Letherhead's allegations, 7 October 1691, TNA T1/15/46, ff. 184–85.

68. *An Abstract of the Proceedings of W. Carter* (1694), 26.

69. Ibid., preface, "To the Merchants, Clothiers and Drapers &c." Carter prints therein a letter from a supporter describing his earlier efforts to get Parliament to take action against abuses of aulnagers. For one such effort, see *CJ* 9:462–63 (27 March 1678). It appears none of these succeeded.

Chapter 3. "A Tool with so Devilish an Edge"

1. The side changing is recounted in J. P. Kenyon, *Robert Spencer, Earl of Sunderland, 1641–1702* (London: Longmans, 1958).

2. John B. Hattendorf, "Churchill, John, First Duke of Marlborough (1650–1722)," *ODNB*.

3. Single-sheet broadside beginning "London, the 29th day of September. This day the citizens being met at Guildhall . . . ," [1696]; see also *The Request of the Citizens of the City of London in the Common Hall Assembled to Their Representatives in Parliament* [1696]; Vernon to Shrewsbury, 1 October 1696, *LI* 1:12. Jacobite prisoners are discussed in chap. 4.

4. James Ormiston to Trumbull, 9 August 1695, BL Add. 72532, ff. 177–79.

5. Kingston to Trumbull, 10 August 1695, BL Add. 72570, f. 69.

6. Paul Hopkins, "Sham Plots and Real Plots in the 1690s," in *Ideology and Conspiracy: Aspects of Jacobitism, 1689–1759*, ed. Eveline Cruikshanks (Edinburgh: J. Donald, 1982), 91. King William's Dutch favorite, the Earl of Portland, also developed a network of spies, but he was far more concerned with agents on the Continent who are beyond the scope of this study. David Onnekink, *The Anglo-Dutch Favorite: The Career of Hans Willem Bentink, 1st Earl of Portland, 1649–1709* (Aldershot: Ashgate, 2007), 168–73.

7. Shrewsbury to Portland, 28 June, 12 July 1695, NUL PwA 1380, 1381.

8. On Fuller, Tobias B. Hug, *Impostures in Early Modern England: Representations and Perceptions of Fraudulent Identities* (Manchester: Manchester University Press, 2009), chap. 8; George Campbell, *Imposter at the Bar: The Life of William Fuller, 1670–1733* (London: Hodder and Stoughton, 1961).

9. For the £100, Nottingham to Jephson, 2 July 1690, *CSPD 1690–91*, 46; Secret Service payments, 4 July 1690, *CTB* 17:579 (1702). For account given to Portland, NUL PwA 446a. Unfortunately, the document is not dated, and no dates are given for expenses. Its reliability is questionable. A not entirely

compatible alternative account of Fuller's expenses was given to Parliament: *LPD*, 67–68 (9 December 1691). Neither of Fuller's accounts is fully trustworthy. Still, if we assume Fuller is probably underrecording what he was paid on both occasions, then the quantity of money he does acknowledge having received is especially striking.

10. For the cipher and letters from Fuller to Delaval, NUL PwA 447–450. Request for vessel, Fuller to "My Lord" [Tillotson], 6 July 1691, NUL PwA 454.

11. Fuller to "My Lord," 8 May, 6, 30 July 1691, NUL PwA 451, 454, 455; Campbell, *Imposter at the Bar*, 79–80.

12. Carmarthen to William, 3 February 1691, *CSPD 1690–91*, 243–44; paper by Crone, c. May 1691, headed "Memorandums of Some Particular Discourses," *HMC Finch* 3:325–26; Preston to William, [end of April 1691?], ibid. 3:311.

13. Nottingham to William, acknowledging Halifax's offense was at worst only misprision of treason, 26 June 1691, *HMC Finch* 3:128; *LPD*, 53 (30 November 1691).

14. *LPD*, 67–68 (9 December 1691); *GD* 10:202–6.

15. *LBHR* 2:326, 331, 346.

16. *LPD*, 24 (24 February 1692).

17. *LPD*, 67–69 (9 December 1691); *GD* 10:203–6 (9 December 1691).

18. Nottingham to Robert Waller, 24 March 1692, *HMC Finch* 4:41; Nottingham to Blathwayt, 25 March 1692, ibid. 4:43–44. Shrewsbury's certificate, dated 15 April 1692, is printed in William Fuller, *A Brief Discovery of the True Mother of the Pretended Prince of Wales, Known by the Name of Mary Grey: To Which Is Added a Further Discovery of the Late Conspiracy against His Majesties Sacred Person and Government, &c., and Deposed to a Committee of Parliament* (printed for the author, 1696), following p. 48. Fuller alludes to it in many of his writings: see, e.g., *A Trip to Hampshire and Flanders* (printed for the author, 1701), dedication.

19. "Fuller's Letter to the House of Commons," [8 November 1692], BL Add. 42586, f. 194.

20. Richard Holland to Nottingham, 12 October 1693, *HMC Finch* 5:264–65; Kingston to Trumbull [July 1695], *HMC Downshire* 1:505–6.

21. Kingston to Trumbull, 10, 12 August 1695, BL Add. 72570, ff. 69, 78. More correspondence from Ormiston is in BL Add. 72533, ff. 33–34, 45–46, 163–64, 209–10, and BL Add. 72534, ff. 63–64.

22. Stuart Handley, "Talbot, Charles, Duke of Shrewsbury, 1660–1718," *ODNB*; Trumbull Diary, Saturday, 18 October 1696, and Sunday, 17 October 1697, BL Add. 72571, ff. 55v, 62. One witness was insufficient to convict a

defendant for treason after the 1696 Treason Trials Act went into effect. The implication of this cryptic diary entry is that Vernon was reassuring a Jacobite suspect that he need not worry about being convicted.

23. For more about Smith, see Rachel Weil, "Matthew Smith vs. the 'Great Men': Plot Talk, the Public Sphere, and the Problem of Credibility in the 1690s," in *The Politics of the Public Sphere in Early Modern England*, ed. Steve Pincus and Peter Lake (Manchester: Manchester University Press, 2007).

24. Matthew Smith, *Memoirs of Secret Service* (A. Baldwin, 1699), viii.

25. Ibid., 44, 57, 67–69. Quotations are from letters from Shrewsbury to Smith, printed by Smith in that text.

26. Ibid., 76.

27. Vernon to Shrewsbury, 24 September 1696, *LI* 1:2–3; Richard Kingston, *A Modest Answer to Captain Smith's Immodest Memoirs of Secret Service* (J. Nutt, 1700), 16; Matthew Smyth, *Remarks upon the D—— of S——'s Letter* (printed and sold by the booksellers of London and Westminster, 1700), xv; *Memoirs of Secret Service*, 149.

28. Fenwick's information, first paper, 6 November 1696, *CJ* 11:577–78. William III to Shrewsbury, 10 September/30 August 1696, in William Coxe, *Private and Original Correspondence of Charles Talbot, Duke of Shrewsbury* (Longman, Hurst, Reese, Orme and Brown, 1821), 145; Portland to Shrewsbury, 10 September/30 August 1696, ibid., 146.

29. Vernon to Shrewsbury, 24 October 1696, *LI* 1:28; *CJ* 11:579 (6 November 1696).

30. See esp. Vernon to Shrewsbury, 24 November, 1, 5, 8, 10, 12, 17 December 1696, *LI* 1:70–71, 90, 103–5, 108, 114–15, 117, 128–32; Somers to Shrewsbury, 10 December 1696, Coxe, *Private and Original Correspondence*, 439–41.

31. Shrewsbury's letter to the House of Lords, 13 January 1697, is printed in Smith, *Remarks upon the D—— of S——'s Letter*, xiii; Somers to Shrewsbury, 12 January 1697, Coxe, *Private and Original Correspondence*, 459; Somers to Shrewsbury, 16 January 1697, ibid., 463; Somers to Shrewsbury, 20 January 1697, ibid., 463–65.

32. *Remarks upon the D—— of S——'s Letter*, 21–25.

33. For Kidd scandal: Robert C. Ritchie, *Captain Kidd and the War against the Pirates* (Cambridge, MA: Harvard University Press, 1986); Smith, *Memoirs of Secret Service*, vii.

34. The pamphlets are: Richard Kingston, *A Modest Answer to Captain Smith's Immodest Memoirs of Secret Service* (J. Nutt, 1700); Matthew Smith, *A*

Reply to an Unjust and Scandalous Libel, Intituled A Modest Answer (1700); Richard Kingston, *Impudence, Lying, and Forgery, Detected and Chastiz'd* (1700). For Kingston's attacks on Smith, see esp. *A Modest Answer*, 7, 14, 31, 32. For Smith's attacks on Kingston, see esp. *Reply to an Unjust and Scandalous Libel*, 36–38.

35. Vernon to Shrewsbury, 27 February 1700, *LI* 2:454; Vernon to Shrewsbury, 22 June 1700, *LI* 3:93; case and petition of Matthew Smith, BL Harley MS 6210, ff. 138–47.

36. Vernon to Shrewsbury, 10 June 1697, *LI* 1:261–62; *Remarks upon the D—— of S——'s letter*, ix–x.

37. Steven Shapin, *A Social History of Truth: Civility and Science in Seventeenth-Century England* (Chicago: University of Chicago Press, 1994).

38. M. W. Beresford, "The Common Informer, Penal Statutes, and Economic Regulation," *Economic History Review*, n.s., 10:2 (1957): 221–38; Mark Goldie, "The Hilton Gang and the Purge of London in the 1680s," in *Politics and the Political Imagination in Later Stuart Britain*, ed. Howard Nenner (Rochester, NY: University of Rochester Press, 1997); "An Act for the More Effectual Suppressing Prophane Cursing and Swearing," printed in [Edward Stephens], *Phinehas: or, The Common Duty of all Men* (Richard Baldwin, 1695), 13; John Beattie, *Policing and Punishment in London, 1660–1750: Urban Crime and the Limits of Terror* (Oxford: Oxford University Press, 2001), 230–31. One example of numerous proclamations offering rewards, in this case for discovering the forgers of Lord Nottingham's seals, is *By the King and Queen, a Proclamation. Whereas in Order to the Holding a Correspondence with Their Majesties Enemies* (Charles Bill, [9 March] 1693). For reward to discover Assassination plotters, 22 March 1696, *CSPD 1696*, 96.

39. Isaac Newton, draft memo to Treasury commissioners, TNA MINT 19/1, f. 438.

40. Kingston, "A Journey into Kent and Sussex," BL Add. 72570, ff. 50–51; Kingston to Trumbull, 24 November 1695, *HMC Downshire* 1:589–90.

41. Petition and "An Abstract of the Services Done by William Chaloner," BL Add. 72568, ff. 47–49; James Johnston's account, [22 June 1694], NUL PwA 1375.

42. James Johnston's account, [22 June 1694], NUL PwA 1375.

43. For Lancashire witnesses, "Aaron Smith's Account of What Moneys He Received for Carrying on the Prosecutions, and How He Has Paid and Distributed the Same," 15 February 1695, Parliamentary Archives, HL/PO/JO/10/1/471/881 (c).

44. Proceedings on petition of Edward Anely and John Blackburne, 27 November 1693, *CSPD 1693*, 409; TNA T1/25/18, ff. 81–83.

45. Petition of Henry Oulding, TNA T 1/60/67.

46. For Darby, Northern Assizes Depositions, 1691, TNA ASSI 45/16/1/21.

47. Aaron Smith's report about Banahan, TNA T1/54/19, f. 78; Robert Alcock's petitions: 5 May 1697, TNA T1/45/6; 9 June 1697, TNA T1/45/85; 8 September 1697, TNA T1/47/59.

48. For Scott and Read, Vernon to Shrewsbury, 17 December 1696, *LJ* 1:129.

49. For possible spying by Crymes in 1692, Information of Henry Crymes, [before 14 July], 1692, *HMC Finch* 4:311–12; Nottingham to Lords Justices of Ireland, 14 July 1692, *CSPD 1691–92*, 369. For Crymes's activities in 1695, see "Papers of Mr. Crymes," dated 6 and 8 August, BL Add. 72533, f. 83. The paper is printed in *HMC Downshire* 1:464–65 but is mistakenly dated 6 and 8 April. It is possible that Spenceley is the William Spenceley who kept a coffeehouse and was tried for seditious words in 1693 after having said that six thousand men were coming to make a descent on England. Trial of William Spenceley for seditious words, 26 April 1693, *OBO* t16930426–84. For Crymes in prison, Crymes to Trumbull, 18 September 1695. For Crymes's revelations of Assassination Plot, first made on 15 February 1695, see John Gellibrand to Trumbull, 15 February 1696, BL Add. 72534, ff. 164–65; Crymes to Trumbull, 17 February 1696, *HMC Downshire* 1:623; Gellibrand to Trumbull, undated, ibid. 1:626; NUL PwA 2506.

50. Paul Hopkins, "Prendergast, Sir Thomas, First Baronet (c. 1660–1709)," *ODNB*.

51. Crymes to Trumbull, 25 February 1696, *HMC Downshire* 1:627; list of prisoners in custody of messenger, 23 June 1696, *CSPD 1696*, 242; note about Crymes, 19 May 1696, BL Add. 72535, ff. 169–70; Crymes to Trumbull, 16 June 1696, ibid., ff. 211–12; Trumbull to James Butler, 1 August 1696, *CSPD 1696*, 316.

52. Crymes to Trumbull, 6 November 1696, BL Add. 72536, ff. 146–47. For payments: Crymes to Trumbull, 6 November 1696; Trumbull to Exchequer, 14 December 1696, *HMC Downshire* 1:716.

53. Crymes to Trumbull, 21 December 1696, BL Add. 72537, ff. 6–7 (Trumbull's comments are in an endorsement, 23 December); Trumbull to Ellis, 30 September 1697, BL Add. 28895, ff. 154–55; Secret Service payments, 7 March 1698, *CTB* 17:823 (1702).

54. Vernon to Shrewsbury, 4 September 1697, *LI* 1:338. Vernon to Portland, 14 September 1697, NUL PwA 1471. I am grateful to Abigail Fisher for an unpublished seminar paper that first called my attention to the material discussed in this section.

55. Tim Wales, "Thief-Takers and Their Clients in Later Stuart London," in *Londinopolis*, ed. Mark S. R. Jenner and Paul Griffiths (Manchester: Manchester University Press, 2000), 67–85; Beattie, *Policing and Punishment*, esp. chap. 5; Tim Wales, "Lovell, Sir Salathiel (1631/2–1713)," *ODNB*. Vernon to Mr. Mountstevens, 24 September 1698, BL Add. 40772, ff. 135–36.

56. Vernon to Portland, 3, 10 September 1697, NUL PwA 1468/1, 1470.

57. Chaloner's "Abstract of Services," BL Add. 72568, ff. 47–49. On Gibbons: Wales, "Thief-Takers," 76–77; Vernon to Shrewsbury, 28–29 September 1696, *LI* 1:9. Chaloner's ties with Gibbons are confirmed in "Minutes at the Examination of William Chaloner," 3 February 1696, BL Add. 35107, ff. 30–31.

58. Trial of Matthew Coppinger for theft, 20 February 1695, *OBO* t16950220–35; Newton, "Answer to Mr. Chaloner's Petition," TNA MINT 19/1, ff. 497v–498.

59. Trial of William Newbolt and Edward Butler for treason, 6 September 1693, *OBO* t16930906–78. Chaloner is not named in the Old Bailey account as the witness against Newbolt and Butler, but he took credit for their conviction in his "Abstract of Services," BL Add. 72568, ff. 47–49. Moreover, Chaloner was assaulted by John Herbert and William Purchase because, as asserted at their trial, "he was a witness against William Newbolt, Edward Butler and Thomas Farr": Trial of John Herbert and William Purchase for assault, 6 September 1693, *OBO* t16930906–67. Newton's comment is made in "Chaloner's Case," TNA MINT 19/1, f. 501.

60. *The English Guzman; or, Captain Hilton's Memoirs, with Several Other of the Grand Informers* (R. Oswel, 1683); Goldie, "Hilton Gang"; *Guzman Redivivus: A Short View of the Life of Will. Chaloner, the Notorious Coyner* (J. Haynes, 1699), 3.

61. Chaloner's "Abstract of Services," BL Add. 72568, ff. 47–49; Somers to Portland, 2 May, 2 July 1605, NUL PwA 1177, 1179; certificate of Aaron Smith with Trumbull's endorsement, 12–14 November 1695, *HMC Downshire* 1:583.

62. "Minutes at the Examination of William Chaloner," 3 February 1696, BL Add. 35107, ff. 30–31. Notes of a second examination, dated 1 April 1696, are in BL Add. 72567, ff. 25–26. The undated petition from Chaloner in BL Add. 35107, f. 29, appears to allude to this second examination and to events following the 3 February examination recorded on ff. 30–31.

63. Chaloner's petition, BL Add. 35107, f. 29. This seems to have been written after one or both examinations before the Privy Council; LJ minutes, 14 May 1696, *CSPD 1696*, 177.

64. Holt to Trumbull, [May 1696?], *HMC Downshire* 1:667; warrant for Chaloner's pardon, 18 January 1696, *CSPD 1696*, 22. For Chaloner's demonstration to Arnold's committee, *CJ* 11:774–77 (8 April 1697); William Chaloner, *Defects in the Present Constitution of the Mint Humbly Offered to the Consideration of the Honorable House of Commons* [1697].

65. On Price, 14 December 1695, *CSPD 1695*, 124; Vernon to Shrewsbury, 4, 7 September 1697, *LI* 1:331, 341. The story of the trunk of plate comes second- or third-hand and is somewhat garbled in the sources: Vernon to Shrewsbury, 7 September, *LI* 1:344; Vernon to Portland, 14 September 1697, NUL PwA 1471.

66. Vernon to Portland, 14 September 1697, NUL PwA 1471.

67. Robins to Trumbull, 12, 26 May 1698, BL Add. 72538, ff. 203–4, 209–10.

68. Robins to Trumbull, 11 August 1697, BL Add. 72538, ff. 45–46; Trumbull Diary, 8, 11–12 April 1697, BL Add. 72571, ff. 57v–58r, 58.

69. For Northamptonshire rising: Vernon to Shrewsbury, 17 June 1697, *LI* 1:268–69. For Price's accusations of Lansfield: LJ minutes, 7 August 1697, *CSPD 1697*, 291; Robins to Trumbull, 11 August 1697, BL Add. 72538, ff. 45–46. For Trumbull's prior knowledge: Henry Crymes to Trumbull, 6 November 1696, BL Add. 72536, ff. 146–47. For Gargrave: Vernon to Shrewsbury, 4 September 1697, *LI* 1:336. For Yarmouth: Vernon to Shrewsbury, 24 August 1697, *LI* 1:316; John Miller, "Robert Paston," *ODNB*.

70. Vernon to Shrews, 24 August 1697, *LI* 1:315–16; LJ minutes, 4 September 1697, *CSPD 1697*, 350–51.

71. Vernon to Shrewsbury, 17 June 1697, *LI* 1:268–69; LJ minutes, 10, 24 August 1697, *CSPD 1697*, 297, 326.

72. 31 August 1697, LJ minutes, *CSPD 1697*, 337–38.

73. Vernon to Shrewsbury, 2 September 1697, *LI* 1:328–30.

74. Vernon to Shrewsbury, 31 August 1697, *LI* 1:319–26; LJ minutes, 31 August 1697, *CSPD 1697*, 337–41; Vernon to Shrewsbury, 31 August 1697, *LI* 1:319–26.

75. Vernon to Shrewsbury, 9 September 1697, *LI* 1:349–50; Vernon to Portland, 10 September 1697, NUL PwA 1469; Vernon to Shrewsbury, 14 September 1697, *LI* 1:370.

76. Vernon to Portland, 10 September 1697, NUL PwA 1470.

77. Ibid.; Vernon to Shrewsbury, 9 September 1697, *LI* 1:354–55.

78. Vernon to Shrewsbury, 7 September 1697, *LI* 1:343–44; Vernon to Portland, 10 September 1697, NUL PwA 1470.

79. Vernon to Shrewsbury, 23 September 1697, *LI* 1:396; LJ minutes, 23, 24 September, 7 October 1697, *CSPD 1697*, 391–93, 396–97, 416–18; Vernon to Shrewsbury, 7 October 1697, *LI* 1:420.

80. Vernon to Portland, 7 September 1697, NUL PwA 1469; see also Vernon to Shrewsbury, 7 September 1697, *LI* 1:347.

81. Vernon to Shrewsbury, 21 September 1697, *LI* 1:393–94.

82. Vernon to Portland, 10 September 1697, NUL PwA 1470; Vernon to Shrewsbury, 9 September 1697, *LI* 1:354.

83. Vernon to Shrewsbury, 7, 9 September 1697, *LI* 1:343, 350–51; Vernon to Portland, 10, 14 September 1697, NUL PwA 1470, 1471.

Chapter 4. Identity, Honor, and Gender in the Narratives of Informers

1. Sheila Fitzpatrick, "Signals from Below: Soviet Letters of Denunciation of the 1930s," *Journal of Modern History* 68:4 (December 1996): 831–66 (quotation on p. 866). Jan T. Gross, "A Note on the Nature of Soviet Totalitarianism," *Soviet Studies* 34:3 (July 1982): 375. Joanna Innes, *Inferior Politics: Social Problems and Social Policies in Eighteenth-Century Britain* (Oxford: Oxford University Press, 2009), chap. 7.

2. Proceedings on petition of Cornelius Sodington, 31 March 1697, *CSPD 1697*, 81. On Mary Cook, Vernon to Williamson, 26 November 1697, ibid., 487; warrant, 26 November 1697, ibid., 489. Trial of James Weames for seditious words, 3 September 1690, *OBO*, t16900903-50.

3. "Extracts of letters out from Norwich relating to papists," BL Add. 28941, ff. 23–24.

4. Anne Hancock to John Wildman, BL Add. 61690, ff. 134–35.

5. "Extracts of letters out from Norwich relating to papists," BL Add. 28941, ff. 23–24. The extracts are dated 28 February, 2, 9, and 13 March; Richard Haddock to Nottingham from Portsmouth enclosing information of Dorothy Damram of Portsmouth taken 2 July 1690, Leicestershire RO, Finch MSS (*HMC Finch* 2:332–33); warrant for Mrs. Smith, 3 July 1690, *CSPD 1690–91*, 47.

6. *LBHR* 2:236 (29 May 1691).

7. For Marks, newsletter, 29 June 1697, *CSPD 1697*, 218, LJ minutes, 29 June 1697, ibid., 218–21. LJ minutes, 1 July 1697, ibid., 223; Vernon to Shrewsbury, 29 June 1697, *LI* 1:300. For a similar case of a witness with little

concrete to report being dragged before authorities by a third party, see LJ minutes, 11, 12 November 1697, *CSPD 1697*, 467–68, 471.

8. Informations of Thomas Pearne and Elizabeth Webb, 30 March 1695, BL Add. 42596, ff. 140–41; abstract of testimony, ibid., ff. 137–38.

9. Informations of William Thurloe, Edward Milles, and Elizabeth Webb, 30 March 1695, BL Add. 42596, ff. 139–41.

10. Paterson to Brockman, BL Add. 42586, f. 228; information of Arthur Gibbons, 30 March 1695, BL Add. 42596, f. 145; abstract of testimony, ibid., ff. 137–38.

11. Paterson to Brockman, BL Add. 42586, f. 228; abstract of testimony, BL Add. 42696, ff. 137–38.

12. Paterson to Brockman, 3 March 1695, BL Add. 42586, ff. 228, 234.

13. Abstract of testimony, BL Add. 42696, ff. 137–38; Paterson to Brockman, 15 March 1695, BL Add. 42586, ff. 247–48. For Skarr's profession, paper signed by John Skarr, 31 March 1695, BL Add. 42596, f. 151.

14. Paterson to Brockman, 26 March, 18 November 1695, BL Add. 42586, ff. 257, 273.

15. Informations of Elizabeth Bent and Mary Newton, 5 August 1690, *Records of the Borough of Leicester*, vol. 7, *Judicial and Allied Records, 1689–1835*, ed. G. A. Chinnery (Leicester: Leicester University Press, 1974), 25 (item 22.9).

16. Joshua Bowes to Trumbull, 29 June 1696, BL Add. 72535, ff. 226–27.

17. William Watson to Brockman, 5 December 1691, BL Add. 42586, f. 146; Brockman to Francis Jeffreys, 1 December 1691, ibid., f. 144. For similar sentiments, see Jacob Janeway to Brockman, 23 November 1691, ibid., f. 135.

18. Brian Austen, *English Provincial Posts, 1633–1840: A Study Based on Kent Examples* (London: Phillimore, 1978), 44–48; Paper by Woodgate, BL Add. 42586, f. 240; BL Add. 42596, ff. 157–58.

19. Wildman to Woodgate, 29, 30 January 1690/91, BL Add. 42586, ff. 119, 121–22; Viscount Sidney to Mr. Sotherne, 12 February 1691, *CSPD 1690–91*, 255. Crofts is here described as the commander of the *James* galley but is surely the same person.

20. Woodgate to Brockman, 28 August 1695, BL Add. 42586, ff. 269–70; Wildman to Woodgate, 3, 26 February 1691, ibid., ff. 123–25, 125–26.

21. *To the Honorable House of Commons. The Case of John Woodgate, Late Post-Master of Canterbury* [1699]; proceedings on libelous publication, 22 April 1699, *CJ* 12:659–60; Cotton and Frankland to Woodgate, 13 December 1694, BL Add. 42586, ff. 221–22.

22. British Postal Museum and Archive, PO 1, piece 1, 113–16. The signatories are Basil Dixwell, John Knatchbull, James Oxendon, William Honywood, and William Brockman. Copy of a letter from Basil Dixwell to Lord Portland, 23 January 1695, BL Add. 42586, ff. 226–27.

23. William Lowndes to Frankland and Cotton, 27 February 1695, BL Add. 42586, ff. 231–32; Frankland and Cotton to Woodgate, 28 February, 8 March 1695, ibid., ff. 233–34, 238.

24. M[ary] Woodgate to John Woodgate, 1 April 1695, BL Add. 42586, f. 262; Jacob Janeway to Brockman, 16 March 1695, ibid., f. 249; Woodgate to Brockman, 28 August 1695, ibid., ff. 269–70.

25. Testimonies of Manley, Frankland, and Cotton, proceedings on libelous publication, 22 April 1699, *CJ* 12:659–60.

26. John Robins to Trumbull, 19 November 1696, BL Add. 72536, ff. 169–70; proceedings on libelous publication, 22 April 1699, *CJ* 12:659–60; *To the Honorable House of Commons. The Case of John Woodgate, Late Post-Master of Canterbury* [1699].

27. *To the Honorable House of Commons. The Case of John Woodgate, Late Post-Master of Canterbury* [1699].

28. Proceedings on libelous publication, 22 April 1699, *CJ* 12:659–60.

29. "Memorial of Robert Paterson," Brockman Papers, BL Add. 42597, f. 17. See also Paterson to Brockman, 22 April 1695, BL Add. 42586, f. 266.

30. Robert Paterson, 22 April 1700, BL Add. 42597, ff. 52–53; "Memorial of Robert Paterson," ibid., f. 17.

31. "Memorial of Robert Paterson," BL Add. 42597, f. 17; Paterson to Brockman, 22 April 1695, BL Add. 42586, f. 266.

32. Paterson to Brockman, 3, 26 March 1695, BL Add. 42586, ff. 234, 257.

33. Paterson to Brockman, 18, 19 March 1695, BL Add. 42586, ff. 251, 252; John Baron to Brockman, 4 April 1695, ibid., ff. 260–61.

34. St. Clare and Baron to Brockman, 10 April 1695, BL Add. 42586, ff. 264–65; Romney to Excise Commissioners, April 1695, ibid., f. 271; Paterson to Brockman, 22 April 1695, ibid., f. 266.

35. Proposals "for the better discovery of three suspected persons," [October 1696], BL Add. 72569, ff. 125–26; affidavit of Robert Paterson, 21 November 1696, BL Add. 42597, f. 19. On Deery, Robert Paterson, 22 April 1700, ibid., ff. 52–53.

36. John Morgan [to Shrewsbury], 29 March 1690, *CSPD 1689–90*, 529–30; Morgan to Shrewsbury, 5 April 1690, ibid., 540. James Ormiston to Trumbull,

9 August 1695, BL Add. 72532, ff. 177–79. Ralph Dutton to Trenchard, 20 May 1694, *CSPD 1694–95*, 142.

37. Everard to Nottingham, 29 August 1691, *HMC Finch* 3:367. On Mr. Platt [Kingston] to Nottingham, September or October 1692, ibid. 4:478.

38. Banahan to Shrewsbury, 30 September 1689, *CSPD 1689–90*, 280; Shrewsbury to the mayor of Bristol, 17 October 1689, ibid., 294; information of Owen Banahan, 16 August 1694, *HMC Downshire* 1:446–48; Aaron Smith's report about Banahan, TNA T1/54/19, f. 78.

39. Shrewsbury to King, 10 July 1694, *CSPD 1694–95*, 218.

40. Ibid.; Shrewsbury to Admiralty, 26 July 1694, *CSPD 1694–95*, 240.

41. Taaffe's recantation, 15 June 1688, LPL 1029/11–12; Taaffe's examination in House of Commons, *HMC Kenyon*, 333; Taaffe to Tenison, 23 March 1689, with enclosure of letter addressed to Taaffe, LPL 1029/17–18.

42. On serving Mass, deposition of Mary Conjett and Katherine King, 24 April 1689, LPL 1029/4; Taaffe to Tenison, 23 March 1689, with enclosed letter addressed to Taaffe, LPL 1029/17–18. See also LPL 1029/16 for Taaffe's escape from prison in Calais. For Taaffe's information on St. Ange, 29 March 1689, *HMC Finch* 2:196–97.

43. Taaffe to [Tenison?], 2 June 1689, LPL 1029/5.

44. Trial of Patrick Harding for treason, 11 December 1689, *OBO* t16891211–54.

45. Examination of John Taaffe, BL Add. 36913, ff. 177–78; P. A. Hopkins, "The Commission for Superstitious Lands in the 1690s," *Recusant History* 15 (1980): 265–82; Edith Lutwych, "Abstract of Her Case," TNA T/1/27 #60, f. 246; petition of Richard Norcross, BL Add. 36913, f. 188.

46. Paper marked "Earl of Nottingham," headed "1690" beginning "On Thursday 25 September," in Gloucester RO, Lloyd-Baker MSS, D/3549/2/4/12.

47. Ibid.; Bellomont to [William Lloyd], cover letter to depositions of Anne Chevet and Anne Claude Archer, 17 July 1691, Gloucester RO, Lloyd-Baker MSS D/3549/2/4/12.

48. For letters in French, Taaffe to Tenison, 23 March 1689, LPL 1029/17–18; letter from Taaffe describing escape from Calais, LPL 1029/16. For "French Mary," Shrewsbury to mayor of Dover, 28 November 1689, *CSPD 1689–90*, 334.

49. Bellomont to [William Lloyd], cover letter to depositions of Anne Chevet and Anne Claude Archer, 17 July 1691, Gloucester RO, Lloyd-Baker MSS D/3549/2/4/12.

50. Deposition of Anne Claude Archer, 16 July 1691, Gloucester RO, Lloyd-Baker MSS D/3549/2/4/12.

51. Petition of James Archer addressed to Arlington [1672–74], *CSPD 1673–75*, 80–81. In January 1681 the £350 due in arrears to James, now deceased, was ordered to be paid to Anne; she had to wait until November, however, to receive the full sum. Order for payment, 18 January 1681, *CSPD 1680–81*, 136; *CTB 1681–85*, 162, 312. For rewards or lack thereof, see also 22 April 1684, *CSPD October 1683–April 1684*, 393; 22 December 1685, *CSPD February–December 1685*, 417.

52. Deposition of Anne Archer, 16 July 1691, Gloucester RO, Lloyd-Baker MSS D/3549/2/4/12.

53. Bellomont to [William Lloyd], cover letter to depositions of Anne Chevet and Anne Claude Archer, 17 July 1691, Gloucester RO, Lloyd-Baker MSS D/3549/2/4/12.

54. Information of M. Girard, 22 April 1692, *HMC Finch* 4:96.

55. Information of John Taaffe, 21–29 April 1692, *HMC Finch* 4:107–10. Volume editor notes that informations by Archer and Taaffe are in the same hand.

56. Ibid.

57. Ibid.

58. Information of John Lunt, sworn before John Trenchard, 27 June 1694, *HMC Kenyon*, 298; Taaffe's examination in House of Commons, ibid., 348.

59. "The names of persons employed to take up persons impeached as also of the informers with an account of what they were or have been," LancsRO, DDKe/HMC/921; deposition of Agnes Barker, 11 June 1694, TNA E134/6 W&M/Trin9.

60. Deposition of Agnes Barker, 11 June 1694, TNA E134/6 W&M/Trin9; deposition of William Barker, 11 June 1694, TNA E134/6 W&M/Trin9.

61. Testimony to Lords, *HMC Lords 1694–95*, 449. See also affidavit of Agnes Barker, 10 February 1695, in R[ichard] K[ingston], *True History of the Several Designs and Conspiracies against His Majesties Sacred Person and Government* (Abel Roper, 1698), 226–28. "The names of persons employed to take up persons impeached as also of the informers with an account of what they were or have been." LancsRO, DDKe/HMC/921.

62. Testimony to Lords, *HMC Lords 1694–95*, 449. See also affidavit of Agnes Barker, 10 February 1695, in Kingston, *True History*, 226–28.

63. Bridget Molineux to Thomas Legh, 11 October 1694, Jacobite trial file, LancsRO, DDKe 8/6.

64. For Mainwaring, Barker to Kingston, 14 September 1695, BL Add. 72533, ff. 75–76; for Page, William Barker to Richard Kingston, 4 September 1695, ibid., ff. 52–53.

65. William Barker to Richard Kingston, 29 September 1695, BL Add. 72533, ff. 120–21. The other letters are all in ibid.: 4, 14 September, 6 October 1695, ff. 52–53, 75–76, 147–48.

66. William Barker to Richard Kingston, 4, 29 September 1695, BL Add. 72533, ff. 52–53, 120–21.

67. Copies of Taaffe's manuscript narrative can be found in Tenison's papers, LPL 1029/24; in the Kenyon papers, LancsRO, DDKe/acc. 7840 (and printed *HMC Kenyon*, item #981); and in Oxford University, Bodleian Library Carte MS 228. It was printed in *A Collection of Scarce and Valuable Papers* (George Sawbridge, 1712), vol. 1. I cite from this printed edition.

68. *An Acct. of the Tryalls at Manchester October 1694*, ed. Alexander Goss, *Chetham Society* 61 (1864), 23; "Taaffe's Narrative," in *A Collection of Scarce and Valuable Papers*, 1:555.

69. *An Acct. of the Tryalls*, 26, 23.

70. "Taaffe's Narrative," 1:553–54.

71. *LBHR* 4:46 (18 April 1696); list of prisoners, 23 June 1696, *CSPD 1696*, 242. Captain Barron to Ellis, 3 June 1697, BL Add. 28924, f. 237. Paul Hopkins, "Taaffe, John (b. 1646/7, d. after 1728)," *ODNB*. Solomon Smith to Ellis, 18 February 1697/8, BL Add. 28882, f. 124.

72. For La Fore, Shrewsbury to mayor of Dover, 31 October 1689, *CSPD 1689–90*, 310; for Nash, Nottingham to mayor of Rochester, 31 May 1692, *CSPD 1691–92*, 306. Newbolt and Butler are named as witnesses against Griffith by William Chaloner in his "Abstract of Services," BL Add. 72568, ff. 48–49; see also trial of William Newbolt and Edward Butler for treason, 6 September 1693, *OBO* t16930906-78. For Anderson, *LBHR* 3:113 (8 June 1693). For other instances of witness coercion, see Kingston to Nottingham, September or October 1692, *HMC Finch* 4:478; John Mason to Nottingham, 14 November 1692, ibid. 4:501–2; and Kingston to Nottingham, 2 December 1692, ibid. 4:518–19.

73. Excerpts of intercepted correspondence, endorsed "About John Crofts," 19 August 1696, BL Add. 28880, ff. 280–81. Government officials also believed that Crofts was ready to inform: Henry Spence identified him as someone "who being discontented may be made use of for further discoveries," Spence to Trumbull, 19 July 1696, *HMC Downshire* 1:680. Crofts appears on lists of prisoners for 23 June and 15 November 1696, *CSPD 1696*, 242, 438.

74. Clarendon's Diary, 8–9 June 1690, *Correspondence of Henry Hyde, Earl of Clarendon*, ed. Samuel W. Singer (Henry Colburn, 1828), 2:317; *LBHR* 2:63–64 (22 June 1690). For the arrest of the astrologer John Gadbury, see Nottingham to Southwell, 11 June 1690, *HMC Finch* 2:294; 10 June 1690, *CSPD 1690–91*, 30.

75. *LBHR* 2:164 (23 January 1691). Kingston to Nottingham, 30 November 1692, *HMC Finch* 4:515. Newsletter, 24 January 1693, ibid. 5:19; *LBHR* 3:19 (24 January 1693).

76. Kingston to Trumbull, 8 August 1695, BL Add. 72570, f. 65. For the Batemans, Shrewsbury to Blathwayt, 9 October 1694, Yale University, Beinecke Library, Osborn MS Shelf b. 317; [Robert Ferguson], *A Letter to Mr. Secretary Trenchard, Discovering a Conspiracy against the Laws and Ancient Constitution of England* (n.p., 1694), 42.

77. Preston [to Earl of Devonshire], 2 May 1691, *HMC Finch* 3:43–45. Preston had laid the groundwork for this rhetoric earlier, when having been told to prepare for his execution he had responded, according to Luttrell, that "he had lived hitherto by the King's mercy, and had that assurance of his life," *LBHR* 2:212 (16 April 1691); John Callow, "Graham, Richard, First Viscount Preston," *ODNB*.

78. Nottingham to Sidney, 5 May 1691, *HMC Finch* 3:46–48; Crone to Nottingham, 3 May 1691, ibid. 3:323.

79. Crone to Nottingham, 3 May, [5 June] 1691, *HMC Finch* 3:323, 329.

80. Crone to Nottingham, [25 May, 5 June 1691], *HMC Finch* 3:328, 329.

81. Crone, "Memorandums of Some Particular Discourses," [May 1691], *HMC Finch* 3:325–26.

82. For washballs, statement of Matthew Crone, *HMC Finch* 3:339. For Mrs. Clifford vs. Lady Oglethorpe, Matthew Crone's information, c. 8 May 1691, ibid. 3:327–28.

83. Paul Hammond, "Titus Oates and Sodomy," in *Culture and Society in Britain, 1660–1800*, ed. Jeremy Black (Manchester: Manchester University Press, 1997), 85–101.

84. Rachel Weil, "'If I did say so I lyed': Elizabeth Cellier and the Construction of Credibility in the Popish Plot Crisis," in *Political Culture and Cultural Politics in Early Modern England*, ed. S. D. Amussen and M. Kishlansky (Manchester: Manchester University Press, 1995), 189–209. For Mrs. Hansard, Vernon to Shrewsbury, 12, 19 April 1698, *LI* 2:51, 64–65.

85. Anne Brown, LMA CLA/047/LJ/13/1696/003; information of Alice Barton, 18 July 1690, BL Add. 42596, f. 74.

86. For Webb, abstract of testimony [1695], BL Add. 42596, ff. 137–38. Information of Elizabeth Wattell, 20 November 1701, BL Add. 42597, f. 33; Edward Northey to Vernon, 27 November 1701, *CSPD 1700–1702*, 454; Vernon to Northey, 5 December 1700, ibid., 461. Gender was not the only issue: Northey thought the fact that Wattell had already revealed her dislike of Bliss was

relevant, but he also thought that Wattell's dislike only made Bliss's speech more reckless.

87. To obtain these numbers, I searched the *Old Bailey Online* database for the offense "seditious words" and the dates 1689–1702 and discarded two records that were of arraignment only. Identifiably male witnesses appear in the trials of Michael Ferrer (t16900115–27), Francis Paleing (t16940221–34), Joseph Sheares (t16890703–6), Richard Francis (t16950508–32), and James Weames (t16900903–50). Identifiably female witnesses appear in the trials of Ann Knot (t16920831–36), Sarah Ghoste (t16891211–39), and Jacob Duchfeild (t16931012 31).

88. Anonymous to Dorset, KHLC U269/C120/5; Anne Hancock to John Wildman, BL Add. 61690, ff. 134–35.

89. For attacks on Kingston, Robert Ferguson, *A Letter to the Right Honourable Sir John Holt, Kt. Lord Chief Justice of the Kings Bench; Occasioned by the Noise of a Plot* (n.p., [1694]), 19–20; Matthew Smith, *A Reply to an Unjust and Scandalous Libel* (1700), 36–38; for Price, Vernon to Portland, 3 September 1697, NUL PwA 1468/1.

90. See, e.g., petition of John Woodgate, British Postal Museum and Archive, PO 1, piece 1, 113–16; petition of Owen Banahan, 28 June 1697, TNA T1/54/19, ff. 80–81; petition of William Chaloner, TNA MINT 19/1, f. 497; petition of Henry Oulding, TNA T 1/60/67; petition of Robert Alcock, 5 May 1697, TNA T1/45/6; proceedings on petition of Edward Aneley and John Blackburne, TNA T1/25/18, ff. 81–83.

91. Bowes to Trumbull, 29 June 1696, BL Add. 72535, ff. 226–27. "Memorial of Robert Paterson," BL Add. 42597, f. 17.

92. Ann Hughes, "Gender and Politics in Leveller Literature," in Amussen and Kishlansky, *Political Culture and Cultural Politics*, 162–88.

93. John Macky to John Ellis, 29 September 1698, Dover, BL Add. 28883, ff. 193–94.

94. Information of John Taaffe, 21–29 April 1692, *HMC Finch* 4:107–10.

Chapter 5. Credit and Credibility in the Worlds of Richard Kingston

1. Kingston's attacks on Smith are *A Modest Reply to Captain Smith's Immodest Memoirs of Secret Service* (1700) and *Impudence, Lying, and Forgery Detected* (1700). For Fuller's charges against Nottingham, see William Fuller, *A Further Confirmation That Mary Grey Was the True Mother of the Prince of Wales* (printed for the author, 1696), 4. The biography is *The Life of Wm. Fuller, alias*

Fullee, alias Fowler, alias Ellison, &c. by Original a Butcher's Son; by Education a Cony-Wool-Cutter; by Inclination an Evidence; by Vote of Parliament an Imposter; by Title of His Own Making, a Colonel; and by His Own Demerits Now a Prisoner at Large Belonging to the Fleet. The First and Second Part ("Printed to prevent his further imposing upon the public," 1701). On Peterborough, *Remarks upon Dr. Freind's Account of the Earl of Peterborow's Conduct in Spain* (James Woodward, 1708). No author is given on the title page, but Kingston was arrested on orders of the House of Lords as the author of it. W. A. J. Archbold, "Kingston, Richard (b. c. 1635, d. 1710?)," rev. M. E. Clayton, *ODNB*.

2. [Robert Ferguson], *A Letter to the Right-Hononrable* [sic] *My Lord Chief Justice Holt, Occasioned by the Noise of a Plot* (n.p., [1694]), 19–20. [Robert Ferguson], *A Letter to Mr. Secretary Trenchard, Discovering a Conspiracy against the Laws and Ancient Constitution of England: with Reflections on the Present Pretended Plot* (n.p., dated 9 October 1694), 28.

3. Paul Hopkins, "Sham Plots and Real Plots in the 1690s," in *Ideology and Conspiracy: Aspects of Jacobitism, 1689–1759*, ed. Eveline Cruikshanks (Edinburgh: J. Donald, 1982), 92. He is dubbed a "trusted and able government spy" in Archbold, "Kingston, Richard (b. c. 1635, d. 1710?)."

4. The early works are Richard Kingston, *Pillulae Pestiltiales; or, A Spiritual Receipt for Cure of the Plague* (Edw. Brewster, 1665); and R[ichard] Kingston, *Vivat Rex* (Joseph Hindmarsh, 1683). For connection to Lucas, see Kingston to Nottingham [1692?], *HMC Finch* 4:536; "Paper about Marshall" (received from Lord Lucas), [4 June 1692?], ibid. 4:204. For Nottingham's changing opinion: Nottingham to Portland, 10 June 1692, ibid. 4:217; Nottingham to Portland, 19 August 1692, ibid. 4:407; [Kingston] to Nottingham, September or October 1692, ibid. 4:478.

5. Kingston to Nottingham, 9 November 1692, *HMC Finch* 4:500–501.

6. Kingston to Nottingham, 21 July, 11 or 12 September, 9 November 1692, *HMC Finch* 4:330, 452, 500–501.

7. Comber to Nottingham, 12 October 1692, *HMC Finch* 4:485. For context, see Paul Monod, "The Jacobite Press and English Censorship, 1689–95," in *The Stuart Court in Exile and the Jacobites*, ed. Eveline Cruikshanks and Edward T. Corp (London: Hambledon, 1995).

8. Lois G. Schwoerer, "Propaganda in the Revolution of 1688–89," *American Historical Review* 82 (1977): 843–74; Richard Kingston's information, 28 September 1692, *HMC Finch* 4:474–75.

9. Kingston to Nottingham, [1692?], [August 1692], [September or October 1692], *HMC Finch* 4:536, 437, 478; information of Richard Kingston,

c. 4 April 1693, ibid. 5:72; Kingston to Nottingham, 7 November 1692, ibid. 4:499. Dr. King is William King, bishop of Derry, the leading Irish defender of the Revolution of 1688. Charles Leslie, the Irish non-juror, did publish a reply to King's *The State of the Protestants of Ireland under the Late King James's Government* (Robert Clavell, 1692). On the exchange, see S. J. Connolly, "King, William (1650–1729)," *ODNB*.

10. Kingston to Nottingham, 29 July, [13 or 14 August] 1692, *HMC Finch* 4:352, 391. See also Nottingham to Portland, 27 August 1692, ibid. 4:426.

11. Kingston to Nottingham, [August 1692], *HMC Finch* 4:437–38.

12. Kingston to Nottingham, 2 December 1692, *HMC Finch* 4:518–19; "To Mrs. Ann Merryweather," c. 17 January 1693, ibid. 5:13–14.

13. For attendance at meetings, see Kingston to Nottingham, March or April 1693, *HMC Finch* 5:70; Kingston to Trumbull, 21, 30 June 1695, *HMC Downshire* 1:483, 489. For meeting emissaries and reading letters, see Kingston to Nottingham, [April or May 1692], [11 or 12 September 1692], *HMC Finch* 4:113, 452–53; information from Richard Kingston, [28 September 1692], ibid. 4:474–75; Kingston to Nottingham, 16, 21 January 1692/3, ibid. 5:13, 17–18.

14. Kingston to Nottingham, [April or May 1692?], *HMC Finch* 4:113; information from Kingston, [28 September 1692], ibid. 4:474–75; Kingston to Nottingham, [September or October 1692], ibid. 4:477–78.

15. Kingston to Nottingham, [September or October 1692], 16 January, 14 March 1693, *HMC Finch* 4:477–78, 5:13, 60–61.

16. Much pertinent archival material on Nottingham's spies is reproduced in *HMC Finch* 5, pt. 2 (Secret Service Papers).

17. "Copy of a Letter from France," [June 1692?], *HMC Finch* 4:273–74.

18. Trumbull to Portland, 25 June 1695, BL Add. 72532, f. 88. Examples of reform projects include paper "received from Captain Baron 11 June 1695," containing proposals for stopping "dangerous persons" going in and out of the port of London, BL Add. 72569, ff. 16–17; "Proposals Humbly Offered to Their Excellencys and Lords Justices of England for Ye Better Restraining of Dangerous Persons Going and Coming into Ye Kingdom by Gravesend and Ye Coast of Kent and Sussex," ibid., ff. 18–19; "Mr. Carter's Paper," 25 January 1697, ibid., ff. 150–51.

19. Trumbull to Portland, 25 June 1695, *HMC Downshire* 1:484; "Suggestions for an Intelligence Service," 15 May 1692, *HMC Finch* 4:160–61; Kingston to Trumbull, *HMC Downshire* 1:725.

20. "Abode of Several Messengers," BL Add. MS 72570, ff. 63–64.

21. Kingston, "A Journey into Kent and Sussex," BL Add. 72570, ff. 50–51.

22. Ibid.

23. Ibid. For similar accusations, see Kingston to Trumbull, 22 July 1695, *HMC Downshire* 1:514–15.

24. Richard Kingston, *Tyranny Detected, and the Late Revolution Justified, by the Law of God, the Law of Nature, and the Practice of all Nations* (John Nutt, 1699), 12–15.

25. Robert Ferguson, *Letter to Holt*, 19–20.

26. Kingston to Trumbull, undated, [May 1695?], [July 1695?], [after November 1695?], *HMC Downshire* 1:602, 473, 505, 601.

27. James Ormiston to Trumbull, 9 August 1695, BL Add. 72532, ff. 177–79; Kingston to Trumbull, 10, 12 August 1695, ff. 69, 78.

28. J[ohn] K[nighton] to Tenison, 17 August 1695, *HMC Downshire* 1:536–37. Portland to Trumbull, 5/15 August 1695, ibid. 1:528–29.

29. The mysterious gentleman's behavior is described in the information of James Griffin, 31 March 1695, BL Add. 42596, ff. 146, 136r. The note appearing to identify Kingston as the mysterious gentleman is f. 136v.

30. The last datable letter from Kingston to Trumbull is 21 February 1696, *HMC Downshire* 1:624. There are two later letters from Kingston in Trumbull's papers lambasting Shirley Prettyman (a freelance informer whom Kingston came to suspect of being a double agent), which may indicate continuing service to the government: Kingston to Prettyman, 18, 19 May 1696, ibid. 1:663. Still, there is nothing from Kingston in Trumbull's papers after May 1696.

31. Relevant letters to and from Vernon about Fuller's fraud include BL Add. 40772, ff. 27, 69–72, 92, 213–16, 227–28.

32. Kingston, *Life of Wm. Fuller*, 51–55; William Fuller, *The Whole Life of Mr. William Fuller; Being an Impartial Account of His Birth, Education, and Relations* (sold by the booksellers, 1703), 71–72.

33. R. K. [Richard Kingston], *A True History of the Several Designs and Conspiracies against His Majesties Sacred Person and Government as They Were Continually Carried on from 1688 to 1697* (Abel Roper, 1698), 40, on the reasons for Lunt not being convicted in 1691.

34. Kingston, *True History*, 73–97.

35. The earliest letter establishing Smith's relationship to Trumbull is Smith to Trumbull, 19 May 1696, BL Add. 72535, ff. 171–72.

36. For Vernon-Kingston contact: Vernon to Kingston, 14, 16 November 1698, BL Add. 40772, ff. 307, 314.

37. Vernon to Shrewsbury, 3, 4 January 1700, *LI* 2:400–401. For "bespatter," Vernon to Shrewsbury, 23, 25 January 1700, ibid. 2:417, 419–20. See, for

similar anxiety about perceptions that Kingston worked for Shrewsbury, Vernon to Shrewsbury, 20 January 1700, ibid. 2:414; and Kingston, *Modest Answer to Captain Smith's Immodest Memoirs*, 4.

38. Vernon to Shrewsbury, 30 January 1700, in *Letters from James Vernon to the Duke of Shrewsbury, 1696–1708: from the Shrewsbury Papers in Boughton House, Northhamptonshire* (microform) (East Ardsley: E. P. Microform, [1980]), vol. 4, letter #26. For Matthew Smith's charge, see his *Reply to an Unjust and Scandalous Libel* (n.p., 1700), 7.

39. Vernon to Shrewsbury, 27 January 1700, in *Letters from James Vernon to the Duke of Shrewsbury*, vol. 4, letter #25.

40. Smith, *Reply to an Unjust and Scandalous Libel*, 36–38.

41. Archbold, "Kingston, Richard (b. c. 1635, d. 1710?)."

42. Kingston, *A True History*, preface, A4; Kingston, *Modest Answer to Captain Smith's Immodest Memoirs*, 4. For Bromfield, *True History*, 6; for Betty Grey, *Enthusiastick Impostors, No Divinely Inspir'd Prophets* (J. Morphew, 1707), 80–82.

43. Kingston to Nottingham, May–June 1692 [or 1693?], *HMC Finch* 4:196–97.

44. Kingston, *Modest Answer to Captain Smith's Immodest Memoirs*, 7–13; Kingston, *Life of Wm. Fuller, alias Fullee*, 44.

45. William Fuller, *Fuller's Non-Recantation to the Jacobites* (printed for the author, 1701), 13; *The Second Part of the Life of William Fuller, alias Fullee . . . by Way of an Appendix* (1701), preface, A3.

46. Kingston, *Life of Wm. Fuller, alias Fullee*, 51–55; William Fuller, *The Whole Life of Mr. William Fuller; Being an Impartial Account of His Birth, Education and Relations* (sold by the booksellers, 1703), 71–72.

47. Kingston, *True History*, preface.

48. Ibid.

49. Ibid.

50. Kingston, *Life of Wm. Fuller, alias Fullee*, preface, 1st and 2nd pages.

51. Kingston, *Impudence, Lying, and Forgery Detected*, 44. For Smith, see *Modest Answer to Captain Smith's Immodest Memoirs*, 8, 32. For Fuller, *Life of Wm. Fuller, alias Fullee*, 66.

52. Kingston, *Life of Wm. Fuller, alias Fullee*, 46–47, 60; *Enthusiastick Imposters* (part 1), 65–66.

53. J[ohn] K[nighton] to archbishop of Canterbury, 17 August 1695, *HMC Downshire* 1:536–37; *The Second Part of the Life of William Fuller*, preface; Kingston, *Life of Wm. Fuller, alias Fullee*, 8–9; *Enthusiastick Imposters*, 1:37.

54. Kingston, *True History*, 43; for similar, see ibid., 44, 45, 47.

55. For the virulent paper, Kingston, *True History*, 117–18; for Clark, ibid., 51.

56. Kingston, *Modest Answer to Captain Smith's Immodest Memoirs*, 6, 10–13, 16; Smith, *Reply to an Unjust and Scandalous Libel* (1700), 13; Kingston, *Impudence, Lying, and Forgery, Detected and Chastiz'd*, 24–29.

57. Kingston, *Life of Wm. Fuller, alias Fullee*, 66; *Second Part of the Life of William Fuller, alias Fullee*, preface.

58. Kingston, *Life of Wm. Fuller, alias Fullee*, 38, 74; *Second Part of the Life of William Fuller*, preface.

59. The full title is: *The Life of Wm. Fuller, alias Fullee, alias Fowler, alias Ellison, &c. By Original a Butcher's Son; by Education, a Coney-Wool-Cutter; by Inclination, an Evidence; by Vote of Parliament, an Imposter; by Title of His Own Making, a Colonel; and by His Own Demerits, Now a Prisoner at Large Belonging to the Fleet*. For Kingston's service to the state, *Impudence, Lying, and Forgery Detected*, 44.

Chapter 6. Loyalty and Credibility in the Lancashire "Sham Plot"

1. *An Acct. of the Tryalls at Manchester October 1694*, ed. Alexander Goss, *Chetham Society* 61 (1864): 41–42. This is a transcription of a manuscript in the possession of Major Blundell of Crosby Hall.

2. [Robert Ferguson], *A Letter to Mr. Secretary Trenchard, Discovering a Conspiracy against the Laws and Ancient Constitution of England: With Reflections on the Present Pretended Plot* (n.p., dated 9 October 1694), 31. Hereafter cited in text and notes as *Letter to Trenchard*.

3. Mark Goldie, "The Roots of True Whiggism, 1688–94," *History of Political Thought* 1 (1980): 195–236; David Hayton, "The 'Country' Interest and the Party System, 1689–c. 1720," in *Party and Management in Parliament, 1660–1784*, ed. Clyve Jones (Leicester: Leicester University Press, 1984).

4. Information of John Taaffe, BL Add. 36913, ff. 177–78; P. A. Hopkins, "The Commission for Superstitious Lands in the 1690s," *Recusant History* 15 (1979): 265–82.

5. Taaffe's testimony at Manchester, in *An Acct. of the Tryalls at Manchester*, 24, 26; "Taaffe's Narrative," in *A Collection of Scarce and Valuable Papers* (George Sawbridge, 1712), 1:556–58.

6. "Taaffe's Narrative," 1:558–60.

7. Lady Standish to George Kenyon, 11 September 1694, *HMC Kenyon*, 305; Thomas Hodgkinson to Roger Kenyon, 19 September 1694, ibid., 306; see also "The Names of the Persons Employed to Take Up Persons Impeached as Also of Ye Informers with an Account of What They Were or Have Been," LancsRO, DDKe/HMC/921, which contains much gossip but names no sources.

8. On Allenson, *An Acct. of the Tryalls*, 26; affidavit of Edward Beresford, 1 February 1695, *HMC Lords 1693–95*, 452–54; for Bankes, "Examinations Taken before the House of Commons," *HMC Kenyon*, 323, 332.

9. Bankes's testimony to House of Lords, 29 January 1695, *HMC Lords 1693–95*, 439–41; Lettice Bankes's and Elizabeth Masters's testimony, ibid., 441–43.

10. [Thomas Wagstaffe], *A Letter out of Lancashire to a Friend in London, Giving Some Account of the Late Tryals There* (n.p., 1694), 12. Ferguson makes a similar charge, *Letter to Trenchard*, 38.

11. Nottingham, "Observations of Some Practices before the Trial," Papers on the Lancashire Plot, Leicestershire RO, D.G. 7/ P.P. 110 (item 6).

12. Warrant, 5 October 1694, *CSPD 1694–95*, 323.

13. *LBHR* 3:366 (4 September 1694); Sir Christopher Musgrave to Robert Harley, 10 September 1694, HMC, *Manuscripts of His Grace the Duke of Portland, Preserved at Welbeck Abbey* (H.M. Stationery Office, 1891–1931), 3:555; [Robert Harley] to Sir Edward Harley, 11 September 1694, ibid., 3:556; [Edward Harley] to Sir Edward Harley, 10 September 1694, ibid., 3:554–55. For Manchester mob, Kingston, *True History*, 130. The adventures of Bankes and Beresford are recounted in *Letter to Trenchard*, 32–33.

14. John Whett of Coventry to Ralph Hope, 16 January 1695, LancsRO, DDKe 8/28; warrant to Job Jones, 5 July 1689, LancsRO, DDKe 8/2; Shrewsbury to mayor of Coventry, 31 July 1689, *CSPD 1689–90*, 204. For Kelly, justices at Manchester to Shrewsbury, 18 October 1689, *HMC Kenyon*, 225–26. For Dodsworth's discovery, Shrewsbury to Sir James Rushout, 27 February, 6 March 1690, *CSPD 1689–90*, 484, 496; Hopkins, "Aspects of Jacobite Conspiracy" (Ph.D. diss., University of Cambridge, 1981), 418–20; *CJ* 10:420 (17 May 1690); *LBHR* 2:42, 35 (15, 23 May 1690); proclamation to apprehend persons in Lancashire and Yorkshire accused by Dodsworth, 30 May 1690, *CSPD 1690–91*, 22–23.

15. For the "real" plots, see Hopkins, "Aspects of Jacobite Conspiracy," esp. 408–40; and T. C. Porteus, "New Light on the Lancashire Plot, 1692–94," *Transactions of the Lancashire and Cheshire Antiquarian Society* 50 (1934–35): 1–64. See also Paul Hopkins, "Sham Plots and Real Plots in the 1690s," in

Ideology and Conspiracy: Aspects of Jacobitism, 1689–1759, ed. Eveline Cruikshanks (Edinburgh: J. Donald, 1982).

16. Rachel Weil, "'If I did say so I lyed': Elizabeth Cellier and the Construction of Credibility in the Popish Plot Crisis," in *Political Culture and Cultural Politics in Early Modern England*, ed. S. D. Amussen and M. Kishlansky (Manchester: Manchester University Press, 1995), 189–209.

17. Shrewsbury to Blaithwayt, 26 October 1694, Yale University, Beinecke Library, Osborn MS Shelf b. 317; for story that Taaffe was suborned, see testimony of Agnes Barker, *HMC Lords 1693–95*, 449.

18. "Aaron Smith's Account of What Moneys He Received for Carrying on the Prosecutions, and How He Has Paid and Distributed the Same," 15 February 1695, Parliamentary Archives, HL/PO/JO/10/1/471/881 (c); Shrewsbury to Blaithwayt, 26 October 1694, Yale University, Beinecke Library, Osborn MS Shelf b. 317.

19. *The Lancashire Sham-Plot. To the Tune of A. Smith* [1694]. Aaron Smith was the Treasury solicitor active in the prosecution.

20. Wagstaffe, *Letter out of Lancashire*, 8, 14.

21. *CJ* 11:223–24 (6 February 1695); *LJ* 15:497–98 (15 February 1695).

22. For the chronology of legal proceedings I have relied on Kingston, *True History*, 154–61.

23. Kenyon to John Legh, 10 November 1695, *HMC Kenyon*, 386; similarly, Richard Edge to Kenyon, 11 February 1696, ibid., 402.

24. Somers to Portland, 2 May 1695, NUI, PwA 1177. For payment and protection to Lunt, Womball, and/or Wilson: Trumbull to Treasury, 2 May 1696, *CSPD 1696*, 162; *LJ* minutes, 16 May 1696, ibid., 180; warrant, 26 November 1696, ibid., 446.

25. *Bishop Burnet's History of His Own Time. From the Restoration . . . to the Conclusion of the Treaty of Peace at Utrecht . . . in Four Volumes* (A. Millar, 1753), 3:194–98.

26. *Declaration of his Highness of Prince of Orange Concerning Papists Not Departing from the Cities of London and Westminster, and Ten Miles Adjacent* (J. Starkey and A. and W. Churchill, 1689). For a large collection of constables' reports for London, see "Petty Constables' Returns of the Number of Papists in Their Respective Wards That Have Not Been Three Years' Householders," 27 February 1689, Parliamentary Archives, HL/PO/JO/10/1/402/6 (e). For Lancashire round-ups, Roger Kenyon, "Account of Lunt," *HMC Kenyon*, 314; Brandon to Shrewsbury, 15 June 1689, *CSPD 1689–90*, 150; Brandon to Shrewsbury, 25 June 1689, *CSPD 1696*, 166–67.

27. On Declaration against Transubstantiation, see Rachel Weil, "Secularization and National Security after the English Revolution of 1688," in *After Secular Law*, ed. Winnifred Sullivan, Robert Yelle, and Mateo Taussig-Rubbo (Stanford, CA: Stanford University Press, 2011). Examples of warrants: 10 December 1689, 10, 15 April 1690, *CSPD 1689–90*, 352, 548, 554. Order by Ralph Assheton, 11 January 1690, *HMC Kenyon*, 235–36.

28. Jan M. Albers, "Seeds of Contention: Society, Politics and the Church of England in Lancashire, 1689–1790" (Ph.D. diss., Yale University, 1988); Geoff Baker, "William Blundell and Late-Seventeenth-Century English Catholicism," *Northern History* 45 (2008): 259–77. For Bradshaigh, see Michael Mullett, "'A Receptacle for Papists and an Assilum': Catholicism and Disorder in Late Seventeenth-Century Wigan," *Catholic Historical Review* 73 (1987): 391–407. A version of Eyre's remark is in *The Jacobite Trials at Manchester in 1694*, ed. William Beaumont, *Chetham Society* 27 (1853): 52.

29. Lionel K. J. Glassey, *Politics and the Appointment of Justices of the Peace* (Oxford: Oxford University Press, 1979), esp. chap. 10; Lionel K. J. Glassey, "The Origins of Political Parties in Seventeenth-Century Lancashire," *Transactions of the Historic Society of Cheshire and Lancashire* 136 (1987).

30. *An Acct. of the Tryalls at Manchester*, 25.

31. Thomas Norris to unknown recipient, 6 August 1694, *CSPD 1694–95*, 255.

32. Thomas Lee to John Trenchard, 20 July 1694, *CSPD 1694–95*, 232–33; Kingston, *True History*, 130.

33. On Brandon's career, J. D. Davies, "Gerard, Charles, Second Earl of Macclesfield (c. 1659–1701)," *ODNB*.

34. Michael Mullett, "Receptacle for Papists," 395.

35. "Lord Brandon's Lord Lieutenancy," *HMC Kenyon*, 234–35; "Observations on Lord Brandon's Lord Lieutenancy and the State of the County of Lancaster" [1689/90?], ibid., 212–13. See also David H. Hosford, *Nottingham, Nobles and the North: Aspects of the Revolution of 1688* (Hamden, CT: Archon, 1976).

36. Kingston, *True History*, 152; Macclesfield to Somers, 21 May 1698, Surrey History Centre, Somers Papers, 371/14/L/22.

37. Account of Manchester trial in Kenyon's hand, *HMC Kenyon*, 309–10; draft speech, probably to be delivered to House of Commons by Roger Kenyon, ibid., 370–71.

38. Thomas Patten's testimony, *An Acct. of the Tryalls at Manchester*, 37–38; E[lizabeth] Legh to Kenyon, October 25, 1694, LancsRO, DDKe/HMC/887; John Heys to Kenyon, 14 August 1696, LancsRO, DDKe 9/69/52.

39. For Tacitus quotation, *No Protestant Plot; or, The Present Pretended Conspiracy of Protestants against the King and Government, Discovered to Be a Conspiracy of the Papists against the King* (R. Lett, 1681), 14; also in *Letter to Trenchard*, 27. On witness bribery, *No Protestant Plot*, 36; *Letter to Trenchard*, 38.

40. "Concerning the Rye House Business," printed in James Ferguson, *Robert Ferguson the Plotter* (Edinburgh: D. Douglas, 1887), 409–37; Ferguson, *Letter to Holt*, 4.

41. *No Protestant Plot*, 10–11; Ferguson, *Letter to Holt*, 3–4.

42. Ferguson, *Letter to Holt*, 6.

43. Wagstaffe, *Letter out of Lancashire*, 14.

44. For an example of Jacobite literature criticizing the suspension of habeas corpus, James Montgomery, *Great Britain's Just Complaint* (n.p., 1692), 29; Ferguson, *Letter to Trenchard*, 8–27.

45. For Nottingham: "Observations of Some Practices before the Trial," Papers on the Lancashire Plot, Leicestershire RO, Finch manuscripts, DG7/PP110. Kenyon's objections to the proceedings are expressed in the account in his hand of Manchester trial, *HMC Kenyon*, 309–10, and the draft speech, probably to be delivered to House of Commons, ibid., 370–71.

46. Mark Goldie and Clare Jackson, "Williamite Tyranny and the Whig Jacobites," in *Redefining William III: The Impact of the King-Stadholder in International Context*, ed. Esther Mijers and David Onnekink (Aldershot: Ashgate, 2007), 177–99; Melinda S. Zook, "Turncoats and Double Agents in Restoration and Revolutionary England: The Case of Robert Ferguson, the Plotter," *Eighteenth-Century Studies* 42 (2009): 363–78.

47. Ferguson, "Concerning the Rye House Business." Ferguson, *Letter to Holt*, 28.

48. Ferguson, *Letter to Trenchard*, 3, 15–16, 28.

49. Ibid., 6.

50. Ferguson, *Letter to Holt*, 12.

51. *An Acct. of the Tryalls*, 28–30.

52. "Account of Lunt," ibid., 310–11; Richard Townley to Captain Beresford, 23 December 1694, ibid., 357–58; Thomas Fleetwood to Kenyon, 3 April 1695, ibid., 379. For Wilson: deposition by John Garlside, LancsRO, DDKe 2/5 (13); statement of John Edwards, vicar of Ruthlan, 8 October 1694, LancsRO, DDKe 9/67/55, f. 2.

53. Ferguson, *Letter to Holt*, 16; Ferguson, *Letter to Trenchard*, 30, 34–37.

54. "Notes to Discredit Witnesses," LancsRO, DDBl 24/18.

55. Allegations of bribery were made in Kingston's *True History*; see, e.g., the affidavit of Thomas Clayton, 260–67.

56. Richard Brooke to Kenyon, 15 October 1694, LancsRO, DDKe 9/67/57.

57. Henry Prescott to Kenyon, 11 October 1694, LancsRO, DDKe 9/67/55; the statements of Bryan and Edwards are in LancsRO, DDKe 6/67/55.

58. Anthony Heathcoat's information, 19 September 1694, LancsRO, DDKe 2/5/13.

59. Bridget Molineux to Thomas Legh, 11 October 1694, LancsRO, DDKe 8/6.

60. "The Names of the Persons Employed to Take Up Persons Impeached as Also of Ye Informers with an Account of What They Were or Have Been," LancsRO, DDKe/HMC/921.

61. "Notes to Discredit Witnesses," LancsRO, DDBl 24/18.

62. The phrase is from Peter Lake, "Antipopery: The Structure of a Prejudice," *Conflict in Early Stuart England*, ed. Richard Cust and Ann Hughes (London: Longman, 1989), 72–79. For late seventeenth-century concerns about the relation of truth to partisanship, see Mark Knights, *Representation and Misrepresentation in Later Stuart Britain: Partisanship and Political Culture* (Oxford: Oxford University Press, 2005), esp. chap. 6.

Chapter 7. Representation, Politics, and Law in the Assassination Plot

1. On recoinage, see most recently Carl Wennerlind, *Casualties of Credit* (Cambridge, MA: Harvard University Press, 2011). On country opposition, see Mark Goldie, "The Roots of True Whiggism, 1688–94," *History of Political Thought* 1 (1980): 195–236; and *Bishop Burnet's History of His Own Time. From the Restoration . . . to the Conclusion of the Treaty of Peace at Utrecht . . . in Four Volumes* (A. Millar, 1753), 3:194.

2. For an overview, see Jane Garrett, *The Triumphs of Providence: The Assassination Plot, 1696* (Cambridge: Cambridge University Press, 1980).

3. *A Continuation of the History of the Plot . . . in Another Letter to a Friend in Oxford* (E. Whitlock, 1696), 4–5.

4. *LBHR* 4:71 (11 June 1696); *A True History of the Horrid Conspiracy* (John Salusbury, 1696), 20; [J. Abbadie], *The History of the Late Conspiracy against the King and Nation* (Daniel Brown, 1696), esp. 65–74; Richard Kingston, *A True History of the Several Designs and Conspiracies against His Majesties Sacred Person*

and Government as They Were Continually Carried on from 1688 to 1697 (Abel Roper, 1698).

5. Abbadie, *History of the Late Conspiracy*, 52, 54.

6. Paul Monod, *Jacobitism and the English People* (Cambridge: Cambridge University Press, 1989); see also his "The Politics of Matrimony: Jacobitism and Marriage Patterns in Eighteenth-Century England," in *The Jacobite Challenge, 1689–1760*, ed. Jeremy Black and Eveline Cruikshanks (Edinburgh: John Donald, 1988), 24–41.

7. Abbadie, *History of the Late Conspiracy*, 178.

8. Ibid., 42.

9. Ibid., 172, 171.

10. Ibid., 64, 169, 13.

11. Ibid., 13, 117, 192.

12. Ibid., 37, 170–71.

13. Ibid., 169, 177–78.

14. Ibid., 37–38, 89–90, 119–20.

15. Ibid., 98–99.

16. Roland Gwynne to Trumbull, 2 April 1696, BL Add. 72535, ff. 81–82. For a similar belief that Parkyns could incriminate more men, see "Reasons Humbly Offered," BL Add. 72569, ff. 171–72.

17. *A Copy of the Association Agreed upon by the Honourable House of Commons on Monday the 24th of February 1695/6*.

18. "An Act for the Better Security of His Majesty's Royal Person and Government," *SR* 7:114–18.

19. For Catholics taking Association, *A Continuation of the History of the Plot . . . in Another Letter to a Friend in Oxford* (E. Whitlock, 1696), 5. See also Pincus, *1688: The First Modern Revolution*, 469–70. For the oath of fidelity, see "Returns of Papists for 1696," LMA MR/R/R/008, sheet #1. On the impact of these changes, see Rachel Weil, "National Security and Secularization in the English Revolution of 1688," in *After Secular Law*, ed. Winnifred Sullivan, Robert Yelle, and Mateo Taussig-Rubbo (Stanford, CA: Stanford University Press, 2011).

20. *ST* 13:33, 58–59.

21. *ST* 13:404.

22. On judicial purges (which were only partly successful), see Lionel K. J. Glassey, *Politics and the Appointment of Justices of the Peace, 1675–1720* (Oxford: Oxford University Press, 1979), 118–27, 282.

23. Order from Trumbull to Mackie at Harwich, and officers at other ports, 23 February 1696, *CSPD 1696*, 50–51; enforcement of act, 25 February 1696,

ibid., 55; seized horses, *LBHR* 4:25 (5 March 1696); order in council to judges, 27 February 1696, *CSPD 1696*, 56; Shrewsbury to deputy lieutenants of Worcester, 21 March 1696, ibid., 94.

24. *A True Relation of the Horrid Conspiracy against the Life of the King* (E. Whitlock, 1696), 6–8. Dating based on internal evidence: it describes the executions of John Friend and William Parkyns on 3 April but makes no mention of the trials of Lowick et al., which took place on 2 April; *A Continuation of the History of the Plot* (E. Whitlock, 1696), 6–8. This postdates the executions of Cranburne, Lowick, and Rookwood, 29 April 1696, which it mentions; *A List of All Those That Were Committed to the Tower, Newgate, Gate-house, King's-Bench, Mashalsea, Fleet since the Discovery of the Horrid Conspiracy against the Life of the King; also Some of Those in the Messenger's Houses and Some since Discharged from the Places Abovesaid* (1696). The date comes from the fact that Peter Cook, who was tried 9 May, is listed as awaiting execution.

25. Nicholas Nolan's petition, LMA CLA/047/LJ/13/1696/008; Thomas Cappock's petition, LMA MJ/SP/1696/10/063; Thomas Hawley's petition, 25 May 1696, BL Add. 72568, f. 71; petition of Major Thomas Hawley for arrears, 18 July 1698, TNA T1/43/6; humble petition of Gilbert Jones, 23 May 1696, BL Add. 72568, ff. 89–90. He states he was confined 28 March.

26. Petition of Thomas Segar, BL Add. 72568, f. 130; list of persons in messengers' custody, 15 November 1696, *CSPD 1696*, 438; Davison's petition, LMA CLA/047/LJ/13/1696/008. Some other petitions in the Trumbull Papers are from David MacAdam (BL Add. 72568, f. 102) and Francis Raye (9 May 1696, ibid., f. 125).

27. For poisoning, *ST* 13:359–61; Douglas/Edwards, *ST* 13:361–62; King's Head staff, *ST* 13:365–66, 374–75; solicitor general's speech, *ST* 13:385.

28. *ST* 13:295–96.

29. Robert Atkyns, *A Defence of the Late Lord Russel's Innocency* (Timothy Goodwin, 1689), 5. The "trapanner" reference is probably to Rumsey, who at Russell's trial had described arriving at Sheppard's house with a message from the Earl of Shaftsbury asking the assembled company (including Russell), "What resolution they were come to about the rising of Taunton?" The ensuing conversation, which Rumsey reported, was thus one which he initiated. As John Hawles put it, "It was well known, it was Rumsey's way to talk extravagantly, in order to accuse those that heard him, if they did not discover it." John Hawles, *Remarks upon the Tryals of Edward Fitzharris, Stephen Colledge, Count Coningsmark, the Lord Russel, Collonel Sidney, Henry Cornish and Charles Bateman*

(Jacob Tonson, 1689), 70. Charnock, in any case, was thinking of Francis De La Rue; *ST* 12:1435.

30. Hawles, *Remarks*, 64–65, 22–24, 32.
31. *ST* 12:1397–98.
32. *ST* 13:118, 72–73.
33. *ST* 12:1403–5. It should be noted that Porter was eventually rewarded and protected by the government, and that his testimony was indeed given in return for something, that is, in return for not being indicted.
34. *ST* 12:1381–84; *ST* 13:72–73.
35. *ST* 12:1384–85; *ST* 13:9–10.
36. For Holt, *ST* 13:111. Historically there had been much confusion as to whether the law required two witnesses in treason trials: L. M. Hill, "The Two-Witness Rule in English Treason Trials: Some Comments on the Emergence of Procedural Law," *American Journal of Legal History* 12:2 (April 1968): 95–111; for Treby, *ST* 13:113.
37. *ST* 13:117–18. The 1696 *Act for Regulateing of Trials in Cases of Treason and Misprision of Treason* (*SR* 7:6–7) is somewhat confusing. Article 2 seems to support the three justices. It states that no one could be indicted, tried, or attainted "but by and upon the oaths and testimony of two lawful witnesses either both of them to the same overt act or one of them to one and another them to another overt act of the same treason." But Article 4 might support Parkyns. It states, "If two or more distinct treasons of diverse heads or kinds shall be alleged in one Bill of Indictment one witness produced to prove one of the said treasons and another witness produced to prove another of the said treasons shall not be deemed or taken to be two witnesses to the same treason within the meaning of this act." Clearly the application of the act hinged on how one defined "the same treason" as opposed to "distinct treasons of diverse heads or kinds."
38. *ST* 13:217–20. The relevant article of the act is #7.
39. For Berkenhead, Vernon to Portland, 30 June 1696, NUL PwA 1460. For manuscript notes on examinations of Hunt, see Hunt's examination, 26 March 1696, NUL PwA 2486; Hunt's second confession, NUL PwA 2487–88; "Hunt's examination and Harcourt Berkenhead's, March 28," NUL PwA 2489; BL Add. MS 72567, f. 119. Another examination of James Hunt occurred 30 June (*CSPD 1696*, 251). For Cook, see Cook's information, 12 June 1696, NUL PwA 1457, naming Berkenhead. For Mrs. Hunt, see 30 June 1696, *CSPD 1696*, 251; Vernon to Portland, 30 June 1696, NUL PwA 1460.
40. Knightley's confession, 22 March 1696, NUL PwA 2482–83; Vernon to Portland, 2 June 1696, NUL PwA 1449.

41. Parkyns, *LBHR* 4:38 (2 April 1696); Hunt's disappearance, *LBHR* 4:123 (8 October 1696); Counter and Bernardi, Vernon to Shrewsbury, 29 December 1696, *LI* 1:152.

42. Goodman's testimony, *ST* 13:354–55.

43. Cook to Tenison, 9 May 1696, LPL 1029/29; information of Peter Cook, 12 June 1696, NUL PwA 1457; Vernon to Portland, 19 June 1696, NUL PwA 1456.

44. For Vernon's view of Cook, Vernon to Portland, 7 July 1696, NUL PwA 1461; Vernon to Portland, 19 June 1696, NUL PwA 1456. Short reprieves: in November and December 1696 alone, for example, there were six separate warrants to grant Peter Cook a reprieve. See *CSPD 1696*, 430, 436, 439, 450, 463, 473 (for 2, 12, 17 November and 1, 15, 29 December).

45. "An Act to Attaint such of the Persons," *SR* 7:165–66. For further acts, "An Act for Continuing the Imprisonment of Counter and Others" [until January 1698], *SR* 7:300; "Act for the Continuing the Imprisonment of Counter and Others" [during His Majesty's Pleasure], *SR* 7:53. See also *A Short History of the Life of Major John Bernardi. Written by Himself in Newgate; Where He Has Been for Near 33 Years a Prisoner of State, without Any Allowance from the Government, and Could Never Be Admitted to His Trial* (J. Newcomb, 1729).

46. Paul Hopkins, "Fenwick, Sir John, Third Baronet (c. 1644–1697)," *ODNB*.

47. Copy of the letter written in black lead (beginning "what I fear has happened"), BL Add. 33251, f. 25r; Fenwick's information (first paper), *CJ* 11:577–78 (6 November 1696); William III to Shrewsbury, 10 September/30 August 1696, in William Coxe, *Private and Original Correspondence of Charles Talbot, Duke of Shrewsbury* (Longman, Hurst, Reese, Orme and Brown, 1821), 145.

48. For deliberations among Shrewsbury et al., see Rachel Weil, "Matthew Smith vs. the 'Great Men': Plot Talk, the Public Sphere and the Problem of Credibility in the 1690s," in *The Politics of the Public Sphere in Early Modern England*, ed. Steve Pincus and Peter Lake (Manchester: Manchester University Press, 2007); for Fenwick's paper and Commons resolution, *CJ* 55:579 (6 November 1696).

49. *The Tryal, Attainder or Condemnation of Sir John Fenwick* (printed at The Hague, 1697), 77–79, 46; paper beginning "I presume I may take it for granted," BL Add. 28941, ff. 154–55.

50. *The Tryal, Attainder or Condemnation of Sir John Fenwick*, 93. Paul Hopkins, "Fenwick, Sir John, Third Baronet (c. 1644–1697)," *ODNB*.

51. *A Short History of the Life of Major John Bernardi: Written by Himself in Newgate, Where He Has Been for Near 33 Years a Prisoner of State, without Any Allowance from the Government, and Could Never Be Admitted to His Trial* (J. Newcomb, 1729), 90–135. For Whig-Jacobites, Mark Goldie and Clare Jackson, "Williamite Tyranny and the Whig Jacobites," in *Redefining William III: The Impact of the King-Stadholder in International Context*, ed. Esther Mijers and David Onnekink (Aldershot: Ashgate, 2007), 177–99.

52. On Harris, *Short History of the Life of John Bernardi*, 92–93. For evidence against Bernardi, see Knightley's confession, 22 March 1696, NUL PwA 2482–83; "Examination of Rookwood and Bernardi," 25 March 1695, NUL PwA 2485.

53. I myself learned of Bernardi only through a brief discussion in Garrett, *Triumphs of Providence*, 255–57.

Manuscript Collections Consulted

British Library

28880–28   Ellis Papers
33251   House of Lords Proceedings on Fenwick Attainder
35107   Privy Council Memoranda
36913   Aston Papers
40772   Vernon Papers
42586–97   Brockman Papers
47608   Fenwick Papers
61689–90   Wildman Papers
72532–38   Trumbull Papers and Correspondence
72567–71   Trumbull Papers

Beinecke Rare Book and Manuscript Library, Yale University

Osborn Shelf b. 317 Shrewsbury to Blathwayt Letters

British Postal Museum and Archive

PO1 Royal Mail Archive

Gloucestershire Record Office

Lloyd-Baker Manuscripts

John Rylands Library, Manchester

Legh of Lyme Papers

Kent History and Library Centre, Maidstone (formerly Centre for Kentish Studies)

U269 Sackville Correspondence (Earl of Dorset)
U1015 Papillon Manuscripts

Lambeth Palace Library

LPL 1029 Tenison Papers

Lancashire Record Office

DDBl Blundell Papers
DDKe Kenyon Papers

Leicestershire Record Office

Finch Manuscripts

London Metropolitan Archives

LMA MR/R Middlesex (Recusants)
LMA MJ/SP Middlesex Sessions
LMA CLA/O City of London Sessions Papers

National Archives (TNA)

ASSI 45 Northern Assizes Depositions
E Exchequer
T1 Treasury Papers
MINT Newton Papers

Nottingham University Library

PwA Papers of Hans Willem Bentinck, Earl of Portland

Parliamentary Archives

HL/PO/JO House of Lords Main Papers

Surrey History Centre

317 Somers Papers

Index

Figures and illustrations are indicated by italic page numbers.

Abbadie, James, 250–251, 253–256
Abjuration Bill (1690), 55
abjuration oath, 37–38
Act for Amoving Papists and Reputed Papists from London (1689), 259
Act for Securing His Majesty's Royal Person and Government (1696), 257
Ailesbury, Earl of, 271–272
Alcock, Robert, 125
aliases, 108
Allen, Henry, 198
Allenson, Mr., 221
Aneley, Edward, 123–124
Anglican Church, 34–35, 37, 40, 171, 222, 228–234
Anne (Princess), 13, 192
anonymous information, 23, 213–214
Aram, Mr., 73
Archer, Anne-Claude, 159, 163–165
Archer, James, 163–164
Armstrong, Thomas, 27, 29, 46, 58
Arnold, Jack, 80, 118, 133–134
Arnold, John, 107
Arrowsmith, Simon, 246
Ashley, Maurice, 84
Ashurst, Henry, 155
Assassination Plot (1696), 248–279; betrayal of, 116; credit of government enhanced by, 25–26; investigation challenges, 270–275; and loyalty oaths, 256–259; and powers of the state, 259–261; recruitment of conspirators, 126; rewards offered for capture of plotters, 121; and rule of law, 262–270
Association Oath, 257, 259
Astry, Samual, 189
Atkyns, Robert, 264, 266
attainder, 22, 28, 31, 58, 272–275
Austen, Robert, 46–47

Bagshaw, Mr., 221–222
bail, 63
Baker, Harry, 170–171, 219–220, 242
Baker, Henry, 94
Baker, Nicholas, 108, 125
Baldwin, Richard, 39
Banahan, Owen, 125, 158–159
Bankes, Leigh, 218, 221–224
Bank of England, 13, 129, 133, 248, 278
Banks, Adam, 143
Baptists, 33
Barclay, George, 248–249, 272–273
Barker, Agnes, 94, 160, 167–170, 246
Barker, William, 160–161, 167–170, 245
Baron, John, 156
Barone, Michael, 16
Barron, Captain, 172
Barton, Alice, 181
Bartram, Major, 126
Bartram, Thomas, 249
Bastinck, Francis, 82–83
Battle of Boyne (1690), 73
Beattie, John, 128
Bell, Ralph, 83
Bellomont, Earl of, 161–163

335

Bent, Elizabeth, 147
Bérault, Peter, 94
Beresford, Edward, 221–222
Berkenhead, William, 270
Bernard, Catherine, 133
Bernardi, John, 50, 271, 273, 275–276, *277*, 279
Beverton, Joseph, 94–95, 102
Billers, Mr., 144
Bill for Securing the Government (1690), 55–56
Birch, Colonel, 47, 52–53, 55
Birch, John, 230
Bird, Major, 154
Blackbourne, Robert, 273
Blackburne, John, 124
Blackhall, Ralph, 153
Blair, Brice, 249, 258
Blincoe, Mr., 154
Blundell, William, 221
Boad, Captain, 156
Bois, William, 249
Bossy, John, 41
Boteler, Philip, 154
Bowes, Joshua, 19–20, 149, 183
Bowles, Margaret, 77–78
Boyle, Robert, 209
Bracton, Lord, 61
Bradshaigh, Roger, 230
Bradshaw, Joseph, 146
Brandon, Charles, 50, 80, 228, 232–233
Brent, Robert, 51, 55
Brett, Dr., 130
Brewerton, Captain, 243
Bridgman, William, 129
Brockett, William, 80
Brockman, William, 114, 145–146, 150, 152, 154–155, 186, 202–203
Bromhead, Meredeth, 81
Brooke, Richard, 244
Brown, Anne, 179
Brown, John, 246
Brown, Tom, 208
Bryan, John, 244
Bulkeley, Richard, 212
Bumford, Thomas, 243
Burden, George, 130
bureaucracy, modernization of, 68–71
Burke, Edmund, 3, 16, 275

Burnet, Gilbert, 248
Butler, Edward, 130–131, 173
Butterfield, Herbert, 16–17

Cade, William, 181
Calvert, Thomas, 154–155
Canning, William, 198
Capel, Henry, 47, 57, 65
Capel, John, 113
Cappock, Thomas, 260
Carmarthen, Marquis of (formerly Earl of Danby), 35, 64, 85–86, 105, 110, 172, 199
Carr, Captain, 88
Carter, Thomas, 244
Carter, William, 89, 91, 95–103
Cary, Peter, 60–61
Cassells, Robert, 273
Castleton, Nathaniel, 81
Catholics: and Counter-Reformation, 5; and Declaration against Transubstantiation, 41; and Exclusion Crisis, 28, 31–32; as informers, 159–173; informers against, 115; and Lancashire Plot, 217, 228–234; and Magdalen College, 43; and national security debates, 39–42; and oaths of allegiance, 258; and Popish Plot, 4; and Superstitious Lands Commissions, 93–94; as turncoat informers, 157
Cellier, Elizabeth, 179, 225
central government, 70–75, 259–261
Chadwick, John, 111
Chaloner, William, 122, 128–139, *132*
Chambers, James, 273
"chameleons," 157–178; Catholics as, 159–173; converts, 157–159; involuntary, 173–178; prisoners as, 173–178; voluntary, 157–159
Charles I, 3, 250
Charles II, 3, 27, 34, 36, 65, 121, 255
Charnock, Robert, 11, 116, 248–249, 262, 264, 266–267, 271
Cheshire, Mr., 245
Chiffinch, Mr., 75
Church of England. *See* Anglican Church
civil liberties, 18, 31, 67, 237
civil service, modernization of, 68–71
Clancarty, Earl of, 80
Clapham, Christopher, 179

Clarendon, Earl of, 174, 177
Clarges, Thomas, 38, 53, 57
Clayton, Robert, 55
Clerke, Frances, 198
Clifford, Alithea, 174, 178
Clifford, Captain, 106
Clifton, Thomas, 234
Coachman, Charles, 198
Cockeram, John, 49
coinage, 13, 129, 131, 136, 173, 251, 278
Cole, Michael, 135
College, Stephen, 30, 54, 58
Colter, Peter, 84
Colt, Harry, 133–135
Colt, Henry, 107
Comber, Thomas, 193
Commins, John, 131
common law, 48
Congregationalists, 33
Conjett, Mary, 163
Conway, John, 244
Cook, Mary, 142
Cook, Peter, 249–250, 262–263, 271–272
Coppinger, Matthew, 129–130
Cornish, Alderman, 29, 54
corruption, 72, 74, 129, 154, 197, 199, 204, 248
Cotton, Robert, 45, 47, 151–153
Cotton, William, 90–91
Council of Nine, 86
Council of Trade, 97
Counter, John, 271, 273
counterfeiting, 13, 129, 138
Counter-Reformation, 5
Court of King's Bench, 49
Court of Star Chamber, 61
Court of the Lord High Steward, 56–57
Coxhall, Thomas, 89
Cranburne, Charles, 250
credibility and credit: and Anglican Church, 171; and anonymous sources, 213–214; and financial solvency, 242; gentlemanly vs. market models of, 120; of informers, 156, 185–187; Kingston's attempts to establish, 207–215; and Lancashire Plot (1694), 217, 241–246; of Lunt, 218; of patriotic entrepreneurs, 97; and politics, 8; Post Office's impact on, 76; of prisoner informers, 175–176; and social status, 211–212, 241; of women witnesses, 181, 183
credit fraud, 8, 242
Crofts, Captain, 151
Crofts, John, 174
Cromwell, Oliver, 250
Crone, Matthew, 109–110, 174, 176–178, 185
Crosse, Godfrey, 150
cruel and unusual punishment, 63
Crymes, Henry, 126–127
Crypto-Jacobitism, 36, 148, 153, 204
Cunningham, Patrick, 124
currency. *See* coinage
Curzon, John, 84
customs service, 70, 74, 92, 97, 108, 156, 197
Cutts, Lord, 274

Dabhoiwala, Faramerz, 22
Damram, Dorothy, 144
Danby, Earl of, 32, 35, 51, 64. *See also* Carmarthen, Marquis of
Darby, Thomas, 124
Davenant, Charles, 69
Davis, Thomas, 172–173, 260
Davison, Barnet, 261
Declaration (James II), 59, 130, 193–195
Declaration against Transubstantiation, 41–42, 228
Declaration of Indulgence (James II), 35, 40
Declaration of Rights, 63
Deedes, Julius, 78, 89
Deery, Daniel, 154, 156
defactoism, 14, 37, 239–240
Delamere, Lord, 94
De La Rue, Francis, 116, 126, 249, 262, 264, 266, 268
Delaval, Thomas, 109, 111, 113
denunciation, 140–141, 202
detention of prisoners, 18, 48–52, 259–261. *See also* habeas corpus
Devonshire, Duke of, 172
Dicconson, Roger, 218, 221, 241
Dicconson, William, 169, 172, 220
disinformation campaigns, 197
divine right of kings, 200
Dixwell, Basil, 80, 151–152
Dodsworth, Robert, 224
Dog Tavern riot, 273

Dolben, Gilbert, 48
Dorchester, Lady, 178–179
Duchfeild, Jacob, 182
Dunbarton, Earl of, 72
Dungeness lighthouse, 72
Dunn, John, 4–5
Dutton, Ralph, 157

Edwards, Charles, 263
Edwards, John, 244
Ellesdon, John, 89
Ellis, John, 107, 142, 172, 184
espionage, 104–105. *See also* informers; intelligence
Ettrick, William, 45, 53, 55
Everard, Edmund, 157
excise service, 68–69, 108, 154–155
Exclusion Crisis, 31–34, 58, 259–260
Exeter Assizes, 124
Eyre, Giles, 218–219, 224, 230, 233, 247
Eyre, Justice, 61

Falkland, Lord, 38
Farmer, John, 50, 81–82
Fenner, Mr., 152
Fenwick, John, 11, 22, 105, 114, 117, 135, 250, 263, 270–275
Ferguson, Robert, *180*; habeas corpus relief for, 49; on informers, 104, 139, 175; and Kingston, 183, 189, 193–194, 203; on Lancashire Plot prosecutions, 201, 219, 225, 234–242, 245; on liberty, 30–31, 276
Finch, Daniel. *See* Nottingham, Earl of
Finch, Nathaniel, 260
Fisher, Richard, 263
Fitzharris, Edward, 58, 65
Fitzpatrick, Sheila, 23–24, 140–141
Fleetwood, Thomas, 242
Foley, Paul, 56
Fountaine, Colonel, 196
Francko, Adam, 80
franking privileges, 79–80
Frankland, Thomas, 151–153
freedom of movement, 18, 28, 88
"French Mary" (Mary Conjett), 163
Friend, John, 116, 249, 256–258, 263
Fuller, William, 11, 108–119, *112*, 123, 188, 192, 203–212

Gabree, Mark, 97
Gadbury, John, 84
Gambetta, Diego, 12
Gargrave, Lieutenant, 134
Garroway, Mr., 59
Gatley, William, 101
Gaylord, Elizabeth, 78
Gee, Edmund, 200
Gellately, Robert, 24
Gellibrand, John, 126, 198
gendered narratives of informers, 179–187
"General will," 20
gentlemanly model of credibility, 120
Gerard, Henry, 156
Gerrard, Charles, 230, 232
Gerrard, Thomas, 168
Gerrard, William, 220
Ghoste, Sarah, 182
Gibbons, John, 129
Gibbs, Ralph, 198
Gibson, Captain, 91
Girard, M., 165
Glassey, Lionel, 87, 230
Godden v. Hales case, 43
Godfrey, Edmundbury, 31
Godolphin, Sidney, 73–74, 110, 117, 273
Goldie, Mark, 66, 238
Golling, Francis, 81–82
Goodman, Cardell, 249, 262, 271–272
Goodrick, Henry, 38
Gorge, Robert, 85
Gosling, William, 80
Grafton, Duke of, 263
Graham, James, 110, 177–178
Great Fire of London (1666), 84
Great Recoinage (1695–1696), 13, 278
Green Ribbon Club, 94
Grey, Betty, 207, 211
Griffith, Henry, 130, 173
Gross, Jan T., 140–141
Grosvenor, Thomas, 38
Grove, John, 59–60
Guise, John, 94, 111
Gunpowder Plot, 255
Gwynne, Rowland, 95, 256

habeas corpus, 18, 22, 28, 48–53, 237, 261
Habeas Corpus Act of 1679, 48–49, 237

Haddock, Richard, 144
Halifax, Marquis of, 35, 64, 105, 110, 172
Halliday, Paul, 49
Hammond, Paul, 179
Hampden, Richard, 47
Hampson, Edward, 84
Hancock, Anne, 143, 183
handwriting identification, 8
Hansard, Mrs., 179
Harcourt, Simon, 38
Harding, Patrick, 161
Harfleet, Cornelius, 212
Harley, Edward, 223
Harley, Robert, 36, 53
Harris, Edward, 89–90
Harris, George, 249, 270, 276
Harris, Tim, 16–17
Harrow, Charles, 143
Hawkins, Thomas, 87
Hawles, John, 43, 47, 54, 64, 266, 268
Hawley, Thomas, 260
Hayes, James, 111, 113
Hayward, Richard, 198
Heathcote, Anthony, 244
Hely, William, 89–90
Henry IV (France), 45
Hermon, Roger, 78
Hewett, Jack, 116, 118
Higgonson, William, 231
Hilton gang, 120
Hindmarsh, James, 146–147
Hobbes, Thomas, 6–7, 10–11, 14, 69
Holland, Richard, 113
Holloway, Richard, 60
Holt, John, 11, 60–61, 131, 163, 222, 224, 258, 266, 268–269
honor in narratives of informers, 149–156
Honywood, William, 154
Hopkins, Paul, 1, 94, 106, 189, 219–220, 224
Hornby, Mr., 73, 155
Hough, Abraham, 92, 102
House of Commons: Fuller as witness before, 110; and indemnity, 46; and Lancashire Plot, 227; Oates's case before, 60–65; and treason trial reform, 53, 56–58. *See also* Parliament
House of Lords: and Lancashire Plot, 227; Oates's case before, 60–65; Smith questioned before, 118; and treason trial reform, 56–58. *See also* Parliament
Howard, Robert, 28, 46–47, 56, 64–65
Howe, Jack, 43, 45, 111
Howe, Scroop, 94
Hughes, Ann, 184
Hulke, George, 78–79
Hunt, James, 94–95, 260, 271

identity fraud, 8, 189
identity in narratives of informers, 140–178
impeachment, 58
incompetence vs. treason, 72–73
indemnity, 35–36, 42–47
informers, 19–24, 104–187; anonymous, 23, 213–214; "chameleons," 157–178; gender in narratives of, 179–187; and government officials, 104–139; honor in narratives of, 149–156; identity in narratives of, 140–178; one-shot informers, 141–149; patriotic, 149–156; and politicization of intelligence, 108–119; truth's relationship to money, 119–127; and value of information, 128–139. *See also specific individuals*
Innes, Joanna, 24, 141
Instrument of Association, 257
intelligence: disinformation campaigns, 197; gathering of, 24–25, 104–105; politicization of, 108–119, 200–206; Post Office's role in, 77, 83–84; private spy networks, 107–108; by secretaries of state, 107. *See also* informers
Ireland, William, 59–60

Jackson, Clare, 66, 238
Jacobean oath of allegiance (1606), 37
Jacobites: and central government, 71; communications network of, 74; currency debasement blamed on, 14; intelligence gathering against, 105–106; Kingston's knowledge of communications network, 195–197; in Post Office, 82; printing and publishing by, 3, 194–195; in professional bureaucracy, 74; and trust, 13; as turncoat informers, 157, 175–176
James II, 1, 3, 18, 32, 34–35, 69, 161–162
Janeway, Jacob, 152
Jeffreys, George, 27–28, *44*, 150

Jephson, Commissioner, 75
Jermy, Francis, 213
Johns, Adrian, 8
Johnston, Alexander, 115, 202, 219, 242–243
Johnston, James, 115, 122–123
Jones, Gilbert, 260
Jones, William, 198
judicial precedent, 63. *See also* law

Kelly, John, 224
Kenyon, George, 221, 233
Kenyon, Roger, 56, 221, 227, 232–233, 238, 240–242
Keyes, Thomas, 249, 262
Kidd, William, 118
King, Edward, 249, 262
King, John, 198
King's Head Tavern meeting, 249–250, 262, 271, 275
Kingston, Richard, 188–216, *191*; accusations against, 183; on Assassination Plot, 251; Barker's work with, 169–170, 186; on Bastinck, 83; credit and credibility in works of, 207–215; Ferguson on, 239; on informers and money, 121; and Jacobite communications, 195–197; on Lancashire Plot, 1, 217, 232; on Ormiston, 106; and policing and surveillance reform, 197–199; and politics, 200–206; and press, 193–195; on Smith, 119; styles of informing used by, 189–193; Trumbull's correspondence with, 107, 113–114; on turncoat informers, 158, 175
Knightley, Alexander, 249–250, 258, 262, 271, 278
Knighton, John, 202, 211
Knights, Mark, 8
Knights of Montgomery, 82
Knoller, Robert, 198
Knott, Ann, 181–182

Lacy, John, 212
Lad, Thomas, 95
La Fore, Mrs., 173
Lancashire Plot (1694), 217–247; credit and credibility issues in, 26, 241–246; informers' role in, 12; loyalty vs. disloyalty question in, 228–234; Lunt's accusations, 159, 219–228; party politics of, 228–234; religion's role in, 228–234; rewards paid to informers, 123; and rule of law, 235–241
Lansfield, Stephen, 127, 134, 260
Latham, John, 158
law: in Assassination Plot, 262–270; and judicial precedent, 63; in Lancashire Plot, 235–241; nature of, 47–48
Law, Mr., 82
Lawrence, James, 84
Lee, Thomas, 38, 231
Legh, Peter, 217, 221, 231, 243
Legh, Thomas, 244
LeHardy, Charles, 89–90
Leslie, Charles, 194
Letherhead, John, 91–93, 101–102
Licensing Act of 1695, 15
Lilburne, John, 184
Lingo, James, 82–83
Littleton, Thomas, 38
local government, 70, 86–93
Locke, John, 3–7, 10–11
London Penny Post, 76, 79, 81–82. *See also* Post Office
Longueuil, Dame de, 163–164
Louis XIV (France), 69, 96, 101
Lovell, Salathiel, 60, 131
Lowick, Robert, 249–250, 263–264, 268
Lowther, John, 54, 92, 111
loyalty: and informers, 19; and Lancashire Plot (1694), 228–234; Post Office positions as indication of, 77–78, 80
loyalty oaths, 14, 35–39, 239, 256–259, 278
Lucas, Colin, 20, 22–23
Lucas, Lord, 144, 190
Lumley, Lord, 230
Lunn, Mr., 81
Lunt, John, 94, 159–160, 165, 167, 170–172, 185, 217–228, 241–243, 260
Lupin, Madam, 183
Luttrell, Narcissus, 27, 50, 72, 110–111, 174–175, 223, 250, 259, 271
Lutwych, Mr., 161

Macclesfield, Earl of, 80, 232–234
Mackenzie, George, 39
Macky, John, 95, 184
Magdalen College, 34, 38, 43

mail, opening of, 84–85. *See also* Post Office
Mainwaring, John, 38
Mainwaring, Matthew, 169
malicious accusations, 142
Mansuet, Father, 164
market model of credibility, 120–122
Marks, Mr., 144–145
Marlborough, Earl of, 21, 86, 105, 117, 192, 273, 279
Marshall, Alan, 24
Marshall, John, 78
Mary (Queen), 86, 248, 273
Mason, Robert, 79–81
Matthews, Edward, 230
Meal Tub Plot, 225
Meldrum, Robert, 273
Merchant Adventurers, Company of, 99
Merriweather, Anne, 174, 195
Mildmay, Carey, 260
Milles, Edward, 145–147
Minors, Robert, 73
modernization of civil service, 68–71
Molineux, Bridget, 244
Molineux, Caryll Viscount, 217, 220, 234, 238
Monk, Francis, 99–100
Monmouth, Earl of, 86, 94, 107, 116–118, 131
Monod, Paul, 251
Montagu, Ralph, 94
Montgomery, James, 263, 271, 276
Montgomery Plot, 83
Mordaunt, Charles. *See* Monmouth, Earl of
Morgan, John, 72, 157
Morisco, Peter, 111
Morland, Samuel, 84–85
Morris, Benjamin, 198
Morris, Charles, 198
Morton, George, 155
Murcott, William, 79, 81

Napier, Robert, 53
Nash, Mrs., 173
National Archives, 107
national security debates, 27–67; and Catholicism, 39–42; and habeas corpus, 48–53; and indemnity, 35–36, 42–47; and loyalty oaths, 35–39; and nature of law, 47–48; Oates case, 59–65; Tory narratives on, 31–35; and treason trials, 53–59; Whig narratives on, 31–35
Newbolt, William, 130–131, 173
Newton, Isaac, 121, 130, 135–136, 139
Newton, Mary, 148
Noel, Thomas, 75, 90, 243, 260
Nolan, Nicholas, 260
Norris, Thomas, 231
Northey, Edward, 181
Nottingham, Earl of: and Anglican Church, 39; correspondence of, 107; and habeas corpus, 49–50; and informers, 83, 114, 177–178; and intelligence gathering, 71, 123; Kingston's work for, 190, 197, 201–202; and Lancashire Plot, 222–223, 227, 231, 238; and warming pan scandal, 162, 188
Nynn, Walter, 88, 145–147, 155, 181–182, 203

Oates, Titus, 21, 31–34, *33*, 59–65, 179, *180*, 183, 236, 251
oath of allegiance (1689), 14, 39–41, 239, 257, 259. *See also* Jacobean oath of allegiance (1606)
Oglethorpe, Lady, 178
Oglethorpe, Theophilus, 165
one-shot informers, 141–149
Ormiston, James, 106, 114, 157, 202
Oulding, Henry, 124
Owling, 89, 100, 200
Oxenbridge, Henry, 81

packet boat operators, 79
Page, Matthew, 169–170
Paine, Neville, 133
Papillon, Thomas, 45, 80, 82–83
Papist Toleration Bill (1689), 41–42
pardons. *See* indemnity
Parker, Benjamin, 142
Parker, Colonel, 123, 204
Parkyns, William, 115–116, 211, 249, 256–257, 267–270
Parliament: and Assassination Plot conspirators, 273–275; and attainder, 58; Chaloner's supporters in, 130; and habeas corpus, 49, 51–52; and impeachment, 58; power of, 17. *See also* House of Commons; House of Lords
Parsons, Henry, 79

Paterson, Robert, 145–146, 150, 153–156, 183, 186, 203
patriotic informers, 93–103, 149–156
patronage, 230
Payne, Neville, 25
Payne, William, 24, 141
Penn, William, 177
Pepper, Paul, 75, 156, 260
Peterborough, Earl of, 188, 206
Petley, Thomas, 97
Philips, Captain, 194
Pickering, Thomas, 59–60
Pike, Thomas, 158
Pincus, Steve, 15–18, 69, 101
plots, 1–4. *See also specific plots*
police reform, 197–199
political informers. *See* informers
politicization of intelligence, 108–119
politics: Kingston's role in, 200–206; of Lancashire Plot (1694), 228–234. *See also* Tories; Whigs
Pollard, William, 147–149
Popish Plot, 4, 21, 31, 33, 39, 63–64, 225, 236
Porter, George, 11, 249, 262, 264, 266, 268, 271–272, 275
Portland, Earl of, 108, 117–118, 190, 202
Post Office, 76–86; appointments to positions in, 77–78; and franking privileges, 79–80; intelligence gathering by, 108, 151; opening of mail by, 84–85; trust in, 70, 81–86
Pownall, John, 243
Prendergrass, Thomas, 116, 126, 249, 262
Presbyterians, 33, 234
Prescott, Henry, 244
Press, 39, 193–195
Preston House of Correction, 230–231
Preston, Lord, 174, 176–177
Prettyman, Shirley, 260
Price, Aubrey, 114, 128–139, 183
Price, Edward, 130
prisoners: detention of, 18, 48–52, 259–261; informing by, 173–178
privateering, 91
Privy Council, 13, 52, 56, 73, 105, 130
Protestant Reformation, 5
Protestants, 33, 73, 231
public good, 100
Puritanism, 3, 33

Quakers, 33
quartering of troops, 88

Read, William, 125, 213
religion, 6, 228–234. *See also* Anglican Church; Catholics; Protestants
Rezneck, Samuel, 53–54
Rich, Robert, 46
Roberts, Captain, 135
Robins, John, 133–134, 153
Robinson, Howard, 76
Robinson, John, 157
Robinson, Robert, 145–147
Roettier, James, 144–145
Rokeby, Justice, 269
Romney, Earl of, 156
Rookwood, Ambrose, 249–250, 269
Rowe, Anthony, 46
Royal Lutestring Company, 95
royal messengers, 72, 198, 238
Royal Society, 7, 10, 211
Russell, William, 28, 29, 34, 53–54, 86, 117, 264, 274
Rye House Plot (1683), 4, 21, 27, 34, 39, 238, 264

Sacheverell Clause, 45, 87
Saffin, George, 87
St. Ange, Captain, 161
Sancroft, William, 40
Sawtell, Edward, 79–80
Sawyer, Robert, 46, 53
Scott, Mrs., 125
Second Conventicle Act of 1670, 120
secrecy, 70, 105
secretaries of state, 107, 114, 122. *See also specific individuals*
Segar, Thomas, 261
Seres, John, 146–147
Seven Bishops case, 40, 160
Seymour, Edward, 110–111
Shaftsbury, Earl of, 34, 235–236
Shales, John, 73
Shapin, Steven, 8, 10, 120, 210–211
Shapiro, Alexander, 53
Shapiro, Barbara, 10
Shaw, Richard, 243
Sherlock, William, 14

Shower, Bartholomew, 55, 264, 269–270, 276
Shrewsbury, Lord: correspondence of, 87; and Customs service employees, 73–75, 82; and habeas corpus, 49; and informers, 113, 116–117, 158–159; Jacobitism accusations against, 21, 114, 128, 273–274, 279; Kingston's work for, 188, 201, 205; and Lancashire Plot, 224, 226; and local government employees, 87
Sidney, Algernon, 29, 34, 53–54, 58
Sidney, Henry, 107
Singleton, Henry, 130
Skarr, John, 147
Skinner, Mary, 182
Skinner, Thomas, 162
Slingsby, Mr., 243
Smith, Aaron, 83, 98, 108, 124, 129, 170–171, 220, 222, 226
Smith, James, 51, 55
Smith, Matthew, 108–119, 121–123, 183, 188, 192, 201, 205–207, 211, 213
Smith, Solomon, 172–173
smuggling, 89–90, 94, 96, 151
social status, 211–212, 241
Societies for the Reformation of Manners, 21–22, 120–121
Sodington, Cornelius, 141–142
Somers, John, 47, 58, 73, 95, 113, 118, 131, 227, 274
South, Henry, 195
Sovereignty, 6–7
Speke, Hugh, 219, 223
Sprat, Thomas, 8
Standish, Lady, 221
Stanley, Rowland, 168, 218, 243
Stephens, Edward, 22
Stepkin, Peter, 94
Stock, Abraham, 83
Stokes, William, 88
Stott, Thurston, 168
Sunderland, Earl of, 105, 274
Superstitious Lands Commissions, 93–94, 103, 160–161, 167, 219–220
surveillance, 197–199. *See also* intelligence

Taaffe, John (aka Father Vincent), 94, 159–173, 185, 218–228, 241, 260
Taaffe, Mary, 165, 185

Tasborough, Mr., 142
Temple, Richard, 47, 73
Tenison, Thomas, 107, 160, 202
Thatcher, Margaret, 16
thief-takers, 128–129
Thompson, John, 38, 56, 60, 111
Thurloe, John, 84
Thurloe, William, 145–146
Tillotson, John, 107, 109
Tomlinson, William, 87, 230–231
Tom, Peter, 198
Tories: and indemnity, 42–47; and Kingston, 200–206; and Lancashire Plot, 226–234; and loyalty oaths, 21, 36–38; national security debate narratives of, 31–35; and Oates case, 62; and treason trial reform, 54
Torrington, Admiral, 73
Tower of London, 72
Townley, Richard, 242
trade restrictions, 8, 88–90, 97
treason: definition expanded, 30; and habeas corpus suspension, 52; incompetence vs., 72–73; trials for, 28, 53–59, 217–218
Treason Trials Act of 1696, 228, 248, 263–264, 267–270, 274
Treasury, 108
Treby, George, 51, 54–55, 57, 269
Tredenham, Joseph, 43, 45
Trenchard, John, 73, 107, 121, 125, 166–167, 170, 200–201, 218, 226, 239
Triennial Act, 15
Trumbull, William, 19, 75, 79, 85, 95, 107, 113–116, 125, 127, 134, 197, 201–202, 205
trust in government, 68–103; and central government's role, 71–75; historical perspective, 4–12; importance of, 5; as issue for Williamite regime, 12–15; and Lancashire Plot, 247; and local government, 86–93; and modernization of civil service, 68–71; and national security, 27; and patriotic entrepreneurs, 93–103; and Post Office, 76–86
Tuff, William, 142
"turncoats." *See* "chameleons"
Turnham Green Plot. *See* Assassination Plot (1696)
Tyrconnell, Countess of, 105
Tyrwhit, William, 158–159

Vallance, Edward, 16–17
Vernon, James: and Assassination Plot, 272, 274; and informers, 95, 107, 114–115, 117–119, 125, 128–129, 134–137, 179, 181; intelligence gathering by, 91; Kingston's work for, 203, 205

Wagstaffe, Thomas, 222, 226–227, 237–238
Wakemen, George, 82
Wales, Tim, 128
Waller, William, 51
Wallis, John, 84
Walmesley, Bartholomew, 161, 220
Ward, Isaac, 81
warming pan scandal, 161–162, 164
warrants, blank or incomplete, 49, 237
Warrington, Earl of, 94, 170
Wartman, Joseph, 80
Watkins, John, 91–92, 102
Watson, William, 150
Wattell, Elizabeth, 181
Watts, Elizabeth, 78–79, 151
Watts, John, 79, 152
Weames, James, 142
Webb, Elizabeth, 145–146, 181–182
Welles, Jeffrey, 79
Wennerlind, Carl, 13
Werden, John, 73
Whig-Jacobites, 66, 276
Whigs: and indemnity, 42–47; and Kingston, 200–206; and Lancashire Plot, 226, 228–234; and loyalty oaths, 21, 36–37; national security debate narratives of, 31–35; and Oates case, 62; and Rye House Plot, 27; and treason trial reform, 54
Whiston, Mr., 144–145

White, G. Edward, 49
Whitelocke, William, 53
Whitfield, Mr., 143, 183
Widdrington, Mr. *See* Lunt, John
Wildman, John, 47, 76–78, 80, 82, 84–86, 151, 279
Williamite regime: and Assassination Plot (1696), 248–279; historiographical context of, 15–19; informers used by, 104–187; Kingston's work for, 188–216; and Lancashire Plot (1694), 217–247; and national security debates, 27–67; trust as issue for, 12–15
Williams, William, 59, 228
Williamson, Captain, 158
Williamson, Francis, 83
Wilson, George, 218, 242, 244
Wilson, John, 153
Winchester, Marquis of, 94
Winnington, Francis, 202
Withins, Francis, 60
witnesses, 53, 181. *See also specific individuals*
Womball, John, 218–219, 227, 231, 243, 246
women: credibility and credit of, 181, 183; as witnesses, 179–183. *See also specific individuals*
Woodgate, John, 150–151, 153–154
Woodward, Catherine, 78
Woodward, Mary, 165
Writtell, John, 94

Yallop, Robert, 142
Yarmouth, Earl of, 134, 138

Zook, Melinda, 238